Urban Disorder
and the
Shape of Belief

Urban Disorder
※ AND THE ※
Shape of Belief

*The Great Chicago Fire,
the Haymarket Bomb, and the
Model Town of Pullman*

Carl Smith

THE UNIVERSITY OF CHICAGO PRESS
Chicago and London

CARL SMITH is professor of English and American Culture at Northwestern University.

The University of Chicago Press, Chicago 60637
The University of Chicago Press, Ltd., London
© 1995 by The University of Chicago
All rights reserved. Published 1995
Printed in the United States of America

03 02 01 00 99 98 97 96 95   1 2 3 4 5

ISBN: 0-226-76416-8 (cloth)

Library of Congress Cataloging-in-Publication Data

Smith, Carl S.
    Urban disorder and the shape of belief : the Great Chicago Fire,
the Haymarket bomb, and the model town of Pullman / Carl Smith.
        p.   cm.
    Includes bibliographical references (p.   ) and index.
    1. Chicago (Ill.)—Social conditions.   2. Disasters—Illinois—
Chicago—History—19th century.   3. Fires—Illinois—Chicago—
History—19th century.   4. Haymarket Square Riot, Chicago, Ill.,
1886.   5. Chicago Strike, 1894.   I. Title.
HN80.C5S57   1995
977.3'11—dc20   94-16704

The paper used in this publication meets the minimum
requirements of the American National Standard for
Information Sciences—Permanence of Paper for Printed
Library Materials, ANSI Z39.48-1984.

To Jeremy and Lucia—
urban disorder
but most of all to Jane—
the shape of belief

CONTENTS

PART TWO

6

From Resurrection to Insurrection / 101

7

Plots and Counterplots / 127

8

Words on Trial / 147

PART THREE

9

Taming the Urban Beast / 177

10

Putting Pullman in Its Place: The Search
for a New Urban Order / 209

11

Making Sense of the Age / 232

Epilogue / 271

Notes / 281
Index / 381

A gallery of photographs follows page 126

Acknowledgments

I have so many people to thank over such an extended period that I hope I have remembered them all. I ask forgiveness of any I may have overlooked.

This book began during a year away from Chicago in California, where I was living in Oakland, working in Berkeley, and fretting over what my family and I would do if an earthquake hit. I tried to deal with my concern by getting to understand it better through a study of the San Francisco earthquake and fire of 1906, which was made wonderfully possible by the splendid resources of the Bancroft Library, then under the gracious direction of the late James D. Hart, whose interest in all things relating to San Francisco (and so much beyond that) provided important early encouragement. Several members of the Berkeley faculty, most notably Gunther Barth, patiently listened to my ideas about urban disaster and pointed me in fruitful directions. This work resulted in an essay published in the *Yale Review*, and I am very grateful to John Kasson, Eric Sundquist, John Stilgoe, Kai Erikson, and Alan Trachtenberg for helping me prepare that essay, and to Neil Harris for encouraging me to think about urban disaster in larger terms. Later on, Paul Boyer, Michael Barkun, Philip Ethington, and, once again, Kai Erikson helped me focus and refine my arguments.

As I continued my research, I found myself less interested in urban disaster than in what I call here urban disorder, and increasingly intrigued by how this subject applied to Chicago in the late nineteenth century. The research that directly resulted in this book began with a National Endowment for the Humanities Fellowship at the Newberry Library. I am not only deeply indebted to the NEH and to the remarkable collections of the Newberry Library but to the whole intellectual community fostered at the Newberry under the leadership of its academic vice president, Richard H. Brown. I would also like to thank the other scholars in residence with me, especially Douglas Wilson and Rima Schultz, and the research staff, including above all John Jentz. Several members of the library staff of the Newberry, notably John Aubrey and the late Michael Kaplan, were very helpful in guiding me to resources of particular value.

The holdings of the Regenstein Library of the University of Chicago, the State Historical Society of Wisconsin, and the Chicago Public Library have also been important to this book, but the most vital resource has been the Chicago Historical Society. I believe that I have besieged the heads of all the collections at one time or another. I am particularly grateful for the help I received from Archie Motley and his staff in Archives and Manuscripts, and from Larry Viskochil and Linda Ziemer in Prints and Photographs, as well as from the Society's exceptionally knowledgeable librarians. An earlier version of a portion of my Haymarket section appeared in the Haymarket centennial issue of the society's journal, *Chicago History,* and I very much appreciate the suggestions of editor Russell Lewis and his associates. The society's Urban History Seminar gave me the chance to share my findings with others and hear their responses, and I would like to thank Michael Ebner of Lake Forest College for inviting me to speak to this group, as well as for his own outstanding work in Chicago and urban history and his continuing interest in my project.

Northwestern University has provided crucial institutional support and offered me a superb array of colleagues. Two deans of the College of Arts and Sciences, Rudolph Weingartner and Lawrence Dumas, enabled me to have the leave time I required, while the Law and Society Program underwrote necessary research travel expenses. At the outset of this project, Howard Becker offered very important suggestions, and further on Karen Halttunen, Christopher Herbert, Kenneth Warren, and Wesley Skogan were similarly helpful. The Northwestern University Library and its staff have been very supportive of my research needs in every small and large way. I would like to acknowledge in particular Russell Maylone, head of Special Collections; Kathryn Deiss, of Interlibrary Loan; Patrick Quinn, university archivist; and Jean Alexander, reference librarian.

My colleagues in the American Culture Program at Northwestern, program director Jerry Goldman and program assistant Phyllis Siegel, have consistently furnished indispensable technical assistance and, more important, moral support. The program made it possible for me to work out my ideas with an extraordinary group of students, including Peter Golkin, who was an invaluable research assistant. I am also grateful for the responses I received from those who participated in the session of the Northwestern English Department's work-in-progress colloquia at which I presented my work, and from the scholars in the NEH summer institute at the University of North Carolina at Chapel Hill on the rise of American modernism that was directed by John Kasson, Joy Kasson, and Townsend Ludington.

It would be hard to thank enough those at Northwestern and other institutions who agreed to read and comment in detail on earlier versions of the manuscript as a whole. The list includes Henry Binford, James Gilbert, Terry Mulcaire, James Oakes, Eric Sundquist, Robert Wiebe, and, most of all, Burton Bledstein. Of great value were conversations on several occasions with Perry Duis and with Ross Miller, who has written his own outstanding cultural history of the Chicago fire. I want to note especially the importance of my many discussions of the meaning of the fire with Karen Sawislak (whose splendid book on the subject will also be published by the University of Chicago Press) and on Pullman with Janice Reiff, whose work brings the model town and those who lived and labored there back to life. Much of the pleasure in pursuing this project has been in talking at length with both of them.

As in every other respect of note, I owe the greatest thanks to Jane S. Smith. Sometimes against her best interests, she has put an immeasurable amount of effort of her own into this book. If there is any better combination of critical intelligence, unflinching editorial skill, and practical sympathy, I have yet to see it.

The eloquent of the earth were already arriving and standing at the edges of the Event, putting it in fitting words. The world already knew of the catastrophe. What would it say?

JOHN McGOVERN,
Daniel Trentworthy: A Tale of the Great Fire of Chicago

Introduction

This book examines the imaginative dimensions of the Great Chicago Fire of 1871, the Haymarket bombing of 1886, and the celebrated model town of Pullman, Illinois, from its founding in 1880 to the famous strike of 1894. By imaginative dimensions, I mean the context of thought and expression that suffuses individual and social life. "Dimensions" is a broader yet more accurate term than "responses" since, to a greater extent than is obvious at first, what may appear to be an intellectual or literary reaction to an event often inseparably precedes and at least partially determines the nature of that event and the manner in which it is described, and so affects subsequent thought and action. I focus on the fire, Haymarket, and Pullman because their imaginative dimensions are very deep and wide, revealing how people in Chicago and across the country thought and spoke about urban disorder, and, through that, about city life at a time when the increasing organization of human activity in cities was so repeatedly punctuated by major disruptions that disorder itself appeared to be one of the defining qualities of urban culture. In so doing, I investigate how Americans discussed the disorderly in relation to the development of an understanding of the meaning of modernity that has carried into our own time.

The City in Disorder and the
Disorderly City

The conflagration that consumed Chicago is the most well-known urban fire in this country's history. The elemental destruction of this particular place at this particular moment proved irresistibly absorbing and immediately assumed the status of legend that it still has today. The city's resurrection from the flames, its ability to overcome and apparently even benefit from adversity, demonstrated to many the vitality of a new national and international economic and political order in which Chicago occupied a critical position. The pious rhetoric in which the reconstruction process was described meanwhile revealed how important it was to Americans in 1871 to see the determination to rebuild the stricken city as reaffirming the sacred purposes on which they believed that the country and their lives were founded, and to which they had so recently rededicated themselves through the struggle and sacrifice of the Civil War. The fire also, however, seemed both to expose and represent some disturbing aspects of the culture of newly dominant cities like Chicago, qualities that were as difficult to suppress as the spread of the flames themselves from building to building, block to block, and division to division. Both residents of Chicago and outsiders would increasingly assert that the development of the city, even apart from this particular disastrous event, had its own incendiary quality that was essential to its nature. A large and apparently chaotic metropolis made up of so many people and interests, dedicated above all to growth, was perhaps impossible to control, no matter how much all the post-fire talk of determination and destiny might suggest otherwise. The social order of Chicago was inherently volatile, and it might burst into flame at any moment.

As the Chicago fire became the defining instance of American urban disaster among many catastrophes of the time, the Haymarket bombing has been the most notorious example of urban violence in a period of widespread upheaval.[1] The fatalities included policemen acting in the line of duty, and they were not just killed but horribly maimed by a dynamite bomb, which was all the more terrifying since the identity of the assailant was never discovered. The bomb hit a cultural nerve. Immediately perceived as a critically representative event at this time of social conflict, it became the focus of a continuing debate over several pressing issues going back to the fire, central among them the instability of a concentrated and mixed urban population. The backdrop of this debate included the emergence of certain modes of thinking and speaking about city life and social disorder that dictated how the eight men charged with the crime were prosecuted, convicted, and punished. Their trial was the place where the state, speaking for and to the people of Chicago, America, and the world, tried to force these defendants to take the blame for the bomb and other civil unrest in a way that reinforced the value and legitimacy of the current order and discouraged opposition to it.[2] The defendants resisted the roles in which they were cast, using their day in court to indict their accusers for creating the sources of the distress for which they were being blamed.

In ways that transcended its own extremely confused particulars, Haymarket seemed to clarify an embattled cultural context, not only revealing major divisions but also, like the fire, offering a set of images and a vocabulary through which to understand these divisions. Following the fire, Americans were obsessed with finding any words that could describe the catastrophe and the city it befell. The Haymarket trial, and the public discussion that surrounded it, were the site of a conflict over whose words and descriptions were the right ones. In the trial and in the period up to the executions, each side went far beyond the immediate issue of guilt or innocence to advance its own social vision while discrediting that of the opposition. Both tried to place the bomb and other events, including the trial and execution, within a larger history that revealed the correctness of their point of view. And both offered messages of alarm and reassurance, explaining why this awful event could take place and how the deeper dangers and dilemmas it revealed could be resolved.

During the tumultuous 1880s, the town of Pullman, located just outside Chicago, seemed to demonstrate that it was possible to have a healthy, humane, prosperous, and productive urban order free of the kinds of conflicts and dangers that the fire and Haymarket revealed, and that this order could be sustained without police or troops, guns or gallows. Having come to Chicago before the Civil War as an ambitious young man and having witnessed many episodes of labor conflict firsthand, George Pullman staked his fortune, his energy, and his reputation on building an industrial town so carefully planned and managed that it would unite labor and capital in social harmony. In order to do this, however, he was convinced that one had to entrust the responsibility for urban order to a single owner (in this case his Pullman Palace Car Company) in possession of all the property and in charge of all the rules.

It is not difficult in hindsight to see that even this well-meaning experiment that was so contrary to American values of individualism and community, and to labor's goal of determining the conditions of life and work for wage-earning Americans, could lead to a strike, especially in a place and a time constantly beset by labor violence and economic uncertainty. What is perhaps harder to understand at first is the overwhelmingly positive commentary that Pullman's enterprise received up to and even after the strike as a solution to the problems posed by the modern industrial city. The model town of Pullman elicited such an endorsement precisely because it seemed to address effectively the same anxieties about modern urban culture that were inscribed in the fire literature and dramatized in the Haymarket trial. The sometimes strained and almost desperate praise for Pullman's project was thus closely related to what Paul Boyer calls the "heightened sense of urban menace, expressed at its most extreme in visions of revolutionary chaos and mass carnage" that "formed the psychic substratum of urban control efforts" in the late nineteenth century. As Richard T. Ely wrote the year before Haymarket, Pullman's experiment was worthy of the closest "attention and discussion" in this time of "dynamite bombs and revolutionary murmurings."[3] If the model town could provide a way out of the apparently inescapable syndrome of urban disorder, then its lead was worth following, even if to do so required, among the other ideas about social reform that it advanced, a major modification in the concept of American citizenship.

When, in 1894, Pullman instead became the center of the most famous strike in an era of labor wars, this development was regarded by many political and business leaders, social commentators, and journalists as a danger to the nation as serious as the Civil War had been a generation before. "In resisting and suppressing such a blackmailing conspiracy as the boycott of the Pullman cars by the American railway union," the editors of *Harper's Weekly* told their readers, "the nation is fighting for its own existence just as truly as in suppressing the great rebellion."[4] Like the fire and the Haymarket riot before it, the Pullman strike became the event through which many Americans tried to make sense of the larger patterns of change and conflict that seemed to dominate cultural life as the country headed into the twentieth century.

While I discuss them individually, I view the fire, Haymarket, and Pullman as closely interconnected for a number of reasons that go beyond the obvious considerations of time and place. Whether many Americans explicitly saw the political unrest surrounding Haymarket in terms of the fire or the importance of Pullman in relation to the bomb is hard to prove, but there is little doubt that the way people imagined each influenced how they thought and talked and acted in regard to the others, and how they understood the nature of their times. Each event had, and was perceived at the time as having, a powerful narrative form, made up of an engrossing interplay of incident and character that was subject to multiple interpretations. These narratives built upon each other, mutually shaping the recollection and anticipation of contemporary experience into a highly conflicted set of ideas and images in which the major theme was the relationship between disorder and modernity. At the heart of it all was the image of the city *in extremis*, the urban creation of civilization and progress, power and order, that was constantly prey to disruption and disaster.

Americans at this time had good reason to have the city so much on their minds. They were living in the middle of the hundred-year period in which, as Eric Monkkonen has put it, America became urban.[5] Between 1870 and 1900, the number of places classified by the census as cities (i.e., having 2,500 inhabitants or more) went from 663 to 1,737, while the population of such places more than tripled, from just under ten million to over thirty million.[6] In 1870 there were fourteen cities with 100,000 or more inhabitants; by the turn of the century there were thirty-eight, including fifteen with at least a quarter of a million. In the hundred years following the first census of 1790, the proportion of Americans living in settlements of 8,000 or more had climbed from 3.35 to 29.20 percent, with almost 7 percent of that increase taking place in the decade between 1880 and 1890.[7]

In this era of urban expansion, no other city grew so quickly and so much as Chicago. Its population in 1900 was nearly sixty times that of 1850 (1,698,575 versus 29,963). Between 1870 and 1890 it moved from fifth to second biggest city in the country. The 1880s were the years of Chicago's mightiest expansion, from half a million to over a million, with an increase of over 125,000 between 1885 and 1886.[8] Indeed, part of the mystique of the city was that it appeared to emerge full-grown out of nowhere—or everywhere—almost miraculously. Less than forty years old at the time of the fire, Chicago seemed to stand for the power of all the new historical, social, and economic forces in an expanding and interconnected commercial and industrializing nation. It was the irrepressible gateway to the West, through which unprecedented amounts and kinds of people, capital, goods, and information flowed.[9]

At the same time, partly because of the fire and this population increase, but also because of the immense changes in transportation, communications, structure of the workplace (both factory and office), and building technology, Chicago's identity was constantly transforming, so that the city that was rocked by the Haymarket bomb was physically as well as demographically very different from the one that had burned down fifteen years before. This combination of sudden titanic growth out of a virtually nonexistent past and continuing constant alteration combined to make Chicago seem a place hostile to traditional ideas of order and stability. The burning of the city commanded more attention than any other of the dozens of nineteenth-century American urban fires (as, likewise, the Haymarket bombing and the Pullman strike were the most infamous events of their kind in a period rife with spectacular acts of urban violence and labor conflict) not only because of its scale but also because, as John J. Pauly suggests, it thrust calamity into the heart of the most promising—and, in some respects, most threatening—city in the nation.[10]

Urban Disorder and the Shape of Belief

Urban disorder is an evocative but elusive term. In common definition, *disorder*, however large or small, is a specific event or resulting condition that is opposed to order—the way things normally are. We assign extreme disorders such names as disaster, cataclysm, calamity, and catastrophe. A *disaster* can be almost any major adverse event, often sudden, while a *calamity* usually implies special suffering or affliction. *Cataclysm* is a markedly violent or overwhelming experience that shakes its object —whether the surface of the earth, the body politic, or the individual soul—in some profound way. In its purest meaning, *catastrophe* is the most extreme form of disorder or disruption, for it implies irreversible and tragic finality. Distinctions quickly become blurred, however, and even amidst the magisterial calm and clarity of an unabridged dictionary these terms are offered synonymously.

One can hardly fault Chicagoans if, at the moment their city hall collapsed in flames in 1871 or the Haymarket bomb exploded in 1886 or troops confronted mobs in 1894, they did not check the appropriateness of their terms. Even excluding such moments of duress, however, the task of finding clear, consistent meanings for any such words in the context of American urban experience of the late nineteenth century is impossible. Cities as large, as mixed, and as rapidly changing as Chicago offered no such thing as a unified vision or voice. I have tried to be sensitive to the political and cultural nature of the characterization of this or that event as a disorder or some related term. As I shall show, the contemporary understanding of the fire, the bomb, the strike, and of Chicago itself as disastrous, cataclysmic, calamitous, or catastrophic derived from existing ideas which were already in place and which affected how people integrated these events and this city into their lives.

None of these urban disorders that struck Chicago were imagined or, in some abstract sense, socially constructed, as anyone burned or blasted or beaten in the course of each of them could readily attest. But we should be aware that the occurrences that people consider most disruptive are those which seem to offer the greatest challenge to their ideas of order. As Mary Douglas has argued, "Everything that can happen to a man in the way of disaster should be catalogued according to the active principles in the universe of his particular culture."[11] The central intellectual drama in the consideration of the nature of disorder is the struggle of imagination to explain what is inexplicable, troubling, or threatening. The imagining of disorder, whether it is accurate or not in its details—and it is often most interesting and revealing when it is most obviously inaccurate—involves the attempt to find the best way in which to absorb those things that challenge the sense of what is right and normal. The best way is the one that helps master experience by finding a way to think and talk about it. What was apparent in discussions of the fire, Haymarket, and Pullman was that they were being used heuristically by people trying to understand the world in which they lived. Thus, the Haymarket bomb, which killed or wounded a few dozen people and caused virtually no property damage, was a cataclysm of a deeper and broader kind than the fire because of its more extraordinary and enduring imaginative reverberations. While the fire forced the physical re-creation of Chicago, the bomb remade the mental map of the metropolis.

Through the last three decades of the nineteenth century, Americans increasingly agreed that the modern American city, and Chicago in particular, was the disorderly embodiment of instability, growth, and change. They also agreed that it was the center of political, economic, and social power in America, and, as such, was contested ground—another reason why it seemed so unstable. In this context, defining whether and in what way this or that event was disorderly, disastrous, and potentially catastrophic was an act of power in a struggle in which different people tried to enforce their often disputed vision of urban order as the one that was most normal, proper, desirable, progressive, and correct. The struggle was over the future of America, with which the rise of the city was so closely linked, and the matters at issue were the rules and principles that formed the basis of this setting, from those relating to wages and working conditions to ones of fairness, truth, and, of course, order.[12]

The passion that characterized the discussion of the meaning of urban life in this period reveals how important the establishing of imaginative control over the city was thought to be. The attempt to define the fluid and contested city, about which people could hold many different and often contradictory ideas, was not just an effort at social empowerment but also of personal belief. Many of the individuals examined here were speaking to a much broader group of Americans who eagerly wanted the city interpreted for them so that they could know what to believe about the world and how to act within it.[13] They were willing to accept that the urban world was often disorderly, but not that their beliefs were incoherent or lacking a sound basis. This meant that they wanted an interpretation of urban experience that seemed neutral, apolitical, and stable, all the more so since the urban setting struck them as so contested, politicized, and unstable. Different groups and individuals insisted that circumstances confirmed their view of experience, or, if they were forced to the defensive, that their view was still adequate to deal with the challenge at hand. And, in the midst of the debate over the proper form and meaning of urban life, all parties sought more than control. They wanted consensus. Social leaders and observers, and the audiences they addressed, wished to find a correct and appealing meaning for Chicago and America on which they felt all could and should reasonably agree, so they could claim that what they stood for was in the true spirit of the nation as a consensual community.[14]

This wish helps explain the continuing centrality of the Civil War in discussions of urban life in the decades that followed. No event cut so deeply into the American psyche as did the war, or was so fondly remembered in terms of high ideals, moral intensity, and the triumph over the profoundest kind of social disorder. As the city came to seem a battlefield on which the fate of America would be decided, a place where finding a broadly unified vision or voice often appeared to be impossible and where social disorder seemed to be a constant condition or threat, there was an immense special appeal in being able to speak self-righteously of being on the side of the defense of the republic against those who would destroy the nation. To many Americans in the urban North, Burton J. Bledstein points out, "the real war for social discipline and rational consolidation had only begun. The Civil War might only be preliminary to the main event."[15]

The question at the time, always implicit in public discussion, was whether what many different people agreed to be disorder was something inherent in the nature of the city or something external that happened to it. One's answer revealed what one thought the city in essence was. While there was always a considerable resistance to the idea that urban life was inevitably disorderly, the period between the fire and the Pullman strike witnessed the emergence of an outlook in which reality, city, and disorder became closely related, if not interchangeable, terms, and all converged in definitions of the nature of experience which Americans took into the twentieth century. Put another way, urban disorder became the shape of belief. As every disruption seemed to enact a potential that was always inherent in modern city life, disorder on a significant scale was integrated into the idea of the normal. And in this view, for better and for worse, the city in disorder was the city at its most urban.

As disorder became part of the definition of urban life, discussions of what this or that disruption meant became considerations of the nature of reality itself. The process, if that is the right name for something so tentative and uneven as the strains of thought that were expressed, was very complicated, but it was directly tied to the developments analyzed here. The fire, the bomb, and the strike were not only extraordinary events in themselves, but also occasions through which to consider such pressing issues as the measure and price of progress, the violent and competitive nature of experience, the unfairness and diffi-culty of life, the need for efficiency and its necessary costs, the means—practical and utopian—of improving the established order, and related questions of what the city and the nation were and what they should be. The attempts to establish a particular view of social experience as authoritative unquestionably worked to define certain events as disor-derly, but as part of any kind of larger effort to direct social action in a way that would avoid future disorder they consistently failed, not only because of the unpredictable nature of city life, but also because to some extent the existence of what many defined as disorder was para-doxically necessary to the very people who condemned it. Here we should be aware of the appeal of the idea of disorder, not just to those dissatisfied with the status quo, but also to those of power and privilege within it. While no one "wanted" the fire or the Haymarket bomb or the Pullman strike, all three events were used in important instances to jus-tify as well as to question the order of things. Their dangers were in sev-eral instances exaggerated and even invented for this purpose, to set the social stage for what were presented as masterly accomplishments, such as the restoration of order in post-fire Chicago, the hanging of the anarchists, the building of Pullman and, later, the breaking of the strike.[16]

Texts and Voices

While most of the materials scrutinized here are spoken or printed sources, several are more accurately described as actions, including pa-rades and demonstrations, meetings and rallies, strikes and other more spontaneous forms of protest, and, of course, the post-fire rescue and relief efforts, the Haymarket bomb, and the building of Pullman. Even these nonliterary phenomena are "literary," however, in the sense that they were meant to express, and were taken to be expressing, certain meanings.[17] More often than not there was obvious (if not always clear) intention behind them, as in the throwing of the bomb and in the hanging of the anarchists held responsible for it, or in the design of Pullman and in the strategies of the striking Pullman workers. The spo-ken materials are the published versions of speeches and other state-ments, including transcripts from trials and hearings. While I exam-ine some personal manuscript materials, such as letters, most of my sources were meant to join in a public discussion, and they therefore ap-peared in print. They mainly fall under the broad categories of journal-ism (newspapers and periodicals) or topical publications (including cir-culars, pamphlets, books, and government, corporate, or institutional reports) that were quickly pushed through the press because of daily deadlines or because their authors and readers believed them to be urgent. Most of the published materials are nonfiction, though there is a small but significant representation of fiction and poetry, as well as drawings, paintings, illustrations, cartoons, and other visual materials.

For economic reasons as well as the desire to have some influence on current events, the authors of these different texts hoped to reach a large audience. This was especially true of those who wrote for newspapers, mass-circulation magazines, and inexpensive pamphlets and books, which relied on improved printing presses, the telegraph (and soon the telephone), and the railroad for both the quick gathering of information and for their own rapid production and wide distribution. The period's sense of urban disorder was largely expressed through these new forms of communication, produced in unprecedented numbers and created by this country's first numerically significant generation of professional authors.[18] The industrial revolution and the rise of cities raised the possibility of disorder of a new scale and kind in a fascinating and unquestionably important social setting—which included a large readership eager to understand itself—while forms of mass communication not only provided a marvelously swift and cheap way to learn about events like the fire, the bomb, and the strike, but also sometimes seemed to create a demand for them. "Authors" of every kind, including politicians, business and labor leaders, reformers, and radicals, conspired with professional writers in fashioning urban disorder out of current events for an eager public at a time when the most engaging news story was life in the modern city. John F. Kasson rightly observes, "Of all the voluminous texts produced in the nineteenth century, among the most massive and challenging were the new metropolises themselves."[19]

The primary means by which all of these people tried to communicate their beliefs was language, and that is the main evidence scrutinized here. As Alan Trachtenberg explains, the forms of language are "of prime historical interest" and "forces in their own right." Language, particularly figurative language and literary convention, is at once descriptive and interpretive, conveying the details of life and an understanding of them. Considered as discourse, a particular literary expression, Hayden White suggests, "is intended to *constitute* the ground whereon to decide *what shall count as a fact* in the matters under consideration and to determine *what mode of comprehension* is best suited to the understanding of the fact thus constituted." This expression is closely related to imagination and belief in that it is itself "a product of consciousness's effort to come to terms with problematical domains of experience," in which primary categories are order and disorder. Language, as a system of figures and forms that convey mean-

ings, is itself based on a concept of order, and is almost always summoned in moments of perceived crisis to stabilize and reassure the
imagination, or at least to explain things in familiar terms.[20]

A study of the imaginative dimensions of urban disorder in Chicago
in the late nineteenth century, or of any other topic, through literary
expression, is, as White and others point out, an exploration of the history of meaning in which language is considered in semiological terms.
As I have already stated, however, this does not imply that social reality
for authors and readers of the time was entirely constructed or determined by the system of ideas and words through which it was expressed. Meaning and experience are constantly intertwined in ways
that reveal an intricate dialectical relationship between extraliterary reality and forms of expression. As the detailed analyses that follow demonstrate, in the face of "problematical domains of experience," people
simultaneously find refuge in, manipulate, and alter the way they discuss and interpret life around them. This extensively affects the life
they and others live, even if they cannot be said to wholly "imagine"
their lives or to constitute or inhabit life entirely through language.
There is no simple way to get at this dynamic relationship between
public event, personal belief, and expression. The history of meaning
is, John E. Toews points out, "a complex process of linguistic creativity
and communicative action that is irreducible to socioeconomic models
and demands the interpretive skills intellectual historians and literary
scholars have developed in the critical reading of the artifacts of 'high'
culture."[21]

This book attempts to apply these skills to a much wider range of
artifacts than those that might be classified under the heading of "high
culture." One of its aims is to consider the kind of play there is between
imagination, idea, and experience, and how much the cultural context
which reveals and is revealed by a particular textual artifact is itself
something that requires interpretation. The description and interpretation of the Chicago fire, the Haymarket bomb, and the rise and
fall of Pullman involved a multileveled form of mediation. Americans
tried to find the best language available through which to talk about
these developments, and in turn used these events to interpret their
culture. The ability to write or speak about such events is very important, for to give something a name is to assert, or at least to try to assert,
control over it imaginatively. In the contemporary discussion of the
fire, Haymarket, and Pullman, there was an elaborate engagement of
language and experience, as Americans struggled to understand the
kinds of changes that were taking place in their country as a whole, and
especially in their cities. These efforts were complicated by the fact that
by its very nature an event that is perceived as disorderly is assumed to

resist any frame, and to be in some measure inexplicable and imaginatively elusive. This resistance and elusiveness are what make it powerful in both its danger and its imaginative appeal, and what link it to the amorphous and ungraspable nature of city life in America.[22]

One of the key tasks in a study such as this is to sort out lively and deeply felt argument from timeless responses and standard rhetoric. Many of the forms of action and expression cited here fit into patterns of human thought and behavior that transcend specific cultural contexts, and I shall point this out in several instances. But whether the people in the particular place and time this book covers adapted certain common patterns to their own experience or said and did something unique and unprecedented, I am looking for what they thought, expressed, felt, and lived as belief. To accomplish this, I am trying to discover their controlling narratives or central mythologies. By narratives and mythologies I do not mean things they made up, but what they sincerely took to be the interconnections and explanations through which they understood their times. I contend that the fire, Haymarket, and Pullman had such imaginative resonance because they were widely accepted as events that tested the value of any narrative or mythology of the way things were.[23]

Even if the texts I examine are too numerous and varied to sort out with precision, it is possible to discern the major voices within them. These fall into three overlapping categories, with many different hybrids. The first voice was that of a Protestant evangelical outlook, both militant and sentimental, concerned about corruption, rectitude, and proper feeling, and eager to see urban community as purified and redeemed. The second was the voice of liberal education and worldly refinement, wishing to view experience as an aesthetically and politically satisfactory drama in which the best citizenry proved themselves calm and brave, reasonable and responsible, wise and generous, disciplined and harmonious. The last voice can be described as professional, bureaucratic, and protoprogressive, believing in rational organization, training, and expertise. All three voices were active and eloquent throughout the period this book spans. The third, somewhat more muted than the first two in discussions of the fire, became increasingly powerful in the decades ahead, though it would never drown out or completely separate itself from the others. The broader context in which these voices spoke was the general movement, never complete or consistent, from a romantic to a realistic sensibility in many areas of social thought and aesthetic expression, with those who contended for power and influence claiming that the view of experience they presented through their narrative of contemporary events was the most real.

These voices were mainly those of the native-born Protestant upper- and middle-class Americans who dominated most political, social, and economic institutions and forms of cultural discourse in this period.[24] The elite members of this group, whose power was reflected in the breadth of the influence of their beliefs and their ability to get them expressed locally and nationally through the press and enacted as public policy, reached maturity around the time of the Civil War, attained positions of leadership within the political, economic, and social structure by the late 1860s and early 1870s, and held on to these positions until the end of the century. Chicago's cultural leaders were mainly men from small towns in the northeast who tried their hand at several different trades or small businesses before coming to the city (generally in the 1850s) and beginning the careers that brought them their self-made success, prestige, and influence. They formed only the second generation of leadership in a metropolis that was barely as old as they were. Like the pioneers who preceded them, they differed from the upper classes in more established eastern cities in that both their status and the place in which they enjoyed it were of such recent derivation. They were, in Frederic Cople Jaher's words, "a new elite in a new community."[25]

Many other somewhat less prosperous and prominent middle-class people—journalists, lawyers, architects, engineers, educators, politicians, government officials, soldiers, and reformers, as well as businessmen—substantially assented to this elite's ideas of urban order and disorder. They had or desired a significant and rewarding place within the current system, which they wanted to be defined, stable, and, above all, orderly. As Burton Bledstein has explained, they "were seeking a professional basis for an institutional order, a basis in universal and predictable rules to provide a formal context for the competitive spirit of individual egos." While they "celebrated their own energy, their capacity for booming, boosterism, and the lust for power," they also desired "respectability, orderliness, control, and discipline" as part of an ethos of personal advancement and social progress. Hence their belief in rules for every sort of economic and social behavior, and in the independent individual as the foundation of society. Daniel Walker Howe notes that they had a faith in an internalized ethic of self-cultivation, self-denial, self-control, and self-improvement based on a correspondence between the ordered individual and an ordered society.[26] But by the middle of the nineteenth century they recognized that the attainment of social or economic status was never certain or permanent (and certainly not in an unpredictable economy and a place as new as Chicago), and they believed that in the city there was a large and unstable population whose attitudes and behavior constantly menaced stability

and order.[27] Events like the fire and Haymarket were threatening because they were thought to be moments of vulnerability when lines of
control and authority might break down, jeopardizing one's position
and promise within the current order. The town of Pullman was likewise appealing because it seemed to propose an urban design that
would reduce or even remove the threat of disorder by effectively reconstructing the social other under elite norms without jeopardizing
class distinctions.

As is evident, I do not claim to examine the beliefs of all Chicagoans
or all Americans, especially the growing number of workers who came
to agree that they could not express or defend their interests as individuals, though I do think that I trace those patterns of belief that most
affected urban life and the way it was discussed in most public discourse through this period.[28] And, while I am mainly looking at those
forms and beliefs regarding disorder and city life that were shared
among the middle and upper classes, I do not mean to suggest by any
means that I have found unanimity or certainty of opinion and expression. On the contrary, I emphasize points where there was a certain internal tension in the discourse. I am also interested in the way forms
and ideas evolved, but here, too, it is misleading to maintain that there
were clear patterns and smooth transitions. It is essential to keep in
mind that both Chicago (and the American city generally) and modes
of thought and expression were never monolithic, and to say again that
both were changing throughout this period. To sort out their mutual
conditioning is to investigate an extremely complicated cultural dynamic. Likewise, I try to acknowledge the qualitative differences between my three major subjects, including the distinctive ways in which
a culture responds—usually more positively—to natural disasters like
the fire than to man-made disorders like the Haymarket bomb and the
Pullman strike.[29]

It is also important to be aware that what might appear here to be a
grim fixation on urban disaster and disorder must be considered as one
of many ways—though, I would contend, a major one—in which cities
were imagined in this period. People from all over America and the
world in overwhelming numbers chose to live their lives in cities like
Chicago and could be simultaneously both champions as well as critics
of urban life. Most of the individuals who speak in these pages were city
people who felt such ambivalence. Indeed, one could argue that the
very success of the city in attracting residents and resources was one of
the things that was most alarming about it, even (perhaps especially) to
those who lived here. It was also very hard for Americans not to see the
astonishing growth of the city and the pace of change in terms of disor-

der, and not to focus on particular episodes of distress as offering special insight on the nature of contemporary reality.

I try to approach the many individuals whose words and actions are scrutinized here in the spirit of understanding, if not exactly sympathy. I am troubled and at times outraged by the extent to which many of the people I examine managed the concepts of urban order and disorder in such a way as to enforce a repressive social vision after the fire, to murder the Haymarket accused, to overpraise the Pullman experiment in spite of its disregard for rights these people claimed to value and then, during the strike, to condemn the workers who stood up for those rights. While I cannot withhold judgment in many instances where I think that it is vital to responsible and meaningful inquiry, I think that it would be hypocritical a century and more later to feign surprise that very few individuals were able to see beyond their interests. I do think that they were genuinely engaged in trying to figure out the circumstances of their times, that they believed urban disorder was an issue they had to confront decisively, and that, even when they overstated the perils at hand, in almost all cases they thought and acted in the ways they did on the level of belief, not simple rationalization and expediency. Like all of us, they were not simply looking for ways in which to weather a particular moment, but for a view of the world in which they could imaginatively live. Aware that this was a period of conflict, they tried to make or find a substantial and coherent community animated by the power of its ideas, a cultural "we" that liked to believe it transcended the contested nature of urban life by agreeing on a definitive way to imagine reality, change, order, disorder, and the city. To find ideas that one could believe in, and modes of language and action through which to speak and live out these ideas, was critical, for to be unable to do this would be to confront a deeper kind of disorder than any that took place on the streets of Chicago.

I have tried to adapt my own form to the clearest and fullest exploration of my broad subject.[30] In Part One, "Fire," after examining the ways the fire literature expressed certain hopes and fears about urban life, I look at how people at the time rationalized the need to apply both direct and more subtle forms of cultural control to the unstable city. Part One concludes with some reflections on how the fire became integrated into cultural memory, including a discussion of how the manner in which Chicago chose to remember the fire was more a consideration of the city's future than of its past. The ways in which people at the time spoke and wrote about the fire helped them explain to themselves what they thought they were doing in the city, and at the same time directly influenced how they would think and act at subsequent moments they perceived as disorderly and dangerous.

The first chapter in Part Two, "Bomb," traces social disorder in Chicago between the fire and the Haymarket riot, with special attention to how a series of events and the language in which they were discussed developed out of each other. The next chapter focuses on the meanings that the police, the prosecution, and most public commentary tried to impose on what all saw as the drama of Haymarket, and the way in which the defendants rejected these meanings and offered other interpretations of their own. The last chapter concentrates on the conflicts that centered on key terms that came up again and again in public discussions of disorder before, during, and after the trial.

Part Three is titled "Strike," but it deals with the model town of Pullman in the entire period between its conception in the 1870s and its dissolution in the late 1890s. This part begins with a look at all the positive expectations for this experiment that were expressed by George Pullman and, more significantly, by the host of visitors and commentators who wanted to be shown that there could be a way to end social strife without social revolution. This is followed by a survey of some of the expressions of doubt that appeared in the years before the strike. Next comes an extended examination of the town in the context of some of the most popular analyses and reform proposals that were contemporary with it and that also confronted the issue of urban disorder and its implications for the nation. This examination includes a look at other Chicago institutions besides the town of Pullman that addressed this issue. Only then do I deal with the strike itself, mainly the views of those who tried to understand the age of which it was a part and how best to address what continuing challenges lay ahead.

Part One

FIRE

TWO

The Great Conflagration

The summer of 1871 was extraordinarily dry in Chicago, with very little rain after Independence Day. More than two dozen scattered fires were reported in the early autumn, the most serious of which broke out on the evening of Saturday, October 7, in Lull and Holmes's planing mill at the center of a neighborhood just west of downtown that had been dubbed the "Red Flash" by local insurance men. This blaze, which was not put out until the middle of Sunday afternoon, consumed four city blocks and caused losses estimated at a million dollars. A major downtown fire in 1857 that killed twenty-two people had convinced the Common Council to replace volunteer companies with a professional department the following year.[1] The 185 firefighters who made up this force in 1871 were spirited and competent, but perilously overmatched by a prodigiously expanding city now populated by over 330,000 people.

The barn belonging to Patrick and Catherine O'Leary behind their home at DeKoven and Jefferson Streets was about ten blocks south of the Saturday night fire, and, like most of the buildings in the vicinity, was flimsily constructed of boards. Indeed, the whole city was largely made of wood, though some newer homes of the well-to-do and a number of downtown commercial buildings were covered with brick and stone. Vast quantities of such highly flammable commodities as lumber and grain were stored not only in the "Red Flash" but also all along the branches of the Chicago River, which divided the city into its South, West, and North Divisions. During the afternoon of Sunday, October 8, a supplier had delivered a new load of hay to Mrs. O'Leary, who conducted a modest local milk trade. While it is likely that what became known as the Great Chicago Fire did begin in or around the O'Leary barn about nine that evening, the story of a cow kicking over a lantern, which was in circulation almost immediately, was the stuff of journalistic invention. The precise cause of the fire was and remains unknown, despite an official inquiry. Wherever the conflagration started, confusion and failure in the signal system delayed its being reported to the watch in the Courthouse across the river in the South Division, and from there to the appropriate fire companies. By the time firemen arrived, they were unable to contain the flames, partly because their equipment was damaged, their ranks depleted (by nearly a third), and their energies diminished from fighting the Saturday night fire. The final fateful element was a strong wind from the southwest that blew over the O'Leary barn in the West Division and toward the downtown. As A. T. Andreas, author of the most exhaustive nineteenth-century history of Chicago, described the situation, "Nature had withheld her accustomed measure of prevention, and man had added to the peril by recklessness."[2]

The fire spread with what appeared to be malicious intention, growing hotter and stronger as it was nourished by what it destroyed. It divided unpredictably into separate parts by hurling out flaming brands on the superheated draft it generated, leaping the South Branch of the Chicago River and striking at the commercial heart of the city. It reached the Courthouse, bounded by Clark, LaSalle, Randolph, and Washington Streets, early Monday morning. Designed by J. M. Van Osdel, the city's first architect of note, this Greek Revival structure contained virtually all municipal and county offices and records. It had grown clumsily along with Chicago since its original central section was built in the early 1850s, and by 1871 it featured a domed tower with a watchman's walk, a clock installed only a few months before the fire, and an enormous bell, which frantically tolled the general alarm.[3] When city officials realized early Monday that the Courthouse was itself doomed, they released the prisoners from the basement jail just before the bell's five tons of superheated iron plummeted through the collapsing tower.

The flames soon crossed the main branch of the Chicago River and entered the North Division, ravaging the neighborhood of large and handsome homes, some with elaborately landscaped grounds and outbuildings, that housed many prosperous "old settler" families who constituted the first generation of Chicago's elite. The fire destroyed Lill's Brewery opposite the yellow limestone Gothic water tower and pumping station on Chicago Avenue that had been designed by Chicago's current leading architect, W. W. Boyington, and dedicated with great ceremony in 1867. Although the flames somehow spared the water tower, which still stands as a monument of the disaster, the roof of the pumping station fell in about 3:30 Monday morning, cutting off the flow of water and dashing what small hope remained of resisting the blaze. Meanwhile, back in the South Division, the luxurious new Palmer House gave way, along with the offices of the *Chicago Tribune*, whose editors throughout the summer and fall had exhorted the Common Council to raise the level of fire protection if they wished to avoid just this sort of disaster. By noon on Monday the North Division fires had reached North Avenue and Lincoln Park. They advanced the better part of a mile to Fullerton Avenue, then the northern limit of the city, when, with rain falling, they finally died out early Tuesday morning, leaving Chicago a steaming ruin eerily lit by the glow from cellar coal piles.[4]

As the fire spread out of control, the mood of the population shifted from interest and concern to alarm and panic. Individuals who worked in downtown buildings that were reputed to be "fireproof," like the one that housed the *Tribune*, or who were sure that their homes were beyond harm's reach, soon realized that there was no place of guaranteed safety. Fascinated as well as fearful, people alternately—even simultaneously—tried to get the best view and flee for their lives. It seemed as if the ground itself was on fire—which in a sense it was, since most of the city's streets and virtually all of its sidewalks were made of wood. Later there were reports of Chicagoans trapped or crushed in their homes, on one of the two dozen bridges that spanned the river, or in the Washington and LaSalle Street tunnels, the latter of which had just opened in early July. The burned-out gathered in dazed and dispirited groups on open stretches of prairie west and northwest of the central city, in the South Division along Lake Michigan, and in the North Division at the south end of Lincoln Park. Another refuge of dubious safety was an area known as the Sands, a patch of lakeshore just north of the river. From these different vantages they could look back upon a holocaust so hot and bright that its elemental power stunned the senses.

Amidst the havoc, a small group of elected and self-appointed leaders attempted to impress some order on the devastated city. On Monday morning, with the downtown still too dangerous to enter and parts of the city still aflame, Charles C. P. Holden summoned the original core of this group to a meeting later in the day at the First Congregational Church. Holden was president of the Common Council, the city's legislative body, and he represented the tenth ward in the West Division, where the church was located. Once assembled later in the day, he and the others turned the church into a temporary city hall and hastily made arrangements for enlisting citizens as special deputies to assure public safety, for supplying food and water to the homeless, and for other emergency needs. Mayor Roswell B. Mason arrived at the meeting a little before three in the afternoon, and he signed a proclamation pledging the "faith and credit of the city of Chicago" to "the preservation of order, and the relief of suffering," as well as to "the protection of property." Other directives established the price of bread, set certain safety regulations, limited the hours of saloons, and forbade hackmen, expressmen, and teamsters, who reportedly had exploited and even robbed desperate homeowners, from charging more than their regular fares.

The scale of the Chicago disaster suited this city obsessed with statistical achievement. The so-called "Burnt District," a map of which appeared in virtually every account of the fire, encompassed an area four miles long and an average of three-quarters of a mile wide—over two thousand acres—with the greatest losses in the heavily residential North Division. The death count was by different estimates around three hundred, and even if this figure was low, the number of fatalities was still surprisingly small. On the other hand, the property damage was staggering. The fire destroyed eighteen thousand buildings, and the financial worth of the losses (many of them never recovered because of the failure of local insurance companies) approached two hundred million dollars, a third of the valuation of the entire city. The fire destroyed the homes of nearly 100,000 Chicagoans, almost a third of the people in the city, and at least temporarily removed the means of livelihood of a large segment of the population whose exact number, like the toll of fatalities, is very hard to compute. Approximately 30,000 left the city (many soon returned) on free passes offered by the railroads. One of the fire's most daunting qualities was how thoroughly it did its work. "It was the *completeness* of the wreck," observed local journalists Elias Colbert and Everett Chamberlin in their history of the fire, "the total desolation which met the eye on every hand; the utter blankness of what had a few hours before been so full of life, of associations, of aspirations, of all things which kept the mind of a Chicagoan so constantly crowded, and his nerves and muscles so constantly driven." The toll in the Burnt Division included over twenty-eight miles of streets and 120 miles of sidewalks (though numerous thoroughfares still had neither sidewalks nor paved streets of any kind), as well as over 2,000 lampposts, along with countless trees, shrubs, and flowering plants in a town that liked to call itself the Garden City of the West.[5]

Writing the Calamity

The catastrophe ignited a literary conflagration as extensive in its own way as the fire. Naturally, the local interest was most intense and per-

sonal. As H. A. Musham, author of the first modern and carefully doc-
umented account of the disaster, explained, "So sudden was the visitation, so complete the destruction it achieved, and so magnificently
awesome the spectacle it presented to the frightened people, that it
etched an indelible though blurred impression on their minds—a picture which time was never able to erase." The result, Musham observed, was that "[e]veryone . . . in Chicago in those fateful days had a
story to tell, and they never tired of telling it,"—in letters, diaries,
memoirs, and other kinds of personal accounts.[6] Whether undertaken
with some prompting or not—and many recollections were committed
to paper well after the fact at the urging of children and grandchildren,
other survivors, old acquaintances, or local history buffs—they were
predictably colored by a sense of an epic occasion, a confidence that the
magnitude of the moment more than justified taking pen in hand.[7]

The personal accounts composed not long after the disaster generally followed a common narrative sequence: the first news of the fire
and the belief that it will be contained; the men of the house heading
downtown to view the blaze and, in several instances, to check on their
offices; the realization that no one is safe, followed by the frantic gathering of family and goods; the retreat (usually in several stages) to some
point of safety; the post-fire scene and mood, and reflections on the
whole experience, colored by a shifting mix of fear and hope, depression and exhilaration. Chicagoans repeatedly focused on the small details amidst the cosmic horror: the putting in good order of a home
about to be destroyed, the obsession with saving the beloved portrait or
rag doll or pet parrot while everything else was relinquished to the
flames, the last look back at a way of life lost forever. These often eloquently understated individual accounts of confrontations with calamity and with the uncertainties of the future possess a moving human
quality that links them in spirit to confrontations with disaster ranging
from the diaries of the London fire of 1666 to John Hersey's
Hiroshima.[8]

Of far greater substance, both in terms of the quantity that was produced and the readership it reached, was the fire literature that was created by a host of professional authors. This includes the outpouring of
sermons and public proclamations and addresses, but mainly the massive newspaper and periodical coverage of the devastation locally (the
leading Chicago papers resumed publishing in makeshift quarters in a
matter of days, and *Chicago Evening Journal* editor Andrew Shuman
managed to find a printer in the West Division who turned out an edition on the day of the fire), nationally, and internationally. Even if they
were uncertain of exactly what was happening in Chicago, newspaper-
men were absolutely convinced that they were covering the biggest

story of their lives, for which there was an enormous and insatiable audience. In a wild scene in John McGovern's novel, *Daniel Trentworthy:
A Tale of the Great Fire of Chicago* (1889), a frantic editor commands his
exhausted reporters, their faces blackened beyond recognition by their
adventures on the streets, "All sit here and write whatever comes into
your heads!"[9]

Perhaps the most impressive measure of the attention and interest
the fire commanded was the dozen or so fire histories, ranging from
cheap pamphlets to clothbound volumes, that went through multiple
editions and were in a few instances over five hundred pages long. The
authors of these works were, like McGovern, mainly local journalists or
out-of-town reporters who came to cover the fire and its aftermath,
though so sure were writers and publishers across the country of a market for such books that some were put together by individuals who
never set foot in the city and who mined their narratives out of news
reports and ingenuity. They worked with astonishing speed, cranking
out these forebears of today's "instant" histories of popular news events
in a matter of weeks. Written for expressly commercial purposes, they
showed none of the rhetorical constraint of the personal accounts. In
their most elaborate versions they included sections on Chicago's rise
to eminence (in one of the most ambitious of these works, Colbert and
Chamberlin's *Chicago and the Great Conflagration,* in print before the
end of November, this prehistory occupied the first twenty-one chapters), followed by descriptions of the city just before disaster struck, of
the long dry summer of 1871, of the Saturday night fire, and of the origins of the blaze in the O'Leary stable.[10] Only then came the main
event, which commonly divided into three major parts. These parts
might be titled "Daring and Danger," describing the perils of the fire
and the failed attempts to contain it; "Flight and Fellowship," the retreat from its terrors into communities of refugees; and "Return and
Resurrection," the reestablishment of routine and the determination to
build a better Chicago. All of this was enriched with an abundance of
illustrations, eyewitness and newspaper accounts, as well as with sections on the actions of leaders, incidents of note, the extent of the
losses, the relief effort, the lessons of the fire (including, of course, the
need for fireproof construction), the current condition of the city, and a
brief survey of great urban fires since antiquity.

The story of Chicago's destruction soon became the subject of gift
books and anniversary issues of newspapers and magazines. Local publishers distributed pamphlets that combined brief histories of the conflagration with directories of "leading houses" in the rebuilding city,
interspersed with advertisements for these concerns. The fire also entered into explicitly imaginative writings, some of which relied heavily

on other printed sources, especially newspapers. Poets near and far, including Bret Harte, John Greenleaf Whittier, and Julia Moore, the inexorably lugubrious "Sweet Singer of Michigan," set themselves to the task of discovering and expressing the higher meaning of this terrible visitation, generating a corpus of verse unrelievedly lofty in tone and abysmal in quality. One of the best-sellers of the period, with sales in its various editions ultimately totaling a million copies, was the Reverend E. P. Roe's 1872 novel, *Barriers Burned Away*, which was still being reprinted after the turn of the century.[11] The New York dime-novel house of Ornum & Company beat Roe to the punch with *The Ruined City; or, The Horrors of Chicago* (1871), featuring a "Full Description of the Great Fire of Chicago, Including the No. of Houses, and Principal Buildings Burnt, Number of Lives Lost; Thrilling Incidents, Amount of Damage Done," and, for good measure, a "Brief Account of the Fire of London." A quarter of a century later Frank Tousey's Five Cent Wide Awake Library issued *The Fire Bugs of Chicago*, suggesting that the Chicago fire was started by the "rascally band" in the title, "and the story of Mrs. O'Leary's cow only circulated as a blind."[12]

Describing the Indescribable

But what were all these different accounts of the fire saying? Given the staggering volume of what was written and published, they reveal surprisingly little about the fire itself that is reliable and definitive in regard to the matter of what exactly had taken place. In his reflections on his sources, H. A. Musham noted that, even ignoring the outpouring of secondary accounts in newspapers, magazines, pamphlets, and books, anyone who was trying to figure out what occurred in Chicago between October 8 and 10 faced a mass of information that, in his words, "defied analysis." The daunting quantity of the fire literature was only part of the problem Musham encountered, since, he also observed, different descriptions and recollections "disagree almost unanimously as to details," making it "very difficult to determine just what happened at critical points of the fire." He might have added that the longer after the fact an individual composed his or her "personal" memoir, the more likely that it was clouded by the passage of time, reshaped by post-fire experience, and inflected by its author's familiarity with other narratives. Musham bemoaned the fact that there were virtually no contemporary accounts of the fire of scientific value.[13]

The same goes for visual records. Historians of Chicago Harold M. Mayer and Richard C. Wade point out that no photographs of the Chicago fire survive, and that perhaps none were ever taken. With the exception of the sketches of noted Civil War artist Alfred R. Waud, the illustrations that appeared in the local and national press, and later in books, were obviously fanciful. A widely reprinted lithograph by Currier and Ives, part of whose stock-in-trade was such disaster scenes, was a humanly inaccessible bird's-eye view from over the lake, in which the flames go in the wrong direction. John McGovern suggested in *Daniel Trentworthy* that the reason for the absence of reliable information was that the event was simply too titanic for anyone's senses to encompass. Unless one was "at least ten miles away, on a high place," McGovern wrote, this "line of fire a mile long" would appear to be "an endless sea of flames" that was "broader than the eye can cover." As a result, he concluded, in spite of the fact that this event had hundreds of thousands of witnesses, "Nobody saw the Chicago fire."[14]

Many others suggested that seeing the fire would have made little difference, at least as far as furnishing an accurate literary record was concerned. According to the Chicago Relief and Aid Society's 1874 report on its administration of aid, Chicago's experience transcended all categories of description. The report contended that if the verbal record of what had happened was fragmentary, incomplete, and contradictory, this was not surprising. What else could one expect to emerge from "the stifling clouds of dust, smoke, and cinders, and the confusion and utter chaos of the night—a night lurid with flames, the reflection of which, in itself, gave to the countenances of these fleeing thousands an awe-stricken and almost unearthly aspect"? Since both trying to see and attempting to describe the fire were impossible, eyewitnesses could speak only of the failed attempt to do such seeing, describing, and comprehending. The hiss and crackle of the flames, the roar of the gale, the collapsing walls, the report continued, "gave tragic coloring to the scene, and leaves the night memorable in the minds of those who witnessed it, as a picture of appalling horror, distinct in its outlines, weird in its dark shadings, but utterly incapable of verbal representation."[15]

Utterly incapable of verbal representation. The inclusion of such a phrase is by far the most commonly shared feature of all accounts of the fire, whether nonfiction, fiction, or poetry. Again and again writers conceded a power to the fire that they said they could not hope to capture in words. It was impossible to describe something so "bewildering, exciting, electrifying, astounding and weirdly stupendous" and that was so full of details that could never all be collected, including so many sights that "petrify the intellect and strangle reflection."[16] It is an easy task to compile a whole anthology of similar statements, many equally overwrought in their special pleading.[17] Such disquisitions on the impossibility of representing this calamity verbally are invariably followed, however, by a lengthy attempt to do just that. Rather than being stunned into silence by the realization that no words could describe the fire experience, amateur and professional writers alike seemed, as Musham said, to be incapable of *not* talking on and on about it, as if to compensate for their professed inadequacy with a massive literary outpouring.

The simplest explanation for the prevalence of these claims of indescribability, followed by a heavy helping of what certainly reads like description, is their conventionality. Their purpose was to convince an audience of the significance of the subject and to win some sympathy for the author, whose virtuosity was revealed in meeting the creative challenge he or she defined as impossible. More particularly, the assertion that an event is indescribable is one of the telltale signs of disaster literature throughout the ages, an essential (and often honest) declaration that a writer must make to get the reader's attention and sympathy and to establish the status of his or her subject as catastrophe, as something that does not readily fit into any existing vocabulary. In addition, terrible events sometimes seem to demand a substantial verbal response precisely because they are unspeakable; talking about them has a therapeutic value as a necessary step toward survival, healing, and renewal. Having passed through a hell on earth that turned their city into a desolate wasteland overnight, all that Chicagoans (and Americans who followed what happened from afar) seemed to have to fill the terrible sense of loss—and its disorienting combination of wonder, horror, dread, confusion, and expectation—was an "indelible" blur, and they dealt with it by trying to fill the absence by talking, writing, and reading about it. It is possible also to generalize in another direction and argue that the body of writing on the Chicago fire is an especially pointed and dramatic example of the fact that the attempt to translate experience into language that can accurately and directly convey that experience to readers is to a greater or lesser extent expressive of its own failure.

These explanations are not satisfactory, however, in accounting for the heft and variety of the fire literature, and they mainly tell us what this body of writing fails to do. What if we take those who wrote about the fire at their word, or loss of words, and agree with them that there was no way to describe it? This leaves us with a pile of pages about the fire higher than the water tower, and with the question of what this pile signifies. If so many people spent so many words in *not* describing the fire, *what* were they writing about? Musham provides a useful suggestion when he argues that while contemporary sources do not offer an accurate physical description of the fire itself, they do give us an "impression." Others much closer to the event suggested something similar. The Chicago Relief and Aid Society account maintained, "The imagination is the only faculty of the human mind equal to any comprehension of the appalling night when Chicago was in flames," while the anonymous author of one of the first instant histories observed that "the burning city itself was the theatre in which the various predominant passions which actuate the human mind were most amply displayed."[18] What the literature of the fire revealed most fully was the complicated way the fire entered the minds of those who wrote and read about it.

The authors of the fire literature tried to explain what had happened for themselves and eager readers everywhere on the level not of fact but, as the Relief and Aid Society report hinted, of imagination. The result was not a history of the fire but an expression of how the writers understood it in relation to their lives. The conflicting quality and overwhelming quantity of their outpouring present a problem to anyone, like Musham, trying to determine precisely how the flames progressed moment by moment and block by block, but the writing itself tells us a great deal about how the authors appropriated the fire to talk more generally about Chicago and to express an understanding of the nature of modern urban experience.[19] The physical means, as well as the literary forms, through which they communicated this understanding, and the imaginative frames in which they tried to make it fit, all reveal how they "saw" the fire and the city.

One of the most striking aspects of the telling of the story of the Chicago fire was how quickly and how widely it was told. The reporting of the city's destruction was a pioneering example of what Richard D. Brown has called the "contagious diffusion" of information. While telegraphic transmission of news dates to before 1850, the advances in communications in the years following the Civil War arguably made the fire the country's first national and international "instant" media event. The city burned down because of the failure to summon nearby firefighters in a timely way, and local citizens were alerted to the impending disaster by the ancient means of a tolling bell, but meanwhile the telegraph, with remarkably few interruptions, enabled much of the rest of the country to learn of Chicago's misfortune virtually as it happened.[20] As has become the rule with the dissemination of disaster news in the modern age of communications, an enormously scattered population far from Chicago probably knew more about the event while it was occurring than many of those actually experiencing it at the time.[21] The family of William Blair, whose Michigan Avenue home survived the fire, experienced this new order of things firsthand, as Mrs. Blair recalled fifty years later. Traveling in the East with her husband and son, Sara Blair first heard the terrible news at a stop in Utica, and then proceeded home against the tide of continued updates from the burning city.[22]

Newspaper editors, following common practice for stories transmitted by wire, headed columns on the Chicago disaster with the words "NEWS BY TELEGRAPH" or "BY TELEGRAPH" to assure their readers of the freshness of the reports. The production of the news of the spectacle thus mixed in journalists' and readers' minds with the event, as the fire, the technology that communicated it, and the information that was communicated merged into one phenomenon. As successive dispatches came in faster than these editors could issue extras, they printed these dispatches—numbering in some cases into the teens—one right after another, separated by datelines that noted the hour, so that readers could witness the fire's advance across Chicago through the columns of their papers. The instant histories, and many accounts published well after the fire, tried to capture the same breathless sense of temporal and spatial immediacy conveyed by the original telegraph reports.[23] People everywhere read about the fire, and about their ability to read about it, so quickly that they could contribute to trainloads of supplies while the city was still burning—a feat that then was reported in the same papers. Once their own newspapers resumed publication, Chicagoans could then see reprinted fire stories originally published in out-of-town papers and national magazines.

What they all were ultimately reading about was themselves as part of a national community of cities in a networked urban nation. The immediate access to stories of the fire told them that they and Chicago were connected, that Chicago's growth had been founded on its importance as the crucial nexus between East and West in the expanding nation as the United States assumed leadership in an international economy. Indeed, the reason so many people wanted and were able to learn quickly about Chicago's destruction was because the rest of the country and the world had invested so much in making it a vital mercantile center with which they needed to keep instantly and constantly in touch.[24] On the same pages through which they could follow the course of the fire, they could read related stories on the turmoil in financial markets everywhere and on how the continued commercial vitality of the stricken city was crucial to the country, as well as commentaries from other papers that similarly discussed the meaning of this catastrophe for everyone. The wide repercussions of the Chicago fire in American public life, the *Nation* commented three days after the flames died out, "is perhaps as striking a proof as we have ever had of the closeness of the relations which have been established between the uttermost ends of the earth."[25]

Mixed Messages

If most commentators agreed that one of the central meanings of the fire was how the cities and regions of the nation were interconnected and interdependent, they reached no similar consensus on how this and other meanings should be expressed. The fire literature, especially the published forms, presented an array of rhetorical styles and literary conventions that clashed with one another.[26] Partly because it was compiled hastily from many different sources, and since its authors were eager to capture the attention of a variety of readers, much of the fire literature, particularly the instant histories, consists of startlingly multivalent texts speaking unpredictably in several different voices. Combining lofty history with interviews, eyewitness reports, sensational anecdotes, official proclamations, and analyses—all supplemented by maps and illustrations and capped off with a title as overpacked as the works themselves—they are at once sentimental and hard-boiled, nostalgic and utopian, sensational and sober, encomiastic and critical. The rhetorical strain often showed, especially when authors made great claims for the significance of the fire. Frank Luzerne, author of one of the most vivid fire histories, threw in every metaphor he could think of. In the space of a single paragraph, Luzerne compared Chicago's fate to that of "tall Troy," Moscow, London, Jerusalem, Rome, and Carthage (all of whose catastrophes, he argued, paled by comparison), as he described the fire as a furious gale, a rolling ocean, a seething and roaring volcano crater, a torrent, a typhoon, lightning, and as an endless assault by heavy artillery.[27]

Such stormy mixtures of style and language reflected a time of transition and uncertainty in thinking and writing about the modern city, a period associated in the broadest terms with the evolution from a romantic to a realistic aesthetic. Viewed in these terms, the most significant (and common) hybrid in the fire literature was the melding in numerous permutations of Gothic-epic-romantic conventions with those of the reportorial-scientific-realistic. On one hand, the lurid spectacle of the destruction of Chicago, with tens of thousands of people trying to escape being burned alive through a terrible night made brighter than day by the hellish flames, seemed to demand the most unrestrained treatment. It was a natural subject for pulp accounts like *The Ruined City; or, the Horrors of Chicago*, which observed, "Scene is no name for it [the fire]. It was a multiplicity of scenes. A wild phantasmagoria in which all the forms and figures that romancists [*sic*] struggle after, were dreadfully produced."[28] But at the same time, the importance of the city of Chicago in the rationalized commercial network of trade communication, and administration demanded accurate facts and shrewd assessments, clearly presented. The accounts in newspapers, magazines, and instant histories refused to make a choice, joining high melodrama with tightly reasoned economic projections, overwritten comparisons of the horrors of Chicago and those of Herculaneum and Pompeii with a detailed breakdown of which insurance companies survived or failed. The *Chicago Times* argued that "[n]othing less than the pen of divine inspiration could outline the prefiguration of catastrophe so grand as that which has befallen Chicago," recounted how the "twin rioters of flame and wind, with their appetite sharpened instead of gorged by the blast among the meaner buildings of the West division and river side . . . fell in dire carnival upon the noble edifices of LaSalle street," and then followed all this with a no-nonsense editorial on the necessity of keeping the downtown where it was and protecting Chicago's credit rating. A. T. Andreas rehearsed the terrors of the unleashing of bareheaded and barefooted "demons" from the Courthouse jail right after informing the reader, in what reads today like modern press release prose, that the bell in the tower "was purchased by the city of Jones & Co., bellfounders, of Troy, N.Y., December 3, 1862, at a cost of $3,688.66," and that it weighed 10,849 pounds and was five feet two inches tall and six feet ten inches across at its mouth. Colbert and Chamberlin devoted an extensive section to "The Science of the Fire," combining a technical analysis of the possible deleterious effects of the increase in the percentage of carbonic acid gas released by such fires with philosophical speculation on whether the Chicago cataclysm was "but one of a series of events, designed by the Great Ruler of the universe to prevent man from progressing too fast or too far, in his forward march toward the perfection of knowledge, and of that power which knowledge confers upon its possessors."[29]

The sometimes rocky marriage of contrasting conventions was one of the hallmarks not only of disaster literature but also of urban writing of the period, less a problem to be resolved than a strategy to be mastered by a Hugo, a Dostoyevsky, a Dickens, and, in the decades ahead, a Theodore Dreiser, whose Chicago is a mix of boundless dreams and inescapable realities. The merging of literary modes in the fire literature opposed a view of experience that trampled on subtlety in asserting the imaginative power of cataclysmic loss of control against a perspective that desired to manage and comprehend disorder through accurate description and careful analysis. Both points of view conceived of the city as new ground in both social and literary terms, and of Chicago on fire as an especially appealing and promising occasion to

try to find a voice and a viewpoint that would enable one to master this
unsettled landscape imaginatively.[30]

At this dramatic moment, and for a long time to follow, the frame in
which the Chicago calamity seemed best to fit was the memory of the
country's most divisive war. An article titled "The Silver Lining of the
Cloud," published three weeks after the fire in *Harper's Weekly,* maintained that "since the war no event has so startled and saddened the
nation." By this time many other discussions of the fire had described it
in terms of the Civil War, and war in general. It is hard to find an account of the fire, particularly one meant for a public audience, that
does not resort to such imagery, that is not dotted with descriptive
epithets like "the fiery foe" and "battalions of flame" and such sentences as "The two main columns sent out detachments which entered
every street with the regularity of an advancing army."[31] This kind of
depiction was as common as observations on how it was impossible to
see and describe the fire accurately and completely. Numerous authors
likened Chicago aflame to a battlefield precisely in terms of its incom-
prehensibility and indescribability. "Nobody could see it all—no more
than one man could see the whole of the Battle of Gettysburg," *Chicago
Tribune* editor Horace White recalled. "It was too vast, too swift, too full
of smoke, too full of danger, for anybody to see it all."[32]

The fire-as-war metaphor, like the trope of indescribability, has a
long history as a literary convention.[33] As impassioned conflicts over
(hotly) contested territory, warfare and urban fire are well-suited counterparts. The intrusion of the Civil War in descriptions of the fire was
virtually inevitable, given how recent and how deeply felt the war was,
and because of its association in the public mind with cities set ablaze.
Speaking of the fire in relation to the Civil War also enabled writers and
readers to displace the problem of indescribability in talking of what
happened in Chicago by comparing it to another epic event that
seemed both to defy description and demand a literary response.[34] In
addition, it provided another way to praise the valor of all those who
survived this heroic struggle and to sanctify the mutual dependency of
Chicago and the rest of the nation. The Reverend Edward Everett
Hale, whose great-uncle was Nathan Hale and whose uncle Edward
Everett had spoken beside Lincoln at Gettysburg (and who himself was
author of the wartime classic, "The Man Without a Country"), reminded his audience at a relief rally in Faneuil Hall that Chicago was
Boston's ally in trade and commerce, and that its misfortune was everyone's. "We are all, as it has been said, linked together in a solidarity of
the nation." He then integrated Chicago's devastation into the current
mission of Reconstruction. "Their loss is no more theirs than it is ours
in this great campaign of peace in which we are engaged," Hale ex-

plained. "There has fallen by this calamity one of our noblest for-
tresses. Its garrison is without munitions. It is for us at this instant to
reconstruct that fortress, and to see that its garrison are as well placed
as they were before in our service."[35]

The close imaginative association of the fire and the war did not
cause but certainly reinforced the distinctively two-sided imaginative
understanding of the fire. The effort to see the disaster in terms of local
and national affirmation found its antagonist in an anxiety that existed
independent of the fire, but which the enormous dislocation and destruction enhanced and gave special urgency. Linking the fire experience to the Civil War enabled writers and readers to find progress and
unity beyond the flames, but it also raised the idea, one that would become more powerful as time passed, that Chicago was a community at
peril because of divisions that threatened to destroy it from within.
Rather than daunt the city, the fire seemed to reenergize all the zeal and
optimism that built Chicago in the first place, but at the same time it
prompted many reflections on the city's past and present that spoke of
serious problems and of other difficult encounters that lay ahead.

THREE

Trial by Fire

Two large and loosely defined clusters of belief regarding Chicago and the modern city emerged from the flames. The first stressed the idea that Chicago's transcendent purpose and special relationship with God and history had been reconfirmed by this ordeal. Most commentators chose to greet the fire, as many Americans had the Civil War, as a special opportunity offered the city to cleanse its soul and devote itself to an enlightened moral discipline that would be a vital step forward in the march toward a final and perfect civilization.[1] By this reasoning, the fire was part of the inscrutable workings of fate, which brought about the dry summer of 1871 and the hot wind of October 8. The scale of the destruction did not indicate the degree of Chicago's venality or misfortune, but the grandeur of its destiny. Greater than the catastrophes that consumed Rome, London, and other world cities, the fire proved that Chicago and America had already surpassed or would soon supersede these other settlements in all respects. The contrasting vision saw the American city, in normal as well as in such obviously exceptional moments as the burning of Chicago, as a center of social conflict, with the eventual outcome—and the future of "civilization"—still very much unsettled. Chicago might hold the key to America's promise, but its social order would have to be carefully guarded since the city was a tinderbox ready to break out in crime, debauchery, and anarchy the moment restraints were relaxed.

These two sets of attitudes vied with each other in many places, moving along axes of uncertainty on which it is possible to chart the imaginative dimensions of the fire. In some ways these opposing attitudes were not very different, since they both were based in a belief in the perils of urban disorder and in the value of social control. Together they shaped a collective meditation on the relation of contemporary events to each other, to the past, and to the future, expressed through literary forms whose purpose was to discover through the fire the nature and meaning of reality.

The Faith of Catastrophe

What exactly had happened in the burning of Chicago? What did the future hold? These were the key questions that the literature of the fire had to answer. In its interpretation of everything from the smallest private action to the broadest public achievement, the affirmative view of what had occurred found expressive form as the story of a series of critical challenges that were decisively met by the city and the nation. If the fear, bewilderment, despair, mental agony, and pain of the fearsome two days could "never be adequately pictured," recalled one writer reviewing how people responded to the terror, neither could "there be properly recorded the courage, the self-possession, the generosity, the mutual helpfulness which also marked the astonishing scene."[2] This view constructed a narrative of the fire as a myth of re-creation in which Chicago was apotheosized into a higher plane of civic being in an epic moment that made it pure, heroic, and modern. The purpose of the myth was to banish the idea that the fire was a threat to what had always been Chicago's most valuable commodity, its future.

The effort to interpret the fire as an act of purification was derived from a prevailing concern, especially on the part of the old settlers and the new business elite, that the moral condition of the city, or at least the reputation of the moral condition, was a source of embarrassment and shame. "Pure" was not an adjective commonly attached to pre-fire Chicago, since the city had a well-earned reputation for tolerating gambling and prostitution.[3] Some commentators in other cities compared Chicago to Sodom and Gomorrah, pointing to the city's materialist spirit as being of a piece with its receptivity to vice. The Reverend Granville Moody of Cincinnati, for example, saw the fire as punishment for the flouting of Sunday and liquor laws, and as "a retributive judgment on a city which has shown such a devotion in its worship to the Golden Calf." This kind of talk of sin and retribution was inevitable in the post-disaster mentality of any Christian nation, and, whether widely and deeply felt or not, was certainly one of the first cultural resources to which several Chicagoans themselves resorted both privately and publicly in an attempt to find a reason for their misfortune. William H. Carter, one of the three commissioners of the City's Board of Works, wrote to his brother, "Boastful Chicago lies prostrate and

with outstretched arms is begging of her sister cities for relief," and customs official Francis William Test soberly told his mother, "We have
been punished."[4]

The most pious of the instant histories, the Reverend Edgar J. Goodspeed's *The Great Fires in Chicago and the West,* railed against all the
breweries, brothels, theaters, "gambling-hells," and violations of the
Sabbath in pre-fire Chicago, before asking rhetorically, "Will vice and
crime riot as they have done, eating out the very vitality of the city? In
the presence of death and woe will men forget the better part?" Mayor
Mason's earliest emergency proclamations concentrated on social and
economic concerns, but he attributed "this terrible calamity" to "the
providence of God, to whose will we humbly submit. . . ." He designated Sunday, October 29, "as a special day of humiliation and prayer;
of humiliation for those past offenses against Almighty God, to which
these severe afflictions were doubtless intended to lead our minds; of
prayer for the relief and comfort of the suffering thousands in our
midst; for the restoration of our material prosperity, especially for our
lasting improvement as a people in reverence and obedience to God."[5]

Remarks like these were, however, a brief and relatively minor counterpoint to the view that not only dismissed the idea of the fire as atone-
ment but embraced the disaster as a sign of Chicago's unique importance. The lead story of the *Chicago Weekly Post* of October 26, titled
"Resurgam," stated, "People who see a Providential judgment in the
destruction have very limited knowledge of Divine economy," while
George Alfred Townsend, in his poem "The Smitten City," dated October 13, 1871, called the admonishments of those who read the fire as
divine judgment "shallow platitudes from fool and foe." In the third of
his twenty-one stilted stanzas, Townsend abandoned a defensive posture altogether and declared pre-fire Chicago a pillar of piety:

> Bright, Christian capital of lakes and prairie,
>   Heaven had no interest in thy scourge and scath;
> Thou wert the newest shrine of our religion,
>   The youngest witness of our faith.[6]

Explaining the destruction of Chicago this way was a somewhat
tricky task since it required minimizing the disaster as an act of God
while stressing the idea of holy purpose. It was important to observers
both locally and nationally, whatever the contradictions, to attribute
the fire to bad luck that could have struck anywhere, while at the same
time connecting the monumentality of the experience to some divine
good divorced from the idea of direct punishment. The discussions of
"humiliation" and "humbling," of the puniness of man, the vanity of
worldly ambitions, and of the simple joy and priceless privilege of a safe

and happy home and hearth that appeared in the fire literature (and
the literature of almost all catastrophes) interpreted the conflagration
not as an indictment of this particular city but as a generalized lesson
for everyone. Local author Alfred Sewell, who is credited with writing
the first of the instant histories, stated that he would not treat "the divine or religious aspect" of the fire, "except so far as to express the opinion that, if the Almighty, in His government of our little world, . . .
employs what theologians term 'special providences,' then it may be accepted as a solemn fact that He smote Chicago not only for its own ultimate good, but as a warning and a lesson for all other cities, if not for all
mankind."7 Sewell's argument, which was implicit in Townsend's
poem and was echoed repeatedly in public and private writings in Chicago and elsewhere, shared the logic of Lincoln's Second Inaugural
Address, which accepted suffering as divine judgment, but, in a search
for harmony and healing, diffused the blame. If anything, the city was
not punished but honored by having been singled out for such a trial.
The larger question, raised tentatively, of whether Chicago in particular or urban culture in general was in need of reformation, was quickly
buried under the theme of "ultimate good."

This analysis thus conceptualized the fire less as a retribution for
past sins than as a forward-looking and virtually instantaneous program of reform that was yet another sign of Chicago's destiny. The calamity seemed to transform this Gilded Age capital into a city on a hill
that was inhabited by a spiritually reborn chosen people who had a cov-
enant with God and history. The rebirth from the fire involved a conversion experience of the highest kind, as N. S. Emerson proclaimed in
the last stanza of his poem "The Stricken City":

> For he who walked of old on earth,
> Is with us in this later birth:
> We lost him in our greed for pelf,
> But to his higher, purer Self,
> He leads us through his golden tide,
> And thus our loss is glorified.

In the months following the fire, this interpretation became the prevalent public reading of the event. Writing in an issue of the *Lakeside
Monthly* marking the first anniversary of the fire, *Chicago Evening Journal* editor Andrew Shuman asked, "Was not the Great Fire a blessing in
disguise?" and then answered his own question:

> If, as some of the severer school of religionists told us, Chicago's baptism
> of flame was an exhibition of God's vengeance upon a wicked, proud,
> and presumptuous community, then it must also be that He soon re-

pented of his severity, and changed the curse into a blessing. . . . But turning from the consideration of individual unfortunates to that of the community and the city as a whole, it may, we think, be truthfully said that, all things considered, the fire will prove a benefit rather than a calamity.[8]

The Triumph of Character

While some resisted seeing what had happened to Chicago as a drama of sin and redemption, virtually everyone who wrote about the fire was eager to read it in a very similar way as a trial of the city's character in which its mettle was tested in a literal crucible and found not wanting. The many stories that immediately appeared in print that emphasized individual bravery and selflessness were tributes to the human spirit that transcended the specific circumstances of the moment, but part of their message was that Chicago in 1871 was a community of valiant citizens who in this worst of times discovered the best in themselves. These stories read like other formulaic fiction or drama in which decisive action by the most honorable and noble triumphs in the end.[9] This is evident in the "thrilling anecdotes" in the newspapers and histories that celebrated the courage of common citizens who were heedless of personal welfare, like quick-thinking Sherman House desk clerk John Hickie and his assistant, who saved the life of an ill female guest by dashing back into "the now trembling building," smashing in her door, drenching her bedclothes with water from a pitcher and basin in the room, and taking her safely away, their own garments and hands badly burned, just a few minutes before this proud structure became "one of the most complete wrecks of the night."[10] Among the popular subjects of the illustrations accompanying the instant histories were highly theatrical renderings of fearless men risking all in aid of helpless women and children, as well as of the last desperate moments of people about to perish.

   More common than its citation of such spectacular acts of bravery was the fire literature's commendation of a quieter kind of courage that was evident in the dignity of Chicagoans amidst terrifying danger. Eyewitnesses insisted on how calm and civil people remained as they retreated from their lost homes. Mary Ann Hubbard, the matriarch of one of the oldest of the "old settler" families, remembered being impressed by "the calm, courteous way in which people talked—if all had been serene and normal they could not have been more patient and respectful." Landscape architect H. W. S. Cleveland claimed in a handwritten account composed a month after the fire that "there was little or no confusion and nothing like a panic. . . . Everybody seemed cool and collected." And Frederick Law Olmsted, reporting on the disaster for the *Nation*, told his readers, "Very sensible men have declared that they were fully impressed at such a time with the conviction that it was the burning of the world," but that, nevertheless, "[a]lmost every one holds the remembrance of some instance of quiet heroism, often flavored with humor."[11]

As is commonly the case immediately following catastrophes in the United States, there was much talk of a refined post-fire "community of suffering" bonded by Christian faith and democratic feeling.[12] Whether they asserted that the fire's effects were so utopian or not, Chicagoans were eager to point out that the destruction certainly seemed to have an egalitarian disregard for class distinctions that was beneficial even to those who seemed to lose the most. Emma Hambleton wrote to her mother a day after the fire, telling her that "in the streets were the families of the richest men in Chicago running, some lost, and many sitting right on the pavement for a moment's breath, dressed in velvets[,] silk, and jewels they were trying to save." She then reflected, if not without some dismay, "The fire was a wonderful leveler, if I may use that expression." Goodspeed spoke more enthusiastically of the undermining of the pride of the rich, who, "in the presence of the universally imminent danger," were "thoroughly glad" to make their escape in "the humblest cart." Colbert and Chamberlin similarly maintained that one of the salutary consequences of the fire would be "the greater necessity for *work*" that would stir everyone into action. In a chapter titled "Good Out of Evil," they developed this theme at length:

> But the best work which the fire has wrought has been upon the character and habits of the people, rather than upon their business, political, or other material affairs. The people of Chicago were, before the fire, fast lapsing into luxury—not as yet to any such degree as the people of New York—but still more than was for their good. The fire roused them from this tendency, and made them the same strong men and women, of the same simple, industrious, self-denying habits, which built up Chicago, and pushed her so powerfully along her unparalleled career. All show and frivolity were abandoned, and democracy became the fashion.[13]

The fire literature repeatedly maintained that the main effect of the flames was to burn away vain inessentials to reveal the sound and solid integrity of the people, not so much reforming Chicago but, as Colbert and Chamberlin's reference to New York hints, bringing the city's citizens back to their best selves. One of the central figures in *Barriers Burned Away* remarks, "That which can vanish in a night in flame and smoke cannot belong to us, is not part of us. All that has come out of the crucible of this fire is my character, myself."[14]

The point of these comments was to testify that Chicagoans had displayed, in the words of one citizen writing a few days after the fire, "American character of the highest type," and thus had proved that their city was a coherent community.[15] Certain particular stories that appeared repeatedly in the fire literature developed this idea in greater depth. These generally evaded any serious critical reflection on the state of the pre-fire city by concentrating on effects and not causes of the disaster, and by seeing the benefits of the fire more as the source of a heightened self-awareness and maturity than as reform. Both personal correspondence and the instant histories singled out as a representative case the fate of Unity Church. Located in the North Division's best neighborhood, Unity's spiritual leader was Robert Collyer, a Yorkshire-born blacksmith who in his mid-twenties had turned to the ministry shortly before emigrating to America in 1850. Collyer had established himself as one of the most popular preachers in the city. An outspoken abolitionist active in the Sanitary Commission during the war, he was widely known as a humanitarian who embodied what many saw as the best Chicago had to offer. The Sunday after the fire he met with the members of his congregation and of several others ("Denominations and creeds were forgotten") by the ruins of his sanctuary in a gathering that one fire history likened to "a convention of early Christians in the catacombs."[16] To post-fire Chicago, this gathering represented the moral and social core of a new urban dispensation that now better understood its responsibility to its own future.

Several writers developed the theme of the multidimensional civic elevation of burned-out Chicago through a number of depictions of Chicago, "the Queen City of the West," as a woman. Colbert and Chamberlin concluded their lengthy history of the fire by comparing the effect worked by the fire on Chicago to the transformation of the "wild and wanton girl, of luxurious beauty, and generous, free ways," when "becoming a wife, a great bereavement, or the pangs and burdens of maternity overtake her, robbing her cheek of its rich flush, but at the same time ripening her beauty, elevating, deepening, expanding her character, and imbuing her with a susceptibility of feeling, a consciousness of strength, and an earnestness of purpose which she knew not before." They then folded this transformation into the mythology of national progress. By the time of the nation's centennial now less than five years hence, when the country would commemorate its unity, achievement, and destiny, the "new Chicago" would "join her sisters in laying the laurel wreath upon the mother Columbia's brow," to be greeted warmly by all of them "and welcomed back from out her vale of affliction as one who had suffered that she might be strong."[17]

The visual interpretations of the meaning of the fire also expressed this idea of fortunate suffering (though not fortunate fall), working in the same vein as many other contemporary representations in America and Europe of the spirit of a particular country, city, or cherished national ideal (such as "liberty," "freedom," or "democracy") as a beautiful maiden with perfect classical features. The most ambitious example of this was a painting by the Royal Academician Edward Armitage, reproduced in different versions by local lithographers, that the staff of the *London Graphic* commissioned and presented to Chicago. In the painting, the nude reclining figure that is stricken Chicago is attended to by clothed sisters of mercy symbolizing Britain and America, respectively flanked by a lion and an eagle.[18]

The fire literature further explored the meaning of the occasion and indirectly offered a prescription for social conduct in its many different references to brides and weddings, including Colbert and Chamberlin's comparison of the city to a once wild and wanton girl who has now acquired the maturity, strength, and purpose of a woman. Several private and commercially produced fire narratives made special note of what happened to the weddings (one involving Robert Collyer's son) that had been scheduled to take place in the days following the fire. Whether or not some of these stories were the fabrication of reporters and illustrators combing through the ashes for one more angle on the fire, their appeal lay in the way they expressed optimistic sentiments about the future of the city. The focus in the wedding tales was on the bride, who, because of the fire, finds herself suddenly unable to obtain a caterer, flowers, trousseau, license, and perhaps even a clergyman. But she shows her pluck and character, as well as her "exceeding sweetness and womanliness" (which together form the female counterpart to the "manliness" that was elsewhere celebrated in the stories of courage and heroism), by fashioning a dignified ceremony from the humble possibilities available. In a story that appeared in the *New York Tribune* and was reprinted in several other places, one Chicago bride makes a cloth-covered soapbox do as an altar, on which she places a slop jar filled with a "bouquet" of autumn leaves. The story followed typical society-page language in describing the bridal gown, but now the point was the way its modesty demonstrated the bride's (and Chicago's) resourcefulness, sincerity, and resilience. The *Tribune* correspondent informed the reader that the bride adorned herself in a white cambric morning dress, a veil borrowed from her married sister, and her intended's gift of a string of "pearls" made from cotton ravelings. As the correspondent pointed out, "it seemed as if the fire had developed as much feminine ingenuity as it had destroyed feminine property."

Such episodes declared that the Chicago spirit was stripped of affectation and rededicated to the responsibilities of the future. In one illustration the bride and groom clasp hands to receive the benediction

of a minister whose Bible rests on the remains of a chimney. This subdued ceremony was a group exercise in the continuity of a determined
and undaunted vital community. The *Tribune* reporter confessed that
she had never seen, "among rich or poor, a sweeter and more holy-
seeming wedding," which ended with the whole congregation dropping to their knees to thank God for their preservation, their "broken
voices and tender heartfelt tones attest[ing] to the reality of the service." Conversing cheerfully with each other at a "marriage feast" of
water and warm biscuit, "all felt that to be poor in such good company
robbed ruin of half its sting."[19]

The novels of the fire were likewise expanded moral melodramas in
which the action moved toward marriage and a settled urban order purified by the fire. Conventional romances, they are full of improbable
complications of plot that become sorted out by the conflagration,
which occurs late in the book when the situation is apparently beyond
human help. In *Spicy* (1873), narrator Melody Belmore is the wife of an
army officer and a member of the comfortable community in the North
Division, and as the novel unfolds she furnishes the reader with such
local color as descriptions of a wartime Sanitary Fair and of the city's
reception of the news of Lincoln's death. The primary consequence of
the fire in the context of the novel is that it removes the obstacles in the
way of the marriage of two major characters. While the book is filled
with mysterious robberies, ghostly figures, hidden identities, family se-
crets, and noble sacrifices, it still somehow manages to be very dull, but
through it all it depicts Chicago as a stable social order whose citizens
are capable of the kind of sacrifice, selflessness, and sympathy that has
sustained this couple and will grace both their and the city's future.[20]

Troubled romance is even more central to Roe's *Barriers Burned Away*.
Pious Dennis Fleet falls for the beautiful and brilliant but haughty and
atheistic Christine Ludolph, daughter of a successful German immigrant art dealer. The fire claims the life of Christine's father and the
family fortune, but it leads to her realization of her love for Dennis and
her conversion to Christ and democracy. "It seems that I have lost so
little in this fire in comparison with what I have gained," she joyfully
admits. What she has gained above all is full citizenship as a Chicagoan
in the city's finest hour. Christine's acceptance through marriage of all
the values represented by Dennis promises the fulfillment of her talent,
beauty, and character.[21]

Humanity to the Rescue

The broadest claims for the beneficial effects of the fire on Chicago—
and on modern America—were made in the many retellings of the

story of how the rest of the nation responded to the disaster. Like many of the anecdotes of how Chicagoans stayed calm and resolute as they saw their world disappear before their eyes, the depictions of the relief emphasized how determination, morality, sympathy, and self-control saved the day, but one of the purposes of these anecdotes was also to bless the postwar economic and political order. The flood of contributions from everywhere seemed to prove that the developing national system through which the country circulated goods, capital, information, and people ultimately served universal democratic Christian sympathy. After all, the same telegraph and rail lines that carried the news and refugees out brought the pledges of relief and the carloads of food and supplies in. The published fire literature reprinted verbatim the wires sent by dozens of mayors, governors, and heads of state pledging the essential resources that sped toward Chicago on the nation's rails. The story of the relief reaffirmed the manifold worthiness of Chicago and America. Americans expressed certainty that the city would inevitably prevail not just because the rest of the world's material progress needed a healthy Chicago, but also because this progress was allied with the finest human sentiments.

One of the most-repeated episodes in the accounts of the relief told of how New York financier Jim Fisk, after hearing the first bulletins of the disaster, loaded up a lightning express for Chicago, demonstrating that the economy that made such private fortunes possible also supported an unprecedented display of charity and generosity. While her husband is still reconnoitering the damage wrought by "the fell destroyer," Melody Belmore tells the reader of *Spicy,* "the importance of our new agents of modernization were being realized by millions of human beings. The railroads, the telegraph, and the deep-sea cables, were mediums by which Christian nations proved that they were indeed Christian to the core." John Greenleaf Whittier, who interpreted the fire as a redemption from the "primal sin of selfishness" and a victory for Christ's "gospel of humanity," concurred:

> A sudden impulse thrilled each wire
> That signalled round that sea of fire;
> Swift words of cheer, warm heart-throbs came;
> In tears of pity died the flame![22]

Chicago, and the new urban order it represented, might be humbled overnight in a way that showed that God and not man was the ultimate ruler of earthly destiny, but through it all the city revealed itself to be astonishingly resilient because of its material and human resources, because of its vital connection to a far-flung yet tightly bound social and economic system, and because this system evidently had the blessing of the same God who in his wisdom chose to afflict Chicago for the nation's own good.

If the fire purified Chicago by burning away all but what was best within it, the challenge of the relief worked a similarly miraculous renewal and reunification of mankind elsewhere. In responding to Chicago's needs, the rest of the country forgot its petty artificial divisions and rediscovered its finest collective self. That "so immense a destruction of actual wealth" did not cripple the economy and discourage the nation "is an inspiring proof both of its sound condition and of its cheerful confidence," wrote the editors of *Harper's Weekly*. Andrew Shuman observed that the terrible blow to Chicago "struck that chord of humanity which vibrates with the sympathetic thrill of a common brotherhood—the chord which unites us all, and makes the great family of man a grand unit in impulse, sympathy and a sense of dependence." It loosened "the cold, clutching grip of avarice" on individuals and "opulent and grasping corporations" everywhere. It brought out the best in "close-fisted Yankees of New England," "slow-plodding capitalists of Canada," "lavish spendthrifts of the Pacific Coast," and the "peculiar people" of Utah. Even further afield, it leavened the souls of Germans "flushed with [their] freshly-earned triumphs in the land of the vanquished Gaul" and of "debt-burdened" and "tyrant-tied" Austria."[23]

The *New York Herald* of October 10 reported that clusters of people pressed against the bulletin boards of newspaper offices, becoming one in their interest and concern: "From the kid-gloved exquisite, laying aside for once his nonchalant air, to the hard-fisted mechanic or apple woman, the same feeling of awe and sympathy prevailed, and from the lips of all, words of pity and kindness could be heard to fall."[24] Discussions of the relief never failed to respond to this rediscovery of common humanity that overcame social divisions, selfishness, and cold calculation. The fire was as blessed a gift to the donors of aid as the relief was to its recipients, for it was the first major opportunity since the war to pledge the nation to the unity for which so much had been sacrificed, and to prove that materialism and competition were not the governing spirits of the time. The rhetoric of relief was more pious than the accounts of the fire, conjuring up images of holy war and crucifixion. Colbert and Chamberlin wrote that yet another indescribable aspect of the fire experience was "the acts in which all Christendom leant over Chicago and poured the precious balm of sympathy into her wounds, and bathed with the wine of relief her parched and blistered lips." There was "no acre of the United States but that some cinder from Chicago had lighted on it and kindled the fire of sympathy." The *St. Paul*

Press declared that the fire was a test that not only Chicago but America had passed, and Henry Ward Beecher added that the worldwide response "shows how the great element of Christian sympathy has unitized the world."[25]

Here again the fire literature construed the whole fire experience as "ennobling." Another enthusiastic commentator declared, "Never was spiritual intuition more active, than in this the day of our calamity." Bret Harte's poem on the fire, written the same day the flames finally went out, began with an image of the city as a noble young queen,

> Blackened and pleading, helpless, panting, prone,
> On the charred fragments of her shattered throne,

And moved toward assurance of salvation for all:

> She lifts her voice and in her pleading calls,
> We hear the cry of Macedon to Paul,
> The cry for help that makes her kin to all.
>
> But happy with wan fingers may she feel,
> The silver cup hid in the proffered meal,
> The gifts her kinship and our loves reveal.

The relief efforts thus blessed all they involved. Former Illinois lieutenant-governor and *Tribune* part-owner William Bross called the "spontaneous outburst" from all over the world a "touching spectacle," and claimed that he had seen "strong men, accustomed to the wear and tear of life, whom the loss of enormous fortunes could not bear down, stand at the corners of our streets with the tears in their eyes as the kindly words came pouring in upon them on the telegraph wires."[26] These tears were the liquid essence of feeling, more vital in saving the city than the damaged equipment of the fire department had been or ever could be.

The Fireproof Booster Spirit

Along with all these expressions of gratitude for the privilege of the fire there were, however, a few demurrals that, while still seeing the calamity in some sense as a valuable "lesson," argued that the most important thing it taught was Chicago's responsibility to itself and the country as a modern urban center. As the shock and euphoria of the days immediately after the catastrophe ebbed, important long-term policy decisions had to be made. Putting aside some of the moral and aesthetic terms in which the fire had been viewed in many accounts, several commentators reflected seriously on the need for new measures to deal with the problems posed by the growth of large-scale industrial cities. They thought that the fire was a blessing not because it purified the soul of Chicago, but because it might bring under control the city's sometimes short-sighted speculative ambitions that had led to the construction of shoddy buildings and inattention to zoning and fire prevention.

The Relief and Aid Society blamed the fire on the city's rapid growth and hasty construction, and on public authorities who out of what had wrongly appeared to be "the necessities of the case" had provided mainly for the needs of "commercial interests rather than for the permanent security of the homes and property of the people." Frederick Law Olmsted similarly criticized Chicago's "weakness for 'big things,'" its pride in its belief that it would surpass New York, and its showy, shoddy, commercial buildings. Mixing morals and mortar in still another battlefield image that figured the American nation as an army, Olmsted contended that the fire might have been prevented, or at least controlled, with "honest architecture" and "good generalship, directing a thoroughly well-drilled and disciplined soldierly force of firemen and police." Eleven months after Olmsted's article was published, the *Chicago Inter-Ocean* stated that it was time to cut through the "fustian and hyperbole" of post-fire encomiums and acknowledge that the burning of the city revealed a civic fault of which the disaster was the correction: "The paramount need was harness, self-restraint, the temperance which comes by experience. What Chicago lacked was not pluck, but thoroughness; not thought or originality, but the embodiment of these in substantial forms."[27]

It should be kept in mind, however, that the people who were saying such things were for the most part spokespersons for the point of view of the leading businessmen both in the city and in financial centers like New York who were largely responsible for the city's rapid growth. These businessmen naturally had a strong desire for the continuation of this growth in ways that would serve their own interests. Their hope was that the fire would convince everyone that what was needed for the benefit of all was an effectively managed city in which their kind of enterprises would be better protected against such catastrophic dangers. They certainly had no desire to quell the booster spirit of Chicago, which, far from being discouraged by this apparent major setback, seemed to take heart from the disaster and expand to new proportions.

Modern discussions of the fire are fond of finding a paradigmatic case in the king of all Chicago boosters, John Stephen Wright, who came to Chicago with his father in 1832 and immediately entered the real estate business. His *Chicago: Past, Present, Future*, published three years before the fire (with a second edition two years later) was not only the culminating work of his career but arguably the masterpiece of the apparently inexhaustible if largely forgotten genre of what Ross Miller has called "Boosterature." Without reading some examples of this enormous body of writing, one cannot fully understand the imaginative power of the idea of the growth of Chicago and of other nineteenth-century cities (and would-be cities).[28] There appears to have been no economic or geographic fact, condition, or development that Wright could not cite as incontrovertible proof that Chicago was destined to be the leading urban center in the whole wide world. His faith could be summed up in one of his sentences: "There never was a site more perfectly adapted by nature for a great commercial and manufacturing city, than this." By the time he wrote *Chicago: Past, Present, Future*, he could claim with some justification that his dream had been made reality. Indeed, the heading of one section is "The Basis of Our Prosperity is No Longer Hypothetical." When, with the ruins of Chicago all around him, Wright was asked skeptically about the prospects of this prosperity now, he is reputed to have predicted that Chicago would grow more in the next five years than had there been no fire.[29]

Wright's response was typical rather than extraordinary among Chicago's entrepreneurs, even if they may have been whistling in the dark. Immediately after the fire, William Bross, his family just burned out of their elegant new townhouse on Michigan Avenue, caught a train to New York. His purpose was to reassure the financial markets, and his major asset at this point was bravado. Upon arrival, Bross told reporters that the fire brought out the "true Chicago spirit" of pluck and determination: "Every one was bright, cheerful, pleasant, hopeful, and even inclined to be jolly in spite of the misery and destitution which surrounded them and which they shared."[30] Bross advised wealthy businessmen in New York and elsewhere to invest their fortunes and their sons in the unprecedented opportunities in Chicago created by the fire, and, like Wright, assured them spectacular returns within five years. This faith animated the first post-fire issue of Bross's *Tribune*. It featured an editorial titled "Cheer Up," which confidently boasted, "As there has never been such a calamity, so has there never been such cheerful fortitude in the face of desolation and ruin." After asserting that "the forces of nature, no less than the forces of reason require that the exchanges of a great nation should be conducted here," it built to a lofty finish:

Let us all cheer up, save what is yet left, and we shall come out all right. The Christian world is coming to our relief. The worst is already over. In a few days more all the dangers will be past, and we can resume the battle of life with Christian faith and Western grit. Let us all cheer up![31]

In two places the *Tribune* could not contain its enthusiasm and broke into capitals, stating first that "CHICAGO SHALL RISE AGAIN,"

following this with the even more determined exclamation, "CHI-
CAGO MUST RISE AGAIN!" The choice of the word "rise" was very
popular among editorial writers, boosters, and poets determined to put
the most optimistic face on this terrible event by viewing the city of Chicago as a spiritual force. Among the songs inspired by the fire was
"From the Ruins Our City Shall Rise" by George F. Root, the Chicago
composer who had rallied the North with "Tramp, Tramp, Tramp, the
Boys are Marching," "Just Before the Battle, Mother," and "Marching
Through Georgia," as well as "The Battle Cry of Freedom." The
chorus of his fire anthem proclaimed:

> But see! the bright rift in the cloud . . .
> And hear! the great voice from the shore . . .
> Our city shall rise! yes she shall rise
> Queen of the west once more . . .[32]

This kind of expression of faith in Chicago's resurrection soon was explicitly objectified in the adoption of the phoenix as the symbol of the
city, and it was the essential message of the figurative language that continued to tie the fire to the Civil War as an experience that tested the
spirits of Americans and, far from dividing and destroying them, ultimately created them anew and revealed their direction, purpose, and
meaning. Like the hero and heroine of Roe's *Barriers Burned Away* and
of all the stories of rescues and marriages and other acts of valor and
faith, Chicago would not only survive but prevail in the years ahead because it now knew that it had the kind of courage and will that enabled it
to triumph over this mightiest of challenges.

Devils and Doubts

But what if darker causes and purposes were behind the fire? Associations of the fire with the forces of Satan abounded in contemporary accounts of the destruction. According to one account, "witnessing the
appalling spectacle was like "looking over the adamantine bulwarks of
hell into the bottomless pit." In one of his several poems on the fire,
N. S. Emerson personified it as

> A demon whose power was stronger
> Than the strength of our puny hands,
> Who paused not to ask for favors,
> But took the wealth of our lands:
> We fought him with desperate courage,

He laughed at our fruitless pain,
We begged him to spare our treasures
Alas! that we begged in vain.[33]

Speaking in this manner hardly undermined the positive interpretation of the fire, but was yet another rhetorical means of declaring the disaster a victory of morality and character over the forces of disorder. Chicago was further ennobled by its having struggled with the devil. It is unlikely that those who discussed the fire this way thought they were doing anything other than talking figuratively.[34]

But the belief that the city had indeed been engaged in a battle with something infernal was in some senses deeply felt. At the same time as the fire literature certified that Chicago had been sanctified and purified, it told another kind of story of how the flames unleashed many dangerous people and encouraged them to do their worst, putting the upstanding members of the population in peril. This narrative substantiated a view of what was wrong with the city as seen from the same middle- and upper-class, native-born perspective that formulated the affirmative view of the fire. Speaking in an only partially veiled way about class and the need to draw the line on the thought and behavior of a social "other," this version of what had happened constructed an idealized stable status quo based on a deep suspicion of urban democracy that viewed the fire as a metaphor for the dangers present in everyday social experience.

Some raised the possibility that real demons in human form were responsible for what had happened. Immediately following the fire, the story circulated that it had been deliberately set by social revolutionaries with direct connections to the Paris Commune, which had been put down in late May of 1871 in a bloody battle that ended with Paris set afire by radicals in a last-ditch act of defiance against the Versailles government, the bourgeoisie, the upper classes, and the throne.[35] The *New York Evening Post* published a poem that wondered out loud about the relationship between the calamities that befell the sister cities of Paris and Chicago:

Did out of her [Paris's] ashes arise
This bird with a flaming crest,
That over the ocean unhindered flies,
With a scourge for the Queen of the West?[36]

In *The Lost City!*, the most melodramatic of the book-length fire histories, Frank Luzerne offered evidence of such a connection, a lengthy "alleged confession" of a "Member of a Secret Organization," worldwide and Paris-based, dedicated to setting other leading cities ablaze as part of a war against wealth and property.[37] Such stories may have suggested that Chicago was the innocent victim of a foreign conspiracy from without, but to see the disaster as an extension of the Commune rather than the Civil War turned it into a story of class conflict rather than of political reunion and reconciliation.

Personal correspondence and newspaper reports in the days following the fire were more preoccupied with crime than international conspiracy, however. Concerned that Chicago's misfortune, regardless of what had caused it, had created a golden opportunity for criminals throughout the country and within the city, they either predicted an outbreak of assaults on life and property or declared that it was already taking place. Cassius Milton Wicker wrote to his family in North Ferrisburgh, Vermont, "With the close of the fire, or rather conflagration, our troubles have not closed. Roughs and thieves from all parts of the country flocked here for plunder." The coverage of this development in print was frequently lengthy and colorful, as professional writers seemed inspired by the chance to describe the secondary terrors of the catastrophe. In all cases the point was how vulnerable Chicago was to these dangers. "The city is infested with a horde of thieves, burglars and cut-throats, bent on plunder, and who will not hesitate to burn, pillage and even murder, as opportunity may seem to offer to them to do so with safety," warned the *Evening Journal* a day after the fire. The *Galena Daily Gazette* (Illinois) published a fire extra with the headline, "Thieves Holding High Carnival!" and reported that "notwithstanding the efforts of the fire patrol," these predators "held high revel," and that "such a carnival of robbery perhaps never took place in a civilized society." Meanwhile, *Harper's Weekly* told of a "new reign of terror" marked by rape, arson, and murder, singling out four "ruffians" who were "well known to the police of every city in the Union—BARNEY AARON, BILL GRACY, JIM MUNDAY, AND JIM BROWN—as vile a set of scoundrels as ever picked a pocket or cut a throat."[38]

One of the purposes of such stories was to offer the same kind of assurances as did many of the tales of bravery and self-possession, to which they were often joined. The reports of terrorists, thieves, and murderers insisted that there was a saving majority of righteous people in Chicago. Most fire accounts that reported outbreaks of criminality called the malefactors "barbarians" to stress the point that they were external invaders. Even if one source of this attack was the city's own "criminal element," this group was small and hardly representative of the city. One of the earliest pulp fire histories talked of such low individuals in terms that emphasized their isolation and antisocial abnormality, their fundamental opposition to all that was spiritually upright, physically attractive, and socially constructive. They were "black sheep and scabbed members of the flock" who were "hideous excrescences on the smooth surface of social life," opposed to the spirit of the "brave and noble-hearted sons of Chicago. . . ."[39]

Bringing Out the Worst

But certain incidents that made their way into the fire narratives were far more unsettling. The most alarming effect of the fire was not that it attracted career criminals, but that it awakened a large underclass to follow its own base nature in ways that threatened the "better" elements in the city. This underclass was clearly identified with the substantial portion of the population whose background was different from that of the Yankee elite and the middle class. What was more shocking than any of the terrible things these people did was that they were able to assert their presence. The *New York Tribune* spoke approvingly of the imposition of a curfew, whatever its inconveniences, since it would restrict "that portion of the twilight population which always comes to the surface at such hours," whose "rascal faces and hang-dog air" now could be seen by day in parts of the city they never ventured before . "It would certainly not be prudent to give the city up to them," the *Tribune* advised, and so at night they are kept in their own haunts on the West Side." Among the commonest features of accounts of the terrors of the night are scenes in which men, women, and boys of a vulgar sort—often characterized as "roughs"—break into saloons and then proceed to commit outrages against wealth and respectability. Fire, whiskey, and the distraction of the authorities amid the general excitement become a dissolving medium that removes whatever restrained these people up to now, causing them to give into "their slavish propensities" and terrorize others.

One of the earliest versions of this kind of wild moment, reprinted in other places, appeared in the *Chicago Evening Post* a week-and-a-half after the fire. Describing the behavior of the inhabitants of a slum neighborhood in the fire's path as "[i]ll-omened and obscene birds of night," it continued in uncertain syntax:

> Villainous, haggard with debauch and pinched with misery, flitted through the crowd collarless, ragged, dirty, unkempt, these negroes with stolid faces and white men who fatten on the wages of shame, glided through the masses like vultures in search of prey. They smashed windows reckless of the severe wounds inflicted on their naked hands, and with bloody fingers rifled impartially till, shelf and cellar, fighting viciously for the spoils of their forays. Women, hollow-eyed and brazenfaced, with foul drapery tied over their heads, their dresses half torn from

their skinny bosoms, and their feet thrust into trodden down slippers, moved here and there, stealing, scolding shrilly, and laughing with one another at some particularly "splendid" gush of flame or "beautiful" falling-in of a roof.[40]

The hollow-eyed hags, so physically repulsive and morally impure, were a striking contrast to the vibrant presence of Armitage's fair and full-bosomed representation of Chicago. They stood in the minds of respectable people for the undifferentiated rabble, who, if not directly responsible for the fire, possessed some half-articulated idea that anything bad that happened to their betters was a good thing. One of the consequences of Chicago's calamity was that it opened up opportunities for such people to invade the better neighborhoods from which their own disorderly habits had rightfully excluded them.[41] Another visual image of the fire, much more in keeping with Armitage's painting than with the story in the *Evening Post*, depicted Chicago as a beautiful young Pre-Raphaelite princess being helped to her feet by four other maidens, symbolizing the other cities and countries that sent relief, each adorned identically with flowing dresses and coronets. The scene is one of apocalyptic destruction. Over fallen Chicago hovers a much larger and profoundly ominous winged female figure holding a torch, while in the murky background the other maidens struggle to keep off with their bare hands a pack of wild dogs with fearsome fangs. Dark birds on the horizon await the uncertain outcome.[42]

Notably lacking in such depictions, and in the fire literature as a whole, is any significant attention to the losses and suffering of even the virtuous members of the lower class and the enormous ethnic communities, mainly German and Irish, that made up a majority of the city's population and included numerous respectable middle-class Chicagoans.[43] Despite the many assertions of universal spiritual awakening inspired by the fire, the authors of the fire commemoratives and instant histories reserved their sympathies mainly for the plight of "the landlord and aristocrat," who was to be pitied far more than "the boor who now jostles him," since his loss of property and prestige was far greater. What discussion there was of the tribulations of the marginal members of society was sometimes startlingly coldhearted. To some commentators the fire was a fortuitous piece of urban renewal that had cleared a few slums and, in so doing, raised property values. One noted that the city had, thanks to the fire, gotten rid of some of its "old rookeries and riff-raff population near the river," while others reported with similar approbation that among the devastated areas were notorious immigrant neighborhoods like Conley's Patch, near the O'Leary cottage.[44]

To the extent that it was victimized by the fire, this riff-raff seemed to get little more than what it deserved. Or so was the message of some of the fire accounts. Luzerne's *Lost City!* spoke of the fate of "women of the baser sort" in their "dens and haunts" drinking heavily and abandoning their children as the fire attacked their "squalid tenement." Those who did try to rescue one "painted Jezebel" were thwarted since "she had inhaled the intense caloric into a stomach already heated with alcohol, and fell dead before one could reach her." Others among the poor died because they evidently lacked the character and resolve to save themselves, which was also why they were poor in the first place. While there was perhaps surprisingly little specific explicit blame for the fire laid to the O'Learys or to the immigrant population they represented, their presence was clearly felt to be a dangerous liability, and whatever misfortunes befell them were their own fault.[45]

More disturbing perhaps was how the fire brought out the worst in supposedly *good* people. Mary Ann Hubbard recollected the "universal thieving propensities let loose" that cost her many of her possessions, some of which she was sure were stolen by her own trusted servants. "I suppose the fact that things were lying around loose and would probably be destroyed by the advancing flames had the effect of weakening any principle of honesty," she reflected, raising the possibility that the fire demonstrated that the city's moral fiber was perhaps not so strong after all.[46] William S. Walker attributed the fire-incited drinking to "physical and mental exhaustion" and "the inexplicable seeking for an assuage of trouble in potent alcohol," and he told (as many others did) of how saloon keepers and liquor dealers, knowing that their stock was lost in any case, rolled "barrels of the poison" out into the street and threw open their doors "to the overwrought and haggard populace." Walker's elevated diction dramatized his shock at the resulting loss of self-possession: "Men drank then whose lips had never before been crossed by alcohol; while those who had hitherto tasted of its Lethe-draughts only on rare occasions, now guzzled like veteran soakers."

The horrors knew no boundaries. Not only "were hardened women reeling through the crowds, howling ribald songs," and "coarse men . . . breaking forth with leering jokes and maudlin blasphemy," but there were even "women of the highest culture tossing down glasses of raw whiskey; ladies with cinder and tear-begrimed faces, pressing the cups with jewelled fingers." The fire seemed to have brought all down to the lowest level: "of rich and poor, well-bred and boors, the high and the lowly, there were few who did not appear to have been seized with the idea that tired nature must finally succumb unless the friendly stimulant was used."[47] Such Gothic scenes were riveting to the middle-class imagination, whose conception of social order was based on internal regulation, and which in its fixation on temperance in this period bolstered the traditional moralistic attack on drinking with "scientific" evidence that alcohol destroyed the prospects of an individual in an orderly society.[48] Those who let themselves go not only jeopardized their own well-being but also the social order which was ready to award money, status, and prestige to those who adhered to its strictures.

It is hard to square these anecdotes of debauchery with an interpretation of the fire as an invading enemy against which the citizenry bravely rallied, let alone with the rhetoric of purification and positive purpose. What makes such stories all the more intriguing is that they, like the O'Leary legend and the Communard's confession, were based less on actual events than in an anxiety about urban society that existed even without the fire. While there was some looting, theft, and drunkenness amidst all the commotion, the tales of such behavior were greatly exaggerated and fed on each other.[49] The personal narratives sound suspiciously like the stories in the newspapers. In most instances their authors confessed that they had witnessed no such atrocities directly, while other trustworthy sources maintained that they were not true at all.[50]

These fictive tales constituted a literary phenomenon of importance equal to that of all the claims of indescribability, but in this case instead of maintaining that they could not put into words all the things that indisputably happened, authors graphically described events that never took place. Why? Paranoid rumors, like the claim of indescribability, are almost always one of the aftershocks of any large-scale disorder, and so it was only natural that they would circulate locally for at least a brief time.[51] Hinting that there was perhaps more fantasy than substance to some of these reports, bookkeeper Eben Matthews still recalled how powerful the rumors were: "In addition to the resident criminal class we were obliged to look out for persons of this character who began to come in great numbers, [which] added to our trouble. At this late date one, who was not an eye witness, can hardly imagine the fear of incendiarism, looting, etc. which prevailed. Stories of all kinds were afloat concerning thefts[,] murder and the like."[52]

But Chicago was perhaps particularly prone to becoming the subject of widely published tales of the eruption of criminal and destructively loose behavior because of a prevailing concern with urban vice and crime, and with a postwar increase in the population of "floaters" and other suspect social types—including immigrants in general—who were drawn to the city.[53] Authors after a commercial audience were eager to exploit this concern and Chicago's existing reputation for loose and illegal behavior, joining their accounts of the fire to a lively literature of urban exposé already in circulation. This literature, which could express both conservative and subversive social agendas, had its origins in Europe but dated in the United States at least as far back as George Lippard's shocking treatment of Philadelphia in his *Quaker City* (1845) and George Foster's worldly-wise *New York by Gas-light* (1850). Such works purported to reveal to their mainly middle-class audiences the shocking and otherwise hidden lives of those, usually the very wealthy and the very poor, who by choice or necessity lived outside the boundaries of propriety.[54] The fire, which burned away all walls and masks and guards, offered an irresistible opportunity for professional writers ready to feed the fascination of respectable readers with those at the margins. Whether or not hordes of criminals descended on Chicago is hard to prove; less in doubt is that a large number of "reporters" tried to make the most of the occasion.

But something more significant was also at work. Observers of the Chicago fire near and far saw in the smoke and flames a fulfillment of their deepest fears about urban life, fears that demanded realization, no matter what the facts, if the cherished prejudices that lay behind them were to be justified. Whether the specific cause of trouble was an international conspiracy of dedicated revolutionaries, an invasion of criminals, the unchecked flow of alcohol, or simply an Irish woman's clumsy cow, the basic problem was the precariousness of the social order. The tales of arson and drunkenness and crime spoke mainly on a symbolic level, revealing a desire for greater control of "dangerous" elements. The anxiety behind this desire was that social chaos, not fire, was the most severe threat to the future of the city.

The Hanged Man, and Evil Unloosed

This anxiety was most obsessively at work in one kind of anecdote that appeared in most fire narratives: the lynching of incendiaries who, even if they did not start the conflagration, accelerated its rapid spread. The motives of these individuals are not fully explained, though they are generally lower-class young men presumably acting out of a general antipathy to property and the settled order. Of all the kinds of stories that came out of the fire, the lynching tales had the highest ratio of number of reports to verified occurrences, of which there were none. Tales of street justice meted out to these arsonists (and to looters of all ages and sexes) appeared in the earliest newspaper dispatches. They figured prominently in the fire histories and the personal letters and memoirs, and were a popular subject for the illustrations that accompanied the histories. On the page opposite the "Confession of a Member of a Secret Organization," Luzerne included a much-reproduced drawing (of which there were several variations) of a group of hearty male citizens hanging a young man from a lamppost. The men work together calmly,

assisting each other in this grim errand with the same kind of cooperative spirit depicted in scenes of rescue. The action takes place against a
backdrop of smoke and fire that the assembled crowd of vigilantes and
spectators ignores while it turns its attention to this spectacle. The caption reads: "Swift Justice. Fate of Thieves and Incendiaries."[55]

Authors and artists tried to outdo each other in their presentation of
these grisly scenes. The "winner" in this strange competition was
George L. Barclay's *The Great Fire of Chicago!*, which included a very
stark drawing of a would-be malefactor hanging barefoot and upside
down, about to be brained by two soldiers, one using a rifle butt and the
other an ax. The illustration is brutal, primitive, and direct, a kind of
ritual exorcism of the devils that beset the city. Such vigilantes typically
are, like the hanged man, members of the working class, though they
are usually a little older. This suggests that Chicagoans of the "better"
sort would not participate in such activities, but also that responsible
citizens of all classes realize that property and order must be defended.
In any case, such scenes should be viewed in relation to the different
portrayals of Chicago as a beautiful young woman in distress. This
male incendiary, who is representative of the dangerously unstable elements of society, is ceremonially inverted, stretched, beaten, and dis-
membered for attempting to ravish the noble maiden.[56]

To read these anecdotes and view the illustrations is to marvel at the
foresight, presence of mind, and cooperative spirit of Chicago's citizens, who, in the midst of fleeing from a cataclysmic fire that destroyed
their every belonging and threatened their livelihoods and their lives,
found time to stop to catch such alleged villains, reach a consensus on
what to do with them, procure a rope, and string them up. There are
so many of these tales that together they conjure up the image of a
post-holocaust cityscape of charred ruins measured out by gallows-
lampposts. But the most remarkable thing about the lynching narratives was that the authors never failed to endorse the action of the vigilantes, thus declaring that it was proper and perhaps necessary to take
the law into "our" own hands in order to defend the city against
"them," the agents of disorder. In a letter to his family and friends written two days after the fire, Phillip C. Morgan, who worked for National
Life Insurance, said of the vandals: "There has been a good many
roughs shot dead and quite a number *hung. Immediately* upon their hellish deeds such as setting new fires and stealing." One fire history more
unabashedly saw the hangings as brave acts of moral resolve that saved
Chicago from the same kinds of beasts that threatened the city in the
more allegorical illustrations: "Let us thank God that many of these
monsters in human shape received the summary punishment they so
richly merited. And not forgetting the quality of mercy, 'which is not

strained,' let us heartily rejoice that in most cases they were shot down like dogs, brained while they were in the act of crime, or hung up high in the streets as a proof of good faith to other members of the unholy pack."[57]

The reports of the lynchings—at once so unforgiving, bloodthirsty, and untrue—were full of contradictions. While reasserting the primacy of public order, they endorsed the most violent and irregular measures in support of that order, carried out under the worst possible circumstances. The same accounts that recoiled from the thought of a reign of terror thus contained a justification for one, as long as the right people had the rope and acted against those who would set the social order aflame. The lynching narratives seemed to say that justice was preserved through the timely action of public-spirited citizens, even if this was accomplished only by ignoring some of the principles through which these same citizens claimed to be a civilized community. The best way to explain the lynching rumors, after conceding their sensational appeal, is on the level of a mass dream—or nightmare—that did not require consistency. These stories were the darker side of the hope that the fire was redemptive, a warning that saving the "life" of the city not only required heroic and selfless acts of rescue but also swift, sure, and even murderous measures against the enemies of society. On the deepest psychological level, authors and readers who participated imaginatively in the stories of hanging needed those arsonists and looters in order to attach their concerns about instability to such figures, and they needed to have them lynched. The fire gave them the opportunity to assure themselves that these needs were real, and that they would be able to identify and take arms against the enemies of society.

The hanged incendiaries were born of concerns that urban order was inherently unstable, that the clarity of perception and action that stability required—the ability to identify and remove sources of disorder as readily as did the vigilantes—was not available. The anxieties about the social order implicit in these narratives were in some ways more obviously present in the wild stories surrounding two other incidents of the fire, the release of prisoners from the Courthouse jail and the gathering of fire refugees on "the Sands." These incidents had some basis in fact, but the authors of the fire literature reworked both of them in order to express certain warnings about the nature of the urban populace and about social democracy.

To leave the prisoners incarcerated would condemn them to be burned alive, but the consequence of humanely letting them go was to allow these unreconstructed wretches to rejoin the law-abiding. William S. Walker wrote of the way the fire had worked a reversal of fortunes in favor of these criminals and against the good citizens of the city: "Happy in the brute consciousness that the ill wind which was showering extermination upon Chicago, had, with consistent ugliness, blown a precious boon to themselves, garroters, thieves, debtors, petty pilferers, and hardened murderers, shot off into the crowds and were seen no more." Once liberated, they set the terrible tone of the night, at least according to such sources as the *Chicago Times,* which reported, "In view of the horrible scenes of incendiarism, robbery, and murder afterward enacted, it is almost a matter of regret that the entire batch of villains were not allowed to experience a hasty roasting." These prisoners, described elsewhere as "yelling like demons," thus came to be identified with the destructive spirit of the fire, which in turn was personified as a satanic being let loose in the city streets.[58]

This drama, in which the lowest and most dangerous elements of society, who had been captured and contained by the civilized order, were suddenly liberated to do their worst, emphasized both the necessity and the vulnerability of social control in the same way as the stories of lynching had. According to one improbable anecdote, the first thing the prisoners did was set upon a wagon full of clothing, which they "emptied . . . of its contents and fled to remote alleys and dark passages to don their plunder and disguise themselves."[59] They could then mingle undetected in the crowds, and amid the distraction and disarray caused by the fire there was nothing to stop them when they inevitably chose to turn on society again. One kind of rumor here dovetailed with several others, as the story of the liberation of the prisoners helped to explain the reports of intemperance, crime, and barbarism, which in turn justified the much-celebrated vigilantism. Beyond that, however, the news of the prisoners' release warned post-fire Chicagoans that anyone among them could be an enemy of society, that the city was a place where such terrible people were indistinguishable from respectable citizens, and that sparing these convicted criminals from what others like them—whether terrorists, arsonists, or Irish immigrants— had caused in the first place was perhaps a less wise policy than allowing them to perish.

Like the anecdotes of the lynchings, the stories of the escapades of the prisoners were untrue.[60] While some inmates were reportedly let go, the authorities evidently did not release the most dangerous criminals, but transferred them elsewhere in chains, and those who were let out, like most other Chicagoans, likely devoted their energies to self-preservation. The rumors of the release did, however, address the real fear that in such a large city with such a mixed population, any stranger might be suspect. The special problems that John J. Flinn said faced the members of the undermanned police force following the disaster sound like those presented to Chicagoans by these escaped prisoners:

> The city was undergoing a complete metamorphosis; locations were obliterated, old landmarks destroyed; the neighborhoods that had been respectable had become disreputable, the slums of anti-fire days had become purified; the streets were almost impossible for months after the fire; shelter and hiding places for criminals abounded in the ruins or in the rising buildings; new faces were in the majority among the criminals, and the most experienced officers had to learn their trade over again, just as if they had been assigned to duty in a new city.[61]

Flinn could have been describing the effects not just of the fire but of the rapid growth of the city, where neighborhoods and personal fortunes could seem to shift almost overnight, and where so many faces were unfamiliar. Chicago was continuously remaking itself into a new metropolis, with all kinds of individuals of questionable motives running free. The fire was its normal condition in intenser form.

"The Sands" was genuine enough even if the fire-related events that supposedly took place there were also largely invented. Situated along the lakefront north of the river and a few blocks east of a number of distinguished North Division homes, the area had a notorious reputation since the 1850s as a morally as well as geographically marginal neighborhood congenial to the most suspect human impulses and activities, notably gambling and prostitution, which were unofficially tolerated by the authorities. In April of 1857, Mayor "Long" John Wentworth, determined to root out vice and corruption, led thirty policemen in a raid on the area. While this dramatic action added to the popular mayor's reputation, it proved to be counterproductive since it scattered the men and women of ill repute all over the city, bringing "into hitherto law-abiding sections the fear and terror which only lawless elements create" and leading to the tacit acceptance of prostitution throughout the city.[62]

The proximity of the Sands to the lake made it a natural point of retreat from the flames. Here, closed off from other escape routes, the burned out "shrank for refuge from the pursuing monster," only to find that the fire seemed to revive the old spirit of the Sands. Or worse. The point that most descriptions of the population on the Sands made was how mixed it was. The fire created an instant democracy, uniting "extremes of wealth and squalor" so that "inequalities of societies were now leveled off as smooth as the beach itself." "Such an assemblage as there congregated," Colbert and Chamberlin maintained, "Chicago never witnessed before and probably never will witness again."[63] The message here was clearly not a celebration of leveling but a reaffirmation of the value and desirability of class distinction and separation, and of the need to be vigilant—forceful, if necessary—in their defense.

Like the liberation of the prisoners, and the fire in general, the community on the Sands pushed the "lowest" Chicagoans up against their betters, with no restraints and no fear of reprisals for acting out the impulses of their base nature. The situation on the Sands dramatized what Andrew Shuman said was taking place in the city as a whole: "There was no Power to control the confused elements, to protect the weak against the strong, or to enforce law, order or justice." Without this "Power," the "confused elements" would reign.[64] Alfred Andreas told of how the well-to-do who were driven from their fine homes "found that they were between two deaths—the burning city on the one side and the lake upon the other," their only hope being "this stretch of sandy purgatory." Small hope it was, Andreas sadly recalled, enlisting the reader to share his own feelings of outrage at the violations of decency that were perpetrated. The fire played a scene that would cause a writer to pause "abashed and heart-sick at the awful task before the worst was told," deeds so foul that "[n]o publisher would be permitted to preserve in types—no man of moral consciousness would place before his family—the volume that told what there transpired." The literary problem now was not the indescribability of what had happened, but its unspeakability.

Speak many did, however, and with a flourish, in an elevated style that was long on figurative language and short on specifics, except to assure the reader that what had transpired was an atrocity against morality. The imaginative transformation of a social, political, and cultural concern into a sexual one, conveyed symbolically and obliquely in the narratives of the lynchings of young male arsonists, was in the stories of the Sands literal and inescapable. "There," Andreas immediately continued, "on the scorching earth, that held the heat and sent it shimmering, ceaseless wave of blasting air and sand from underneath the feet, parching the flesh and drying up the fountains of blood and life, the spirit of infernal revelry prevailed." It was a hell on earth, worthy of the pen of Dante, full of "human creatures" and "maddened animals," where "delicate and refined women, pure and innocent children," "young girls, whose artless lives were unfamiliar with even the name of crime," and "men of well-ordered lives and Christian minds" suddenly found themselves cheek-by-jowl with "brutes in human form, who were not only ready to do acts of crime, but whose polluting wickedness was rank and cast off prison-fumes upon the air." It was as if the Courthouse convicts, by plan or by the destiny of their nature, had directly proceeded to the Sands to work their will on all that was most delicate and fine in Chicago. Here "purest girlhood was forced to endure the leering of the vile." The felons and the fire became indistinguishable fiendish forces:

> The creatures who there tortured the helpless were no longer human—vice had dulled their moral instincts, and despair transformed them, for the moment, into demons. Their orgies were born in malice, they delighted in their sins; they shrieked aloud with glee to see the innocent rush from them, and plunge into the lake, that, for the instant, the sight might be shut out.

These creatures and demons were, if anything, worse than the devil. "Could all the powers of hell itself," Andreas wondered, "devise a keener form of anguish?"[65]

Like the other talk of outbreaks of crime, passages like these recalled depictions of the lurid urban underworld, of ethnic-based riots, and of "the dangerous classes" in fiction, journalism, and social analyses since before the Civil War.[66] In most instances accounts of the Sands presented this gripping drama of defenseless virtue, assaulted by shameless vice, in order to express horror and alarm at the prospect of social mixing. For all its championing of republican values, for example, *Barriers Burned Away* distinguished its hero, Dennis Fleet, from many others in Chicago as a "gentleman," and Roe recoiled from the forced confusion of classes Dennis experiences as he flees through the overcrowded LaSalle Street tunnel. Here "every morale grade was represented." Individuals who led "abandoned lives" are "plainly recognizable, their guilty consciences finding expression in their vivid faces." They "jostled the refined and delicate lady," pushing her against "thief and harlot" in what Roe unabashedly called "the awful democracy of the hour." In this subterranean scene, urban society is revealed as "a strange, incongruous writhing mass of humanity, such as the world had never looked upon, pouring into what might seem, in its horrors, the mouth of hell."

Emerging from the tunnel, Dennis sees other appalling evidence of the peril refined people suffer when forced into contact with the common crowd. Next to "the aristocratic Christine" is "a stout Irishwoman, hugging a grunting, squealing pig to her breast," and nearby is a "hook-nosed spinster [who] carried in a cage a hook-nosed parrot that kept discordantly crying, 'Polly want a cracker.'" These grotesques, barely distinguishable from the animals they bear, are not just repulsive but outright dangerous. The only restraint that they understand is a gun that has come into Dennis's possession:

> At Dennis's left a delicate lady of the highest social standing clasped to her bare bosom a babe that slept as peacefully as in the luxurious nursery

at home. At her side was a little girl carrying as tenderly a large wax doll. A diamond necklace sparkled like a circlet of fire around the lady's neck. Her husband had gone to the south side, and she had but time to snatch this and her children. A crowd of obscene and profane rowdies stood just behind them, and with a brutal jest and coarse laughter they passed around a whiskey-bottle. One of these roughs caught a glimpse of the diamond necklace, and was putting forth his blackened hand to grasp it, when Dennis pointed the captured pistol at him and said, "This is law now."

Roe evidently felt a sublime compulsion to create such confrontations between "us" and "them" that emphasized the challenges piety and character faced in the city. A few pages later Dennis is at the Sands proper, where "again was seen the mingling of all classes which the streets and every place of refuge witnessed." And once more the enforced democracy is abhorrent, the worst aspect of the fire, as decent people who gather to pray or mourn for lost family members must witness "orgies that seemed not of earth. . . . the mad excitement and recklessness which often seize the depraved classes on such occasions, . . . excesses that cannot be mentioned" committed by "these drunken, howling, fighting wretches."[67]

Common to these scenes was the dramatization of the notion that urban virtue, represented by the "delicate lady of highest social standing," was in terrible danger at the hands of these villains, who want to steal her wealth and violate her virtue, which are equivalent acts. The diamond necklace is a sign not of the self-indulgent materialism of Chicago's elite but of its crystalline character that must be defended from attack, and it is spiritual envy as much as lust for unearned wealth that prompts the assault. These beasts have always wanted to do this, but have had to wait until this unexpected moment when this woman's protector—who may be her father, brother, husband, or suitor, but in any case represents moral authority in Chicago—has been separated from her. Left unshielded, she faces suicide by drowning or, far worse, pollution at the filthy hands of her vile attacker. The only thing that can save her from this terrible choice is the timely intervention of righteous male power in the form of Dennis's pistol.

The story of the imperiled maiden who, forced to choose between death and dishonor, is saved in the nick of time by a brave and noble gentleman, was by 1871 another well-worn turn, but the specific fears and hopes that invoked it—and the tales of the hanged man—were felt as real. They combined in the elite narrative of the fire to convey the idea that urban democracy was, if not "awful," extremely volatile. If the recognition of national and international interrelatedness that caused the country and the world to feel Chicago's loss as their own was a source of reassurance, the acknowledgment locally that different groups of people were forced to live together was unsettling. The lurking problem within the city was that the better sort of people who were concerned with the well-being of the community were always at risk of being victimized by the less virtuous, industrious, prudent, honest, and disciplined who also called Chicago home, and who had cows, barns, lanterns, whiskey—and the vote. Reflecting on the losses to the population as a whole in an essay called "Political Economy of the Fire," D. H. Wheeler saw "new reasons for hopefulness" but "also for apprehension." He was concerned "that bad men, and careless good men, are not restrained from careless handling of great social concernments by the magnitude and range of the perils they thus invite, and when fools abound it is not cheerful to feel that any one of them may put us all to grief by one careless action or one piece of negligence."[68] Urban society, like the physical setting it inhabited, could burst into uncontrollable flame at any moment, and must be carefully watched.

Rebuilding a city that was "fireproof" would require a wide range of regulation that would extend well beyond more stringent building codes and a better fire department. Any measures that hoped to be effective would have to be based on preserving and protecting a carefully structured social order. In the years ahead, when the word "incendiary" mainly referred to those who criticized this order in speech and in print, "fireproofing" would come to mean once again turning to the gun and the rope to make sure that such individuals were removed from society. In the meantime, to assure Chicago's immediate future after the crisis of the fire, certain special emergency measures would have to be taken.

FOUR

Social Restraint

Two post-fire emergency measures of social regulation were especially significant not just as public policy but also as expressions of a certain imaginative view of the city. In a proclamation of October 13, four days after the worst of the fire was over, Mayor Mason announced his decision to turn over to the Chicago Relief and Aid Society the administration of "all contributions for the suffering people of this city." Two days earlier had come the official word that he had entrusted "[t]he preservation of the good order and peace of the city" to Lieutenant General Philip Sheridan, the renowned Civil War officer and Indian fighter, now commander of the sprawling Division of the Missouri, which extended from Illinois on the east to Montana, Utah, and New Mexico on the west, and from Canada to Mexico. Upon assuming command in 1869, Sheridan had moved the division headquarters from St. Louis to Chicago.[1]

In both actions, Mason was accepting a number of ideas about what the city was, how it should be governed, and who should govern it. In trusting the common welfare to a private organization managed by a recently established business elite and to a military leader whom, in spite of his Irish Catholic background, this elite saw as one of their own, the mayor enlisted the participation of all Chicagoans in the urban vision of these men. They in turn used the resources and responsibilities entrusted to them to enforce that vision in the face of the kinds of disorder they thought the fire revealed and represented. They addressed their responsibilities with few doubts that they were working for the good of all Chicago. They did not believe that they were acting in behalf of any special interests except those that were so natural and normal that they could not be described as partisan. On the contrary, they claimed that one of their purposes was to avoid and be above politics. But embedded in many of their statements, and in much of the gratitude that they received at the time and after in the fire literature, was the antidemocratic notion that a sound urban order in Chicago required careful organization, inspection, and regulatory procedures that would restrict those disruptive social elements and forms of behavior that had free rein during the fire. Both these statements and the words of gratitude expressed doubts about how the social order might be preserved over the long term, and about whether there was a coherent urban community that could be protected and preserved.

Relief and Aid

Mason and the other officials gathered by Common Council president Holden on Monday, October 9, the day after the fire began, had established a temporary Relief Committee to organize the daunting social service tasks that lay ahead, including the receipt and distribution of the contributions of food, supplies, and money that began arriving from every direction that evening. The Relief Committee included private citizens and members of the Common Council from all three divisions. On both Wednesday and Thursday the leadership of the Relief and Aid Society proposed that their organization assume the Relief Committee's job. Mayor Mason's proclamation accepting this proposal came on Friday.[2] While the Society was far from the only organization to devote itself to fire relief, as the sole one with this official imprimatur it managed all aid not specifically sent to another agency, and the range and quantity of its activities dwarfed other relief efforts.

The Society divided the city into five districts, each overseen by a superintendent and about ninety employees, all reporting to the general superintendent and the Executive Committee. It opened offices and supply depots throughout the city that were connected by telegraph, and it separated its work into different areas—receipt of contributions, shelter, employment, transportation, correspondence, distribution, and health—each overseen by a committee. It spent almost $22,000 on printing and stationery alone, much of this devoted to forms of all varieties that were to be filled out by clients and staff. The committee chairs, who were private citizens with solid businesses or professional practices, worked long hours without pay (an illustration in *Frank Leslie's Illustrated Newspaper* of November 18, 1871, showed a night meeting). The Society's foresight helped prevent further calamities that might have followed the burning of Chicago. For example, the Committee on Sick, Sanitary, and Hospital Measures under Dr.

Hosmer A. Johnson performed some 64,000 vaccinations against smallpox, reportedly sparing Chicago the same serious outbreak of this disease that struck other cities in the months after the fire.[3]

By its own May 1, 1874, final accounting of its work on fire relief, the Society had received just short of five million dollars worth of contributions in cash and goods, and had expended over $4,400,000 of that total, including a little over $540,000 on administrative costs.[4] The achievements of the Relief and Aid Society following the fire were noteworthy for several reasons. Amidst awful conditions the Society successfully carried out an enormous undertaking involving the collection of contributions from literally all over the world and the distribution of relief to more than half the population of the city. The Society's "scientific" and "professional" management of this task, notwithstanding complaints about impersonality and inefficiency, was an important episode in the transformation of philanthropy in America going back to the 1850s. As Lori D. Ginzberg points out, the most important trends in this transformation were the increasingly utilitarian and businesslike conduct of the work of benevolence of all kinds (here the Sanitary Commission during the war furnished the most important example) and a growing emphasis in the postwar years on social control rather than either humanitarianism or social reform.[5] From the point of view of the Relief and Aid Society's leadership, and of the community of right-thinking citizen-readers assumed by the authors of the fire literature, the work of relief required restriction and restraint as much as succor and sympathy. Chicago's rebuilding would have to be based on the reestablishment of a properly hierarchical social order that had been shaken during the fire and continued to be threatened by the "incendiary" nature of the city itself.

The Chicago Relief and Aid Society was founded in 1850, but it had been virtually inactive as recently as the mid-1860s, and the scale of its work since that time had been modest. The Society carefully defined its mission in a way that was typical of other similar organizations in American cities that also aimed at staving off social disintegration associated with the rising number of immigrants—to whom were attributed increased problems with pauperism, vice, and crime—by reconstructing the character of the lower classes through the comprehensive coordination of charity efforts.[6] Most of the Society's clientele in the years before the fire were largely the "deserving poor" who did not seem to pose much of a social threat, including widows, deserted or abused wives, the sick and disabled, and the aged. More of a challenge were the ablebodied unemployed, whom the Society wanted to aspire to live by its norms of how the lower classes should think and act. This meant that they should be industrious and orderly, eager and grateful for jobs at wages their employers deemed fair. Applicants for aid were interviewed in their homes by a "visitor" from the Society. In the ten months preceding the fire, it doled out fuel and provisions—it did not dispense cash because this did not fit with its goal of encouraging self-reliance— to 1,237 families. The Society pointedly refused to assure "the *permanent* support of any class," and only offered "such *temporary* help to the deserving poor" that "will *tide* them over those hard places in life which single handed and alone they are unequal to—discontinuing at the earliest moment that it is possible for them to provide for themselves, thus guarding carefully against encouraging a feeling of dependence upon the society." The goal was thus to bring this "they" back into the circle of the useful and productive "we." The Society believed that the "permanently" dependent were the charge of the state, not of this voluntary charity.

The most difficult problem the Society and similar organizations in other cities had pondered in the years preceding the fire was that presented by those without income, who, in the staff's opinion, refused to make provision for themselves in the expectation that the Society would assist them, and who would not accept work outside the city when it was offered. In its report of 1870, the Society announced, along with its calls for municipal legislation regulating tenements and for a better lodging-house for the destitute, a new rule denying aid to those who had been assisted through a winter and refused job placement. To continue to aid such people would be a disservice to the moral fiber of the individual citizen and the city. "The moment a charitable fund can be looked forward to, and *calculated upon*," the Society explained, "it enervates the expecting applicant, and prevents his making that present effort without which he is undeserving." While sympathizing with the desire of applicants to stay near their homes even if it meant that they remained unemployed, the 1870 report still declared this desire to be "of small moment in comparison with continued destitution and final starvation." Besides, "Something must be done to stem the tide of improvident and destitute people toward this city, or its increasing volume will swallow the charity which you have committed to our hands."[7] The "you" referred to here were the citizens who were the major contributors to the Society, while the "our" referred to the members of the board's Executive Committee, who came from this pool of contributors, and, in their behalf, tried to bring the "they" of the deserving poor back to a condition of useful independence.

In conducting the fire relief, the Society's policy was not to discriminate by race, creed, or nationality, but it nonetheless meticulously classified those it served by country of origin, distinguishing between particular ethnic groups and "Americans." Its army of "visitors" personally inspected and certified the suitability of the thousands of applicants for the resources that the world had sent and which the mayor had put in the hands of the Society. There was no external appeal or review of the organization's decisions. Unlike the original Relief Committee, the Society had no publicly elected officials (except Mayor Mason, ex officio). If the "visits" or other rules delayed the delivery of assistance, this was a necessary consequence of the Society's conviction that one of its central responsibilities was "to detect and defeat imposition" and "to aid in establishing order by withholding encouragement to idleness," not to mention "to guard against extravagant or injudicious distribution, the duplication of relief or pretended want."

In cases where direct oversight was not practical or possible, the Society's application forms demanded a reference from someone who was a credible member of the trustworthy "we" who were the backbone of a stable city. Some of the forms included the instruction, "Have your pastor, priest or some other prominent person sign the following recommendation."[8] The word "prominent" enforced the idea that the flow of resources was to be controlled by people who were acknowledged by both the Society and applicants as being part of what Karen L. Sawislak, the leading social historian of the fire, calls "the stable class hierarchy," at the top of which were the members of the Executive Committee and others like them.[9] At the same time, applicants could receive the largesse in the Society's hands only by making themselves visible to such referees and to the intrusive surveillance of the "visitors," the agents of the Executive Committee.

The leadership of the Society consisted almost exclusively of members of Chicago's Yankee Protestant business and professional elite, but, as Kathleen McCarthy has pointed out, the kind of individuals who made up this group had changed between 1850 and 1871. In the prewar era, they were men who were active not only in the conduct of their own affairs but also in the government of the city. In keeping with their sense of duty to Chicago and to the Society as Christian gentlemen, many of the trustees and their acquaintances themselves served as "visitors," both to verify firsthand that a recipient was in fact one of the "deserving poor" and to establish the personal contact with the less fortunate that they felt was part of their moral duty. The Society's board at the time of the fire included a few individuals outside the world of commerce (most notably Dr. Johnson and Unitarian minister Robert Laird Collier), but its driving spirit was that of such figures as Marshall Field and George M. Pullman, most of whom came to Chicago around mid-century or shortly after and gained control over major industries while still relatively young. The Society's president was clothing wholesaler Henry W. King, though its most active member was corporate attorney

Wirt Dexter, who had preceded King as president and served as chairman of the Executive Committee following the fire.[10]

Steeped in both the spirit of capitalism and the Protestant ethic, these men were modernizers as much as moralizers. It is unfair to say that they cared less than did the preceding generation about saving the souls and lifting the spirits of the poor, but they were more specifically concerned with the problem of maintaining the kind of stable and productive work force required by the unprecedentedly large-scale enterprises of the postwar period—railroads, factories, wholesale houses, department stores—which they owned and ran. Largely detached from the lower classes except as a source of labor, and believing in the modern ideals of expertise and efficiency, they viewed the Society's affairs as an undertaking to be administered like a modern corporation, with a professional director and staff. They believed in the future of Chicago as much as did the old settlers, but they generally did not seek public office, partly because the increasingly complex worlds of business and government both required full-time management, and also because of their disdain for (and displacement from) local party organization that more and more reflected the rising power of immigrants and other individuals the businessmen saw as corrupt and incompetent political operators. As Robin Einhorn argues, they were also suspicious of local government because they feared that it might work toward the downward redistribution of resources.[11]

The fact that these successful men of affairs did not hold elected government positions took on a special importance in the immediate aftermath of the fire. The Society's taking control of the receipt and distribution of aid was an early example of what Jon C. Teaford and Theda Skocpol have seen as a characteristic pattern in American urban politics in the last three decades of the nineteenth century. Teaford points to how business leaders, suspicious of the power of immigrants and their elected representatives in city councils, and eager to fashion a government conforming to their middle-class notions, tried to counter the "erosion" of their authority and "tip the social balance of power toward the 'better elements' of society" by turning to extralegal organizations like the Relief and Aid Society "as alternate organs of expression and influence." Speaking more specifically about welfare policy, Skocpol argues that elite reformers, "disgusted by the vagaries and 'corruption' of patronage democracy and alarmed by the rising costs and complexity of care for dependents in a rapidly industrializing and urbanizing society . . . [i]ncreasingly . . . championed measures designed to take public welfare provisions out of the grip of the patronage-oriented political parties that controlled much of the polity in the post–Civil War decades."[12] The Relief and Aid Society saw its assumption of the administration of the relief as an act of civic self-possession based in a selfless assertion of responsibility for the good of the commonweal against the threat of the continuation of the "awful democracy" of the fire.

Exactly why Mayor Mason accepted the Society's offer to take control of the fire relief, and over what, if any, competing claims, is hard to know for sure, though some likely reasons present themselves. As its leaders themselves explained, the organization's standing as a chartered charitable society and its experience in dealing with temporary relief (albeit on a much smaller scale than in this instance) made it a reasonable choice. Besides, the well-publicized work of the Sanitary Commission provided a strong precedent for private management of public causes through bureaucratic organization.[13] The Society's board included the most influential private citizens in the city, individuals with a proven talent for directing large undertakings and an unquestioned devotion to Chicago and to the idea that its future depended on them. Mayor Mason, who turned sixty-six a few weeks before the fire, was of the pioneering generation of engineers who were essential to the transportation revolution that had opened up the West and made Chicago the railroad capital of America. He had worked on the Erie Canal and had been chief engineer and superintendent of the New York and New Haven Railroad before coming to Chicago to oversee the building of the Illinois Central Railroad. His career as an upper-level manager was much longer than his experience in politics (his first position in public life was his service on the Chicago Board of Public Works, to which he was appointed in 1865). He would have been likely to trust, and accustomed to follow, the instructions of these corporate leaders, especially since his term as mayor was virtually over when the fire struck.

The Relief and Aid Society's own version of how it came to be in charge reads like a cautionary tale about the dangers of the modern city's lack of control over the masses and their elected representatives. The Society distinguished between the unsightly, inflammable buildings which invited the fire and the grander ones for which its leaders were responsible. The latter had suffered from their proximity to all the firetraps, much as the refined ladies on the Sands were menaced by the low presences around them. The Society criticized "the public authorities" who failed to look out "for the permanent security of the homes and property of the people." Elected officials were obviously not ready to take the kind of timely and determined action required for the public good, which the leaders of the Relief and Aid Society unreflectively identified with their own priorities. To the degree that the fire was the fault of men like themselves, it was because they had entrusted control of the city to politicians, a mistake they were correcting in taking over the administration of the relief.[14]

In short, the city in its strictly legal state of government was a threat to itself, and extraordinary and perhaps even extralegal steps analogous to the vigilante justice of the lynching stories and the armed protection of the virtuous by Dennis Fleet in *Barriers Burned Away* were necessary to remedy the situation. So attested the memoirs of manufacturer Eliphalet Blatchford, who rushed home from a business trip in the East when he heard of Chicago's calamity. He arrived to find a summons issued by order of Illinois Seventh Circuit Court judge Erastus S. Williams to serve on a grand jury. When he appeared to answer the summons, Blatchford immediately realized that in this moment of crisis, with the social order hanging in the balance, Williams had forsaken normal procedures, and, more than any imaginary lynch mob, had taken the law into his own hands by assembling what Blatchford called "truly a respectable company" who knew and trusted each other. This gathered elite's first response was to "express our appreciation of the importance of the duty," and to request that Williams "grant no excuses except on the vote of the citizens he had summoned." The judge agreed. Blatchford wondered about the irregularity of these procedures, but, he reflected, "these were not days to stand upon even legal technicalities."[15] The administration of justice was evidently too important a task to entrust to the rules of law.

Most contemporary accounts praised the Relief and Aid Society in equally undemocratic terms for coming to rescue the people not only from the fire but from their two worst enemies: themselves and the politicians they elected. Writing early in 1872, Sydney Howard Gay, who later was the anonymous author of the Society's 1874 report on its own work, praised the organization's leadership for taking care of "a hundred thousand homeless, hungry, and almost naked people." The social volatility of Chicago, the tendency of some residents to turn into beasts unless someone exercised careful and firm oversight, demanded such intervention if "civilization" was to be saved. Chicago's refugee population had been "huddled together in the extremity of distress and terror, to become marshalled on the instant into an organized body, or left to become a starving, fierce, and lawless mob." Illustrations in popular national weeklies, reprinted in books on the fire, showed well-dressed men processing contributions and handing out railroad passes, and fashionably attired young ladies distributing food and clothing, in most (but not all) cases to people who appear to be of a lower social station. The givers of aid were usually more carefully drawn than the recipients. The orderly procedure, with the well-to-do in beneficent control, offered a marked contrast to images in the illustrations of a

week or two before of the wild-eyed pandemonium in which social hierarchies were disrupted. Such scenes provided reassurance that order
had been reestablished.

Gay questioned Mason's decision to authorize the original Relief
Committee in the first place since its membership included politicians,
but then praised him warmly for turning things over to the Society.
They, after all, were men of character and social position "above personal temptation," who among their other achievements rescued the
city from "political adventurers." Because of "the utter corruption of
our city politics," he explained, there otherwise would have been an in-
effective relief program marked by "a desperate scramble for the spoils,
first of officials, and then of the mob." Gay maintained that, had it not
been for the Relief and Aid Society, "the disaster of destruction would
have been followed by the deeper disaster of disgrace and anarchy," just
the kind of civic shame that was barely avoided on the Sands.[16]

Earlier the *Chicago Tribune* had been equally outspoken on the need
for a responsible elite to intervene. The alternative was "the foul brood
of city politicians," whom the paper said aspired to be like the bosses of
New York's Tammany Hall, whose well-publicized corruption was very
much on the public mind. Chicago's would-be Tweed Ring now greed-
ily "counted . . . upon retaining place and putting their enemies under
their feet, with the personal and pecuniary power which the handling of
the relief fund and provisions in kind would give them." Their struggle
for control "was as desperate as the clutch of death." Even more than
the fire itself, their ambition "was the crisis in the fate of Chicago." The
"political bummers" did not give up easily, "but fortunately the Executive Committee of the society were not only men of high standing in this
community," but, like those brave souls who rushed into the fire to rescue the doomed and helpless, they were also "men of firmness and
quick decision" who "entered instantly and vigorously upon the great
work before them, heedless of partisan clamor, deaf alike to threats and
offers of compromise." Highly regarded observers from outside the city
concurred. "In the midst of the most pressing demands of their private
affairs, men of great good sense and well informed have taken time to
devise and bring others into a comprehensive and sufficient organization, acting under well-guarded laws," Frederick Law Olmsted told
readers of the *Nation,* referring to "laws" of effective management
rather than to specific legislation. Rationality, organization, and control were what Chicago needed most. Olmsted's view became the consensus version of what had taken place in the Relief and Aid Society's
taking charge.[17]

While there was corruption in the city and county government, the
self-serving discussion of the threat of boodlers grabbing the relief

resources—like much of the talk of terrorists, criminals, drunks, arsonists, and lynch mobs—imaginatively offered a specific location for "respectable" fears about urban life while justifying the Society's actions. The Relief and Aid Society was a genuinely civic-minded organization that very possibly did administer the world's contributions more efficiently and honestly than could have the city government, which in 1871 was not as prepared to assume such a task as were the men who ran the Society. But the attack on the moral failings of politicians also expressed an impatience with governmental inefficiency, to which politicians were assumed to be indifferent or antagonistic. More important, this attack spoke to concerns about the changes in the electorate—and thus the urban population as a whole—that had brought such men into power. However much they had some basis in fact, such criticisms of elected officials in this period were also a form of what Anne C. Rose has described as a "ritual expiation that contained anxiety and protected the status quo."[18]

But one of the consequences of these criticisms was the acceptance of the notion by the mayor and most influential bearers of public opinion that a self-appointed group of businessmen caretakers with its own social goals was justified in stepping in to manage the whole city through such a crisis when it decided it must do so, and that the citizenry should be grateful that it did. Most of the fire histories of the time and after neglected to report the disapproval of the Society's leadership and its work that was expressed in the period following the fire, including an attack on the floor of the Common Council by Charles Holden calling for the transfer of relief funds to the local government. Nor did they discuss the opposition of leading businessman, including Wirt Dexter, to tariff reductions on lumber and other materials that might have facilitated the reconstruction of Chicago but which jeopardized their substantial investments in building materials.[19]

Belief into Practice

Three areas of the Society's activity revealed most clearly its leaders' views on the dangers posed by the fire and, more fundamentally, on how they thought urban society was and should be arranged. The primary goal of the Employment Committee was to get the working class working again. This goal had two purposes. The first, of course, was to rebuild the city in which the Society's board members and their associates had such a large stake. But employment would also be a guard against trouble, since putting people busily back to work would help prevent the reenactment of the wild behavior on the streets and the Sands. The Society quickly set up a temporary office by the charred ruins of the Courthouse as a labor exchange, formulating policies that tried to force every able-bodied boy or man who applied for aid to take an assigned job. The Society stated in its report that "it was no more than common justice to say that to shirk work and live upon charity by preference was the exception and not the rule among the laboring people of Chicago." Still, the idea that these people had to be watched was everywhere in the language of relief. On October 24, General Superintendent O. C. Gibbs issued a circular to all superintendents, assistants, and visitors reminding them that there was more than enough work to assure that "[a]ny man, single woman, or boy, able to work, and unemployed at this time, is so from choice and not from necessity." He ordered his staff to "at once commence the work of reexamination of the cases of all persons who have been visited and recorded upon your books, and [to] give no aid to any families who are capable of earning their own support."[20]

The practices of the Shelter Committee also revealed the Society's desire to monitor and manage those that it considered the most unstable members of society. It rejected the idea of housing in temporary barracks skilled workers who had been burned out of their own homes in favor of giving them the raw materials to build, or even building for them, single-family houses. The Society offered two different models, the larger of which was sixteen by twenty feet (designed for families of more than three, it also featured a partition that divided it into two rooms). The aim of this decision to provide such housing for valued laborers in a timely way (over five thousand of a total of almost eight thousand of such "shelter houses" were built by mid-November) was to avoid putting a large number of people "into promiscuous and involuntary association"—precisely the kind of association the fire created— that "would almost certainly engender disease and promote idleness, disorder, and vice, and be dangerous to themselves and to the neighborhood in which they might be placed." The Society expressed concern that "mechanics and the better class of laboring people, thrifty, domestic, and respectable, whose skill and labor were indispensable in rebuilding the city" and who had owned their own homes before, would otherwise fall into "depression and anxiety, if not despair."[21]

What barracks the Committee on Shelter did construct were intended for former tenement dwellers who were used to no better. Staff members made sure that police and medical authorities inspected these premises, with the result, the Society boasted, that "their moral and sanitary condition was unquestionably better than that which had heretofore obtained in that class," and thus also was less of a danger to the well-being of the city as a whole. An object lesson in the need to keep

the classes separate was the tension unexpectedly created by the placement of barracks in Washington Park, a patch of green the size of a city
block, around which were the ruins of many of the stateliest of the
North Division mansions, as well as of Dr. Collyer's Unity Church.
The park also faced one of the very few surviving structures in the path
of the fire, the Mahlon Ogden mansion, and the juxtaposition of the
millionaire who had been spared and these masses in their barracks
who had been burned out was the source of considerable comment and
uneasiness.[22]

No aspect of its program revealed the Society's conception of urban
order better than the work of the Committee on Special Relief. This
body was constituted to deal with problems that the other committees
could not adequately cover. The first such problem was the needs of the
sick, aged, and infirm, who could neither work nor make their way
through the throngs that crowded the Society's offices. Most other
areas of special relief, however, involved people of means who had been
hit hard by the fire. Although, as Sawislak demonstrates convincingly,
the poorer classes in Chicago suffered badly in the fire and had the most
pressing need of outside assistance in reestablishing themselves afterward, the Society was in many ways more generous and sympathetic
to the wants of those who had been better off. It distributed almost
$440,000 in "special relief," including funding to skilled artisans and
professionals (from carpenters and masons to engineers and surgeons)
to help them acquire "the needful tools and appliances for prosecuting
some kind of business or industrial pursuit."[23]

The policies of the Committee on Special Relief reflected the belief,
expressed in the fire literature, that the plight of the poor and unwashed
deserved less sympathy than that of the rich (or formerly rich) and refined, since the latter, being more sensitive, had felt the pain of the fire
more profoundly. The respectable both required and deserved special
treatment because they, like the delicate and desperate mother taking
refuge on the Sands, were what made Chicago worth saving. The relief
depots were deemed "unsuitable" not just for the sick and infirm, the
Society explained, but also "for those whose previous condition in life
unfitted them to endure the exposure and suffering incident to such
modes of receiving relief." In the face of such cases, the Society's attitude shifted sharply from suspicion to solicitude, and its prose warmed
from businesslike to poetic. These fire victims, "who were suddenly reduced to conditions of the greatest privation and distress . . . were the
keenest sufferers of all." After all, "[t]hey were not accustomed to ex-
posures and hardships which were easily borne by the laboring people,
and at the same time the change in their condition and circumstances
was greater and more disastrous. They were borne in a single night

from homes of comfort and plenty into absolute destitution. Nothing could exceed the misery which they were compelled to undergo." Many such families, the Society proudly reported, "received aid from the Special Relief Department which was of the greatest benefit to them, and was afforded with a warmth of good-will, and an earnest sympathy and kindness, which served in some degree to relieve the painful experiences necessarily incident to applications for assistance by persons who had previously been independent in their circumstances." The Society recognized, in short, that the regular relief procedures threatened to extend the social indignities and outrages of the fire. It saw as part of the task of restoration not just to parcel out aid, but to make sure that the leveling effects of the catastrophe were short-lived.[24]

The Society's public statements mainly emphasized the importance of character and competence to Chicago's future, but when the organization issued its final report on the fire relief, it also spoke of its task in the same way as had those who described the occasion as a spiritual rebirth into a new dispensation. Recalling the rhetoric of American Puritanism, the report strongly suggested that the Society's leaders and their agents were a new chosen people who answered the call in this critical historical moment to do God's work in the wilderness of Chicago's desolation. This report was outer-directed, addressed to other people like themselves throughout the country, whom the Society saw itself serving as much as or more than it did the victims of the fire. In the opening sentence of the preface to the report, the Society explained that it was "led by sacred considerations to make a full, and we hope, useful report of the manner in which this trust has been discharged." It modestly questioned whether it was equal to the task, though still assuring the "philanthropic world" that its purpose was to express the gratitude of Chicago and "to render in some measure a service to civilization, as well as to perform an obvious duty."[25]

It would be unfair to undervalue the energy, organizational skills, and the magnitude of the accomplishments of the Relief and Aid Society, but it is important to be aware that its leaders and supporters were unable to separate not only the city's welfare and their own, but also social fact and social anxiety. Fifteen years later, A. T. Andreas expressed thanks that "a man of such rugged common sense and brave character" as Mason, who had been elected in 1869 on a "People's Ticket" pledged to restore honesty to public life, "had control of the city government" and "the courage to intrust all moneys, and supplies received by him on behalf of the people of Chicago, to the Relief and Aid Society, instead of to the City Council."[26] So the story of the relief passed into popular memory as an example of how the forces of respectability and civic order, under attack on the floor of the Common Council as well as in the streets and on the Sands, came nobly and magnificently to the city's salvation.

The Army to the Rescue

The popular version of General Sheridan's role in the Chicago fire was similar to the story of the Relief and Aid Society: in his characteristically decisive manner, this bold warrior brought peace and order to a desperate city that was more ravaged than Paris. According to Andreas, "The record of the hero of the civil war eclipses the record of the soldier who inspired anew the failing courage of Chicago's citizens, but the qualities which made Sheridan conspicuous at the front flashed into view amid the tottering walls of this doomed city."[27] Sheridan had returned to his home in Chicago shortly before the fire, following separate trips during which he had met with Bismarck in Versailles after viewing the triumphant entrance of Prussian troops into Paris and then hunted game in Kansas with a distinguished group of New York and Chicago newspaper editors and businessmen. The hunting party's guide was William Cody, already becoming known as Buffalo Bill, whom Sheridan had appointed chief of scouts for the Fifth Calvary.[28]

Once he grasped the magnitude of the fire, Sheridan shifted his attention from the hopeless task of containing the blaze by blowing up buildings in its path to providing protection for the stricken city. The day after the conflagration began, with the flames still spreading, he telegraphed the bad news to Secretary of War W. W. Belknap, who responded by putting the army's supply depots at Sheridan's disposal. Mayor Mason also agreed to Sheridan's recommendation that federal soldiers be sent to Chicago. The general requisitioned relief rations and supplies from St. Louis, and, with Mason's approval, summoned several companies of troops from Omaha and Fort Leavenworth, the latter including companies of the Fifth United States Infantry under Colonel Nelson A. Miles. At the request of Mason, Sheridan assumed command not only of his own men but also of several state militia units, local police, and the First Regiment of Chicago Volunteers, a corps of private citizens who joined the other units in guarding the relief stations, restricting access to the burned district, enforcing a curfew, and punishing profiteers.[29]

Sheridan recognized early on that defending the public imagination was at least as important as protecting Chicago against real villains. He suggested bringing in troops "for their good effect in quieting the apprehension of the people." He acknowledged the need to guard "treasure and property," but only until what he called "public confidence" was restored. Sheridan later claimed that he reluctantly assented to the proposal that he take overall responsibility for public order only after being beseeched by thousands of citizens, and that he did so with the approval of local, state, and national officials. He insisted that he never abused the powers that were thrust upon him against his will. In no instance, he stated categorically, did his men come in conflict with the regularly constituted authorities. Both his report to Secretary of War Belknap and the posthumous biography written by his brother and close associate, Brigadier General Michael V. Sheridan, maintained that all along he believed that his role in enforcing civil order should be limited. His own motives were "as pure . . . as [were] those of the whole world who . . . [sent] their charities to relieve the distress."[30]

Sheridan's version of how he came to have such broad authority seems to be accurate. Most contemporary evidence indicates that local citizens desperately felt the need for the army's visible presence and for him at the head of it. With a mixture of weariness and pride, John DeKoven, cashier of the Merchants' National Bank of Chicago, wrote to his wife of his experience as a volunteer sentry, "I have not had my clothes off for a week, the city is paroled [sic] every night, you should have seen me last night paroling our alley with a loaded revolver in my hand looking for incendiaries for there are many about." Others were likewise alarmed at the extreme vulnerability of the city and the inefficacy of the police, a situation that they were convinced demanded the highly irregular deployment of troops to monitor a civilian population in peacetime. In the same October 11 letter in which he told family and friends of all the "roughs" shot dead or hanged during the fire, Phillip C. Morgan added with excitement, "*General Sheridan* arrived in the city last night some time with *one thousand* soldiers for the protection of the citizens and their property. Also to hold the cut throats, and Black legs in check and deal to them their just deserts &c."[31]

The "Letter from Chicago" in the *Christian Register,* dated October 13, spoke favorably of Chicago being under martial law, "which is well, for thousands of the vilest and basest of the race have flocked to the city bent on pillage and depredation of every sort, and the patrol of citizens has had to be continued, together with the soldiers, to prevent the burning of what is left." The author admitted that it gave "a feeling of security that is indescribable, save to those who have been in such situations, to see the blue coats and bayoneted rifles at the corners of the streets, and we feel that Sheridan takes hold of the work with a stern grip that is not to be mistaken." Frequently quoted by the fire histories in Sheridan's behalf was William Bross's recollection of his response to the arrival of the troops: "Never did deeper emotions of joy overcome me. Thank God, those most dear to me and the city as well are safe."

Bross maintained that without Sheridan's "prompt, bold and patriotic action, . . . what was left of the city would have been nearly if not quite entirely destroyed by the cutthroats and vagabonds who flocked here like vultures from every point of the compass."[32]

The discussions of Sheridan and the army blended with the comparisons of the conflagration with the war, with all the stories of individual heroism, and most of all with the rumors of incendiaries, looters, and criminal invasion. Chicagoans wanted the army above all to guard their lives and property, but they also needed the soldiers to justify their fears, for the military presence would prove that these fears were to be taken seriously. In their eyes, the fact that no great disorder followed the fire did not mean, as Sheridan suggested in several of his reports to the mayor and to his superiors in Washington, that the rumors of post-fire crime and disorder were without a sound basis and that there had been relatively little to be worried about in the first place, but that the army had in fact been needed and was the only thing that prevented further catastrophic damage and social dissolution. The use of troops, however, would be an important precedent for future armed federal intervention to guarantee urban order, or at least to assuage what Sheridan called "the public mind."[33]

Sheridan remained in charge of "the good order and peace of the city" for almost two weeks. This highly visible de facto martial government caused a much sharper and wider public controversy than did the exercise of emergency powers by the Relief and Aid Society, which lasted almost two years. After first appearing to approve of Sheridan's role, Illinois governor John Palmer questioned its legality as an unwanted federal intervention in state affairs.[34] Palmer found several vocal allies for his position in both the state legislature and the city. The controversy found a tragic focus late in the evening of October 20, when Theodore Treat, a twenty-year-old college student on volunteer curfew duty, shot Thomas W. Grosvenor, who died the next morning. Grosvenor was a former Civil War officer and successful lawyer who had been appointed prosecuting attorney by the Common Council. Different versions of what happened circulated in the city, some blaming Grosvenor for being abusive and even drunk in refusing to respond to Treat's procedurally correct warnings, others citing the incident as an inevitable result of Chicago's extraordinary military occupation and amateur patrols. Treat's own defense was that Grosvenor's behavior made him believe that he was dealing with a "rough," suggesting that the shooting would have been more acceptable if Grosvenor had better fit the profile of the villains of the fire literature. Grosvenor may in fact have been a victim of the false reports of rampant criminality that put Treat fatally on edge. Embarrassed by the incident, Sheridan went out of his way in his report to Belknap to specify that Grosvenor had been among those who "very strongly urged" him to take command of the city, and who told him "that the people would force me to assume control of affairs whether I desired to do so or not."[35]

The finger-pointing continued along political lines. Palmer tried to have Mason and Sheridan, as well as Treat, indicted by a grand jury, which instead lauded the general and refused to order anyone to stand trial. While Sheridan continued to insist that he "never for one moment thought of infringing or abrogating any of the civil laws," Governor Palmer, Mayor Mason, federal officials, legislators, and citizens debated whether or not a violation of states' rights had taken place, and if the whole action was unconstitutional. When Sheridan resigned his temporary command October 23, his official reason was not Grosvenor's death or the political controversy that surrounded the military presence, but his judgment that the presence of troops was no longer necessary since Chicago was safe and calm. At the Relief and Aid Society's request and over Governor Palmer's unsuccessful protests, a small number of army troops continued to provide security for the relief supplies.

Early in 1872 a four-man majority of a select committee of seven legislators supported Palmer in criticizing Mason and Sheridan and in protesting to President Grant, but the minority report, which saw Sheridan's actions as perhaps the most crucial exercise of character and expert leadership in the critical days following the fire, more accurately reflected the feelings of leading citizens in the city. It "most heartily" approved and commended "the humane feelings and manly regard for the protection of human life and property which prompted the active energies" of Sheridan and other officials, including Palmer, "who lent their timely and efficient aid during and immediately succeeding this appalling catastrophe." The minority's most remarkable finding, however, was that even if this aid was technically unlawful, it was still appropriate when considered in its broader context. While concurring "in the general proposition that all violation of law should be condemned, and recognizing the fact that much that was done for the relief of the people of Chicago and the alleviation of their suffering at the time referred to was in violation of law," the minority declared, "yet justice, weighing the pure motives that prompted the commission of these unlawful acts, withholds her sentence of condemnation." Eben Matthews spoke more candidly: "Of course such procedure was illegal, but it had the force of public opinion back of it, and so was most effective in giving us the much need[ed] security."[36] As was the case in the praise for the Relief and Aid Society, the implication was that a period of crisis was no time to trust the legally constituted democratic government to maintain law and order. Responsible citizens were obligated to use their own principled judgment to determine the best and most correct course of action, even if to do so in this case involved defending the validity of the social and political system of the city by violating it.

To the membership and supporters of the Relief and Aid Society, and to many like-minded Americans, the relief sent from everywhere was *their* relief, entrusted to their wisdom and charity. The soldiers likewise were *their* army, and they would use this professional armed force in the way they thought best to defend their city. They were willing to overlook constitutional niceties about legal representation and local sovereignty when they felt that the order they desired was at risk. If the very forces they brought in to preserve order and respectability in fact hanged no looters and mistakenly shot their own prosecuting attorney, they would do no more than express regret and still maintain that it was worth it, for the admission of error and irony in the face of so serious a danger could not be allowed.

Culture and Order

Those who commended the decision to call on the Relief and Aid Society and the army were convinced of Chicago's need for enforced discipline and restraint to see the city through the fire, but these were short-term solutions. No one wanted Chicago kept permanently on relief or under martial law. The boosters were confident that the fire was just a momentary setback that in the end would prove to be an asset to the city's commercial development. But what commonality would hold the city together? What would mitigate some of the sources of instability, including the materialistic tendencies of the booster mentality, that had been exposed by the fire? To the several commentators who raised and, with differing combinations of optimism and doubt, responded to these questions, the answer was "culture."

In this period, "culture" was closely associated with certain forms of training, habits, customs, institutions, and forms of production closely associated with the ideal of the refined individual in a civilized society. In his most influential work of social criticism, published two years before the fire, Matthew Arnold had stated that the alternative to "culture" was "anarchy." As Alan Trachtenberg has pointed out, discussions of culture and order in this period are inseparable from considerations of class conflict, for culture—whether it implied higher education, fine art, or everyday etiquette—was understood to be opposed "to unruly feelings, to rebellious impulses, and especially to such impulses showing themselves with more frequency, as the years went on, among the lower orders."[37] These discussions often contained a critique of American democracy, and particularly of business competition, that was voiced not only by genteel intellectuals but even by some who participated in the Chicago booster dream. In an address to the Chicago Historical Society a half dozen years after the fire, attorney Isaac N. Arnold, an old settler and public figure who was active, in many instances as a founding member, in most Chicago civic and cultural undertakings of note, maintained that without "culture, taste, beauty, art [and] literature . . . there is a danger that our city will become a town of mere traders and moneygetters; rude, unlettered, hard, sharp, and grasping."[38]

Expressions of concern of this kind predated the destruction of the city, as many wondered if a modern commercial and industrial settlement like Chicago ever had been or could be a cultured, and, by extension, stable and well-ordered community. In 1837, the same year the country was beset by financial distress and he was elected Chicago's first mayor, William B. Ogden, who had a hand in almost every significant entrepreneurial enterprise in the city, complained that the spirit of speculation "tended to destroy the discriminating distinctions . . . and . . . integrity of character."[39] Throughout the succeeding decades and into the twentieth century, local leaders, including many of the most successful businessmen, actively tried to make the city a place whose importance to its citizens and the world transcended buying and selling. They and many writers and other observers wondered whether its true nature was that of a new and uniquely American humane civilization all its own, or, as its critics maintained, of a glorified trading post that would always be raw, vulgar, and crude. The city's unquestionable financial success, and the admiration, awe, jealousy, and disapproval that its growth inspired, made this a question of interest well beyond the city in the minds of both its admirers and critics.[40] The fire raised this subject in a new and pressing way, as many commentators cited culture as one of the best long-term safeguards against the social instability and danger revealed by the burning of Chicago. At the same time they pondered the social consequences of the fact that the flames had destroyed several of the city's precious few prized cultural possessions, undercutting its aspiration to be considered a civilized community and, more important, weakening whatever controls these possessions exercised.

For example, the cover of the November 11 *Harper's Weekly*, whose subtitle was "A Journal of Civilization," depicted the ruins of nine Chicago churches, effectively conveying a sense of the terrible damage done to such sacred institutions that held the social fabric together. Almost every enumeration of losses in the fire literature listed, along with the fine hotels, public buildings, and mansions that went up in smoke, notable works of art in private and public hands, institutions like Booksellers' Row and the Academy of Design (on whose board were several directors of the Relief and Aid Society), and the treasured historical artifacts, including the original Emancipation Proclamation, that were lost in the destruction of the new "fire-proof" Chicago Historical Society building. The fire literature likewise mourned the destruction of Crosby's Opera House, which had just been completely renovated and was scheduled to reopen Monday evening, October 9, with a series of symphony concerts under the baton of maestro Theodore Thomas.[41]

Several contributors to the fire issue of the *Lakeside Monthly* attempted to assess just what these losses meant to Chicago. In the booster spirit, J. B. Runnion put the best face on the unfortunate turn of events. He confessed that while "it was depressing and saddening to look back upon those things that can never be restored," including books, paintings, manuscripts, and "the thousand and one things whose value was in their intangible contents," he still found it "exciting and inspiring" to consider the future growth of Chicago. Runnion admitted that Chicago's prodigious commercial development was ahead of its cultural progress, and that the city was, for better or for worse, a little rough by eastern and European standards (Runnion's derisive term was "prim New England notions"). But he suggested that these standards were perhaps not really appropriate to this new setting, and he praised Chicago for its metropolitan variety, its "cosmopolitanism in language and customs," its "earnestness in the pursuit of art and culture, in strange contrast with the frigid and affected connoisseur of older cities," and its "discrimination that was forming itself on the very best model of independence."[42] While the fire may have delayed the city's cultural development, it did nothing to destroy its promise, which Runnion saw as substantially based on the kind of democratic diversity that was the source of so much anxiety in other places in the fire literature. By viewing the city in this light, Chicago's promoters could rationalize the shoddy buildings that were firetraps by attributing them to the necessary but natural awkwardness of growth.[43]

Other essays disagreed with such upbeat post-fire analyses of the state of the city. Their authors were concerned with the damage the fire had done by distracting the attention of the "best" people from the work of urban civilization by forcing them to concentrate all over again on basic tasks of city building. Questioning the view that Chicago had found new depths of spirit and character in the fire, Northwestern University President Erastus O. Haven declared that the city needed to be as aware of its intellectual and moral prospects as of its material and statistical achievements, that it "ought to be to the great Northwest what Boston is to New England." "Magnificent wholesale palaces" and

"six or eight story stores and hotels of rock and iron" were not "extraordinary monuments of the sagacity or courage of their builders." According to this educator and man of the cloth, it was schools, museums,
libraries, and churches that reflected "patient thought and intellectual
and moral culture, not necessarily engendered by a scramble for wealth
or an ostentatious display of it."[44] This allusion to the "scramble for
wealth" blamed the city's commercial leaders more than any "roughs"
for contributing to Chicago's cultural thinness and social instability.

These remarks echoed the analyses of the costs of Chicago's hasty
growth offered by Frederick Law Olmsted and several others as they
sifted through the charred ruins looking for meaning. A few bold souls
were quite pointed in their judgments of the consequences of the city's
lack of cultural progress. In the *Lakeside Monthly*'s issue for the second
anniversary of the fire, John M. Binckley criticized Chicago as being
little more than "a sojourner's resort," "a produce and merchandise exchange," and "an agency of Eastern investment." He attacked the city
for applauding only the most "gross and ignoble species of heroism,"
i.e., material achievement. Chicago had reached the point when "not
to be Athenian is to be Boeotian"; it was still building temples of trade
when it ought to be endowing art museums. It honored the "moneyed
dullard" while ignoring "the true, the beautiful and the good" to be
found in art, literature, and science."[45] In his essay "The Chicago of
the Connoisseur," Episcopal clergyman Horatio N. Powers, who was
active in charitable causes including the Relief and Aid Society's Committee on Sick, Sanitary, and Hospital Measures, complained that Chicago's "aesthetic aspect is dispiriting," and that the world properly
thought of the city not as a civilized and self-possessed gentleman, but
as "a huge monster, gorged with pork and grain, and absorbed in the
single thought of business." While there were "homes of refinement"
and cases of "individual culture" in the city, "the ruling spirit is not an
admirable one, and, we trust, not a permanent one." The source of this
difficulty, he charged, was the same business elite that prided itself on
being the guardian of order. Its members saw material success as an
end, not as "simply the stepping-stones to her real glory." Powers continued, "For Chicago to stand for nothing higher than a great magazine
of provisions, would be to degrade her enormous capacities to promote
the higher abilities."[46]

One entry in the *Lakeside Memorial of the Burning of Chicago* went
even further in its criticism. In his essay, "The Political Economy of the
Fire," D. H. Wheeler wondered where such a destructive event would
fit in the life course of the city and its citizens. He took a Darwinian view
in measuring the overall effect of the fire in terms of the loss and gain of
what he called "human energy." While older men would be disheart-

ened and retire from public life because of this titanic setback, Wheeler predicted, places would be opened for younger men of ability. Such a development would be a source of "personal and moral reasons for regret," however, since it would push into trade some young men "who would else have been forced into letters, art, science." The result would be a "persistency of the old direction of force" that signaled "an absolute loss and a new danger" since "whatever retards the natural movement to higher forms of energy, whatever arrests the progress of a society to a higher life, gives to the lower order of activities facility for crystallization and lessens the probability of a better life." Yet again the analogy of the battlefield was relevant, but now with negative connotations. "On a smaller scale," Wheeler wrote, "the fire repeats the greatest of the burden of the war by subtracting from the education of a generation." The conflagration was no blessing in disguise, but a tragedy for the city's development. "It is not well for us to be taught in the school of pain," he contended, "until it is true that we cannot learn in a better school." Since the fire had diverted men capable of "better" things into trade, "Many a prop is gone from under the civilizing institutions that rose somewhat too slowly in Chicago."

Wheeler then went directly to the consequences of the absence of "civilizing institutions" on the city as a whole. "Whatever educates, as books, newspapers, magazines, higher schools, and churches, suffers out of proportion [from the fire] because material wants are imperious," he warned. "Just because we can hide here such a large proportion of our loss, we shall the sooner recover the shows of our prosperity; but it is a loss—this of education—which has no compensation, and torments the thoughtful spirit with painful apprehensions." The reason for this was that those elements of culture that were casualties of the fire, the things that would be the last and the hardest to be restored, were not only necessary to make Chicago a place where one was proud and glad to live, but also were the very things that would hold it together against the dangerous disorder to which an excessively materialistic society was always prone. They were indispensable to the task of turning a predatory and contentious society like Chicago into a community. "The vast army of counter-jumpers, bartenders, and political bummers," Wheeler explained, using the same kind of terms others had used to describe the sort of people from whom the control of the relief and the city itself were rescued, "is recruited from among the imperfectly educated young men—the young men who have neither book learning nor trades, and want all forms of discipline and culture."[47] Wheeler's comments restated a fear very similar to that expressed in the fire literature's depictions of scenes of chaos in the streets: the problem with urban life, illuminated by the flames but present at all times, was the constant threat of those "lower" forces within the urban population and within each individual to everything that was "higher and better."

Wheeler's remarks lacked the sensationalism of the stories of the lynchings and other barbarisms, the self-righteousness of the accounts of the administration of the relief, and the paranoia behind the declarations that Sheridan saved Chicago, but his reflections shared an important quality with all of these in that they were less a realistic assessment of the situation at hand than a projection of anxieties about city life that the fire crystallized and provided with an occasion for expression. While the disaster undoubtedly rearranged lives and careers and destroyed churches and schools and other cultural institutions, it is not easy to calculate to what extent it caused individuals who would otherwise have been artists, intellectuals, aesthetes, good Christians, and "civilized" citizens to become counter-jumpers, bartenders, and political bummers.[48] This linking of the idea of culture to notions of progress and of "higher" and "lower" would provide the rationale for all kinds of efforts of education and uplift in the years ahead. The wealthy Chicagoans (among whom again were several of the directors of the Relief and Aid Society) who established or expanded the city's major post-fire cultural institutions—including its major museums, libraries, manual training schools, major universities, and the World's Columbia Exposition—turned to this form of philanthropy partly in the hope of exercising social leadership. In their eyes, among the purposes of institutions of culture, which they saw as complementing and not conflicting with their commercial ambitions for Chicago, was the need to overcome the "thinness" of the city's "civilization" and, equally important, to prevent those kinds of social behavior they believed were dangerous and unseemly.[49]

The Reverend E. J. Goodspeed included in the most comprehensive of his several fire histories a short speculative chapter titled "Utopia," which summarized many of the hopes and fears of those individuals who were so eager to have the Relief and Aid Society and the army step in, and who worried about the state of culture in the city. Goodspeed envisioned a morally and socially progressive Chicago rooted in middle-class and native-born Anglo-Saxon Protestant values, where education would be a universal right, temperance the law, gambling and harlotry banned, honesty in public office the rule, and the Sabbath kept sacred. "Literature, science, and art," he continued, allying these cultural endeavors with all the social values he honored, "should enjoy every encouragement and be made to minister, not, as in Paris, to the worse portions of our nature, but to the ennobling, gratification, refinement, and culture of the whole community."

How could all this be realized? Goodspeed had the answer: through the appointment of "a commission of true, honest, public-spirited citizens, to whom all general affairs were entrusted, with power to make laws for the city, and determine the character of its future." This commission "would doubtless greatly change many things, and introduce reforms and establish customs of incalculable benefit to all coming generations." Chicago would then surpass all previous settlements and indeed become the new American city on a hill, its influence "borne by the billow and the breeze" to remote districts, "and men would turn to us as the mariner to his compass or chart, for laws, sentiments, principles and fashions, and the whole conduct of life. Our example would be such that the Republic, energized and purified, would pulsate with new life, and her glorious career would prolong itself to the end of time."

The Reverend Goodspeed's dream, like all the rhapsodizing about purification and revitalization, presented more evidence that the great fire, as catastrophes often do, had reinspired the timeless millennial dream of a finer order. What he did not say was that the closest actual approximation of his commission of public-spirited citizens ruling in trust, and without election or oversight, was the board of the Relief and Aid Society, fortified by control of its storehouses and by the disciplined force of the United States Army. The desire for such a Chicago "Utopia" would become more powerful in the years ahead. But for now Goodspeed himself seemed to discount the possibility of transforming it into reality in modern Chicago: "In the nature of things this is impossible, and all Utopias exist but in the brain of enthusiasts, never probably to issue into living realities, while men are prone to error and sin."[50]

FIVE

The Fire and Cultural Memory

No matter what anyone thought the fire meant, for good or ill, everybody agreed that it marked a moment of major transition in Chicago history. James W. Milner told a friend less than a week after the event, "an age has closed, and a new epoch . . . is about to begin." This "new epoch," Milner added ominously, is "obscured in doubt and uncertainty." The following day Cassius Milton Wicker wrote to his family, "Everything will date from the great fire now." Four decades later, Frederick Francis Cook confirmed their predictions in his memoir, *Bygone Days in Chicago:* "As in our national life the old regime is divided from the new by the Civil War of 1861," he explained, "so in the minds of Chicagoans the city's past is demarcated from the present by the great fire of 1871. In respect to both it is a case of 'before' or 'after.' " The local population seized upon the disaster as an historical marker that would help them frame and understand urban experience and this period of rapid change in terms of the fire's own unpredictable and dramatic, violent and destructive, decisive and irreversible qualities.[1]

Of Time and the Fire

As time passed, there were those who looked back on the fire wistfully. For some individuals, including a few of the old settlers, it became the focus of their nostalgic yearnings for a better day that could never be reclaimed. Writing near the turn of the century, the aged Mary Ann Hubbard complained, "Chicago was a much pleasanter place to live in then [during the antebellum period] than it is now, or has been since 'The Fire.' The people with whom we associated were all friendly and

kind, sharing each other's joys and sorrows, and enjoying simple plea-
sures. The Sabbath was kept holy, and the people were mostly such as
we wished to associate with." To Mrs. Hubbard, as to so many older
people in all times and places, the best was what had been, not what
would be, and what others called progress was a regrettable decline.
Life was better in the old days because Chicago was a simple and moral
human community that did not have the kind of people "we" didn't
like, or at least "they" were not so obtrusive. The implication was that
these people somehow came with the fire or the fire forced "us" to live
with "them," with unhappy and unpleasant results.[2]

Some of this nostalgia, expressed with more subtlety, was in the earliest accounts of the fire. A description of the destruction of the North
Division residence of the Isaac N. Arnold family, which appeared in the
Evening Post and was reprinted in several other newspapers and fire histories, expressed a longing for a finer world now beyond recapture. The
gracious Arnold home took up the entire block bordered by Erie,
Huron, Rush, and Pine (now Michigan Avenue) Streets, and it contained a library of eight thousand history, literature, and law books, as
well as a Lincoln and Civil War collection that was one of the much-
mourned cultural casualties of the fire. The house was also well known
for its lush and varied landscaping. The different versions of the account lavish attention on the lilacs, elms, barn, and greenhouse that
were trappings of a settled village life, already under siege before the
fire, that would no longer be possible in the rebuilt modern city.

The fire signaled the passing of this old order through its destruction
of two emblems of that world in the Arnold garden. The first was the
"simple but quaint fountain . . . beneath a perfect bower of overhang-
ing vines." The fountain was fashioned from a large boulder that featured a rudely carved face of an Indian chief from an earlier era in
Chicago history. The second was a nearby sundial with the Latin inscription, *Horas non numero nisi serenas* ("I reckon only fair hours"),
which "was broken by the heat or in the melee which accompanied the
fire," so that "the dark hours which have followed pass by without its
reckoning."[3] Gone from Chicago was its former harmonious relationship with domesticated nature represented by the fountain, the "perfect bower," and the happy inscription. The accounts of the loss of this
little Eden seemed to sense that post-fire Chicago would have other
uses for precious real estate than rambling grounds and bowers, and
that it would follow the frenetic man-made pace of the time clock, not
the sundial.

The predominant view of the fire, however, was decidedly forward-
looking and optimistic. As if it were theirs by right, Chicago's boosters
claimed possession of the official public memory of the fire, which they

dedicated entirely to the golden future, downplaying much of the earlier talk of piety, character, efficiency, and culture. They continued to
declare to all that the destruction of Chicago was the best thing that
ever happened to the city. Chicago Board of Trade secretary Charles
Randolph quickly picked up the booster flag from John S. Wright in
proclaiming that God, geography, and history were on Chicago's side.
"Nature has seemed to especially designate the banks of the little bayou
on which man has built Chicago as a proper and necessary place for the
exchange of commodities," Randolph declared. While "some may find
their burden greater than they can ever stagger under," he contended,
others, "with the aid of the outstretched helping hands from the four
quarters of the globe," would "repair the waste places, rebuild the lev-
elled landmarks, and raise from the ashes of Chicago past, a city more
grand, more substantial, and in every way more adapted to the needs of
what the world has come to recognize as the necessities of Chicago future."[4] In this statement, grandeur and substance unseated simplicity
and quaintness as desirable urban values, all under the iron rule of "necessity," whose more appealing synonym was "progress."

     Another commentator, who clearly saw the city's future through the
eyes of the Yankee elite, proclaimed that Chicago's recovery was not
only "the proudest manifestation of the concentration of all Anglo-
Saxon energy and enterprise, but also . . . the shining type of the
progress of the Nineteenth century." He went on to assert that the fire
surpassed the Franco-Prussian War as an event of significance, creating
as it did "a new starting point for the memories of the rising generation."[5] The fire was certainly the starting point in the cultural memory
of modern Chicago, which adapted history to its own needs and purposes. The greatest imaginative feat of remembering was to claim that
the epic disaster at once gave the young city what it most lacked—a history and a tradition—and devalued the past. This involved a paradox
that required a good deal of evasion and repression. The paradox was
based in the much-repeated notion that the scale of the disaster demonstrated the greatness of Chicago, which earned recognition as a world-
class city by burning to the ground.[6] W. W. Everts, the most prominent
Baptist minister in Chicago, took as his text for his sermon, "The Lord
thy God turned the curse into a blessing unto thee, because the Lord
thy God loved thee," and then told the story of a Chicago businessman
traveling in Switzerland before the fire who came upon a map of the
United States that marked the location of Milwaukee but not Chicago.
Everts then asked his congregation if they thought this could ever happen now. "Do you think another map will be published on this globe
without Chicago? Do you think that there will be any intelligent man
who will not know about Chicago?" The answer was obvious. "Oh no!"

As was the lesson: "Then if material progress be a blessing at all, you see what a distinction has been brought about by the fire."[7] The disaster literally put Chicago on the map by wiping it out.

The fire had thus bestowed on the city a portentous moment of origin that involved the obliteration of its actual past and the directing of all energy and attention toward Chicago's prospects in a modern social and economic order. The catastrophe, instead of shutting down its future, encouraged the destruction of its memory of its pre-fire history as surely as it burned the records in the Courthouse, the artifacts in the Historical Society, and the precious books in Isaac N. Arnold's library. While several of the fire histories included a chronicle of Chicago from the Indian settlements through the Civil War, they also emphasized how completely this earlier era was burned away, and was now dead, distant, and irrelevant. For many, Chicago's past was all condensed into this fiery moment out of which its glorious future was born. This idea was reinforced by boosters, above all the "rising generation" of business leaders, and accepted without reflection by the continuing flow of immigrants from the rest of the country and the world who had no imaginative association with the Chicago that was. They would all start anew in a fresh context full of great expectations. The final paradox was that the first task of cultural memory would be to forget.[8]

Among the Ruins

To make all this possible, the fire literature in several instances reconstructed the destruction of Chicago as a kind of historical node, a unique moment in time when, it seemed, an old order was instantly gone and a new one appeared in a flash of flame. As Colbert and Chamberlin reported, the burned-out heart of the city was completely inaccessible the day after the fire because of the lingering heat and the "still tumbling walls." No railroad or other traffic went in or out of this transportation center, "There was no gathering together of the people on this day," or "other of the signs of life" which were characteristic of this busiest of cities, "for there was nowhere to gather." "In short," they explained, "the day seemed a *dies non*—a day burnt out of the history of the city."[9]

The fire literature discussed this extraordinary transitional moment in its many passages on the city's ruins, especially in accounts written shortly after the fire, when the rubble had cooled but was not yet cleared to make way for new building. "The town is beginning to fill with aesthetic sight-seers," reported one journalist. "The artists of the illustrated papers are seated at every coign of vantage, sketching for dear life against the closing of the mail." The fragments left standing offered objects for reflections on the meaning of the event. F. B. Wilkie argued that by walking among the "yawning walls, broken columns, shattered chimneys, and slender, smoke-stained arches" that "extended everywhere in a wilderness of undisturbed profusion, . . . one could best appreciate the character of the catastrophe." Wilkie went on, "All the characteristics of chaos and destruction seemed present, and none failed to present themselves as a reward for patient and extended study." One of the most remarkable features "was that found in the complete obliteration of all recognizable characteristics of places and localities," as if there were some "resolute purpose on the part of the spirit of destruction" to wipe everything away. In terms of thoroughness of devastation, he compared the burnt district of Chicago to Herculaneum after the eruption of Vesuvius. Local property owners, he contended, could not find their own buildings, and visitors could not tell that the downtown had been inhabited land.[10]

But the ruins also seemed to objectify the way that the very thoroughness of the fire somehow recreated the city overnight by giving it a history that began with the removal of the past. The ruins were read in a manner that interpreted the destruction of Chicago as creating instantly those things that some feared the "thin" culture of the city most sorely lacked because of the brevity of its history and its materialistic spirit. As if in direct response to those who would bemoan Chicago's (and America's) cultural immaturity and absence of traditions, several authors offered the ruins. In his description of the eerie cityscape of destruction, O. A. Burgess could have been speaking explicitly to Nathaniel Hawthorne's famous complaint, published twenty years earlier, about the difficulty of writing romance in America, where there was "no shadow, no antiquity, no mystery, no picturesque and gloomy wrong." Hawthorne contended that "Romance and poetry, like ivy, lichens, and wall-flowers, need Ruin to make them grow." Here was ruin, Burgess asserted, and all the romance one could wish for. "No fabled story of antiquity," he declared, "no ruined castles or antiquated towers, no moss-covered monuments, no ivy-clad columns of past gra[n]deur though tinged with the rosy hue of fiction and glimmering with the highest flight of a fitful imagination, were ever half so grand as the ruins of Chicago today."[11]

E. J. Goodspeed's aesthetic and philosophical ruminations on the scene combined the central points of Wilkie's and Burgess's comments. "No city can equal now the ruins of Chicago, not even Pompeii, much less Paris," Goodspeed boasted. The fire simultaneously removed an undistinguished past and presented a new and improved one that was equal to the splendor of the ages. When one wandered among the ruins, Goodspeed wrote in a passage that recalled the grab bag of mythologi-

cal allusions in the fire literature's descriptions of the conflagration itself, "the beholder cannot dispel the illusion that he is the victim of
some Aladdinic dream, and that he has been transported with the
speed of light, by the genius of the lamp or ring, and set down among
the ruins of the Titanic ages."[12] To Goodspeed, the fire seemed to defy
and dismiss time, which "works slowly," by setting "before our eyes the
ruins of a world in the compass of a single night." He noted further,
"Here all time is reproduced in a moment," as Chicago's own "time" of
rapid and careless growth was at least temporarily forgotten.

Other writers who contemplated the ruins were similarly inspired.
Sheahan and Upton included in their lengthy history a six-page essay
subtitled "Chicago by Moonlight" that evoked the magic and mystery
of the scene. The two authors shared with their readers their sense of
the way the ruins seemed to carry those who beheld them through
space and time, giving the city an aura of history it heretofore lacked by
transforming it into somewhere else that was finer and better: "In this
indefinite light all things are old, and all things are strange. It is no
longer Chicago, the sky above is clear and starry enough to look upon
the Rhine and Arno, instead of the Chicago river. Telegraph posts are
transfigured into burned and branchless trees, and in this blue land of
supreme fancy, the prosaic and the commonplace have disappeared
forever." Several of the histories contained illustrations depicting
lonely individuals among the ruins in scenes that recalled paintings and
views in travel books of figures dilating thoughtfully on the proud remnants of the old world.[13]

Commentators appeared not to notice that the implication of their
flights of associational fancy was that Chicago's ruins had little character of their own, that their appeal was based on the fact that they resembled other places. If the burned and broken remnants of the old city
elicited any reservations about the value of Chicago, such thoughts did
not find direct expression. The booster imagination had little patience
for public doubt, and it focused its attention to how quickly a new city
was rising from the ashes of the old. The sublime ruins were soon un-
ceremoniously reduced to rubble and shoved into the lake to expand
the available land on which to build a Chicago in which the fire had no
meaning except as a starting point, on the other side of which there was
little worthy of either reverie or reverence. The speed with which Chicagoans replaced the ruins quickly became absorbed into the mythology of the city's energy and dynamism. Sheahan and Upton told of a
man frantically pushing past other passengers at the East St. Louis depot, insisting that he must get on the next train to Chicago "if it costs
me my life." When asked the reason for his haste, he responded, "I
must get to Chicago tomorrow on this train, or those people up there

will have built up the whole d ____d town again, and I won't see them ruins ____!"[14]

Some of the smaller objects that did not become landfill found other purposes more suitable to the irrepressible Chicago spirit of entrepreneurship that could turn almost anything into a marketable commodity. There was an active trade in souvenirs of the fire, such as charred chunks of noted buildings or twisted clusters of plates or spoons welded together by the infernal heat. These were less remnants of the city that was than signs of the transforming power of modern Chicago that, in its stockyards and mills and factories, could turn any raw material into a product to purvey to the world. The fallen Courthouse bell was melted down into tiny replicas that were sold along with little certificates of authenticity, and one resourceful entrepreneur opened a saloon that was supposedly constructed entirely out of materials salvaged from the fire. The Relic House, as it was called, went through a series of changes of owner, use, and even location before it was finally demolished in 1919. An illustration that graced several fire histories depicts a street-smart waif out of Horatio Alger (whose first novel, *Ragged Dick,* was published four years before the fire) who peddles a small doll to a well-dressed family. Nearby is a pile of rubble into which is stuck a sign advertising the removal of the business formerly on the site to another address outside the burnt district. In this and other similar illustrations, members of the wealthy and respectable elite here seem to be buying their city back from the lower classes, who have taken temporary possession because of the fire.[15]

Out of the Ashes

The fire literature expressed the idea of Chicago's prodigious capability to survive and be reborn through another of its representations of the fate of young women during the fire. Published accounts, letters, and illustrations told of "numerous cases of ladies who trying to escape on foot, were overtaken by the pangs of maternity, and upon the street, or in front yards, became mothers." Luzerne claimed that "not less than eight hundred cases of premature birth have already been made known," adding that, like every other aspect of the fire, these births involved extremes of human experience "that no strength of language can adequately describe." Nevertheless, he made the attempt: "The poor women, away from their natural protectors, with no friends at hand, and without even the commonest attention from strangers, so absorbed was everyone in the immediate danger to life and property, were left, in all their helplessness, to encounter the most critical period in their lives—rendered a thousand fold more momentous by the appall-

ing character of the surroundings."[16] While one purpose of these stories was to emphasize the apocalyptic horror of the fire by describing
how helpless mothers and babies suffered miserably in terrible circumstances in little hells like the Sands, these tales also reinforced the idea
of the city as phoenix, indicating that a whole new urban dispensation
rose miraculously out of the old.

The future-oriented booster attitude shaped the way the fire was of-
ficially remembered for a generation and beyond. An attempt to erect a
monument to the fire and to old Chicago came to nothing, while other
much larger projects whose aim was to celebrate the new city pros-
pered.[17] Outsiders who puzzled at Chicago's upbeat official commemorations of its own destruction failed to understand that the viewpoint
of these often elaborate ceremonies was prospective, not retrospective.
In June of 1873 the city hosted a jubilee week to note the progress of the
rebuilding. A few months later it marked the second anniversary of the
fire in even grander style with the Inter-State Industrial Exposition,
which ran from September 25 to November 12 in Chicago's version
of the Crystal Palace, an immense modern exhibition building constructed mainly out of iron and glass and crowned with three cupolas. It
was designed by W. W. Boyington, architect of the Grand Pacific Hotel
and the first LaSalle Street Station as well as of the Water Tower, and
located on the east side of Michigan Avenue between Adams and
Jackson streets. Until the early 1890s, when this emblem of revival itself
gave way to the current Art Institute of Chicago, the Exposition Building hosted many other major events.

Of the twenty-five directors of the Exposition, a crucial handful, including lard manufacturer Nathaniel K. Fairbank and lumber merchant Thomas Avery, as well as Wirt Dexter, were also on the Executive
Committee of the Relief and Aid Society, and they saw this event as a
natural continuation of their efforts as public citizens and private entrepreneurs to assure Chicago's future. While the purpose of the Industrial Exposition was to promote the commercial possibilities of the
states of the Old Northwest as well as Chicago, it also offered displays
of the fine arts and natural history of the kind whose loss many accounts of the fire bemoaned. The most impressive exhibit set before the
visitors, however, was the resurrected city. In the years to follow, business leaders would continue to mount impressive trade fairs, often
accompanied by glossy-paged self-congratulatory commemorative
publications, culminating in the grandest fair of all, the World's Columbian Exposition of 1893.[18]

The fire was thus reduced to a self-contained marvel or curio, made
all the more marvelous, curious, and distant by the removal of virtually
all its traces. When October 9 rolled around, a reporter or two might try

to locate Kate O'Leary, mainly to make her the butt of an anti-Irish joke and to demonstrate how far the city had come.[19] In the fall of 1878, the Griswold Opera House advertised for the "FIRST TIME IN THIS CITY" a "very Realistic and Sensational PANORAMIC & DI-ORAMIC DRAMA" titled "Chicago Before, During & After the Fire," featuring a 1600-foot "grand panorama" plus "the most startling dramatic effects unequaled in the world." The poster for the show included scenes taken directly from the illustrations in the fire histories: the wild exodus over the Randolph Street bridge, a daring rescue by brave firemen, a shooting in a saloon—and a lamppost lynching.[20]

A completely successful escape into boosterism and spectacle was not possible, however. There could be no instant reprieve from the anxieties about Chicago society and culture expressed in the fire literature, even by some imagined moral economy in which a second chance was somehow "paid for" through the suffering caused by the appalling calamity. There was in the boosterism a desperate kind of wishful thinking, a desire to escape the conflicts of historical experience and avoid the difficulties of the present by embracing the future, where nothing has yet happened and so the possibilities are without limit. Some of the less reassuring messages of the fire about the nature of that future were inescapable, however. In a country as varied, complex, and interdependent as that which contained places like Chicago, it sometimes seemed as if a whole city or nation could be put seriously at risk by the actions of almost anyone. The larger moral of Mrs. O'Leary was not so much that it was dangerous to admit these Irish immigrants into "our" midst. Indeed, they were among the most important groups in the building and the rebuilding of Chicago, whether the native-born elite liked it or not. These people would have to be dealt with, since they were part of the system.

The most important lesson of the unhappy accident in the barn was that urban order was so vulnerable that, in the words of a popular song, a cow could kick over Chicago, setting off a night of horrors locally and threatening to bring down the whole system of modernity in which the city had assumed so important a position. The public mood could be skittish and brittle, and any bad news, feeding on fear and anxiety, could have large consequences near and far. Inside Chicago, the rumors of thieves and incendiaries led the city to the assumption of special powers by the Relief and Aid Society and the United States Army. Beyond, the burning of Chicago caused financial havoc. Remarking on the collapse of stock prices following the fire, the *Nation* attributed this to "the keen scent of Wall Street," which "discovered the gravity of the evil at an early hour," with the result that "the owners of railroad securities so long upheld by the manipulations of gigantic rings and combinations, eagerly rushed into the market as sellers, producing a panic and excitement almost equal in intensity to that of the famous Black Friday of 1869."

New York's instant access to information about Chicago, which enabled it to ship relief supplies while the city was still ablaze, thus set off a secondary calamity of sorts. The would-be safety net of national commerce in which Chicago was a vital element was also a precarious economic web made up of an overextended banking system, great corporations "under the control of reckless Wall street gamblers," inflated real estate, national finances "in a nebulous state of transition," and confused political institutions. "[W]ith all these unfavorable circumstances pressing on the community," the *Nation* explained, "the destruction of so large an amount of property at Chicago has a most disastrous effect, and tends to destroy credit in every direction, and to precipitate a panic." The fire seemed to have revealed rather than caused the chaotic financial condition of the country, and the commotion on the trading floor reproduced the situation in the streets.

The overall effect of the burning of Chicago on business, the article continued, "is perhaps as striking a proof as we have ever had of the closeness of the relations which have been established between the uttermost ends of the earth. Calamities, and especially great calamities, are fast ceasing to be what is called local—they are now all general." Referring to the aroused feeling which was the central subject of the sentimental tributes to the relief effort, the *Nation* insisted on practical truth: "No serious disaster can overtake Chicago or St. Louis without making London feel something more than sympathy." That something was the uneasy recognition that in the modern age of cities there was no such thing as an isolated catastrophe. "It appears almost probable," the article went on, "that there will, before long, be no privileged places any more than privileged persons, and no place, in short, any more peaceful or secure against alarms and anxieties than any other place." The sobering conclusion: "The Happy Valley is a thing of the past."[21]

There were a number of important realizations wrapped up in these thoughts. The fire had perhaps put Chicago on the map as a major city, but it also served notice that the dangers of modern life went a good deal beyond those posed by bad building techniques. Tomorrow promised more trouble, not liberation or redemption from the restrictions and sins of the past, but additional entanglements, complications, and conflicts.[22] In its scope, suddenness, and destructive power, the fire spoke of the scale, mystery, instability, and uncertainty of urban life. In its indescribability it offered an unsettling way of perceiving the world it consumed. The fire had, among other things, rearranged and intensified the old categories for understanding the nature of experience. It offered actual events "more romantic than the veriest fiction," Frank Luzerne warned his readers, events whose "realities" could "only be written as it was, with a pen of fire." Chicago's calamity seemed to force a shift in thinking about the new reality the fire appeared to create and reveal. Luzerne repeatedly employed the term "reality," as well as several closely related words. He maintained that his account dealt "with realities alone," but that "it was almost impossible for the compiler to divest his mind of the impression that he is recording a horrid phantasmagorical vision, rather than the facts of real life," and that if Luzerne failed in being true to the realities of his subject, it would be in not being "phantasmagorical" enough. The *Chicago Times* likewise spoke of the "terrible reality of the scene," while the *New York Sun* remarked that the eyewitness reports it published "seemed like an overwrought tale of fiction rather than the grim and terrible reality that all knew it to be."[23]

In this period of so many transitions and conflicts, including the contention between the romantic and the realistic imagination as the most valid interpreter of experience, reality was here linked to "overwrought" fiction, and to terror, and beyond that to the central image of a proud young city on fire, which became in turn the representation of a new and unsettling actuality. The dominant imaginative interpretive view of the fire was based on the ideas of resurrection, purification, revival, and renewal, but not without the very real possibility of catastrophic destruction of a world which contained within itself the elements that could undo it. As powerful and even as justified as was the booster dream, it could not dispel this fear, which the fire literature imagined as the fair city in distress at the hands of incendiaries and demons who would defame, defile, and destroy her unless good citizens were vigilant and forceful. All too soon the ritualized hanging of the enemy of the people would move from dark fantasy to real event and occupy center stage in the public imagination. The most terrible reality of the fire was that the unspeakable and the indescribable had happened, furnishing a vocabulary and a conceptual framework for a troubled future.

Part Two

 BOMB

SIX

From Resurrection to Insurrection

The boosters were right. The fire accelerated rather than slowed Chicago's evolution from bustling mercantile center to manufacturing and trading colossus. In the next two decades its population more than tripled in size to over a million, surpassing all other American cities except New York. The disaster, as Christine M. Rosen explains, contributed to "a permanent reorganization of residential, commercial, and industrial land use patterns that turned an old-fashioned walking city into a comparatively modern nineteenth century industrial metropolis in less than two years time." Property values generally rose until the depression of 1873, as the business center in the South Division doubled in size, rose in height several stories (the skyscraper revolution with which the city was soon to be identified was still a decade away), and became more completely dedicated to commercial enterprises, which were now more segregated than before by type. In the words of a local commentator writing in 1872, Chicago property now stood "better classified, and its future more distinctly marked, than could have been possible before the fire."

Most heavy industries, including the Union Stock Yards, which had opened on Christmas Day of 1865, had been assembled outside the burnt district, and the fire encouraged the continuation of this trend. Except for the passenger depots, which were quickly rebuilt, the train traffic in this leading railroad city was not seriously damaged. The demand for prime commercial space, the destruction of much of the pre-fire housing stock in and near the downtown, and improvements in rail transportation pushed both workers and the more well-to-do further from downtown. As in other cities, the desire on the part of the middle and upper classes to separate themselves from the laboring population led to their movement to the periphery of the city and to the blossoming suburbs, or at least to parts of the city that were more socially homogeneous and clearly divided from less desirable ones than the better neighborhoods had been before the fire. Untouched by the disaster was the most important element in Chicago's growth, its location, which made it more accessible than any place on earth to resources and markets at the very moment when America was taking over world leadership in industrial enterprise.[1]

Newspaper stories, magazine articles, and special publications that appeared on the first and succeeding anniversaries of the Great Chicago Fire justifiably marveled at the resurrected city. But several of the concerns about urban order that the fire had raised, and the ways in which these concerns were expressed, both shaped and were nurtured by new developments that aroused still greater anxieties, which in turn continued to influence the perception of events and events themselves. Against a background of economic difficulties that lifted public uncertainty about the future to a precarious level, Chicago experienced a series of alarming disruptions that seemed to possess an irresistible momentum of their own. Public officials, business leaders, contributors to periodicals, newspaper reporters, and even some labor leaders blamed much of the trouble not on the current order but on a few individuals they characterized as "incendiaries," as troublemakers whose mental processes were twisted by subversive and violent strains of European radical thought that had no application to working and living conditions in America. Unless some strong actions were taken, these troublemakers and their followers would terrorize their betters and launch a new and more intractable civil war centered in the modern industrial city, where all the destabilizing elements of society were thrown most dangerously together.

This outlook helped produce the kind of disorder it supposedly hoped to suppress. Far from backing down, numerous ethnic and labor groups organized and even armed themselves to protect their interests, turning Chicago into a battlefield. Most of the fighting was done with words—speeches, articles, broadsides, and proclamations—and various forms of often carefully staged and deliberately confrontational actions and shows of power. Behind all this angry rhetoric and urban "theater" was the desire by all parties involved to dramatize and thereby validate their view of current social reality and of the nature of urban order and disorder. The Haymarket bombing revealed how deadly serious the conflict had become.

The End of the Post-Fire Consensus

A month after the fire, Chicagoans overwhelmingly elected *Tribune* owner Joseph Medill mayor on the reform-minded Union Fire Proof ticket, but the fragility of any citywide political consensus became apparent by early in 1872.[2] In mid-January a heavily ethnic group of workingmen demonstrated against proposed restrictions on flammable (and inexpensive) building materials as discriminating unfairly against labor and immigrants by making it almost impossible for many of them to afford to own a home in the city. They demanded attention by organizing a parade that ended at the seat of civic power, a Common Council meeting in the temporary city hall, where their most unruly members threw bricks, an approved building material, through the windows. That the protesters saw the regulations as serving class interests was apparent in their banners, which bore such phrases as "Leave a Home for the Laborer" and "Don't Vote Any More for the Poor Man's Oppressor." That the wealthier native-born population viewed the demonstration in some of the same sometimes paranoid and nativist terms that were expressed in the fire literature was equally clear in newspaper stories that deemed this incident the work of "the scum of the community," "mongrel firebugs" who themselves "never owned a foot of ground, and never will, if they do not spend less money for beer and whiskey." Such stories compared this gathering to the urban mobs of France and England, and charged that it was under corrupt, irrational, and foreign control. The *Tribune* deemed the demonstration "a temporary reign of terror," and "one of the rare tastes of Communism that has been thus far vouchsafed to the American people."[3]

In May the building trades unions organized a rally to allay such fears while calling for fair wages, but harmony proved difficult to achieve. What Karen Sawislak describes as the "uneasy peace" between construction workers and their employers came apart in the early fall with strikes by carpenters and bricklayers.[4] To make matters worse, Mayor Medill reluctantly gave in to pressure from "reformers" who demanded that he enforce a long-neglected Sunday ban on alcohol. The fire histories that had exaggerated the amount of bestial behavior during the conflagration and blamed it on the free flow of liquor constituted a kind of temperance literature. In the same spirit, the "respectable" (i.e., native-born and middle- or upper-class) citizens who pressed for the enforcement of the ban saw it as a way to protect Chicago from new outrages by regulating the low and dangerous habits of those in the population whom they perceived as objectionable and threatening. The main targets were the beer gardens and saloons favored by German and Irish workers on their only day off.

Even middle-class members of these two ethnic communities saw this campaign as an attack on their culture for being inherently alien, inferior, and "disorderly." As committed a proponent of the public order as Irish-born John J. Flinn, who was ready to blame shiftless laborers for urban crime, viewed the revived temperance movement as an ill-advised expression of the "sentiments of the better classes" that aimed "to revolutionize the customs of more than two-thirds of the people" (including the American-born children of Irish and German immigrants) at the risk of violating fundamental rights and increasing rather than reducing social unrest. For the moment at least, opponents of cultural pluralism lost out. In 1873 an unprecedented coalition of Germans and Irish formed the heart of a "People's Party" that elected American-born Harvey D. Colvin mayor over a "Law and Order" candidate.[5]

Colvin was a man of small distinction who ran a corrupt administration that contributed to the dissolution of the People's Party and to much confusion in Chicago politics through the mid-1870s. But the most devastating source of social discord was the economic downturn that began with the panic of 1873 and lasted until the end of the decade. As shelter against the winter, the homeless and hungry found refuge by sleeping in police stations. By the close of the year and into 1874, unemployed laborers were participating in rallies and marches that demanded a program of public works jobs from the city and the distribution of the funds still in the keeping of the Relief and Aid Society. These protests, which engaged a broad range of ethnic groups, were orderly and peaceable at first. The city government pleaded poverty but agreed to assemble a committee of nine aldermen to help the jobless appeal to the Society, which was rumored to have up to a million dollars left (Wirt Dexter told the mayor that the figure was closer to $600,000, which he claimed was diminishing fast). The Society agreed to help the genuinely destitute, but rejected the demand for a public works project. This led in turn to unrulier demonstrations outside the Society's headquarters on LaSalle Street, during the course of which the crowd chanted "Bread or death" and threatened to demolish the Society's offices and to seize the Inter-State Exposition Building. Some workingmen charged that the Society's directors were abusing a public trust, perhaps even embezzling the relief funds. Papers sympathetic to the Society published stories defending its policies, offering anecdotes of cases of "imposition" by fraudulent applicants, and characterizing the protesters as "our communists."[6]

In spite of the panic of 1873, newcomers continued to arrive in the city. Whatever difficulties awaited there, they believed that the prospects were better in Chicago than where they came from. By November

the depression had cost seventeen-year-old Louis Sullivan his job in the
Philadelphia architectural firm of Furness and Hewitt, and within a
week he was seated in a Pennsylvania Railroad car crossing the Alle-
ghenies, determined to test his fortunes in Chicago.[7] Albert Parsons
was eight years older than Sullivan when he made exactly the same trip
from Philadelphia to Chicago at virtually the same time. Born in Ala-
bama and raised in Texas, Parsons had joined the Confederate Army at
thirteen. After the war he became involved in the kind of defiantly un-
popular and dangerous causes that absorbed him throughout his adult
life. He edited a newspaper that supported the effort to win political
rights for freedmen, married a former slave, and held various elected
and appointed positions in Texas. With the return of local Democrats
to power in 1873, he decided to settle in the North. His wife, Lucy, met
him in Philadelphia, and they proceeded from there to Chicago. Once
in the city, Parsons joined Typographical Union Number 16, which had
been established in 1852 as the first trade union in the city. Parsons's
skills secured him temporary work on the *Inter-Ocean* and then a regular position on the *Times*.

Sullivan's and Parsons's careers in post-fire Chicago followed very
different directions. Sullivan became one of the major figures in Chicago's rise to eminence as a center of modern architecture. Partly
because of his passionate and iconoclastic personality, his life was embattled and troubled, but his personal and professional struggles could
not begin to compare with those of Albert and Lucy Parsons, who soon
were deeply involved in radical politics. Albert Parsons's response to
the protests of the unemployed was to examine the actions of the Relief
and Aid Society for himself, only to find that "the complaints of the
working people against the society were just and proper." The plight of
labor in the North reminded the pro-Reconstruction Texan of the condition of the former slaves in the South, and he became convinced that
"there was a great fundamental wrong at work in society and in existing
social and industrial arrangements." Thus began what Parsons called
his "interest and activity in the labor movement" that ended on November 11, 1887, when he and three other men were hanged on the gallows of the Cook County Jail for their role in the Haymarket bombing a
year and a half earlier.[8]

Battle Lines

Through the mid-1870s both union and radical activity, and the level of
rhetorical and physical violence on all sides, rose sharply in response to
layoffs and wage reductions. Labor advocates and agitators like Parsons predicted class uprisings against "arrogant capitalism," while the

major dailies, influential periodicals, and business and political leaders became more shrill in throwing immigrants, tramps, union organizers, and communists together as enemies of public order whose activities must be answered with force. Some antilabor spokesmen promised these latter-day social "arsonists" exactly the same fate they dreamed up for their alleged counterparts in 1871. "Every lamp-post in Chicago," the *Tribune* grimly assured its readers in late November of 1875, "will be decorated with a communistic carcass if necessary to prevent wholesale incendiarism or prevent any attempt at it."[9]

The social turmoil that was always close to the surface of the rebuilt city exploded most fearfully during the series of violent railroad strike actions across the country during the summer of 1877. The strikes began in Maryland and West Virginia in mid-July and reached Chicago within a week. On July 21, three days before local switchmen on the Michigan Central struck, Albert Parsons and other members of the socialist Working-Men's Party, an uneasy alliance of different groups that had been organized the year before, staged a rally attacking railroad executives and their allies for enslaving the worker. Parsons condemned the abuse of labor-saving machinery by exploitative employers, and he called for the institution of the eight-hour day. He was the principal speaker at a large rally on the evening of Monday, July 23, in Market Square, which was located at the intersection of Market (now Wacker Drive) and Madison Streets, where he urged workers to avoid violence and to work within the political system by joining unions and voting for prolabor candidates.

In spite of these appeals for restraint, violence soon broke out, though its major source was neither the socialists nor labor unions, but volatile crowds of discontented rowdies and "roughs" of the kind conjured up in the fire literature. On July 24, police broke up another Market Square rally of the Working-Men's Party. The next day, a large mob destroyed two Burlington & Quincy locomotives, and officers fought with strikers near the McCormick Reaper Works on Blue Island Avenue. As trouble spread, the police were joined by units of the Illinois National Guard, created for such purposes only a year before. In addition, on Wednesday afternoon, July 25, Companies E and F of the United States Army's Twenty-second Infantry arrived at the Chicago, Milwaukee, and St. Paul depot. These troops, "tanned and grizzled, with unwashed faces and unkempt hair, their clothing covered with dust an inch thick," were met by General Sheridan's subordinate, Lieutenant Colonel Frederick D. Grant.

The soldiers announced their presence in Chicago by marching through the center of the city to the Inter-State Exposition Building on the lakefront that the "army" of unemployed had threatened to take over three years earlier. The famous detective Allan Pinkerton, whose agency's major clients now included corporations that saw labor organizers as fell enemies to be rooted out, boasted that these Indian fighters were "quite as ready to meet communists as to follow Sitting Bull." They were cheered by crowds who saw this combined force, all under the command of the son of Ulysses Grant, as their deliverer from urban rebels and redskins.[10] Their arrival recalled the much-heralded appearance of troops following the fire and provided another precedent for the deployment of the United States Army in Chicago during the Pullman strike in 1894. The most infamous of the 1877 railroad-strike clashes in Chicago were the series of violent skirmishes between the authorities and mobs of angry men, women, and children that took place the next day by a railroad viaduct at Sixteenth and Halsted. From organized labor's point of view, however, the worst moment occurred elsewhere that morning when, without provocation or warning, the police raided a peaceful meeting of furniture workers on West 12th Street. By Saturday the 28th, the Chicago portion of the national strike had run its course. The Board of Trade reopened, workers returned to their jobs, and the trains began running again.[11]

The strike further encouraged a line of law-and-order thinking that would lead to the Haymarket bomb. This view interpreted the current protests in the same way as the fire literature had treated the attacks on people and property that were allegedly perpetrated amid the chaos caused by the fire. According to different spokesmen for big business, the latest violence was based in momentary public excitement that was being manipulated by a small group of social vandals. Writing in the *North American Review* late in 1877, Pennsylvania Railroad president Thomas A. Scott, one of the "railroad kings" Albert Parsons named as enslavers of the workingman, attributed "the recent disastrous disturbances" to "[n]othing but the insanity of passion, played upon by designing and mischievous leaders." President Hayes labeled the 1877 strikes an insurrection, while others were eager to term them "the American Commune." Allan Pinkerton agreed, laying the disorders to the same sources as those that devastated Paris in 1871: "a horde of bad men, . . . and human beings so devoid of all conscience, pity, or consideration, that it is hard to look upon them as possessing the least of human attributes."[12]

These expressions of alarm were almost invariably accompanied by a call for repressive measures in language very similar to that employed in October of 1871. To the imagination of business leaders, the strike was almost as threatening to the union as the Civil War. Scott maintained that "no thoughtful man can argue in favor of delay by the proper authorities in dealing with lawless and riotous assemblages."[13]

Taken together, the events of 1877 further established the belief in the
mind of many Americans of property and position that their place in
society, and society itself, were under attack, and that the protection of
what they saw as the social order justified, even demanded, the suspen-
sion of certain freedoms and the summoning of the militia and the army
to deal with labor unrest.

Few upstanding Chicagoans who shared this belief recognized at the
time (or after) the incendiary nature of their own attitudes. One exception was John J. Flinn, who, though critical of Mayor Monroe Heath for
not being more vigilant, admitted that all the "deputations running
here and running there" were "generally helping to precipitate the
trouble which they were struggling, in an idiotic sort of way, to avoid."
On Wednesday, July 25, Mayor Heath issued a widely hailed proclamation, requesting, as Roswell Mason had asked, "all good citizens" to
organize for patrol duty, and for 5,000 "good and experienced citizens,
composed as largely as possible of ex-soldiers," to report for "such general duties as may be assigned them." The Common Council gave the
mayor a blank check for expenditures "to enforce law and protect lives
and property." At the same time Heath warned "idlers and curious
people" off the streets, and ordered the law-abiding "to arrest all disorderly persons and take them to the police stations in the vicinity." Some
businessmen, including Marshall Field, armed their employees for the
defense of the city and loaned horses and delivery wagons to the police.

In perhaps the most significant event in the evolution of the attitudes
that looked back toward the fire and pointed toward Haymarket, on the
afternoon of July 25 (about the same time the federal troops arrived) a
large gathering of "leading businessmen" and "law-abiding people
generally," including "some of the most substantial citizens and merchant princes of Chicago," crowded into an emergency meeting in the
Moody and Sankey Tabernacle a block northeast of Market Square.
They were called to order by the Reverend Robert Collyer, the popular
minister who had worshipped with his North Division parishioners
amid the ruins of Unity Church following the fire, and those present included many other prominent citizens who would have important roles
in the events surrounding Haymarket. Among them were Congressman Carter Harrison, mayor at the time of the bombing, and Leonard
Swett, an eminent lawyer and one-time associate of Abraham Lincoln
who a decade later helped prepare the unsuccessful appeal by Parsons
and his codefendants. After choosing dry goods merchant Charles B.
Farwell as their chair, this body discussed the need to arm and organize
"responsible" citizens. In the course of the meeting, Harrison urged all
employers to resume business the next morning to protect the great
mass of laboring men (and their employers) against the dangerous ef-

fects of idleness, whiskey, and the few "idlers, thieves, and ruffians" who made up the core of the mob. Swett supported the summoning of troops and suggested that the group back Mayor Heath's call for volunteer patrols. Collyer proposed an organization of a force of no less than 30,000 special constables and the raising of a million dollars to finance it. He moved his listeners by telling them that this was the most serious moment he had experienced in his twenty years in Chicago, and that, "as God lives," he was ready to die "in defense of order and of our homes against these men."

Others offered their own fevered proposals to save the public order. The Board of Trade called on Congress to increase the size of the standing army, which Marshall Field said should always be at the ready for such emergencies. The strike also hastened the construction of armories in America's cities and the training of soldiers and police against "urban insurrection." Local businessmen, some of whom (including George Pullman) had been active in the Relief and Aid Society, formed a "Law and Order League" of citizen-soldiers prepared to assist Chicago in this latest hour of vulnerability when the same kind of situation as that on the Sands following the fire now seemed to threaten the entire city. The "Military Committee" of the Citizens Association, in which Field was a driving force, raised funds for the militia and in 1878 donated two Gatling guns to protect Chicago against "outsiders" within.[14]

The railroad strike had other important consequences locally. The desire of the authorities to blame the disturbances on particular "incendiaries" and scheming opportunists rather than on economic distress and class conflict made Albert Parsons a social outlaw to Chicago's business leaders. They considered him a worse danger than any of the criminals set loose from the Courthouse or who came from elsewhere to prey on post-fire Chicago, since he was not just an enemy of property but of the whole system that created and protected it. The papers singled Parsons out as a strike leader, while Pinkerton criticized his "flippant tongue," which the detective said enabled this troublemaker to "tingle the blood of that class of characterless rascals that are always standing ready to grasp society by the throat," while at the same time endowing him with "that devilish ingenuity in the use of words which has permitted himself to escape deserving punishment." It was because of Parson's "baleful influence," more than any other reason, "that the conditions were ripe in Chicago for all manner of excesses."[15]

In actuality, Parsons, who up to this time had preached against violence, was far more a victim than a perpetrator of the troubles of late July, which demonized him as the equivalent of the young arsonist from whom the city had to be rescued by righteous violence in 1871. By his account, when he went to work at the *Chicago Times* office the day after his address in Market Square, he found himself discharged and blacklisted. Soon after, two men who said that Mayor Heath wanted to speak with him supposedly took Parsons instead to see Superintendent of Police Michael Hickey, who threatened and insulted Parsons as he interrogated him in front of a hostile group of officers. These policemen called out, "Hang him," "Lynch him," "Lock him up," while Superintendent Hickey blamed Parsons for the disturbances in the city. Hickey let Parsons go, but not before advising him in language that harked back to the narratives of the fire and prophesied things to come, that "those Board of Trade men would as leave hang you to a lamp-post as not." That evening, deeply upset, Parsons went to the *Tribune* office to try to find work and talk to some of his fellow printers, but three strangers, one armed with a pistol, threw him out of the building and threatened his life. He was without regular work for the next two years.[16]

Meanwhile, newspapers and periodicals were describing places like Chicago not just as social firetraps ready to burst into flame, but, in the words of a Pennsylvania congressman, as volcanoes about to erupt. The modern industrial city was the place where all the volatile elements in America were thrown most dangerously together, and it could blow up at any moment, destroying any exceptionalist claim that America was free of the social strife of the old world. "Unless our experience is to differ entirely from other countries,—and it is not easy to see why it should, with the increasing population of our large cities and business centers, and the inevitable assemblage at such points of the vicious and ill-disposed," Tom Scott solemnly declared, "the late troubles may be but the prelude to other manifestations of mob violence, with this added peril, that now, for the first time in American history, has an organized mob learned its power to terrorize the law-abiding citizens of great communities."[17]

Virtually no one at the time acknowledged that labor and "the mob" were expressing their anger at anything more than specific working conditions, that workers were attacking the unwritten but well-understood "rules" of a social system they did not create and whose "order" seemed arranged against them. As Shelton Stromquist explains, the railroad strikes across the country both "foreshadowed nearly two decades of deepening labor conflict on the railroads" and were "the baptismal rite of a broader, urban working class not bound by differences of trade or skill." What workers were seeking in their protests and attempts to organize was a new balance of power in which they exercised more control over the terms of their lives. Failing that, the depth of the discontent was such that they were prepared to walk off the job and even in some instances overturn locomotives and hurl sticks and stones at formidably armed soldiers and police who represented a social and economic order which they perceived as the real source of distress. David Montgomery asserts that while the character of the strikes of 1877 varied a great deal from place to place, "everywhere the first target of the crowd's fury was the interlocking directorate of railroad executives, military officers, and political officials, which constituted the apex of the country's new power structure."[18] Whether through disciplined organization or mob action, when workers and malcontents attacked any part of the directorate, they were striking symbolically as well as literally at this power structure and trying to demonstrate their own might.

The Chicago Anarchists

According to Parsons, the tactic of scapegoating and persecuting individuals like him only reaffirmed their commitment to radical causes. "The events of 1877," he later recalled, "gave great impulse and activity to the labor movement all over the United States, and, in fact, the whole world."[19] But the history of worker activity and political protest from 1877 to the mid-1880s was far more complicated than Parsons's comments suggested. It was marked by conflicting agendas and changing alliances of different labor leaders and organizations amidst unpredictable currents of public opinion and national and international financial conditions. Whatever their many differences with each other, however, as workers recognized more clearly that incorporation and industrialization had widened the social, economic, and psychological distance between capital and labor to the extent that the gap was virtually unbridgeable, they more forcefully resisted the extent to which employers controlled the workplace. The American economy improved by the beginning of the 1880s but took another downturn by the middle of the decade, with more than three times the strikers and strike activity in 1886 than in any year between 1881 and 1884.[20]

This period witnessed major disagreements not only between capital and labor, but also among union spokesmen and the several subgroups of American socialists committed to the labor cause. The radical socialists with whom Parsons most closely worked, who were at most a very small fraction of the labor movement, adopted the position that the system could not be reformed through the ballot and other nonrevolutionary means.[21] Parsons, convinced that any system besides that of free association of individuals in a cooperative relationship with each other was inescapably oppressive, became a convert to anarchism. He and his fellow anarchists pondered whether or not to work with labor unions, specifically whether to join in the revived eight-hour movement. Many remained committed to the idea of unions as vital organizations in the restructuring of society, but they moved back and forth on the question of eight hours, seeing it as a promising political cause but questioning whether speaking of hours at all implied an acceptance of the wage system.[22] Probably the thorniest and certainly most highly charged issue among radical activists, however, was the debate over violence as a tactic, whether revolution by word should shift to revolution by deed.

While Chicago came to be known as the center of anarchism in the United States, different local factions associated and disputed with each other in shifting alignments within and across generational, ethnic, and ideological lines. Albert Parsons was in the vanguard of the American Group of Chicago anarchists, editing its newspaper the *Alarm,* which began publication in October 1884. In the same year, August Spies, who had arrived in Chicago from Germany in 1873 at the age of seventeen, became editor of the *Arbeiter-Zeitung,* the leading German-language anarchist newspaper in Chicago. More militant splinter groups held their own meetings and issued separate publications.[23] But few Chicagoans or other Americans outside the movement distinguished between shades of belief among anarchists, between anarchists and communists, or, for that matter, between radicals and protesters or labor organizers of almost any kind. As far as most government officials, managers, office workers, professionals, clergymen, and intellectuals were concerned, labor and political activists who tried to organize the workers in strikes or boycotts interfered with the individual right to work of honest, industrious, and independent workingmen, whose welfare would be best served by trusting their bosses. Any dissenter might as well be an anarchist, and every anarchist was a public enemy.

Urban daily newspapers and national periodicals immediately assumed the worst about the rise in union activity and worker dissatisfaction, condemning strikers as savages while continuing the demand for the repression of "malcontents" that was expressed so passionately in 1877. The presence of such malcontents was hard to miss, since they were eager to display themselves in the public eye as spokesmen for "the people." In Chicago, "respectable" citizens uneasily eyed the socialist picnics in city parks and the small rallies on the lakefront that were addressed through the 1880s by speakers including Parsons, Spies, and Samuel Fielden, an English-born member of the American Group. They viewed with special concern and contempt mass demonstrations such as the March 22, 1879, commemoration of the Revolution of 1848 and the Paris Commune of 1871 that attracted a crowd estimated at thirty thousand or more, made up mainly of immigrant workers and their families, including several armed and trained ethnic paramilitary

organizations whose drills, the *Tribune* observed, drew the most attention from those at the rally.

The demonstrators staked their claim to having a voice not only with
their numbers but by parading through the downtown as the soldiers
did in 1877, their destination the same Inter-State Exposition Building
to which the soldiers had marched. The building was so packed that
much of the scheduled program of speeches, music, and dancing had to
be rearranged, especially when one of the featured speakers, Albert
Parsons, could not be found in the throng. "Those who labored under
the belief that there were but few Communists in our midst, and that
they were not worth taking notice of," wrote the *Tribune* the next day,
"could have easily satisfied themselves of their error if they had gone to
the Exposition Building and witnessed the Commune celebration held
in that structure." Elected officials tried to outlaw the more militant
organizations of workers, such as the Lehr-und-Wehr Verein, the Bohemian Sharpshooters, and the Irish Labor Guards, whose growth had
been spurred by the action of the police and soldiers in 1877. Each
posture of "self-defense," whether by workers or the authorities, inspired the other side to overreact in the rising spiral of mutual
preparedness.[24]

Two demonstrations from the mid-1880s stood out in the way they
revealed how radicals in Chicago tried to dramatize on the city streets
their critique of the current order. On Thanksgiving Day of 1884, despite terrible weather, about three thousand demonstrators gathered in
Market Square to hear speakers including Parsons, Fielden, Spies, and
Michael Schwab, associate editor of the *Arbeiter-Zeitung*, remind them
of the bitter irony of the day for most workers. They then set off on a
spirited march past the homes of their wealthy "oppressors," who
called out the militia a year later when the demonstration was repeated.[25] In April of 1885, the anarchists tried to flaunt their numbers
and their colors directly in the face of the "Board of Trade men" about
whom Police superintendent Hickey had warned Albert Parsons eight
years earlier. The occasion was the grand dedication of the board's new
building in the heart of the financial district. The ceremonies extended
over three days, and were intended to celebrate the indispensable value
of the Board of Trade to the commerce of Chicago, America, and the
world. The anarchist protest against the Board's own carefully staged
spectacle purposely created the kind of juxtaposition of haves and have-
nots later depicted in the novels of Frank Norris and Theodore Dreiser.
It took place on the evening of a "promenade concert," which was to be
followed the next day with the dedication proper and a sumptuous banquet for five-hundred worthies that, at twenty dollars a plate, cost more

than many workers brought home in two or three weeks—if they were employed.

A speaker at that banquet stood near a confectionery model of the Statue of Liberty and offered a version of American history and contemporary life that the anarchists had long been attacking as false.[26] He enthusiastically praised the openness of society in the United States, declaring that, except for Asians, "we invite the oppressed people of the world to come here and enjoy the benefits of this grand system of National Government. They come here because they can own their own consciences, their own speech. Here they can have free labor, abundant reward for their labor." Employment and advancement in all fields, he assured his listeners, were based only on merit and were available alike to all nationalities and classes. This speech was followed by toasts to the United States, the state of Illinois, the army, the New South, the clergy, guests from across the sea, and, of course, the city of Chicago, "[t]he young, vigorous, blooming daughter of the prairie."

At the anarchist rally that began a few blocks away in Market Square, Parsons delivered a very different speech about the meaning of the Board of Trade, which a call to the rally termed "the grand temple of Usury, Gambling, and Cut-Throatism." Parsons denied that there was anything like an open and free society in America for the worker, and he warned that violent means might be required to protect freedom from predatory institutions like the Board of Trade and the capitalist system for which it stood. His inflammatory argument was similar to the one made at the Moody and Sankey Tabernacle in 1877 by the people he opposed, only he spoke of the need for armed force to destroy the current order while they had agreed on the importance of the same measures to defend it. "If we would achieve our liberation from economic bondage and acquire our natural right to life and liberty," Parsons told an enthusiastic group of listeners estimated at about a thousand people, "every man must lay by a part of his wages, buy a Colt's navy revolver, . . . a Winchester rifle, and learn how to make and use dynamite." This and other addresses were followed by a procession toward the Board of Trade, with the marchers singing the Marseillaise. At their head were several women, including Lucy Parsons and American Group member Lizzie Holmes, waving the red and black flags of revolution and anarchy.

They were blocked from reaching their destination by police commanded by two men who would be important figures in the unfolding story of Haymarket, Captain Frederick Ebersold and Lieutenant William Ward, and so they returned to the building at 107 Fifth Avenue (now Wells Street) that housed the offices of both the *Alarm* and the *Arbeiter-Zeitung*, where Parsons, Spies, and Fielden again spoke. The *Tribune* reported that Spies "for about ten minutes murdered the German language in an attempt to prove that dynamite, bloodshed, and rapine were the only means by which the starving masses could obtain their rights." Afterwards, in a widely reported incident that Spies would soon have reason to regret, the anarchist editor showed the press what one reporter described as "a large piece of alleged dynamite and a long piece of fuse which [Spies] said he had intended to place under the Board of Trade Building if he had been permitted to get near it." The same correspondent also claimed that a dozen of Spies's supporters flashed guns, and that another unnamed person showed him a container of nitroglycerine and assured him that "every man in that parade had some of these." The morning after the banquet, the *Tribune* dwelled on the ingratitude of the workers at the rally. "They parade at night with their black and red flags in the very shadow of the buildings which have furnished them full employment and menace the lives of their owners and threaten the destruction of the buildings with dynamite which they were paid to construct!" the *Tribune* exclaimed in exasperation and disbelief. "What do the leaders of this unreasoning, ignorant, inconsistent association mean?" Both radical and establishment newspapers agreed, however, on a hyperbolic figurative language in which to demonize the other. "OUR VAMPIRES" read the headline on the story of the demonstration in the *Alarm,* while the *Tribune* proclaimed, "THEY WANT BLOOD."[27]

Bomb-Talking

The purposely threatening words and actions of Parsons and Spies during and after the Board of Trade rally were typical of the anarchists' increasing fascination with violence. Fundamentally opposed to government and legislative law of any kind, they were obsessed with all forms of power wielded in society, whether in a good cause or not. "Power is might, and might always makes its own right," Parsons later explained. "Thus in the very nature of things, might makes itself right whether or no."[28] Since their use of this language figured so critically in their later arrest, trial, and execution for the Haymarket bombing—the bulk of the 136 exhibits submitted by the state at their trial consisted of things they had spoken or published—it requires careful examination.

By the mid-1880s, anarchist rhetoric in Chicago discussed individuals, events, and ideas in spectacular, theatrical, and explicitly violent terms. As the anarchists pointed out, this trend was also apparent in the language of defenders of the established order, who were willing to accept the legally dubious application of force to save the current system from those who would attack it. Substitute the word "revolutionaries"

or "insurrectionists" for "oppressors" and "enslavers" in some sentences in anarchist speeches and publications, and they would be hard
to distinguish from the intemperate calls by those in power for wiping
out radicalism. But many anarchist statements had a manic intensity
that was all their own. Lucy Parsons's notorious "Word to Tramps,"
which appeared in the first issue of the *Alarm* in 1884 and was distributed widely in leaflet form (it became People's Exhibit 18 at the trial),
sardonically offered words of "advice" to the thousands of unemployed
who were despondent because all around them they saw displays of
wealth that were signs of their exploitation. If you are thinking of suicide, she counseled, don't waste this action by drowning yourself in the
lake. Instead, learn the use of explosives and then "stroll you down the
avenues of the rich and look through the magnificent plate glass windows into their voluptuous homes," where "you will discover the *very
identical robbers* who have despoiled you and yours." This was the
proper stage for the last act of a despondent victim of capital. "Then let
your tragedy be enacted *here*," Lucy directed. "Thus send forth your
petition and let them read it by the red blare of destruction."[29]

   As writings like this revealed, the anarchists' saw armed assaults on
the current order as counterattacks against even greater and more pervasive aggression. The reasoning behind this view was a combination of
Jefferson, Marx, and secular apocalyptic millenarianism. It held that
the current system was one of legalized economic oppression administered by a government of capital's agents backed by police and soldiers.
The ability of the few to enslave the many this way was not sanctioned
by principle but by "[t]he right of might of *force*," read the *Alarm*. To
respond in kind to clubs, Gatling guns, and other "props" to authority
was necessary as well as justifiable. In the face of this armed resistance,
the state and its institutions would perish by their own means of domination.[30] The special appeal of dynamite to the anarchist imagination
followed naturally, since this weapon promised to shift the balance of
power in society almost magically. Parsons was fond of citing a report to
the president and Congress by General Sheridan, by this time commander of the army, in which he spoke of signs of social disturbances
that he hoped could be avoided "if both capital and labor will only be
conservative." Sheridan, quoted in the *Alarm*, went on: "Still, it should
be remembered *destructive explosives are easily made*, and that banks,
United States sub-treasuries, public buildings and large mercantile
houses can be readily demolished, and the commerce of entire cities
destroyed by an infuriated people with means carried with perfect
safety to themselves *in the pockets* of their clothing." The paper exul-
tantly read Sheridan's warning as an inspiration to the radical cause. In
dynamite, invented in the late 1860s and used by European political

terrorists several times through the early eighties, American anarchists claimed to have been presented with an ally that was at least as formidable as the one Chicago's businessmen had found in Phil Sheridan. In an accompanying editorial, the *Alarm* could barely contain itself:

> Dynamite is the emancipator! In the hand of the enslaved it cries aloud: "Justice or—annihilation!" But best of all, the workingmen are not only learning its use, they are going to use it. They will use it, and effectually, until personal ownership—property rights—are destroyed, and a free society and justice becomes the rule of action among men. There will then be no need for government since there will be none who will submit to be governed. Hail to the social revolution! Hail to the deliverer—*Dynamite*.[31]

The anarchist leaders became carried away with such language, as if these incantations alone could remake the world by their plan. More than the vote had ever been, dynamite—accessible, portable, and powerful—was a devastating tool of instant reform, an appallingly effective equalizer in the hands of a committed radical who wanted to hurry along the democratic process. At the same time, it was a mighty deterrent against future oppression that would, in its own way, end social conflict. "Dynamite is a peace-maker," the *Alarm* declared, "because it makes it unsafe to wrong our fellows."[32] And, like it or not, as Sheridan himself had pointed out, it was part of a new urban reality.

This kind of "bomb-talking," and the bravado behind Spies's brandishing a stick of dynamite to reporters in the *Arbeiter-Zeitung* office after the Board of Trade demonstration, unquestionably terrified many people. As writer Floyd Dell later astutely pointed out, however, bomb-talking was something different from bomb-throwing. Like so many other aspects of Haymarket, it is best understood as a kind of performance especially suited to anarchist politics and the romantic sensibility behind them, as an attempt at personal empowerment through rhetoric to which radicals resorted from a position of weakness, from what Dell called a "sentimental interest" in the "Idea" of dynamite as unstoppable weapon. Its destructive force could literally blow into little pieces any agent of concentrated power, whether this agent took the form of a political or business leader, a building like the Board of Trade, or a cordon of police. It would thus simply and suddenly exorcise all social demons and end the oppression plaguing the city, making possible a perfect cooperative order. To wave even just the idea of dynamite about and to emphasize its cheapness, accessibility, and destructive capability was a confidence builder that would attract attention and possibly scare employers and the authorities into concessions.[33] Most of all, perhaps, talking about bombs made anarchists (and plenty of their enemies) believe that they were a force to contend with, and that their social vision was possible, practical, and real.

Into the Haymarket

On other occasions that soon followed the Board of Trade demonstration, the bitter antagonisms of the time went beyond verbal exchanges and street theater into deadly confrontations. On May 4, 1885—a year to the day before the Haymarket bombing—the Illinois militia fired on unarmed striking quarrymen at Lemont, southwest of the city, killing at least two people. In early July the Chicago police, who for a time had exercised restraint in labor disturbances, indiscriminately clubbed citizens during a strike against the West Division Railway Company. The fiercest of the officers was Captain John Bonfield. When summoned before Carter Harrison, who was now mayor, Bonfield supposedly told him, "Mr. Mayor, I am doing this in mercy to the people. A club to-day, to make them scatter, may save the use of a pistol to-morrow." Although labor leaders and citizens of different political persuasions, including Spies and Fielden, demanded Bonfield's dismissal, he was soon promoted to inspector of police, second in command to the new superintendent, Frederick Ebersold.[34]

Continuing financial distress and labor violence reinforced a public mood of anxiety and distrust that had a perverse energy of its own. Police trained for new uprisings, and private citizens carried pistols. Radicals continued to boast in print and speech about the effectiveness of dynamite and other explosives in evening the odds, leading to stories in the papers about bomb plots against leading citizens. The city's state of mind seemed permanently stuck in the same kind of paranoid condition it was in immediately following the fire. Assessing the current state of affairs, some of the country's most thoughtful and open-minded cultural leaders warned of social catastrophe. In the November 1885 issue of the *Century Magazine,* for example, the liberal clergyman Lyman Abbott surveyed the condition of the country and offered some words of warning and hope in an article titled "Danger Ahead."[35] As Tom Scott had done in 1877, Abbott idealized the American past to highlight his concern that the nation, "which two centuries ago had hardly a social rift," was "now as full of social crevasses, broad and deep, as the snowy sides of the Alps." He traced the problem in part to the decline of social homogeneity with the arrival of recent immigrants unschooled in self-government, including some who with good reason carried with them "an inherited hate of both state and church; a disbelief in man which is more dangerous to society even than that disbelief in God which always accompanies it."

While Abbott was wary of unions, he may well have displeased some of the *Century*'s readers by telling them that honest workingmen joined these organizations as a better alternative than to submit passively to tyrannical capitalists, speculators, and corporate leaders, who took far greater wealth out of the world than they put in and who were backed by the power of the state. No wonder, then, that danger lay ahead, that communist organizations, previously unknown, were now "fatally prolific . . . , and with the destructive instruments which modern science has put into their hands, threatening civilization in Germany, France, Great Britain, and the United States." He further advised, "In a warfare between classes for the possession of property, civilization has every advantage. In a warfare by anarchy against all property, the anarchist has every advantage."

Abbott's forecast of the future was especially bleak for modern industrial urban centers, which he called the "natural nests" of radical groups. Every year, Abbott observed, "the burden grows greater and the danger of revolt more threatening. The low growl of the thunder is already to be heard in great cities; the lambent flame already runs along the clouds; the bitter cry of outcast London is faintly echoed from New York and Cincinnati, from Chicago and St. Louis, and from a hundred smaller manufacturing towns and mining villages." On two sides of a narrow valley, labor and capital were marshaling their forces, and that of labor, while "loose in organization," carried "a discontent in its heart which a great disaster might easily convert into bitter wrath,—armed by modern science with fatally efficient equipment for destruction, and officered by leaders often both unscrupulous and daring."[36]

The next several months provided considerable substantiation for Abbott's observation, "Every morning paper brings us the report of some strike or lockout, which is like the shot of a single picket along the line; and now and then we are startled by a riot such as that at Cincinnati, Chicago, or Cleveland, which is like a skirmish between the advance guards."[37] Much of the skirmishing was tied to a rash of strikes and the eight-hour cause, whose supporters were planning demonstrations nationwide on the first of May. At the end of April of 1886, headlines in Chicago read, "STRIKES FROM EVERY HAND," and the stories that followed expressed concern that if local businesses went to eight hours they would suffer in the competition with New York and other cities that did not. The battle lines seemed clearly drawn on May 1, with tens of thousands of workers off their jobs in Chicago alone, many participating in demonstrations throughout the city, including a great parade along Michigan Avenue in which Parsons took a prominent part, all under the surveillance of the police, state militia, and Pinkerton detectives. An editorial in the *Chicago Mail* of May 1 named

Parsons and Spies as the villains of the conflicts that seemed sure to follow. "Mark them for today. Keep them in view," the *Mail* advised. "Hold them responsible for any trouble that occurs. Make an example of them if trouble does occur."[38]

On the evening of Tuesday, May 4, about two thousand Chicagoans, mainly workers, gathered at a rally just north of the Haymarket, Chicago's wholesale produce area, located where Randolph Street crosses Desplaines Street a few blocks west of the Chicago River. Like Market Square, this was a popular meeting place—it had been the scene of a protest against Captain Bonfield's brutality during the West Division railway strike. Now the cause was an incident that had taken place the day before and was reported throughout the agitated nation. Responding to a fight between strikers and scabs outside the McCormick reaper works, officers had killed at least two workers. August Spies, who witnessed the struggle, rushed back to the office of the *Arbeiter-Zeitung* where, in his outrage, he dashed out a bilingual circular that in its English section urged workers to "rise . . . and destroy the hideous monster that seeks to destroy you." The wording of the German version was even more impassioned. Meanwhile, at the First Regiment Armory on Jackson Street, companies of guardsmen went through their street and riot drill and finished assembling a Gatling gun that had arrived only the day before. "A large quantity of ammunition accompanied the weapon, which will be kept in readiness for instant service," read a newspaper article.[39]

The May 4 rally was poorly organized and began late. The broadside that called people to attend assured "Good Speakers," but none of the three who did speak—Spies, Parsons, and Fielden—had taken part in the planning, and Parsons had only just returned from Cincinnati.[40] He had no knowledge of the meeting or of the events that precipitated it, and he was fetched to attend after it had finally begun. Despite the loose structure of the gathering, a mood of angry and fearful expectation surrounded the Haymarket. In preparation for the meeting, Inspector Bonfield, always ready for confrontation, assembled his men in the Desplaines Street police station, a half-block below Randolph. Mayor Harrison, a Democrat who was more sympathetic to labor than many prominent citizens thought wise, showed up at the rally to order it dispersed if it threatened to get out of hand.

As the meeting progressed, this possibility seemed to become remote. It was after ten when Parsons finished up and Fielden, the last speaker, began. By this time Harrison had concluded that the rally was not a threat to public order, and that he need not stay any longer. On his way home he stopped at the station house to tell Bonfield that the meeting was "tame." Even the next day's *Tribune* described Spies's address as "remarkably mild." A sudden change for the worse in Chicago's fickle spring weather convinced most of those still left—including Parsons, who had come with Lucy and their two young children—to call it an evening. By half-past ten only a few hundred people remained when Fielden, who had told his listeners that he would be brief, urged them in standard anarchist rhetoric to "throttle" and "kill" the law that enslaved them, and to "impede its progress." If not, he continued, "it will kill you."[41] The report of this remark to Bonfield by one of the plainclothes policemen sent to monitor the meeting, and the departure of the re-straining presence of Mayor Harrison, evidently convinced the inspector to hurry his force of some 170 policemen toward what remained of the rally. Captain William Ward, who as a lieutenant had helped Ebersold thwart the demonstration at the Board of Trade opening a year earlier, commanded, "In the name of the people of the state of Illinois," that the meeting disperse "immediately and peaceably." Bewildered by the appearance of the police at the close of an apparently anticlimactic meeting that seemed to be breaking up on its own, Fielden replied that the gathering was peaceable. Ward then repeated his command.

At this point someone threw a small homemade dynamite bomb made of two crudely molded lead hemispheres into the lines of police. It hissed as it flew through the air, then exploded with terrible effect, almost immediately killing Officer Mathias Degan and wounding several dozen others. The explosion set off a wild riot of clubbing and gun-fire, virtually all by Bonfield's men, who in the disarray shot several of their own number as well as many members of the scattering remnants of the rally, including Samuel Fielden and Spies's brother Henry. Within the next few days the police death toll had risen to seven. The count of dead and injured among the civilians, like the identity of the bomb thrower, was never determined.

Following the bombing, the police, with the approval of State's At-torney Julius S. Grinnell, conducted a well-publicized roundup of radical activists that brazenly disregarded individual rights and due pro-cess.[42] The most aggressive of the police officers was Captain Michael Schaack of the Chicago Avenue Station, who in 1889 published the most complete, if obviously slanted, contemporary history of Hay-market.[43] The police seized and questioned virtually anyone suspected of having radical sentiments, and they confiscated bombs, bomb-making equipment, and other weapons from anarchists' homes. On May 27 a grand jury indicted ten anarchists for the murder of Degan, though charges were dropped against one, William Seliger, who tes-tified for the state, while another, Rudolph Schnaubelt, escaped trial by fleeing the country. The indictment included sixty-nine counts in all, naming Schnaubelt as the bomb-thrower and the rest as accesso-

ries. Parsons evaded the police dragnet, but the seven others—August
Spies, Samuel Fielden, Michael Schwab, Oscar Neebe, George Engel,
Adolph Fischer, and Louis Lingg—were arraigned on June 5.[44] Given
the unpopularity of their ideas to begin with and the public outrage at
the bombing, they had difficulty finding counsel. They were very fortunate that the distinguished attorney and highly decorated Civil War veteran William P. Black agreed to head a team of four lawyers for the
defense. Captain Black (as he was still commonly called) took the case
on principle, and his career subsequently suffered heavily as a result.[45]

Proceedings began on June 21, less than seven weeks after the bombing, in the courthouse that had been constructed shortly after the fire a
few blocks north of the Chicago River. The opening day witnessed one
of the trial's most remarkable events, when Parsons came out of safe
hiding in Wisconsin to declare his innocence and stand with the other
accused. From Parsons's surrender to the jury's August 20 guilty verdict, the trial in Judge Joseph E. Gary's court was so unfair and irregular that it remains one of the most shameful proceedings in American
history. It can be understood only in terms of the willingness of the citizens of Chicago and of the nation to accept, even to expect and demand, decisive action to preserve what they saw as social order. It was a
show trial in every sense of the term, intended not only to point out to
other would-be agitators their likely fate, but also to convince the public that the established system of authority was right and effective.

In a laudatory biographical sketch written a year before the bombing, Alfred Andreas stated that Gary was an efficient judge who was
"noted for the rapidity of his decisions and for his great dispatch of
business, evidently holding with Emerson that it is more important to
the public that cases should be decided, than that they should always be
decided correctly."[46] This was certainly true of his conduct of the Haymarket trial. When bailiff Henry Ryce filled the pool with men who admitted their belief in the defendants' guilt, Gary refused to dismiss such
individuals for cause, forcing Black to use up his 160 peremptory challenges and to accept a hostile white-collar jury made up mainly of clerks
and salesmen. Gary rejected protests that the pool of jurors contained
virtually no workingmen and later muzzled the defense while giving almost unlimited latitude to the state.[47] He also allowed the prosecution
to try the eight men together rather than separately, rushing the judgment when public opinion was more concerned with speedy action
than legal niceties, and reinforcing the idea that these men were in
conspiracy.

The carefully rehearsed and, in some cases, paid testimony of key
prosecution "witnesses," particularly that of a man named Harry
Gilmer, who claimed he saw Spies light the bomb and Schnaubelt

throw it, was easily refuted, forcing State's Attorney Grinnell to con-
cede that he could neither prove that any of the accused anarchists, including Schnaubelt, had thrown the bomb nor say conclusively who
did. Instead, he offered a narrative of what had happened in which the
accused were conspirators who had encouraged the use of the murderous bomb, even if there was no hard evidence of a specific plot
and, without the identity of the bomb thrower, no way to know why he
acted. According to Grinnell, the inflammatory rhetoric of the accused
had wrongfully and with malicious intent caused the deaths of the brave
defenders of the public peace. This argument turned sedition into murder and made no distinction between word and deed. The judge, jury,
and the world were more than eager to accept it. The accused, who to a
significant extent did not all like or even know one another, thus found
themselves cast into the roles of tightly-knit ringleaders and merciless
incendiaries in a plot to perpetrate a deadly bombing that in fact surprised most, if not all, of them as much as anyone.

By Illinois law the jurors prescribed the penalty, and they sentenced
Neebe to fifteen years at hard labor while condemning the seven others
to death. The fire literature invented arsonists on the loose, and it prescribed the rope as the swift, sure, just, and necessary answer. Fifteen
years later, a Chicago jury agreed. Once again incendiaries threatened
to destroy the city, and once again rope would hold it together. The
defense appealed the verdict to the Illinois Supreme Court, which
heard the pleas in March and upheld the verdict in September 1887.
The accused made a final appeal to the United States Supreme Court,
which at the beginning of November decided not to review the case. In
the months and weeks before the final execution date of November 11,
1887, an international movement for clemency attracted a long and impressive list of supporters, including some members of the Chicago
business community, most of whom took care to distance themselves
from the defendants while criticizing the severity of the sentence and, in
some cases, the conduct of the trial. The clemency campaign suffered a
startling setback when, a week before the scheduled hangings, guards
found explosives in Lingg's cell. Nevertheless, on November 9 the Amnesty Association presented a petition signed by 41,000 Chicagoans to
Illinois governor Richard Oglesby. American Federation of Labor president Samuel Gompers was one of several moderate union leaders who
made the journey to Springfield, and he warned Oglesby that martyr-
ing the convicted men would only energize the radical movement,
which would ultimately weaken both the cause of labor and the social
order. He compared their case to that of Jefferson Davis, a far more
dangerous and deadly rebel, who had been imprisoned for only two
years and then released.[48]

While passions had cooled somewhat since the post-bombing cry for a "rain of lead" and the cracking of anarchists' skulls, the voices that called for mercy were distinctly in the minority. Most editorial comment from throughout the country demanded that the executions go forward. The *New York Tribune* called for the "sharpest and sternest application of force" against "foreign Anarchists," while a lead editorial in *Frank Leslie's Illustrated Newspaper* devoted to the executions declared, "There is no doubt that all right-thinking citizens will approve such a vindication of the supreme law of the public safety, so long and so insolently defied by the class of malignants to which these Anarchists belong." And the *Nation* intoned, "The lesson of all this is, that the only opinions which a civilized community can treat with either respect or indifference are opinions which, even if embodied in action, would not menace its existence."[49] Governor Oglesby heard the different petitioners out and then commuted to life imprisonment the sentences of Fielden and Schwab, who had appealed to him, which the other condemned men refused to do. The morning before the scheduled hangings, Lingg escaped the gallows by setting off a smuggled dynamite cap in his mouth, blowing away the lower portion of his face. He somehow survived his ghastly injuries for several hours, until he finally expired in the middle of the afternoon.

Fearing eleventh-hour conspiracies of dynamite and murder, the whole city was on edge in a way that surpassed the "mental excitement" of 1871 and 1877. Journalist Charles Edward Russell recalled that "the nervous strain upon the public had become almost intolerable. The stories circulated, printed, and believed in those days seem now to belong to the literature of bedlam." One of the rumors had 20,000 armed anarchists ready to assault the jail and blow up major buildings. Russell remembered seeing a gun store on Madison Street still open at ten in the evening, "crowded with men buying revolvers." Although his own inquiries convinced him that there never was any basis to the widespread fears, the "spectacle" seemed at the time not "in the least strange but wholly natural and laudable. The dread of some catastrophe impending was not alone in men's talk but in their very faces and in the air." On the morning of November 11, when Russell and his fellow witnesses to the execution looked up beyond the scaffold, they could see silhouetted in the windows of the jail policemen bearing rifles and bayonets, guarding the building "like a precarious outpost in a critical battle." Security procedures required reporters to enter the jail, which was just north of the courthouse, at six in the morning and then wait almost five hours in the jailer's office before filing into the courtyard where, shortly before noon, the hangings took place. Even some seasoned hands became sick from the tension. In the city outside, soldiers stood beside guns and cannons, while special guards watched over the principals in the prosecution and central places of business, including the Board of Trade.[50] The press commented on how bravely the condemned men carried themselves, as, draped in white shrouds, their arms and ankles strapped and their wrists handcuffed, nooses around their necks and hoods over their faces, each shouted a final declaration from the scaffold. Parsons, the last to cry out, had just implored, "Let the voice of the people be heard!" when the trap dropped. Two days later a solemn funeral procession of twenty thousand workers, with several times that many spectators, gathered the coffins of the dead men one-by-one at their family's homes, and, under the vigilant eye of the authorities, bore them to the Wisconsin Central Railroad terminal for the journey to Waldheim Cemetery in suburban Forest Park, ten miles west.[51]

The Enduring Image

From the time it first appeared in the issue of May 15, 1886, Thure de Thulstrup's *Harper's Weekly* illustration of the fateful moment in the Haymarket has been the authoritative visual representation of the event, commonly reproduced in all accounts of the case and in many surveys of the period published up to the present day.[52] The drama is seen from just above street level, looking slightly down on workers in the foreground who are fleeing toward the viewer while one of their number boldly exchanges gunfire with the advancing police. There are wounded on both sides. Behind the front ranks of officers is a large white cloud produced by the exploding bomb. Meanwhile, on the left a bearded figure, presumably Fielden, his right fist raised angrily in the air, harangues the crowd from the platform, so lost in his own words that he is apparently oblivious to both the blast and the gunplay.

It is an even more impossible scene than any illustrations of the Great Chicago Fire: the speech that ended before the bomb was thrown, the bomb itself, and the riot that followed are occurring simultaneously yet independently of one another. But it is a very accurate picture of how the event was perceived in the popular imagination, which had come to see social and political protest, class warfare, and cataclysmic violence, all set against the backdrop of the industrial neighborhoods of American cities, as a single phenomenon. This nightmare had, after all, been inscribed in the public mind for some time. It was in Lyman Abbott's warning about "the low growl of thunder . . . already to be heard in great cities," as well as in his remark that labor carries "a discontent in its heart which a great disaster might easily convert into bitter wrath." It was in Bonfield's terse justification of the clubbing of innocent citizens during the 1885 street railway strike. And it was in the paranoid concerns dating back to 1877 and, before that, to the wild rumors after the fire, that blamed all the trouble on incendiaries who were poised to bring the whole city down. As terrible as it was, then, there was some awful comfort in the violence in the Haymarket, for it seemed to justify all the warnings, rumors, and tough talk by giving the ambient fears about the social order an actual moment and event around which to cohere. And, now that the moment had arrived and the event had occurred, there was a ready response that had already been articulated in the fire literature that had hanged imagined incendiaries on lampposts, in Superintendent Hickey's warning to Albert Parsons that the Board of Trade men would string him up, and in dozens of other speeches, editorials, and magazine articles. The march of the condemned anarchists to the gallows was the scripted finale, now to be performed for real after so many rehearsals in the public mind.

It is no wonder, then, that people would see de Thulstrup's illustration as a true depiction, or that competent jurists like Grinnell, Gary, and the justices of the Illinois and United States Supreme Courts would willingly participate in such a travesty. Nor is it surprising that businessmen secretly pledged $100,000 not only to aid the families of the policemen killed or injured at Haymarket, but also to pay Captain Schaack to hire spies and informers in his continuing hunt for alleged subversives.[53] What had actually happened in the Haymarket, like the miscarriage of justice at the trial, was almost irrelevant, a technicality quickly disposed of as part of the larger purpose of making the accused responsible for the conflicts of the time. The anarchists stood for the precariousness of social stability in an age of major dislocations, economic distress, massive inequities, and unknown prospects. They were hanged because both cities and dynamite existed, and, taken together, this was frightening.

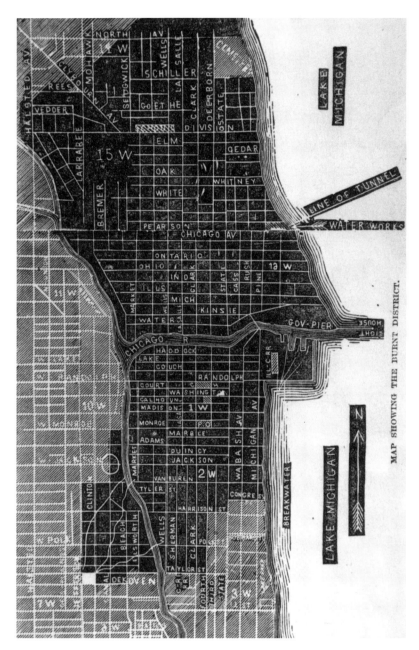

"Map Showing the Burnt District." Such maps were a common feature of the fire histories and of the post-fire business guides to the city. They offered indisputable graphic evidence of how completely the fire had destroyed the commercial heart of the city in the South Division and the residential area in the North Division. Sometimes authors superimposed maps of different urban fires on each other to give readers a sense of the relative extents of the devastation. The white square on the bottom left is the site of the O'Leary barn, while the light patch on the lakefront in the upper right marks a cemetery (now at the southern end of Lincoln Park) that became one of the gathering places for fire refugees. This map is taken from Frank Luzerne's *The Lost City!* Special Collections Department, Northwestern University Library, Evanston, Illinois.

The fire provided scenes of high melodrama on both a small and large scale. In one of the many vivid images from Luzerne's *Lost City!*, a desperate father tries to save his family by tying his children in their bedding and throwing them from the window, while others leap to their fates. Meanwhile, residents of the South Division flee with their lives and belongings through the crush on the Randolph Street Bridge as the firestorm consumes their city. The latter scene is from *Harper's Weekly* of October 28, 1871. Special Collections Department, Northwestern University Library, Evanston, Illinois.

The "awful democracy" of the fire. Chicago's tragedy served as a leveling force that threw all sorts of people together, first in the wild scramble to get to safety, and then in the communities of homeless survivors. In the lower illustration, the depiction of the pandemonium in the streets from *Leslie's Illustrated* of October 28, 1871 (Chicago Historical Society ICHi-02909), shows a wide range of selfish and selfless acts amidst the general panic. The upper drawing, from the cover of *Harper's Weekly* of the same date, centers, as did several other illustrations and passages from the fire literature, on a vulnerable young mother, who embodies all that was endangered by the fire, as she ponders the uncertain future. Northwestern University Library, Evanston, Illinois.

The city as beautiful young woman in distress was the theme of a number of the allegorical depictions of what had happened to Chicago. Above, in an engraving in *Every Saturday* of November 4, 1871, that was based on a painting by Alfred Fredericks (Chicago Historical Society ICHi-02915), Chicago's sister cities both revive her and fend off the savage hounds that would prey on her in this moment of weakness, as an ominous spirit of the fire hovers overhead. In Edward Armitage's 1872 version, England and America minister to the fallen city, who was more discreetly draped in the several adaptations of this image by other artists. Chicago Historical Society ICHi-02971.

This illustration was one of several like it throughout the fire literature, which heartily endorsed such vigilante justice. As the great fire burns indistinctly in the background, the fate that reportedly awaited thieves and incendiaries is vividly realized. Such undocumented scenes were projections of a popular imagination inflamed by the high drama of the event and by free-floating fears about urban unrest. Chicago Historical Society ICHi-02906.

The ties of sympathy in a networked urban nation. In the top image, from *Every Saturday* of October 28, 1871 (Chicago Historical Society ICHi-02916), men in the reading room of the Fifth Avenue Hotel in New York discuss the latest newspaper reports, conveyed by telegraph, of Chicago's distress. Below, in another illustration that was reprinted in several places, financier Jim Fisk himself takes the reins of a six-in-hand to collect provisions for immediate shipment by rail to fire victims. Chicago Historical Society.

The work of relief. In these images, both from the November 4, 1871, issue of *Leslie's Illustrated,* middle-class Chicagoans participate in the distribution of goods sent from around the nation and the world. In the first, fashionably attired ladies hand out clothing and even help fit working-class children in what appears to be a church building (Chicago Historical Society ICHi-02894). In the second, the pastor of Grace Church leads in the distribution of food (Chicago Historical Society ICHi-02885). Judging from their clothing, the recipients of aid in both instances include members of the middle as well as working classes. Note the armed guard at the left in the second illustration.

HARPER'S WEEKLY

A JOURNAL OF CIVILIZATION

Vol. XV.—No. 776.]   NEW YORK, SATURDAY, NOVEMBER 11, 1871.   [WITH A SUPPLEMENT. PRICE TEN CENTS.

Entered according to Act of Congress, in the Year 1871, by Harper & Brothers, in the Office of the Librarian of Congress, at Washington.

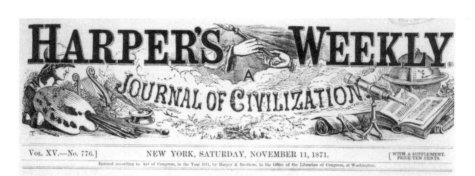

UNITY CHURCH—DR. COLLYER.

NEW ENGLAND CHURCH—CONGREGATIONAL.

ST. JOSEPH'S PRIORY—GERMAN CATHOLIC.

ST. PAUL'S CHURCH—UNIVERSALIST.

CHURCH OF THE HOLY NAME—ROMAN CATHOLIC.

ST. JAMES'S CHURCH—EPISCOPAL.

METHODIST CHURCH BLOCK.

FIRST PRESBYTERIAN CHURCH—SOUTH SIDE.

SECOND PRESBYTERIAN CHURCH.

THE RUINED CHURCHES OF CHICAGO.—Photographed by William Shaw, 137 Twenty-second Street, Chicago.—[See Page 1056.]

The cover of the November 11, 1871 issue of *Harper's Weekly*. This not only presented nine aesthetically appealing studies of Chicago's ruins, but also suggested how widely shared was the loss and how hard the catastrophe had struck at those sacred institutions of culture and "civilization" that bound an orderly urban society together. Northwestern University Library, Evanston, Illinois.

Reconstituting the city. Above, the Reverend Robert Collyer preaches outdoors to a puri-fied Christian democratic community gathered at the ruins of his church. Below, "an enterprising young merchant," sitting in an emptied safe amidst the rubble, sells fire relics to a respectable family, indicating that Chicago's entrepreneurial spirit was undaunted by the disaster but perhaps also that the better classes would have to "pay" to reclaim the city. Both illustrations appeared widely. The first is from *Harper's Weekly* of November 4,1871, while the second is from E. J. Goodspeed's *History of Great Fires in Chicago and the West.* Special Collections Department, Northwestern University Library, Evanston, Illinois.

The recreated fire as dramatic spectacle. Note how the broadside borrows the imagery of popular illustrations from the time of the fire that stressed the themes of chaos and control, including the dangers of intemperance and the importance of swift justice. Soldiers seem to guard (or at least ignore) the crowd that performs a lamppost lynching. A fire hose is cleverly integrated into the overall design. Chicago Historical Society ICHi-06185.

Thure de Thulstrup's version of the critical moment of Haymarket, which covered two full pages in *Harper's Weekly* of May 15, 1886, became the authoritative visual image of the event. Chicago Historical Society Library.

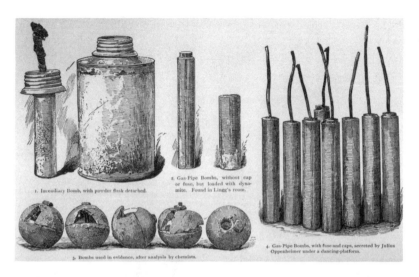

The urban terrorists and their infernal machines. The press and other popular literature presented such scenes of underground gatherings of secret brotherhoods of destruction, as well as pictures of their appalling arsenals. State's Attorney Julius Grinnell introduced these fearful weapons, along with anarchist banners, into the courtroom to help convince the jury of the dangers of allowing such men to remain free on (and under) the streets of Chicago. Both illustrations are from Michael Schaack's *Anarchy and Anarchists.* Northwestern University Library, Evanston, Illinois.

One of a few closely related depictions of the trial, this one from Schaack's *Anarchy and Anarchists*. Judge Joseph Gary sits behind the jury, surrounded by a few of his special female guests, who witness his and Grinnell's manly defense of government and law against the forces of anarchy. Northwestern University Library, Evanston, Illinois.

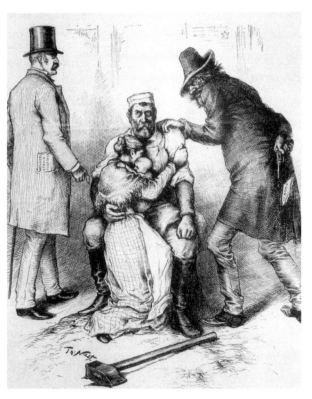

A gallery of Thomas Nast from *Harper's Weekly*. In the image on the top left of the previous page (May 8, 1886), the whip-wielding boycotter orders the laborer to stop work, even if his family suffers, since "*I must show my power.*" Top right (May 15), the noble craftsman must carry the bloated agitator. Bottom left (May 22), he is trapped between being fired by the silk-hatted capitalist (with a pamphlet in his pocket labeled "EMPLOYERS STAND TOGETHER") if he doesn't go to work and shot by the disheveled and gun-toting anarchist (whose pamphlet, sticking out like a tail, reads "TO ARMS") if he does. Notice that the worker is skilled and experienced, and that his tools are forced to remain idle. Bottom right (June 5), one of the many depictions of the anarchist as dirty, captioned "THE HARDEST BLOW YET TO THE ANARCHISTS. Deprived of a privilege of which they were never known to avail themselves." Above (May 29, June 5), characterizations of the anarchist as cowardly and alien, both centering on caricatures of Johann Most. In the first, the anarchists "drill" by hiding under beds, as their crazed leader rants and waves his ragged sword. In the second, the anarchist who brandishes his guns and bombs while he tramples on the flag must choose between "LIBERTY (to go if you do not like the institutions of our Republic) OR (commit murder and you will be punished with) DEATH." Northwestern University Library, Evanston, Illinois.

FRANK LESLIE'S ILLUSTRATED NEWSPAPER

No. 1,672.—Vol. LXV.]   NEW YORK—FOR THE WEEK ENDING OCTOBER 1, 1887.   [Price, 10 Cents.

NO. 1. MRS. NINA VAN ZANDT SPIES.   NO. 2. AUGUST SPIES.

ILLINOIS.—"MURDERERS' ROW," IN COOK COUNTY JAIL, CHICAGO, SHOWING THE CELLS OF THE CONDEMNED ANARCHIST, THE "DEATH WATCH," AND THE PRISONERS RECEIVING VISITORS.
FROM A SKETCH BY WILL E. CHAPIN.—SEE PAGE 102.

Awaiting the hangman. Another popular Haymarket subject was the "death watch" in the Cook County Jail as the date of the execution—November 11, 1887—approached. Illustrators presented numerous jailhouse scenes, including the prisoners sitting in their cells or visiting tenderly with their children, and Louis Lingg's dramatic suicide. One of the most sensational continuing stories was the death-row marriage of August Spies and Nina Van Zandt, who are seen here in the insets on the cover of the *Frank Leslie's Illustrated Newspaper* of October 1, 1887. Chicago Historical Society ICHi-16156.

This complex illustration appeared, among other places, in George McLean's *The Rise and Fall of Anarchy in America.* The insets at the top depict the Cook County Courthouse and Jail. The main sequence moves from the reading of the death warrant (upper left) to the march to the scaffold (upper right), to the adjusting of the nooses (lower left) and the hanging before the assembled witnesses (center). In the lower right we see the news of the executions reaching the respectable and law-abiding public to which the entire drama was played. Note how this audience is very similar to the one represented by the middle-class men who read the news of the Chicago fire in the Fifth Avenue Hotel. Northwestern University Library, Evanston, Illinois.

"Liberty is not Anarchy." Thomas Nast's decisive judgment on the anarchists took a full page in *Harper's Weekly* of September 4, 1886, shortly after the jury pronounced its guilty verdict and sentenced seven of the eight defendants to death. A heroic female figure representing the nation crushes these little men who had presumed to threaten her. Northwestern University Library, Evanston, Illinois.

The opposing sites of cultural memory. Albert Weinert's statue to the anarchists in Waldheim Cemetery, unveiled by Albert Parsons, Jr., in 1893, became a shrine of American radicalism (Chicago Historical Society ICHi-16157). The much-embattled police statue was designed by Charles F. Batchelder and unveiled by the son of slain officer Mathias Degan in 1889. It is surrounded in May of 1963 (it was then situated about a block south and west of the bombing and half a block from its original location) by representatives of the church, the police, descendants of the officers who marched on the Haymarket rally, local businessmen, and the Cook County Sheriff's Junior Posse. Chicago Historical Society.

The Model Town. Two illustrations that accompanied Richard T. Ely's "Pullman: A Social Study" in the February 1885 *Harper's New Monthly Magazine*. Above, the viewer looks northeast, with the Hotel Florence nearby, the main Palace Car works in the distance in front of Lake Vista. There is a glimpse on the right of some of the best housing, and the inset offers a map of the whole town, with the east at the top. While there are workers in the foreground, the setting is tastefully genteel. The bottom illustration looks southwest across the public square just west of the hotel toward the Arcade and, on the left, the Greenstone Church. The housing was concentrated east of this area. Northwestern University Library, Evanston, Illinois.

The White City. Whatever else businessmen, reformers, and labor leaders disagreed about, they generally concurred in thinking that the World's Columbian Exposition, which ran in Jackson Park from May to October of 1893, represented an ideal, if not *the* ideal, urban order—clean, harmonious, uplifting, and well-regulated. Above, the central Court of Honor of major exhibition buildings, with the Statue of the Republic standing regally in the Grand Basin. Below, the crowds in front of the Administration Building on Chicago Day, the anniversary of the fire, celebrating the city's recovery from catastrophe. Special Collections Department, Northwestern University Library, Evanston, Illinois.

The culmination of Chicago Day, and perhaps of the entire fair, was the Grand Columbian Carnival, featuring tableaux and floats, a grand reunion of the states enacted by youths and maidens, a monster concert, and a fireworks show, here presided over by the queenly spirit of Chicago, the city motto, "I WILL," inscribed on her breastplate. Such urban pageantry was popular throughout the late nineteenth and early twentieth centuries—similar events were mounted at the fire's fiftieth anniversary in 1921—as an affirmation of the cultural unity and order that sometimes seemed in doubt. Chicago Historical Society ICHi-06185.

Labor war in Chicago. Above, the cover of *Harper's Weekly* of July 14, 1894, showing "King Debs" willfully blocking the "Highway of Trade." In some illustrations Debs and his supporters (including Governor Altgeld) were depicted as jesters (the suggestion of that is here also) who would toy with the public good, in others as dangerous anarchists. Below, one of the illustrations that Frederic Remington prepared for his series of articles in *Harper's Weekly* on the army occupation. This scene, from July 21, 1894, depicts the infantry in the stockyards confronting the rabble, who cry, "To Hell with the United States Government." Northwestern University Library, Evanston, Illinois.

Military order in Chicago. Above, a sketch of the troop encampment on the lakefront, framed by treetops and with the city apparently in the distance, is remarkably peaceful (Chicago Historical Society ICHi-04916). Below, the Illinois National Guard lines up in front of the Arcade Building (Chicago Historical Society ICHi-22195).

Plots and Counterplots

The trial and executions that followed the Haymarket riot were "written" and "performed" to be viewed and reported in a way that would fulfill the authorities' and the public's aesthetic as well as legal standards for justice. The very staginess of the course of events was what made them seem most satisfying. At the time of the trial, the overwhelming majority of Americans, including many working people and virtually all middle-class citizens, ignored or applauded the procedural irregularities of the case in order to view the participants imaginatively and simplistically as actors in a morality play. Judge Gary later wrote, "We who participated in the trial did not know until it was ended with what interest we were watched by all Christendom," but this claim was disingenuous, for his and State's Attorney Grinnell's conduct of the case indicated that they were fully aware of the public interest in the trial, its spectacular quality, and their roles in moving the entire drama toward the desired conclusion.[1]

Both the prosecution and the defense recognized they had to address the fears that were aroused by the explosive tendencies of modern urban culture. The times and the city raised fundamental issues about life, liberty, government, and society that demanded a detailed cultural explanation as well as a legal resolution. The task and opportunity posed to each side was not just to convict or acquit the defendants, but to advance a persuasive interpretation of current events that would speak to these issues by offering a coherent and realistic program for urban order. Both the anarchists and their accusers contended that they were forcing the other to see the true way things were for the first time. The challenge of radical thought, Parsons reminded everyone at the trial, was precisely that it asked people to confront social disorder, "to discuss it, to reason, to examine it, to investigate it, to know the facts, because it is by this alone, that violence will be prevented and bloodshed will be avoided." Schaack meanwhile boasted that after the bombing the anarchists "had begun to discover . . . that there was a law in the land, and that its majesty would be vindicated. They were confronted with stubborn, serious facts, and they realized that they were in a world of perplexities."[2] The prosecution tried to make the trial the occasion on which it would establish beyond question that society as constituted was in reality stable and sound. The defendants gave their last breath to arguing that the current system was both precarious and unjust.

Center Stage

State's Attorney Grinnell exploited the spectacular possibilities of the trial with the highly questionable use of sensational evidence— including every sort of anarchist article and letter he could find that advocated violence, the gory garments of the police killed or injured in the Haymarket, and an arsenal of the kind of fearsome explosives that aroused the public's fear and anger—virtually none of which was connected with the case at hand. He completed the scene by dressing the courtroom with sloganeering banners in English and German that were displayed at radical rallies.[3] The accused and their defenders were certainly aware of the way every detail of their trial was being carefully staged. On the day the verdict was read, Parsons balked at a rearrangement of the courtroom that had him facing members of the police. "I don't want to be stared at by these officers. I didn't come here to be made a show of," he protested. In two widely circulated pamphlets, one of the "respectable" critics of the proceedings, M. M. Trumbull, attacked the trial by comparing the prosecution's tactics to "the style and manner of the minor theaters."[4] At the same time he permitted the prosecution such theatrics, Judge Gary kept a tight rein on the attempts by Captain Black to dramatize his arguments. On one occasion he abruptly told the defense, "Sit down, and don't make scenes." When Black, hoping to demonstrate his client's innocence, tried to choreograph Parsons's voluntary surrender at the opening of the trial, Grinnell successfully interrupted by asking the judge to order the fugitive's arrest.[5]

The defendants certainly needed no convincing of the importance of the dramaturgical dimensions of experience, as is evident from their countless rallies, parades, and demonstrations, including the Haymarket meeting. And, in a way probably unanticipated by the state, they recognized that as a public performance the trial presented them with an extraordinary opportunity. If their indictment deprived them of their freedom and forced them into a part defined by their enemies, it gave the anarchists something they had been desperately seeking for some time: an audience and the spotlight. Their case may have been a lost cause before it began, but it was also the chance of a lifetime. They moved from fleeting mention in trailing paragraphs on labor agitation into front-page headlines and illustrations, from obscurity in mostly ill-attended rallies to center stage in the theater of the city. When they found themselves in the middle of what had become a national and international spectacle, they presented their case not so much before judge and jury but, as did the prosecution, before the court of public opinion. The best occasions to do so came when they testified in their own defense in July, and in their final statements before sentencing in early October, seven weeks after they were convicted. These statements took up three extraordinary days. Parsons spoke last and longest, trying Gary's patience by taking all of eight hours to explain his entire social vision, pausing occasionally to ask without success for a brief rest. At the other extreme, Louis Lingg was brief and defiant. "*I despise you*," he concluded, "*I despise your order; your laws, your force-propped authority.* HANG ME FOR IT!"[6]

Contemporary illustrations of the executions reveal the extent to which those who reported it understood this grim ceremony, as well as the trial that preceded it, as a drama played to an audience. One illustration of the event consisted of five scenes representing the last minutes of the anarchists' lives in a complicated visual narrative sequence. In the upper left the sheriff reads the death warrant to Parsons in his cell, and in the upper right they begin "the march to the scaffold." Next, on the lower left, the four doomed anarchists stand on the gallows as the last noose is adjusted. The view is from behind them, so that in the background, facing the viewer, are the rows of assembled witnesses. The fourth illustration in chronological order, which is prominently set in the center, reverses the viewpoint. Now the vantage is from above and behind the witnesses toward the executed anarchists, who hang dead and limp from the gallows-stage. The final scene, on the lower right, is titled "Latest News," and depicts a newsboy hawking the extras that report the execution to a crowd of well-dressed men in the lobby of a hotel.[7]

This concluding vignette might seem to be disconnected from the taut sequence that links the other four, but the point so well illustrated by the complex design was that Haymarket and the reporting of it were one cultural event. The journalists who witness the execution act as surrogates for the rest of the "nation of spectators," who are the ulti-

mate audience for this demonstration of the moral as well as legal authority of the social order and its power to exercise that authority.
These spectators are the 1886 version of the righteous "we" of the fire
literature. They are represented in the illustration by the middle-class
men who buy the newsboy's papers, on whose pages the execution is
rendered in affecting language that makes anyone who reads it part of
the cultural performance that is Haymarket.[8]

Making the Case

The case which the prosecution presented from the trial through the
appeals had a multitude of authors, who, until the period just before
the executions, completely drowned out the few scattered voices who
spoke on behalf of the defendants.[9] State's Attorney Grinnell found
many powerful backers outside the courtroom whose opinions, expressed before, during, and following the bombing, affected the handling of the case. Among the most influential were the large employers
who had been the special target of the anarchists' invective and who
had furnished Schaack with funds to conduct his investigations. Some
of Schaack's major sponsors, whom he characterized as "public-
spirited citizens who wished the law vindicated and order preserved in
Chicago," were among those who had "saved" the city after the fire and
had rallied to its defense in 1877. These included Marshall Field and
George Pullman. Field, one of whose salesmen was foreman of the
jury, later used his considerable influence to impede the movement for
clemency in the days before the execution. Six weeks after the hangings, the Chicago Bar Association held a dinner in Judge Gary's honor
at which Wirt Dexter, head of the Executive Committee of the Relief
and Aid Society after the fire, applauded Gary for his heroic conduct of
the trial.[10]
    The local and national press was also of primary importance in shap-
ing as well as reporting the dominant understanding of Haymarket in
the public imagination. Unlike the fire, which was experienced firsthand by a few hundred thousand people of all classes, the bombing was
witnessed by a few hundred workers and police. Information was available to almost everyone else only through the papers (it is not clear how
many reporters who covered the story were actual eyewitnesses). In
Chicago and every other city, Haymarket was a front-page story, and
the slant of the articles went virulently against the defendants, convicting the anarchists in print before they were even indicted. Those who
consumed these stories included the men on the jury list, who freely
admitted prejudices that were based on their reading. The only signifi-

cant criticism directed at the authorities by the papers was that they had not taken preemptive measures that might have prevented the Haymarket rally from happening in the first place. The press was proud of its role in Haymarket, and seemed at moments to be consciously aware that it was making as well as reporting history. The *Tribune* editors would probably have taken as praise the critical observation made by English socialist Edward Aveling, who visited the convicted anarchists during his tour of America and later observed, "If these men are ultimately hanged, it will the *Chicago Tribune* that has done it."[11] Several journalists and self-described "eyewitnesses" quickly produced a handful of inexpensive and highly sensational instant histories, mainly based on material cribbed from the dailies.[12] While all these works condemned the defendants and extolled the police and the prosecution, they differed from a small group of more substantial and explicitly polemical accounts published after the trial whose primary purpose was to establish the correctness of the proceedings as well as to exploit the continuing interest in the case. The most notable book of this sort was Captain Schaack's *Anarchy and Anarchists*, which, at almost seven hundred pages, was by far the most comprehensive and extensively illustrated contemporary examination of Haymarket. Like the fire histories that contained a long prelude and a listing of other similar disasters, Schaack's book included a section on radical terrorism in Europe in the years before the Haymarket bomb. Dedicated to Gary and Grinnell, this work featured a substantially verbatim record of the trial and, of course, a highly favorable account of the police investigations conducted by its author.[13]

Haymarket was also tried in the churches, as ministers near and far condemned anarchism as a violation of God's law and called for the restoration of the worker to the Christian faith. Their sermons, which no doubt relied heavily on the newspapers for their facts, were in turn the subject of numerous newspaper articles, some of which quoted them extensively as expressions of informed public opinion. Several also appeared in pamphlet form. One such sermon was "Christianity and the Red Flag," preached at the Union Park Congregational Church by the Reverend Frederick A. Noble the Sunday following the bombing. Noble, whose church and ministry were known for their sensitivity to the needs of the masses, had no sympathy for the alleged conspirators. Taking as his scriptural text the passage from Isaiah, "Their feet run to evil, and they make haste to shed innocent blood; their thoughts are thoughts of iniquity; desolation and destruction are in their paths," Noble informed his congregation, "This is an ancient description of a modern anarchist." As the date of the execution neared,

Hortensia Black, wife of the chief defense counsel, was appalled to hear a woman say "that every minister in the country would intercede in their behalf if these men would become converted."[14]

The bombing quickly became a subject of xenophobic and antiradical popular fiction. Even before the verdict, the New York Detective Library issued *The Red Flag; or the Anarchists of Chicago,* complete with a lurid cover featuring a portrait of a stolid anarchist against a menacing backdrop of guns, daggers, and explosives. Among more respectable American literary figures, William Dean Howells was the only outspoken critic of the conduct of the case. Howells tried to get his fellow writers to join him in signing a letter published in the *New York Tribune* a week before the hangings that asked for support of his petition to Governor Oglesby requesting clemency. Although he was the acknowledged leader of the national literary community, Howells was angered and disappointed to find that not a single other American writer joined his appeal. Among the prominent authors who spurned him was John Greenleaf Whittier, now almost eighty, who through a career distinguished for its high moral principles had spoken out for abolition, female suffrage, and freedom of speech, as well as against capital punishment. One of his ardent readers was Albert Parsons, who used Whittier's poem "The Reformer" as the epigraph to a short book he wrote on anarchism when he was in prison.[15]

As the voice of public opinion, State's Attorney Grinnell argued that the stakes in the trial went far beyond the guilt or innocence of these particular men. Their punishment would not only remove them from society but, as many claimed the fire had done, would purge and strengthen the social order. When he said that he could have with equal justification charged many others, he as much as admitted that he was acting on a symbolic level, that the eight defendants were arrested and indicted for what they represented as much as for what they did. As he stated explicitly, it was anarchy more than any individual that was being tried. At the same time he made the remarkable assertion that both law and government were "on trial." He contended that the real crime at hand was not murder but the attempted subversion of legal authority in the urban polity that was Chicago, and that the trial was a fateful struggle between order and disorder. Grinnell's assistant, George C. Ingham, told the jury that in punishing the defendants for the death of Matthias Degan, the state of Illinois "attempts to vindicate itself, and so it is that the great question which you are to answer by your verdict is whether the law of the State of Illinois is strong enough to protect itself."[16] It was now time to take a stand and save the city with the same courage that had preserved it through the travails of the fire and the railroad strikes. A guilty verdict, and the executions that would soon follow, would be a long overdue reassertion of the city's character and resolve that would reestablish order and assure a safe and prosperous future. The centerpiece of the state's explanation of Haymarket, vital to its defense of the current order, was that the bomb was an irrational aberration, a result essentially without a cause except in the psychopathology of these villains, who had engaged in what the *Tribune* called, in still another theatrical metaphor, "a deliberate, rehearsed conspiracy" against the social order. Grinnell and Gary shaped the trial accordingly to emphasize this "reading" of recent events and current social reality. The grand jury maintained that it had seen "conclusive" evidence that there was "no real connection" between the "Anarchist conspiracy" and legitimate labor disputes, which could be readily settled without significant social and economic change. The conspiracy had "simply made use of the excitement incident to those troubles as its opportunity" to spread disorder. This "force of disorganizers had a very perfect organization of its own" under the control of those who published the *Arbeiter-Zeitung* and the *Alarm*, and who "were manipulating this agitation from base and selfish motives," namely, the desire for power and money. The large majority of their followers were naive "dupes."[17]

In developing these points, writers out to condemn the defendants relied on some of the conventions of sensational treatments of the urban underworld that had earlier been employed by the authors of the fire literature when they spoke of the dangerous types who threatened to rise from the lower depths and take over the city. Now readers heard of supersecret meetings in dim cellars where groups with names like "Brothers of the Strong Arm" hatched their conspiracies and concocted their fearsome explosives. As for public disorders like that at the McCormick works, these were caused, the *New York Times* asserted, not by working conditions and wage disputes but by anarchists who roused workers "to a pitch of frenzy by incendiary speeches and bad beer." In the terror of the moment, these stories were swallowed whole by most readers. In his recollection of the mood of Chicago in the late spring of 1886, attorney Samuel P. McConnell noted that the widespread feeling was that persons and property would not be safe until the anarchists were punished. "No one seemed to doubt that there was a large organization back of the bomb throwing, with a design to overturn the government and destroy the lives and property of the well-to-do."[18]

The central purpose of this fear-mongering was not only to isolate these troublemakers and appeal to an inflamed public mind but also to justify, as being for the worker's own good, the current social and economic hierarchy that was based on wage labor and marked by class divisions. In the fire literature, the endangered city was an innocent virgin or young married woman of refinement. Now the supposed representative citizen at risk was the "good" worker, who needed to be defended against the same kind of low villains who were the enemies of virtue. What made the current moment much more dangerous than the time of the fire was that the enemies of order were not scattered social dregs and predators who surfaced in a disaster, but a cunning and tightly organized group who were willing to use strikes and bombs to set off a social cataclysm. And they were out not only to destroy lives and property, but to degrade the republic.

What the prosecution was trying to do here was characterize labor organizers in general and anarchists in particular as a particularly sinister version of the old middle-class bugaboo of antebellum America, the confidence man, "whose game," as Karen Halttunen explains, "was to profess an interest in the public good in order to disguise and carry out his own selfish purposes." Lacking fixed principles and capable of voicing whatever line seemed suitable at the moment to advance his ends, he was an insincere trickster whose "greatest offense was that he usurped power from the legitimate leaders of American society." And he was most dangerous in times of great social instability, when the minds of the masses were disturbed and they might follow false leaders toward their own and society's ruin.[19] The problem with the worker was that he lacked the intelligence and social awareness of his betters and could be duped, seduced by the beer and slogans of the anarchists, into abandoning his proper place of worth in society. What he needed most was to develop his character under the kind of training and tutelage that only honest labor for a good employer would provide.

In his history of the case, Schaack called socialist and anarchist leaders "ingrates to society," which they wished to turn upside down in their hopes of establishing "[a]narchy in the midst of the state, war in times of peace, and conspiracy in open day." Schaack, as had many others, accused them of subverting all social values, and of being especially dangerous to honest workers. Anarchists, he explained, hated the wage system that was vital to American prosperity, productivity, and progress, and "only join in the demands of law-observing and peace-loving labor as a means to one end—opportunity for disturbance." They attracted some simpleminded followers because of the natural "fascination about any scheme that promises ease without labor," which was impossible and undesirable. "The state of society they seek to establish," Schaack contended, "may be highly beneficial to a class which, under any conditions, lacks sobriety, frugality, thrift and self-reliance; but just where the general mass of humanity is to be bettered or elevated, socially, morally or politically, is a point not satisfactorily explained."[20]

Judge Gary made similar points at the trial and after. Before formally pronouncing the sentence, he offered a few words in the "faint hope" of reaching not the incorrigibles before him in court, but "the ignorant, deluded and misguided men who have listened to your counsels and followed your advice." It was "not the least among the hardships of peaceable, frugal and laborious people," Gary observed, "to endure the tyranny of mobs who, with lawless force, dictate to them, under penalty of peril to limb and life, where, when and upon what terms they may earn a livelihood for themselves and their families." In his 1893 article on the trial in the *Century,* Gary maintained that one of his key purposes in writing was "*to show to the laboring people, of whom the anarchists claimed to be the especial friends, that the claim was a sham and a pretense, adopted only as a means to bring manual laborers into their own ranks; and that the counsel and advice of the anarchists, if followed by the workingmen, would expose them to the danger of becoming, in law, murderers*" [emphasis his]. He insisted that "the real passions at the bottom of the hearts of the anarchists were envy and hatred of all people whose condition in life was better than their own, who were more prosperous than themselves."[21]

Even those who could claim to be committed advocates of labor and immigrant interests insisted, along with Schaack and Gary, that the anarchists did not represent the wishes or welfare of honest labor. This "lawless element," the *Louisville Courier-Journal* told its readers a month before Haymarket, "does not speak for the intelligent and industrious workingmen of America, and the spirit which animates it must be put under control. In this suppression of violence, in this subjection of lawless men, no class has so deep an interest as the workingmen themselves." This paper, whose politics were Democratic, praised the Knights of Labor for issuing statements condemning the violence at Haymarket. The German-language *New York Staats-Zeitung* pointed out that such "barbarous and unwarrantable acts" as the Haymarket bombing were caused by the "delusive utterances" of a "cowardly and unprincipled" few and did not represent the immigrant community, whether working-class or not, any more than they represented the voice of labor. There were "not so many hundreds of Germans in this herd as there are millions in this Union."[22]

Some conservative voices, however, used the occasion to attack all outspoken labor organizers as dangerous subversives. Among the most forceful characterizations (more accurately, caricaturizations) of such men as the enemies of the public order and the honest worker appeared

in the drawings of Thomas Nast for *Harper's Weekly*. On the cover of the
issue of May 15, Nast, always suspicious of unions and radicalism, depicted the American workingman as a forthright individual forced to
carry on his back a whip-carrying, shaggy-haired, and bloated-bellied
figure Nast labeled "AGITATOR." The worker, who was far better
groomed and fit (although older) than his slovenly burden, was stooped
and sweating. The caption read, "TOO HEAVY A LOAD FOR THE
TRADES-UNIONS. THE COMPETENT WORKMAN MUST
SUPPORT THE INCOMPETENT." A week later Nast pictured the
noble craftsman with his wife and infant pressed against his broad chest
for protection as he sat in the midst of a terrible dilemma. On one side is
the silk-hatted employer, who warns, "If you don't go to work, I must
fill your place," while on the other is the unkempt anarchist, who
threatens, "If you go to work, I'll make it hot for you." The workingman's massive sledgehammer rests idle on the ground, showing that
both his and the nation's energies and earning power have been paralyzed by his dilemma. Nast titled the drawing "BETWEEN TWO
FIRES."23

Blaming labor distress on a handful of agitators and anarchists implied that the current troubles had been blown out of proportion. Yes,
the worker had some cause for complaint against capital, but what was
needed were some small readjustments, not strikes and revolution. The
agitator, no laboring man himself but a professional troublemaker, was
a parasite who took bread out of the mouths of the worker's children.
The best course for labor was to trust to capital, and the best policy for
capital was to be worthy of that trust. And who exactly was the anarchist, besides being the worst sort of agitator? The answer was as pur-
posefully imprecise as ever, based less on a careful scrutiny of radical
thought than on a need to invent a villain who could be blamed for urban disorder. While he could be defined as this or that person, a Spies
or a Parsons, he was less a particular individual with a certain set of
beliefs than an all-purpose repository of amorphous notions devised
from a combination of wishful thinking and repressed fears in order to
prove that the source of all the trouble most fully evidenced by the
bomb was an evil and unprincipled conspiracy. Different writings on
Haymarket (Schaack's book was the outstanding example) included
impressively detailed if skewed histories of anarchism, socialism, communism, and political terrorism going back to the French Revolution,
intended to connect Haymarket to misguided miscreants elsewhere.
But most commentators did not want to understand who the Chicago
radicals were, because to know them in depth would be to credit them
as being complex human beings rather than one-dimensional villains.
It was better not to make distinctions, but to throw them all into the

Cook County Jail until that happy moment when they, and all the troubles for which they were blamed, could be marched to the scaffold and ritualistically removed from society.

Few argued that the bomb was, as many had regarded the fire, a blessing in disguise, but in his sermon just after the riot Frederick A. Noble wondered if the tragedy might have been a favor to society since it finally woke people up to the deadly quality of the conspiracy against them. After Haymarket only those who were "willfully blind" could not see that these "advanced Socialists, Nihilists, Anarchists, or whatever they choose to call themselves are not merely noisy agitators . . . but out-and-out destructionists" intent on "mingling in a common ruin, government, and law, and property, and home, and church, and school, and business, and everything which lies at the basis of civilization as it exists in the most advanced nations of the earth to-day."[24] It was not the shortcomings of the order they attacked that excluded them from it; it was their own laziness, willfulness, and godlessness.

The prosecution, the police, and most of the public thus wanted to characterize the anarchists in two contradictory ways. It was important on the one hand to express confidence that the conspirators were few in number. To speak otherwise would be to admit that their cause had some broad popular support and perhaps even some justification. And if there were a lot of them, hanging these few would not be an effective solution to current difficulties. On the other hand, unless they could be described as a substantial threat, it was hard to justify the intensity of the police investigation, the seriousness of the charges, or the public uproar. Schaack called the anarchists "a minority of a minority," who were far better at bluster than action, but at the same time he argued that a half dozen determined terrorists like Engel "at a critical time could upset a whole city," and that demagogues like Parsons and Spies had to be removed.[25]

There were at least three arguments that addressed this contradiction. The first was the view that these few individuals were a threat because of their incendiary rhetoric and their influential positions as editors, speakers, and organizers. It was not the lockout, the hiring of scabs, or the police, but Spies's deceitful eloquence that had caused the riot outside the McCormick works the day before the Haymarket rally. "With fiery invective, [Spies] wrought up the feelings of the mob to a pitch of reckless frenzy," Schaack explained, describing the editor's serpent-like ability to lead good men astray: "In the climaxes of his envenomed utterances, he held the multitude with a charmed spell, and he evoked their highest plaudits when he counseled violence as a means to redress their grievances." Judge Gary made much of the fact that the accused were very effective orators who held even him spellbound with

their words. If men and women of even "a high order of intelligence, of
pure lives, amiable in their dispositions, seemed under a spell to them,"
Gary asserted, then the effect on working people of their speech was
much more dangerous, since this audience "did not share in the luxuries, and were not able to participate in many of the comforts, of life
which they saw around them" Gary charged that Spies in fact regarded
working people as "stupid and ignorant." It was out of contempt for
them as well as for all society that he used his rhetorical skills to convince them "that anarchy offered a heroic remedy for the inequalities of
life, the evils of which, real or fancied, fell upon them." Gary wondered
out loud, "Who can estimate the effect? The wonder is that a tragedy
was so long delayed."[26]

The second reason for attributing so much danger to so small a
group was dynamite, along with all the incendiary articles, proclamations, platforms, circulars, and books written by anarchists (notably
the notorious Johann Most) that called for its use.[27] Commentators
pointed out that dynamite was an instrument of progress that would
advance the cause of civilization just as had the discovery of fire. But,
like fire, it had to be kept out of the wrong hands, for in the clutches
of a terrorist it was even more dangerous than the arsonist's match.
Schaack devoted a whole chapter to Alfred Nobel's invention, paying
special attention to the bomb that killed Czar Alexander II in 1881 and
the subsequent trial and execution of the nihilists who plotted his
death. As the anarchists boasted and Haymarket proved, dynamite enabled a single individual lurking in the shadows on a crowded street to
overwhelm with one blow a whole force of the sworn defenders of the
peace.

The final reason was the nature of the modern city. Grinnell, Gary,
Schaack, and many others justified the prosecution of the anarchists
because of their view of urban society as a precariously delicate and
nervous system where these terrorists were gathered in their greatest
numbers and could do incalculable harm. Here they were all too free to
plot almost invisibly in their secret hideouts and in the smoky back-
rooms of beer halls. The city's concentrations of people, large businesses, capital, and technologies that linked them all together—now
far greater than at the time of the fire—made it especially susceptible to
the new terror of dynamite. Rallies like the meeting in the Haymarket
were an invitation to trouble, for they exposed the public to the kind of
deadly violence that could be practiced by a few individuals of "malignant heart." "The hissing fiend," wrote George McLean in reference to
the Haymarket bomb, "hurled by some practiced hand to perform its
hellish mission, fell directly between two of the ranks of our brave and

noble officers, and exploded with a detonation which seemed to shake the city from center to circumference."[28]

The bomb was the fire all over again in the most condensed form imaginable, causing more destabilization and terror in a moment than the conflagration had brought about in thirty-six hours. While the extent of physical destruction it inflicted was just a pinpoint in comparison to the broad field of the "Burnt District" of 1871, it left a much bigger mark than had the fire on the landscape of the imagination. It blasted away with appalling ease the rows of officers who stood for all the best the city had to offer, highest among them the values and virtues of order. "ORDER, HEAVEN'S FIRST LAW," was the one-line epigraph of McLean's *The Rise and Fall of Anarchy in America*. Suddenly the anonymous bomb-thrower was not a solitary malcontent attacking a political system, but a satanic rebel against divine harmony. What was at stake on the battleground of the city was the body and soul of the country.

The logic of this view justified the call for repressive measures. "Decent people" were "amazed and horrified," the *Chicago Tribune* reported, telling of Mayor Harrison's meeting with a delegation of leading merchants and manufacturers from the Citizens' Association that was similar to the emergency gathering in the Moody and Sankey Tabernacle during the labor turmoil of 1877. In this latest crisis, Harrison followed the example of his predecessors Roswell Mason and Monroe Heath, issuing a proclamation restricting freedom of assembly and reaffirming the primacy of law. The *Tribune* meanwhile said that it was time to end the "ill-considered toleration" that had allowed Haymarket to happen, to confront radicalism with order, and to "organize to meet it with all the power of the law and put it down." Otherwise there would be more loss of life and property. "These alien Communists must be made to know that American law shall be obeyed, or anarchy and arson will prevail," the *Tribune* asserted, tying the bomb and fire together. It was also time for more police and stronger laws. In its Decoration Day editorial three weeks later, the paper joined many others that viewed Haymarket through the memory of the Civil War. "The Republic is more firmly grounded today than it was in 1860," the editors proudly observed, for the "only danger" before it was "personal-liberty-destroying Socialism and foreign anarchy, which are menacing law, property, government, the pulpit, the home, and public and private rights." The editors assured their readers that when these alien systems were thoroughly stamped out, as the forthcoming trial promised they would be, the "Republic will advance upon a new career of greatness and free itself from the last danger that threatens it."[29]

The out-of-town papers and the national press concurred. The only way to stop "the propagation of incendiarism and outrage," observed the *New York Tribune,* was with "the sharpest and sternest application of force." The *New York Times* advised, "The promptest and sternest way of dealing with such outbreaks as that among the Chicago Anarchists is the wisest and most merciful." *Nation* editor E. L. Godkin similarly addressed the issues at hand: "When we get outside the law, and begin to allow ever so little intimidation or coercion to be practiced by either individuals or organizations for purposes of their own, we begin a descent at the bottom of which is anarchy—that is, arson, pillage, and murder, revolvers, rifles, and bombs." Political cartoonists across the country offered vivid visualizations of the idea that the state should and must complete the drama by responding to anarchic violence with the kind of force and conviction that reaffirmed the public order. The cover of the *Pictorial West* for August featured a drawing in which the central figure was the same female representation of the city that appeared in the fire literature. But now she is no longer frightened and unable to defend herself. Irate and determined, she wrestles an unkempt "Anarchist Agitator" to the ground with her strong left hand, while in her right she holds a sword called "Justice."[30]

It was Thomas Nast, however, who in September of 1886 once again produced the most compelling visual expression of public opinion. In his version of the same kind of scene, he brilliantly restricted the view only to the capable hands of this heroic and powerful female figure. The left hand, the third finger of which is graced with a wedding band on which is the word "UNION," holds a battle sword on which is inscribed "U.S." The right hand grasps upside down between its firmly clenched fingers the seven condemned anarchists, who are desperately squirming in a hopeless attempt to escape. While both images took advantage of public familiarity with Bartholdi's Statue of Liberty, which was to be dedicated a month later, Nast's more successfully conveyed the idea of how puny and pathetic these malefactors were, and how sure and controlled were the anger and might of the state.[31]

In his brief remarks before pronouncing sentence, Gary articulated this idea explicitly, picking up Grinnell's idea that law and the state were themselves in the dock in this case. "Any government that is worthy of the name," he explained, "will strenuously endeavor to secure to all within its jurisdiction freedom to follow their lawful avocations in safety for their property and their persons, while obeying the law; and the law is common sense." He asserted that this latest and most profound trial of national character had been won, for it demonstrated that the American people "will never consent that by violence and murder their institutions shall be broken down, their homes despoiled and their property destroyed." The accused men had been convicted "after a trial unexampled in the patience with which an outraged people" gave the defendants "every protection and privilege of the law" that the anarchists had "derided and defied." The principles and integrity of the law now required that these men be executed. Schaack tried to put the matter in similar abstract terms of principle. He closed the first chapter of his book with the claim that he and his fellow officers "entertain[ed] no animosity against these men," but were "bound by our oaths and by our loyalty to the State and to society to meet force with force, and cunning with cunning. We are the conservators of the law and the preservers of the peace, and the law will be vindicated and the peace preserved in spite of any and all attacks." In his history of Haymarket, McLean agreed:

> But pitying justice wept with drooping head o'er the stern necessity which called for the interposition of her iron hand having discarded the scepter for the rod. When the hand of outraged law and justice is raised the blow must fall in order to vindicate the majesty of the law. America has set the foot of the Goddess of Liberty upon the neck of anarchy and crushed the serpent brood.[32]

Several Chicagoans expressed pride rather than shame that the test of justice and law and order and government had taken place where it did. On the day the verdict was pronounced, the *Chicago Daily News* boasted, "Chicago is the central point toward which the eyes of the world are directed. It is a dull day when some great event does not transpire here." "We live in Chicago," Assistant State's Attorney Ingham told the jury, "the metropolis of the great Northwest, the very center of the highest and best civilization on earth." The guilty verdict would vindicate the vision of inevitable greatness expressed in the booster literature. The Haymarket case, Schaack explained further, "was one which not alone interested Chicago, but touched the stability and welfare of every city of any considerable size in the United States." As a result, "The eyes of the whole country were riveted on Chicago," Schaack declared, "and the outside world was eagerly watching the results of a case, the first in America, to determine whether dynamite was to be considered a legal weapon in the settlement of socio-political problems in a free republic."[33] In the state's version of the Haymarket drama, the message of the final scene on the scaffold was that the answer was no.

Turning Things Around

The defendants and their more passionate supporters, so obsessed with social justice, and so deeply immersed in the literature and lan-

guage of romantic revolution that they seemed to have no other vocabulary through which to express themselves and explain the times, used
the peculiar opportunity presented by the trial to do some "plotting" of
their own that was quite different from the conspiracy of which they
were accused. In their narrative interpretation of what was happening,
their persecution and even their execution were, paradoxically, em-
powering acts that marked them as unquestionably significant and
proved all their ideas to be true. To their partisans, their trial and hanging signaled the fundamental instability of the state, its self-destructive
reliance on lies, force, and violence to hold it together. The condemned
men were martyrs, who had given their lives for democracy and
freedom.[34]

Aware of the weakness of the case against their clients on strictly legal grounds, the four-man defense team tried to focus the jury on the
fact that the prosecution's whole story was wrong. The trial was not
about law or anarchy or city life, but about the murder of Matthias
Degan, and there was no proof that the accused had a hand in this act.
They contended that the conspiracy charge was nothing but a hook on
which to hang the vague and unlegislated offense of radical dissent.
The defendants were selfless social reformers whose "crime" was not
causing disorder but calling attention to it. At the trial, attorney Moses
Salomon declared that the evidence revealed "conclusively" that the
anarchists were "men of broad feelings of humanity, that their only desire has been, and their lives have been consecrated to, the betterment
of their fellow-men." Before the executions many of those favoring
clemency, like William M. Salter of the Ethical Culture Society, conceded that the condemned men were guilty perhaps of sedition, but
certainly not of conspiracy and murder.[35]

The anarchists themselves, aware that any strategy to win acquittal
was certain to fail, scorned their lawyers' tactics and in effect concurred
with the prosecution that the proceedings against them involved a
dangerous conspiracy, and that the law and government and the modern urban order they supported were indeed on trial. Some of the defendants' statements could have come out of the mouths of Gary or
Grinnell. For example, in an interview published in the *Daily News* two
months before Haymarket, Parsons was quoted as saying, "The labor
question is up for settlement. It demands and commands a hearing.
The existing disorders threaten not only the peace, but the destruction
of society itself."[36] While agreeing that the prosecution was using the
right terms to describe contemporary experience, however, the anarchists contended that their accusers had not applied these terms
correctly. The anarchists' version of the plot of the drama unfolding
around them was that their accusers were committing precisely the

kind of criminal act of which they stood wrongly indicted. Elected officials, the police, the prosecution, the judge, and the newspapers—all in service of a capitalist elite out to reassert its immoral power—had conspired against them as part of a larger class war and in order to cover their own role in creating the current disorders. The trial, with its inevitable guilty verdict, was the result of a "plot" in which their enemies had devised this caricature of the anarchist to delude and frighten labor, provoked the bombing (Parsons even charged that a hired agent provocateur threw the bomb), and then fabricated the conspiracy indictment. The real facts were suppressed, Spies declared before sentencing, "and *we were accused and convicted by the real conspirators and their agents.*"[37]

Parsons offered a more specific refutation of the conspiracy indictment when he referred to a recent speech by Illinois governor Richard Oglesby that described current conditions as a "social volcano." "What did he mean?" Parsons asked. "If he had made that remark at the Haymarket he would be in this box here to-day, and turned over to the hangman." The minions of capital had fomented trouble with the full knowledge that to do so aided monopoly and hurt organized labor. "Their speeches, their utterances, their newspapers openly counseled and advised by 'speech and print' just such things," Parsons explained, turning Judge Gary's loose interpretation of conspiracy against government and business leaders. "The question, to use your honor's language," he told Gary, "is 'not whether they did it with their own hands, but whether they (the monopolists) set causes at work which did end in the Haymarket tragedy?' By their own proposals I have shown you that they did."[38]

The trope of ironic reversal was the distinctive feature of Haymarket as imaginative and rhetorical event. It was in substantive ways at the heart of the anarchist challenge to the assumptions on which their trial and the social order were based. In maintaining that the terms the prosecution applied to them were more appropriate to their enemies, the anarchists asserted that the common understanding of these and other terms was exactly the reverse of the truth, and, more important, that their own narrative of events, and the urban vision behind it, offered the most accurate understanding of the meaning of the troubling conditions of the day. The representatives and supporters of the state were at best dangerously misguided and at worst murderously hypocritical, either failing to understand the nature of experience or not really believing what they themselves were saying. In either case, the anarchists asserted, the state's motive was to preserve the deeply flawed and repressive status quo.

The anarchists relentlessly resorted to the strategy of reversal in order to make their case to the world. They maintained that they were the opposite of what their enemies said they were, and that the state was the opposite of what it claimed it stood for, since it had acted in the way it charged the anarchists with behaving. They declared over and over again that they were uncompromisingly allied with liberty, peace, dignity, reason, opportunity, progress, freedom, and order. In contrast, the "system" was in fact opposed to its own official ideals and completely out of control, if its supposed goal was to create and sustain a humane social order. The sentence of the court, Parsons argued, "is the verdict of passion, born in passion, nurtured in passion, and is the sum totality of the organized passion of the city of Chicago." This passion served a state of affairs that was a monumental and pathological contradiction in terms. The police were criminals, law was lawlessness, the current order was disorder. By this reasoning, "civilization" was savagely uncivilized, justifying itself through the barbarous murder of noble and selfless men in exchange for the lives of the policemen it had caused to be maimed and killed.

To put these charges in terms of the stories that came out of the fire, the anarchists were arguing that now an army of incendiaries was hanging the city's saviors. If anarchy was to be equated simplistically with mindless terrorism, then the factory owners and police and newspapers and prosecution were anarchists. There was in fact no free competition or individuality or progress in the United States, only monopoly and enforced obedience that characterized an advanced and warlike stage of industrial capitalism inevitably doomed to the kind of violent catastrophe of which the bomb was symptomatic. The preservation of the state, said Spies, "means the preservation of vice in every form. And last but not least, it means the preservation of the class struggle, of strikes, riots, and bloodshed." Hence his repeated indictment of his accusers with the charges that they raised against him: "You, who oppose the natural course of things, *you* are the real revolutionists. *You* and *you* alone are the conspirators and destructionists!"[39]

This rhetorical strategy was hardly original. It had been most masterfully employed in this country a generation earlier in the classic American anarchist text, *Walden,* and was a favorite device of the accused and their allies well before Haymarket. It was fundamental to Lucy Parsons's embittered characterization of the rich as hypocritical robbers, to the heavy irony lacing the placards and speeches at the Thanksgiving and Board of Trade demonstrations, and to the paeans to dynamite as the dawn of peace and equilibrium. During and after the trial, however, reversal became the major line of defense and explanation of what had happened in the Haymarket and of what was happening in the courtroom and all across America. "Anarchism does not mean bloodshed; does not mean robbery, arson, etc.," Spies declared before sentencing. "These monstrosities are, on the contrary, the characteristic features of capitalism." He went on: "Anarchism means peace and tranquillity to all." "Anarchy, therefore, is liberty," Parsons proclaimed in his autobiography. "[It] is the negation of force, or compulsion, or violence. It is the precise reverse of that which those who hold and have power would have their oppressed victims believe it is." Their supporters pronounced Parsons and his codefendants the victims of "judicial" massacre, murder, and assassination. The prosecution's addresses to the jury, M. M. Trumbull charged in his post-trial analysis, were "anarchy in legal robes, vindictive and crimson as the speeches for which the defendants themselves were tried." Trumbull went on to accuse the state of inverting the truth in its whole line of argument: "Never before, except in burlesque, was the meaning of words reversed as in the Anarchist trial. Logic stood on its head, and reasoned with its heels."[40]

The enemies of the anarchists recognized the effectiveness of the rhetoric of reversal and tried both to expose it wherever possible and make use of it themselves. Impatient with protestations like Trumbull's and with the lengthy appeal process, E. L. Godkin made much of the irony of anarchists pinning their hopes on legal procedures. "The appeal of an Anarchist to the Supreme Court, or to any court," he wrote in the *Nation*, "is a grotesque mixture of opposing ideas and conceptions of the social status." Eager to maintain possession of the high moral ground and to deny it to the condemned men, their critics tried to wrest from them the mantle of martyrs and lay it on the police. Other sorts of reversals offered by champions of the current order, however, seemed unintentionally to make the anarchists' point. A drawing by A. R. Cassidy that appeared in the *Graphic News* a month after the bombing set a militant Miss Liberty on a makeshift platform in a crowded street in a scene that purposely resembled the setting of the Haymarket rally. Only now things were turned around. Her bare feet trample the dishonored flag of anarchy, and armed men near her scatter in fear as she prepares to hurl a smoking bomb labeled "LAW." The anarchists might have taken some small satisfaction at this image of the state's emblem of liberty as a bomb-thrower, and of law as the bomb.[41]

The wholesale effort by the prosecution and its supporters to stigmatize the defendants with certain labels, and the anarchists' efforts to turn the meanings of these labels around, involved a great deal more than verbal sparring. The point the anarchists were making was that the current system of domination was so complete that the most basic vocabulary of the state, not just its laws, was part of an order in which supposedly neutral forms of cultural regulation and expression were in fact summoned to the service of oppression. Language, like society it-self, needed to be cleansed and liberated to express accurately the needs of humanity and not of massed property, to speak the truth in-stead of the kinds of lies offered by the perjured "witnesses." Through all their broader arguments, the two sides became involved in a deadly serious war of words in which they hoped to establish the legitimacy of their particular social vocabulary and of the social vision behind it. Be-neath all the rhetoric was the issue of just what was the social order, what was the city, and what was the United States.

EIGHT

Words on Trial

Words like "law," "order," "conspiracy," and "anarchy" came up so often in so many ways throughout all the discussions of Haymarket that their meanings quickly blurred. Several somewhat less overworked but equally loaded terms offer clearer insight into the fundamental concerns of those who participated in the case and who followed it closely, illuminating at the same time the dynamic relationship between language, imagination, and experience in 1880s Chicago. Three such words were "foreign," "manly," and "natural." On their face, these terms (and close variations) might not appear to have a clear relation to each other or much of a bearing on this criminal trial involving murder and dynamite, but the way they were used reveals that they were all closely connected to how the accused and their accusers construed the bomb and the meaning of political identity and social action in the city. The discussion of "foreign" in regard to Haymarket centered on the question of just who were the true citizens of Chicago, the concern with the "manly" considered the nature and character of this citizenry, while references to "natural" were part of a debate over the basic principles of legitimacy and authority that should govern these people in this kind of place. Those who used these terms believed that establishing their own definition of them was of utmost importance precisely because these words were already the subject of intense but still unresolved public discussion about deciding what they meant in contemporary social life. In the complex cultural dynamics of Haymarket, the bombing became the occasion to try to fix certain meanings and so gain at least imaginative control over the conditions of the tumultuous urban present.

Foreigners All

Of the three terms, "foreign" was the one that was most often invoked and to which Haymarket seemed to have the clearest relevance. The public discussion of the bombing merged with a continuing consideration of the foreign in the United States, with particular reference to urban culture. This discussion included some of the old Jeffersonian suspicion of urbanization as a trait of European culture to be avoided, but it mainly consisted of expressions of concern that heretofore "American" cities were now being overrun by immigrants of a new and different kind. Newspaper editors, contributors to journals, and authors of novels and cultural analyses spoke of the metropolis as a place that had been so invaded by outsiders that as a social and political entity it was becoming "foreign" to the American nation.

To many of these commentators, the bomb justified contemporary anti-immigrant fears that blamed the continuing economic distress and the rising tide of labor trouble on the enormous influx of people, and, most specifically, non-English-speaking political and economic refugees from Germany and southern and eastern Europe, to American cities. The rhetorical jousting about foreignness expressed an uneasiness about what was perceived as the dangers of such a concentrated, mixed, and ever-changing society. By 1890, close to 450,000 of Chicago's nearly 1,100,000 residents would be of foreign birth, with almost 80 percent of the population either themselves born abroad or of non-"American" parentage. Even the "native" residents of the city were largely from places other than Chicago. At the time of the fire, about 30 percent of American-born Chicagoans (who made up only slightly more than half of the city's residents) were originally from Illinois, and this number rose to just under 40 percent by 1890.[1] Such figures were not unique to Chicago. As David Montgomery has pointed out, 77 percent of the population of Detroit in 1890 had at least one parent who was foreign-born (almost 60 percent of that city's manual workers were themselves immigrants from Europe). Of the 2,855,000 newcomers from Europe who arrived in America between 1880 and 1885, more than a third were from Germany and almost 850,000 were from Ireland and Scandinavia.[2]

Virtually everyone directly involved in Haymarket had come from somewhere else. Not only the eight defendants, but all twelve jurors, seven of the eight attorneys (including Black and Grinnell), and Judge Gary were born, and in most cases raised to adulthood, outside Chicago. Defense attorney Sigmund Zeisler came from Germany and Assistant State's Attorney Edmund Furthmann was from Austria, while Police Superintendent Frederick Ebersold was born in Bavaria, Captain Schaack in Luxembourg, and Inspector Bonfield in Canada (of Irish immigrants). The leading citizens who funded Schaack's witch-hunt and who vehemently opposed clemency after the conviction were also adopted sons of the city whose honor and well-being they saw themselves defending against outsiders. Marshall Field was from small-town Massachusetts and George Pullman from western New York, and both had arrived in Chicago as young men. Joseph Gary, who had lived in upstate New York, Missouri, New Mexico, and California before coming to Chicago, was thirty-five when he settled in the city. Carter Harrison, a Yale-educated Kentuckian, was thirty years old when he arrived in the town that would elect him mayor. At issue in the trial was the definition of the community that they were all making together. It is little wonder that Chicago's elite, especially those who had seen it burn down in 1871 and almost come apart in 1877, was so anxiously defensive. Hanging the anarchists seemed to deal effectively with the doubts that any man-made social disorder raises, especially in a constantly changing community of newcomers that lacked the confidence of a long history and firmly established traditions and that seemed so precarious and cataclysmic.

The attack on the anarchists as foreign took several forms, the most common and obvious reinforcing the prevalent strains of xenophobia at the time. John Higham observes that for years afterward "the memory of Haymarket and the dread of imported anarchy haunted the American consciousness."[3] This was because the prosecution and its many allies did all they could to emphasize that everything about the accused—their place of birth, the anarchism they preached, the dynamite they threw—was literally foreign. In one of the first instant histories of Haymarket, Paul Hull noted that Chicago had been for some time "the central distributing point" in the United States for European immigration, but that in the last decade this "made it peculiarly the abiding-place of the only human material from which social peace in America has anything to fear." These were refugees from European despotism who had unfairly and unfortunately turned the city into a repository for "the feverish spirit of human resentment against laws of life, of property, and of conduct which it has no hand in making or enforcing." Too many recent arrivals had too little appreciation for "the new civilization into which they have come and into which they should assimilate," and from them came "this band of ignorant villains and designing demagogues that has bred riot and bloodshed in Chicago." "The Anarchists of Chicago are exotics," the foreign-born Schaack charged, and the discontent they sowed was "a German plant" that in "our garden" was "a weed to be plucked out by the roots and destroyed, for our conditions neither warrant its growth nor excuse its existence."[4]

The prosecution and its supporters repeatedly distinguished between the "good" immigrant, who successfully adapted to American institutions and thereby found happiness within the existing order, and the unreconstructible troublemakers who imported to this country foreign notions that were perhaps justifiable in the nations of their birth but had no application to America. This was a close variation on the argument that strikes were the result of a few bad men misleading "good" workers. Hull, for example, expressed the fear that the same "desirable stream" that brought "sober, industrious, economical" immigrants also carried "the scum and dregs" (other observers called them "offscourings") of countries where despotism bred paupers and conspirators. Like so many others at the time, he urged the kind of stern and swift punishment for such malefactors that would send an unmistakable warning to any others who tried to plant the seeds of what Schaack called "alien revolt" in America. In its editorial on the jury's verdict, the *Tribune* described the decision as "tantamount to a declaration that American law is powerful enough to protect society against the conspiracies of organized foreign assasins [*sic*] and to insure the blessings of a good and free government to all classes of people." This declaration would draw the line that determined the limits of acceptable thought and action, telling anarchist sympathizers loudly and clearly to "speedily emigrate" or be silent. It was "a warning to the whole brood of vipers in the Old World" that they could not abuse American hospitality and freedom "without encountering the stern decrees of American law."[5]

As part of their effort to distinguish the good immigrant from the evil foreigner, the anarchists' accusers went beyond the charge of literal foreignness to code these eight men as alien from humanity itself. The prosecution and the press described them as beasts and infidels, unfit for decent society. "There is not one of them, gentlemen," Assistant State's Attorney Francis W. Walker assured the jury in his opening argument, "that bears upon his face the stamp of sensibility or of heart, and there can be no argument made when they talk about the motive to justify murder and the advice of murder, only from the malignant heart." They were predatory monsters who "feast over the description of how to poison easiest, as the hyena does over the corpse of the dead."[6] They were also savage Indians. Schaack described the "crazy" and "bloodthirsty" women among the anarchists as "squaws," and the secret meetings at which they incited their men as "war dances." This was an especially live metaphor at the time, since during the Haymarket trial came the news of the capture of Geronimo near the Arizona-Mexico border by troops led by Nelson Miles, now a general. Like the feared and hated Indians, Schaack implied, the anarchists were hostile

and dangerous savages who only understood force and who had no justifiable claim to American space.[7] In addition, Schaack and others depicted radicals as physically repulsive (except for those, like Spies, who
vainly and slyly used their looks to attract unwitting followers). The
point of all this vilification was to portray these people as maladjusted
freaks whose ideas were not to be taken seriously by progressive and
"normal" American society.[8]

In the most elaborate coding of the defendants as "foreign," many
different commentators went to great lengths to depict the defendants,
and most radical dissenters, as "dirty." This was obvious in Nast's and
other artists' caricatures of labor agitators. The contemporary fiction
that dealt with social unrest, no matter what its literary quality, stressed
how filthy such malcontents invariably were, and journalists often
noted with sarcasm that soap and water might well be the most potent
weapons in any would-be "class" war.[9] This fixation on dirt was critical
to the imaginative attempt to cast the radicals and their cause as foreign
and inimical to a sane and stable social order. Mary Douglas observes
that "ideas of dirt also express symbolic systems," that dirt is "matter
out of place" in the dynamic relationship between "a set of ordered relations and a contravention of that order." Douglas explains, "Dirt
then, is never a unique, isolated event. Where there is dirt there is system. Dirt is the by-product of a systematic ordering and classification
of matter, in so far as ordering involves rejecting inappropriate elements." Her point that "our pollution behaviour is the reaction which
condemns any object or idea likely to confuse or contradict cherished
classifications" offers a very persuasive explanation of the desire, after
the fire, of Chicagoans concerned about the threat of a social "other,"
so often described as unclean, to see the disaster as an act of purification. It is even more convincing in telling why "respectable" Americans
were obsessed fifteen years later with defining the radical agitator, who
sharply challenged prevailing conventions and standards of social
thought and behavior, as dirty.[10]

The defendants and their attorneys responded to these several
charges of foreignness with what amounted a comprehensive critique
of Gilded Age America. They pointed out that simply coming from
somewhere else did not prove their guilt in the case at hand, as the prosecution seemed to imply. "The charge is made that we are 'foreigners,'"
Parsons told the court, "as though it were a crime to be born in some
other country." In his summation, defense attorney William Foster,
who had only recently moved to Chicago from Iowa, reminded the jury
that justice paid no heed to nationality, advising them that the prosecution was trying "to wring from you a verdict founded on prejudice." He
noted that in any case all the defendants except Lingg had been in

America for several years. Spies advised the court that he had been a resident of Illinois as long as Grinnell, "and probably have been as good a citizen." In an "Autobiographical Sketch" prepared in jail, Spies told of his upbringing as a child of a government administrator in Germany, then added with bitter sarcasm: "I admit I ought not have made the mistake, ought not have been born a *foreigner*. Probably, I might have avoided the fatal mistake, had I prior to my entry upon the stage of life possessed the requisite power of divination. I might then have known that I was about to commit a monstrous crime—a crime, punishable by death 30 years hence in Chicago."[11]

Parsons and Spies were forwarding several interrelated ideas. First, their claim to "Americanness" and even to middle-class "respectability" was as good as anyone else's. They were idealists of good background who earned their livings as small businessmen, journalists, and skilled craftsmen.[12] Second, the sources of revolutionary disruptions like the Haymarket bombing were within the current social and economic order, not outside it. And, finally, in a very real sense this "order" was itself "foreign" to the first principles of the country. In advancing these points, they tried to turn the stigma of "foreign" against their accusers. To Adolph Fischer it was the "police-Apaches" who proved themselves to be the real savages. They "had spilled workingmen's blood" at the McCormick factory and "thirsted for more." Under "chief Geronimo Bonfield" they got their wish, committing at Haymarket—here Fischer threw in another historical atrocity—their "intended Bartholomew night." Spies, objecting to being called an "enemy of civilization," proclaimed that it was the police and prosecution who were bestial and demonic hypocrites who called themselves good Christian citizens while making this "trial" into a satanic rite: "There comes the star-spangled Mephisto, Bonfield, with his noble guards of 'Liberty;' there comes the savior of the state, Grinnell, with the visage of a Sicilian brigand, there comes the hireling juror, and there comes the vast horde of social vultures. *Unisono* is the anathema. *Unisono* is the cry—'To the gallows!'"[13]

Both sides were aware that what was of utmost importance in all this parrying was not just to characterize the other as foreign, but to make the claim that their cause and their actions represented the defining values and traditions of the "true" America and of "the people." To this end the prosecution implied that the accused's most serious offense was not murder but treason. Grinnell and his associates compared the anarchists to the assassins of Lincoln and Garfield, but more often likened their crimes to the Confederacy's rebellion against the sanctity of the Union. In his opening statement, Grinnell charged that the accused were not to be confused with responsible social critics, who, whatever their grievances against American institutions, still believed in liberty, free speech, the Declaration of Independence, and the rule of law. By contrast, these men on trial were of "a certain class" who believe that "our Constitution is a lie." He then compared the anarchists' actions unfavorably with the firing on Fort Sumter. That violent assault on the nation "was a terrible thing to our country," but at least it was "open warfare." It was "nothing" when considered against "this insidious, infamous plot to ruin our laws and our country secretly and in this cowardly way." Grinnell immediately went on, "[T]he strength of our institutions may depend upon this case, because there is only one step beyond republicanism—that is anarchy."[14] To stand firmly united against the accused was defend the country all over again.

All of this talk of foreignness and treason found a special focus for both sides in the case of Albert Parsons. The prosecution and the press reserved their harshest criticism for Parsons because he was *not* literally a foreigner. As he proudly pointed out, Parsons was, if anything, more "American" than his accusers, since his forebears had arrived in 1632.[15] To those eager to condemn him, Parsons's pedigree made his treachery so much the worse. Some suggested that he was a posturing fake who was only trying to draw attention to himself. Reporting the execution, the *New York Times* wrote, "The stolidity of the German criminals, though in their demeanor also there was something theatrical, was much less repulsive than the posing of PARSONS, and it marked them as much more dangerous and implacable conspirators than the vain, loose-tongued American." But to others Parsons was more dangerous since he seemed to demonstrate that a thoughtful American might have some reason to adopt anarchist ideas, which was an unacceptable notion. Attorney William Black commented ironically in his closing statement that, to Parson's accusers, "It was a horrible thing that an American should sympathize with the common people; that he should feel his heart respond to the desires of oppressed workmen." The only "acceptable" explanation was that Parsons was an aberration who represented no large body of opinion in America, since no "real" American could become an anarchist.[16]

The accused responded to their being associated with rebellion and treachery by condemning "the un-American utterances of the capitalist press" and by calling exploitative employers "slaveholders." Spies began his autobiography by noting the absurdity of such antidemocratic figures as "Merchant Princes, Railroad Kings, . . . Factory Lords," and their agents branding individuals like him as barbarians and savages who had no respect for "free American institutions." It was the anarchists' enemies who were "foreign" to the real America. He and the others tried as best they could to demonstrate how they were anything but alien to America and its best interests. They, not the authorities, embodied the hallowed ideas which their accusers espoused but did not believe. They repeatedly noted the fidelity of their own precepts to those of the Founding Fathers, all of whom, they declared, would have been hanged in Judge Gary's court. They claimed special kinship above all with the ideas expressed in the Declaration of Independence, which they interpreted as a virtual anarchist manifesto. The *Alarm* never tired of citing this document's defense of rebellion against oppression and Jefferson's justifications for throwing off despotism: "Our forefathers have not only told us that against despots force is justifiable, because it is the only means, but they themselves have set the immemorial example."[17]

Of all the "American" precedents for their ideas and actions that the anarchists claimed, the most potent and controversial was the example of John Brown. In his closing statement, William Black declared, "John Brown and his attack on Harper's [*sic*] Ferry may be compared to the Socialists' attack on modern evils." Brown, he and others argued, justifiably committed acts of violence in the name of republican principles and was martyred for refusing to accommodate those who would compromise American values. Black recalled for the court that many of the staunchest and most respectable champions of the union had rightly defended Brown's actions. Leonard Swett, who assisted Black in appealing the Haymarket case to the Illinois Supreme Court, gave the Brown parallel another twist in trying to refute the conspiracy argument. He reminded Chief Justice John M. Scott that both of them had once supported Brown's cause, and then asked, "Are [we] now liable to arrest, prosecution and conviction, as aiders and abetters of John Brown's offense? If we are not, the law laid down in this case is wrong, and the reason we are not, is because [we] were guilty of no criminal agency in connection with him."[18] The implication of the Brown parallel was that the same kind of courageous action that had been applauded a generation earlier by people of conscience and character was now a capital offense in Chicago, and that the only explanation for this was that the country had somehow changed and had become unmoored from its principles. Was America, particularly the version of urban America of those who backed the prosecution, "foreign" to its own cherished self-conceptions? Was Samuel Fielden possibly right when he warned, "*The nineteenth century commits the crime of killing its best friend. It will live to repent it*"?[19] The so-called "foreigners" awaiting execution were America's best hope for redemption since they faithfully believed in its ideas.

At the trial, defendant George Engel told of his joy at his arrival in

Philadelphia in 1873, having left Germany with his family for "the land of liberty." He was determined to be the kind of "good" immigrant his accusers wanted all newcomers to be. After facing the possibility of starvation in "this 'free republic,'" however, he asked himself what were the sources of this misery. "I then began to give our political institutions more attention than formerly," he explained. "My discoveries brought to me the knowledge that the same societary evils exist here that exist in Germany."[20] But to most Americans, the distortion of justice was preferable to an open acknowledgment that the social order was the source of the bomb. Attorney Black reminded the jury that it was local conditions, not European socialism, that exploded in the Haymarket. More important than convicting these eight men, or perhaps *the* point of convicting them, was to prove that he was wrong.

Real Men

Even as they were said to betray cherished American political values and institutions, the Haymarket defendants were accused of a crime more horrible still—they were traitors to the ideal of manhood. As in so many other instances, the anarchists threw their accusers' charges back at them. No matter who was speaking, the argument was the same, and it presented another way to divide society into the admirable "we" and the unconscionable "they": we are men; they, who are not men, have threatened our manhood (more precisely, "manhood" as we define it); it is time to be stern and sure, to prove our manhood by standing up to them, with force if necessary; when we stand up to them, they will back down, further proving that we are real men and they are not. Depending on the situation, "man" was opposed to any of many terms that were more or less interchangeable. These included coward, thief, hypocrite, woman, boy, bully, beast, and several others, all of which implied a person who lacked honorable "manly" qualities. It was important to establish that one's enemy was unmanly, since by doing so one could discredit not only him but all that he stood for.

Chicagoans, and many others, had discussed the fire of 1871 as a reprise of the Civil War. With their homes and businesses threatened by this ruthless invader, the manly held their ground, literally under fire, and rescued their city. In 1877 civic leaders had said that it was time to confront these "roughs" whose only courage came from being part of a mob. But the invocation of manhood at Haymarket was at the same time broader and more focused. At this point in American experience, manhood had become part of the cultural vocabulary in which almost any issue was discussed. Of greater direct importance was that the changes most fully experienced and represented in cities like Chicago through the troubled 1880s seemed to jeopardize the values associated with the idea of "manly."

What did "manly" mean at the time of Haymarket, particularly when invoked in public rhetoric? It implied that one possessed certain abstract qualities such as courage, bravery, and power, often demonstrated through the domination of—and the refusal to be dominated by—women and weaker men. But a man was also someone who had certain rights, privileges, and obligations, above all the freedom and responsibility to manage his own life and take care of those who depended on him. He was a self-reliant citizen who was responsible for his own success or failure in the effort to prove himself capable and his life significant. The intensity of the discussion of the manly indicated how many people sensed that manhood was under siege in urban industrial America in the late nineteenth century. Labor leaders spoke out on how large-scale industrialization had made the individual worker helpless and dependent, while middle-class Americans who worked in offices or who owned their own businesses were concerned that large corporations and swings of the economy placed their status in constant jeopardy. Although different groups disagreed with each other on just what were the sources of this instability and what should be done about it, they all believed that a person who did not control his life was not a man.[21]

The anarchists contended, as did less radical spokesmen for labor, that the capitalist elite, aided by new manufacturing technology and supported by the law and "legal" government ("the coward's weapon"), had institutionalized the wage and class system. Far from being free and open, as Schaack had described it, this system deprived the worker of his sense of worth as both a public and private man. The massing and the mechanization of industry devalued the worker's craft, destroying his individual bargaining power and, with it, his mastery of his own life as an economic, political, and social being. This in turn jeopardized his ability to fulfill his traditional role as husband and father by diminishing his earning power, undermining his sense of independence, and breaking his pride. All the strike activity, demonstrations, and the Haymarket bomb defended the worker's manhood from this assault. As for his right to vote, this was meaningless as a form of effective social action and political change. "The ballot can be wielded by free men alone," the *Alarm* proclaimed in February 1885, "but *slaves* can only revolt and rise in insurrection against their despoilers." A few months later, an author identified as "Cato" concluded, "It is time for laborers to stop groveling at the feet of their capitalistic master, and to assume an independent manly position, to assert their rights and to prepare to take them."[22]

The anarchists' appeals to male pride appeared in the most powerful passages of their calls to action. Spies's notorious "Workingmen, to Arms" broadside, written in passionate haste after he witnessed the McCormick riot on May 3, likened workers to blacks in the South, who for years had endured "humiliations," including the surrender of their children to the "factory-lords." Spies compared those workers brave enough to go on strike to the bold slaves who defied the bondsman by making their escape toward freedom and full possession of their male identity. The workers' "crime" was that they had showed "the courage to disobey the supreme will of [their] bosses," i.e., to act as men. And now, in response, the capitalist "masters" had "sent out their bloodhounds—the police" to the McCormick plant. The brief final paragraph of the broadside described the need for action not just in terms of liberation, but also in relation to male acts of procreation and valor, with allusions to sources ranging from Greek mythology to nineteenth-century European political revolution and the American Civil War: "If you are men, if you are the sons of your grand sires, who have shed their blood to free you, then you will rise in your might, Hercules, and destroy the hideous monster that seeks to destroy you. To arms we call you, to arms!" The original version of the circular prepared the next morning summoning workingmen to Haymarket ended with the line written by Adolph Fischer: "Workingmen Arm Yourselves and Appear in Full Force!" At Spies's insistence this imperative was removed and the edited text was distributed, but a few copies of the original version somehow got into circulation and were later used as evidence against the defendants. In court, defense counsel William Foster called the revised version "the emasculated circular."[23]

While the anarchists rallied workers to reclaim their manhood from their bosses, the prosecution and its partisans saw themselves as embodying the highest forms of the manly as they confronted the forces of disorder. In praising the police as brave heroes and martyrs, George McLean stated that "an era so active in thought and impulse is always perilous to the nation," requiring "strong men, wise and calm in the midst of her greatest storms." The nation had to reestablish the standard of male honor set when the country was newly founded and populated by "manly forms, marked by intellectual dignity, and bearing in their countenance the unmistakable insignia of true and noble manhood."[24] To make his point, McLean implicitly—and perhaps unintentionally—questioned the popular ideology of progress upon which the current strife cast doubt. His remarks hinted that, regardless of the anarchists, the state of contemporary urban manhood marked a decline from an earlier standard when men were men. His purpose was not to cast doubt, however, but to portray Haymarket as a moment of crisis that had reinvigorated the best qualities of the urban community by creating a field of action for "true and noble" men.

In the eyes of those who shared McLean's view, the anarchists were unmanly. The literature of the fire had expressed horror at the venality of cowardly members of the population who were suddenly free to work their will on the Sands because the real men whose presence usually held them in check were busy trying to save the city, which was imagined as an innocent woman in need of manly protection. In the same vein, the unsubstantiated elements of anti-anarchist Haymarket narratives emphasized how brave and fearless the police, prosecution, and jury were in the face of these violent terrorists, and how timid the anarchists became as soon as there was genuine danger in the air. The first newspaper stories of the bombing contended that the "wind-bag orators who had harangued the fire-eaters earlier in the evening were not the leaders after business began, but they slunk away and were out of danger." Later on, the best evidence of the accused's lack of manly courage when confronted was in their frightened faces as they awaited the decision of the jury. During the trial a letter to the *Tribune* complained about how these "brutes," "poisonous reptiles," and "fiends" had spent their time in court "[l]aughing, jesting, cursing, flirting" while "their satanic deeds were disclosed." Now, "the braggarts who a few short weeks before were boldly proclaiming the doctrines of Socialism and Anarchy" were "pale and trembling wretches. . . . Bold and fearless as lions they appeared when indulging in flights of incendiary oratory. Like dumb, obedient beasts they bowed in submission before the most powerful scourge the law can wield—the death verdict."[25]

The prosecution, press, and police maintained that the cowardice of the anarchists marked their whole way of life, not just their actions, at Haymarket and after. Far from being motivated by their desire to protect and provide for their families, they had long since abandoned such manly obligations. Schaack wrote at length of a man named Otto Baum, who rarely worked and was "one of the desperate Anarchists who made the air blue with imprecations against capital." Baum's behavior was not exceptional but "a type of a very large class of Anarchists," who "would call the better class of people tyrants, because they did not fill his pockets with plenty of money so that he could get drunk as often as he desired, but in his own household he was the meanest of tyrants." According to Schaack, Baum went into hiding following the bombing, and only after the trial "crawled out of his hole, like a coon does in the spring-time." But Baum's worst fault lay not in what he did,

but what he failed to do: "He never troubled himself about wife or children, but hung around saloons guzzling beer and breathing vengeance
against the police and society." His neglect of his husbandly duty
forced his wife back to work a week after giving birth to their youngest
child, and he rewarded her "uncomplaining toil" with "abuse and cru-
elty." Only the humane intervention of the authorities against whom
Baum railed rescued her from this domestic tyranny. Having given up
hope that the Haymarket verdict might reform him, she supposedly
went to the Chicago Avenue Police Court with her infant in her arms to
swear out a warrant for his arrest, which led to a fine and a jail term.[26]
The moral of the story was plain: there was no need to deal with the
anarchists on the level of ideas, which were merely a feeble justification
for their antisocial and unmanly behavior. They were irresponsible, errant children, pathetic souls made dangerous by their inclination toward mischief and error, their access to explosives, and the complex
social order of the city.

The anxieties about manhood that were connected to Haymarket
figured most sensationally in the fixation of both accused and accusers
on heroic violence and sexual violation. The former was most obvious
in the bomb-talking on one side and the cries for swift and severe punishment on the other. Each discourse reflected a desire to correct the
problem of urban disorder with a dramatic display of power. To the anarchists, revolutionary violence would miraculously explode and reconstruct the flawed social order. To the prosecution and the public,
the noose would reestablish that order. In both cases, to commit such
acts was an almost irresistible way to assert that "we" had not abandoned control of our lives to "them," that our willingness, with whatever eagerness or reluctance, to take extreme measures was a sign of
our refusal to be ruled by others.

The language of sexual violation that entered the discussion of the
meaning of Haymarket was also used to characterize as unmanly what
"they" had done, or tried to do, to "us," and thus discredit one set of
ideas and interests while legitimizing another. Describing social disorder in terms of the honorable and dishonorable exercise of male sexual
power, as in most instances where social or political issues are sexually
coded, was calculated to arouse strong emotions. No matter who was
doing the talking, the real subject was the threat of class difference in
the city. Here again, the most vivid Chicago precedent for this kind of
sensational fear-mongering was the scene on the Sands featured in the
fire literature, when all that was good and pure in the urban community, under attack from those ruled by greed, envy, and lust, was saved
by manly action.

In the period just preceding Haymarket, it was the anarchists who more frequently resorted to the imagery of sexual violation to describe social relations in the city. In several instances their use of this language was elaborate and explicitly dramatic. In March of 1883, the *Fackel,* the German-language Sunday edition of the *Arbeiter-Zeitung,* reported on the plans for the Commune Celebration, which had come to be a major occasion for German workers in Chicago. The culminating event of the evening was to be the presentation of *The Proletarian's Daughter,* "a play about life today" written by W. L. Rosenberg, whose drama of the year before, *The Nihilists,* featured performances by Spies, Schwab, and Neebe. The summary of the plot indicated that the play was a timely reworking of an old story: "The play starts out in a factory town where a strike has just broken out. The heroine of the play is Maria, a proletarian child with strong moral principles, who gives herself in love to the son of the factory owner, Bensdorf, only to be deceived by him." The reporter assured readers that "we're not dealing with any of those caricatures of workers which all too often mar the stage, but rather with men who have understood their class situation."[27] Thus, even though the play was ostensibly about a woman, its purpose was to help males in the audience reach this understanding about their situation as men. Maria's reaction to her discovery of the "base character" of her former lover is an act of retributive violence—she shoots him down. Unexpectedly, the jury acquits her. It is ironic in the scope of hindsight that includes the Haymarket trial that the play, which is set in Germany, ends with Maria emigrating to freedom and fulfillment in America.

The pages of the *Alarm* carried similar "real-life" stories with much unhappier outcomes, including an account published late in 1884 of the appalling experience of a teenage working girl named Martha Seidel, who was allegedly taken to the Chicago Avenue Police Station on the charge of petty theft. Seidel soon found herself closeted with "one Patten," the official in charge, "and there, during the long moaning night, endured all that a mountain of bestial flesh, insane with lust, restrained by no fear, secure of immunity, could inflict upon her shuddering helplessness." When he had taken his pleasure, Patten then ordered her held on an outrageous bail. The horror of the situation mocked the idea that Chicago was a moral and humane community:

> Help there was none in this great christian city, and the virgin violated in the sanctuary of law, semi-conscious, half-dead, memory a blank from that fatal Tuesday night, was duly receipted for at the county jail, there to wait until it was the grand jury's pleasure to throw her into the local hopper, and after that the state's attorney is to let the upper and nether millstones of law do the work.
>
> In the jail the abuse she had burdened became known. In its lifeless, superheated air her bruised and mangled body lost power of resistance,

and succumbed to the effects of the shock it had sustained. Swollen and inflamed her organs refused their natural functions. She passed from convulsion to convulsion incessant, continuous, as her sickened soul sought to escape from its dishonored treatment. The attending physicians. [*sic*] in alarm sent with all speed for Dr. Dluthard their chief [probably Theodore J. Bluthardt, who held the post of county physician]. His examination revealed the fact that a horrible outrage had been committed; that its commital was recent; that the girl, before it, was virgin. By the free administration of opiates, the black horror with which her memory was shrouded [*sic*] from her consciousness, and in the oblivion of a litherel [*sic*] sleep the recupuating [*sic*] forces of nature successfully struggled for her life, and so she yet lives, this flower of womanhood, if it can be called life, to lie in the jail hole on a rude cot, and vaguely brood over the dim consciousness of an incredible, unspeakable wrong.[28]

This narrative, along with *The Proletarian's Daughter,* vividly expressed its author's understanding of the "realities" of a much larger set of circumstances. The account represented the whole working class through the body of Martha Seidel, whom this cannibalistic "christian" city treated as yet another piece of raw material for the factory system that was supported by the law. Between the jail, the grand jury, and the state's attorney, she was, like the worker, ground through the "mill-stones," "bruised" and "mangled" in "lifeless, superheated" conditions and turned into an object that could be "duly receipted" and thrown in a "hopper." Any semblance of her selfhood was obliterated, she lost all power of resistance, and her "dishonored" body collapsed. Meanwhile, the supposed helping agents of the state were brought in not to offer sympathy and care but to drug this poor working girl into insensibility, dulling her memory while doing nothing to relieve the abiding pain and horror that were the chronic condition of the worker.

In the pages of the *Alarm,* private capital was "the Social Moloch" that "grows with what it feeds upon," while Cyrus McCormick, Jr., was "the very picture of human depravity and viciousness, only common to people who have exhausted their vitality and manhood by unbounded licentiousness." The issue published a month before Haymarket melodramatically described the worker as "the victim of the rapacity of some unscrupulous knave" who employed him, and angrily depicted the relationship between the factory owner and employee explicitly in terms of scheming seduction and cowardly sexual violation that demonstrated the impotence of the worker:

Though your daughter fall a prey to the lechery of her capitalistic master, or his precious son; though she be ruined and led into haunts of vice and crime by false promises and glittering allurements; though she die as a common strumpet in the lowest slums, while her betrayer con-

tinues to plume himself on his conquests and irristible [*sic*] fascination—
still be patient. Be forgiving. Abide by the law. Comfort yourself with the
reflection that it is a common thing after all, and why should you kick up a
row about it. Do not resort to violence. Be reasonable, poor fool; do you
not know that this is simply one of the privileges of the rich and
powerful?[29]

Only through vengeful violence would labor resurrect its manhood and
save itself against the brutal voluptuary of capital that had no regard for
human decencies and the sacred ties of society. In contrast, the anarchists tried to demonstrate their principled self-discipline. While the
popular press portrayed the anarchists as destructive, antisocial cowards who had abandoned the responsibilities of manhood, the Haymarket defendants countered that it was specifically in defense of
family that they adopted the cause in the first place. Even the hostile
press marveled at the touching domestic scenes in the courtroom and
jail, where the children of the accused came to visit and sat in their laps
as the proceedings unfolded.[30]

For its part, the prosecution used the language of sexual violation to
describe the defendants as immoral evildoers who contaminated innocent and unsuspecting workers. They claimed that the real purpose of
Parsons and Spies was to lead honest laborers down the road to destruction and damnation, away from the upright family of man in
which they could live happy and fulfilling lives. The prosecutors called
those who followed the indicted anarchists weak and ignorant dupes,
whose honor (and opportunity to live a respectable and fulfilling life
within society) could be protected only by responsible citizens like the
father-employer. Nor were workers the only ones threatened by anarchist despoilers; everyone was vulnerable, for the future of society was
as dependent on virtuous labor as it was on pure womanhood. This seduction imagery not only feminized the worker, it also vaunted the
manhood of the paternalistic elite who guarded the entire city, so often
pictured as a virgin, against these cowardly rapists and seducers.[31]

In one of the many questionable aspects of his conduct of the trial,
Judge Gary tried to emphasize the manliness of his own exercise of authority by inviting female friends and acquaintances to sit beside him at
the bench, which he had festooned with flowers. Early in the trial, one
paper reported that, "as has been the case all the week, Judge Gary has
been banked by a parterre of feminine flowers. His whole platform, his
desk, his chair, his footrest, his chambers have either been set with
flowers or filled with women."[32] Gary was eager to have pretty and respectable ladies near him so that they could watch and even amuse each
other and distract him as he managed the whole spectacle of defending
the virtue and honor of the community against those who would de-

spoil it and bring it to ruin for no other reason than to satisfy their own base and destructive desires. Gary's "feminine flowers" symbolized what was being protected and the audience to which the whole drama was played, like the noble maidens in tales of chivalry who look on anxiously as their honor and happiness hangs in the balance of the battle between good and evil combatants.

In the unsettled period just before Haymarket, some the most ephemeral literature employed the language of manhood to express elite fears and hopes about urban disorder. In the issue of May 1, 1886, the *Chicago Tribune* reprinted a "seasonable tale" from the *St. Louis Globe-Democrat* titled "The Knight and the Lady: A Romance of the Strike," which read like a counter-variation on *The Proletarian's Daughter*. The title was a play on words, for the hero of this piece of short fiction is both a member of the Knights of Labor and a brave man of principle who wins the damsel and the day. Engineer Donald Chapman is the noble Knight who is in love with Marian Poole, daughter of Colonel Poole, the general manager of a railroad against which Donald and his fellow Knights are striking. While some unionists argue that it is time to resort to violence, Chapman disagrees, and he convinces the membership of the need for patience and order, except for a few incorrigibles who plan an attack on Colonel Poole that Donald foils.

The Knights expel these errant members, who are not prosecuted by the law. Poole then explains his position: he will listen to complaints and try to correct injustices, but all he wants is to be allowed to run his railroad as he pleases without hurting anyone or permitting himself to be obstructed, and any worker who does not like it can simply quit. "All this was so simply reasonable that public sentiment was won to his side," and soon the railroad is able to resume operations. According to the work schedule, Donald is the engineer who should drive the first locomotive, but better things are in store for this modern knight. When the train pulls out, he is aboard, but he "occupied instead a position on the rear platform of the sleeper; and beside him stood Col. Poole's daughter, with that crowning radiance in her face which a woman achieves only through the joy of a wedding journey."[33]

It does not take a great deal of ingenuity to understand the messages in this little tale. Donald is an upright Anglo-Saxon of middle-class bearing, a representative of labor at its idealized best. The impasse with Colonel Poole was the result not of economic exploitation and social imbalance, but of a failure to communicate. Once workers and the public realized that capital desires free enterprise that allows competent and responsible workers to sell their skills as they please (like individual entrepreneurs with a product to market), the whole misunderstanding happily collapsed. There is no hint that "pooled" capital has, or even desires, any advantage. If the worker will only open his eyes, he will see that the system nurtures not continued violation of the worker but the utopian possibility of the marriage of labor and management that will be blissfully consummated as they are both carried along by the engines of progress. They can be partners in a fruitful union in which terms like employer and employee are forgotten.

The massive denial and repression of obviously contradictory evidence was the most striking feature of this little story. On the front pages of the same issue of the *Tribune* in which "The Knight and the Lady" appeared, alarmist reports on labor demonstrations filled the columns. The future did not promise anything like a social order modeled on the harmony of classes found by Donald Chapman and Marian Poole in their honeymoon sleeper. Once the urban bomb exploded, Grinnell, Gary, and their twelve carefully selected jurors would reject such wishful thinking and take the path that almost every editorial writer and political commentator in the country directed. They would assert the power that was properly theirs, defend their country against this rebellion, and see to it that such unmanly conspirators would never get the city in their clutches.

The fact that people viewed Haymarket in this way helps explain why there was such a strong public reaction to the bizarre and fascinating death-row courtship of August Spies and Nina Van Zandt, the twenty-four-year-old daughter of a Chicago businessman. One of the fashionable young women who attended the trial, Van Zandt stood for all that Gary was trying to defend against the anarchists. During the course of the proceedings, however, she supposedly became convinced of the innocence of the accused, and she certainly became infatuated with Spies. She visited him in prison, and soon she was working with him on his autobiography. The two evidently decided to wed when Cook County Sheriff Canute Matson sharply restricted visits by those not related to the condemned men. They were married by proxy in late January 1887. Such an unlikely and shocking love story was bound to draw the fervid attention of the press, but the opprobrium the couple endured was extraordinary. That Spies was an attractive man who looked like a member of the comfortably-situated middle class ("In general appearance," a reporter wrote, "he would pass for a well-paid dry goods clerk or floor-walker") made his romantic conquest of a woman like Van Zandt perhaps more explicable but also more disconcerting.[34] Like Parsons's indisputably "American" lineage, Spies's handsome figure indicated that not all anarchists were "dirty" and disreputable-looking, and that there was no way to tell them from anyone else on the city streets. Even worse, if an anarchist might look like a "respectable" person and might even steal the heart and mind of a woman of quality, maybe a "respectable" person could be an anarchist.[35]

The press pictured the marriage as another instance of Spies's conceit and self-indulgence, proof that even behind bars he was a threat to society. The couple's attempts to wed despite the efforts of the sheriff and the advice of Spies's attorneys became a sideshow to the central drama of the anarchists' trial, and manhood was its major theme. One letter published in the *Daily News* commended Matson for his "manly stand," while another in the *Tribune* said the marriage exposed Spies as "a coward who wants to place an innocent woman between himself and a well-deserved fate." He was a heartless rake, "an unscrupulous libertine who hopes, under a sickly sentimental construction and administration of the law, to get satisfaction for his animal lust by sacrificing a young woman who seems to have as little understanding of the true essence of marriage as her intended husband, who has never expressed and acknowledged any respect for that institution upon which our entire system of society is founded." The *Tribune* called the affair "a shocking display of cowardice on the one hand and personal weakness on the other." Miss Van Zandt was romantically morbid and unaware of the consequences of her actions, "[b]ut for August Spies there can be but one sentiment among those who lay claim to a spark of manhood. The part he is playing is that of the craven."[36]

In her preface to the autobiography she helped Spies prepare and publish, Van Zandt tried to explain her actions, revealing that her parents supported her. Like Spies and his fellow defendants, she made much of the hypocrisy of those critics who were trying to "protect" her: "Had I committed every crime denominated in our criminal code, these 'chivalrous, gallant American gentlemen' could not have villified [*sic*] and denounced me more than they did." She maintained that had she been "'some obscure, foreign girl,'" no one would have cared, and if she had married an "old, invalid debauché, with great riches," the same "'moral' gentlemen" "would have lauded me to the skies." She placed at the beginning of the volume a portrait of herself as the embodiment of female virtue. Elegant and appealing in a gown that bares her shoulders, she gazes upward, looking very much like depictions of the vigilant maiden of liberty.[37]

As the date of the hangings approached, the prisoners and their defenders kept pointing to the trial as the best proof that the supposedly benevolent and responsible authorities were destroying the very values of family and civic virtue they claimed to defend, while the convicted anarchists were moral and restrained, prepared to die like men rather than forsake their principles. Albert Parsons wrote a letter to his children two days before his execution, with instructions that it be read every year on the anniversary of his death. In this farewell he spoke proudly of his manly courage, deeming himself "*a self-offered Sacrifice upon the Altar of Liberty and Happiness.*" He continued, "To you I leave the legacy of an honest name and duty done." According to Lizzie Holmes, when Parsons's wife and children tried to see him one last time on the morning of the execution, they were not only prevented from doing so but were themselves physically humiliated in yet one more abuse of power that revealed their enemies to be unmanly. Lucy Parsons desperately pleaded to no avail with the police guarding the prison to let them in. Instead, "sweet little Lulu," "manly little Albert," along with Holmes and Lucy herself, were hauled off to Captain Schaack's Chicago Avenue station where they were all "stripped to the skin and searched" (albeit by a police matron). "And thus it was," wrote Holmes, "that while organized authority was judicially murdering the husband and strangling 'the voice of the people,' the wife and children were locked up in a dungeon, that no unpleasant scene might mar the smoothness of the proceedings."[38]

Natural and Unnatural

The Haymarket debates over who was "foreign" and who "manly" were part of a more profound battle for possession of the meaning of the word "natural." The first two terms were most often used to refer to particular individuals. The concept of "natural" was employed by parties on both sides, as it usually is when it enters political discussion, to maintain that their social philosophy was in harmony with the higher laws of the creation. At the same time, they characterized their enemies' ideas, and actions based on these ideas, both as unnatural and as the source of the current social disorders.

The state's "natural" argument against the accused was straightforward. The anarchists and their kind were dangerous misfits who were trying to pervert the natural social order that prevailed in America.[39] At the trial, Judge Gary, who took it as an article of faith that the existing framework of social and economic relations was based in reason, justice, and "common sense," refused to disqualify prejudiced potential jurors for cause, since it was normal and healthy, as well as "natural," for them to be hostile to the defendants. It was also only natural that any government worthy of the name would act to protect itself by convicting and hanging the anarchists. After all, these social radicals were the source of such "unnatural" cataclysmic events as the strikes of 1877 and the Haymarket bombing that turned society, in the words of Governor Oglesby and others, into a volcano. In the sermon in which he called those responsible for the bomb "out-and-out destructionists," the Reverend Frederick Noble warned that they meant "to sweep through modern society with the disastrous fury of a cyclone," annihilating "everything which lies at the basis of civilization as it exists in the most advanced nations of the earth to-day."[40]

The anarchists meanwhile hammered away at this civilization as being anything but settled and natural. The agents of the state opposed "the natural course of things" and thus were the truly dangerous and destructive revolutionists. The authorities oppressed the individual and caused him to compete in a society based on unnatural force. But science and progress had produced dynamite as the restorer of equilibrium, and the coming collapse of the state would be the natural result of this unnatural repression, to be followed by the natural peace of anarchy, which was the only true order. In an editorial from the spring of 1885 titled "What We Want," the *Alarm* developed these points at some length, claiming that anarchy, not the current order, rested on a "scientific and common sense basis," rather than on the "foolish and insane principle" of private property. The abolition of statute law and its makers would allow "the laws of nature to have full sway." This in turn would result in "a free system, with science for its guide and necessity for its impelling force." With everyone "freely producing and freely consuming," all would have what they reasonably needed, with many other beneficial results, including the end of poverty and ignorance, and permanent peace and plenty.[41]

On the same occasion in which he called statute law the "coward's weapon," Parsons continued, "Man's legal rights are everywhere in collision with man's natural rights; hence the deep-rooted and widespread unrest of modern civilization." This was the most direct and explicit of many statements that contended that current disorders revealed the fundamental flaws of the current order, which was unnatural and disorderly. In his death-row autobiography, Parsons declared through his own version of millennial Marxism that when labor became liberated the state would "of necessity" fall away and a beneficent anarchist order would arise. "[N]atural leaders" would "take the place of the overthrown rulers" and "liberty" would succeed "statute laws." This was no visionary dream to Parsons, since he was convinced that "the crisis" that would precipitate revolution was "near at hand." "Necessity," which was itself an all-powerful law of nature, would force the issue, pushing away the unnatural barriers of statute law and government. "Then whatever is most natural to do will be the easiest and best to do. The workshops will drop into the hands of the workers, the mines will fall to the miners and the land and all other things will be controlled by those who possess and use them."[42]

Where the defenders of the status quo described nature as essentially placid or even static, the anarchists perceived the natural world as one of constant change and potentially violent upheaval, especially if anyone tried to go against nature by "ordering" it. They embraced the identification of themselves with tumultuous natural force, since this made it possible for them to see their cause as the extraordinarily powerful corrective to instabilities of the kind the system tried to enforce. Spies, who was the most eloquent of the defendants in the use of images of natural disaster to describe social conditions, told the court before sentencing that the change he preached was irrepressible and unavoidable precisely because it was natural. "Revolutions are no more made than earthquakes and cyclones," he declared. "Revolutions are the effect of certain causes and conditions." Blame lay with the "ruling class" for its belief that it could "dictate a stand-still to eternal forces." After addressing his enemies as the real conspirators and revolutionists, he continued his indictment, "You, in your blindness, think you can stop the tidal wave of civilization and human emancipation by placing a few policemen, a few gatling guns, and some regiments of militia on the shore—you think that you can frighten the rising waves back into the unfathomable depths, whence they have arisen, by erecting a few gallows in the perspective."[43]

Spies directly connected the social unrest of the day to the natural disaster which had devastated Chicago fifteen years earlier. There was far less hope now of preventing a social holocaust by hanging the accused than there had been for stopping the literal conflagration that had devastated the physical city. The holocaust of which he spoke was a primordial force: "Here you will tread upon a spark, but there, and there, and behind you and in front of you, and everywhere, flames will blaze up. It is a subterranean fire. You cannot put it out. The ground is on fire upon which you stand."[44] Spies's point was that the greatest danger to the community was indeed from within, since its worst firetraps and fault lines were social. In his eyes Haymarket furnished evidence for one of the paradoxical lessons of complex social organizations: disorder cannot be excluded or prevented because it is part of the system itself, and the effort to contain disruptions may well have the opposite effect. A post-fire Chicago might try to pass stricter building codes, but it could not fireproof against radicalism, a natural fact revealed by the bomb's terrible light.

Drama without End

Try as the prosecution, the press, and the public might to brand the defendants, their ideas, and their methods as foreign, cowardly, and unnatural, they agreed with the anarchists' view that the Haymarket bomb was a sign that something was deeply and unnaturally wrong with American society. They were prepared to hang these men in order to deny that this was so, but their almost desperate impatience and the resulting miscarriage of justice in which they all participated only indicated the depth of their fears. Trying to confront the defendants with the hard reality that the law would act to defend itself, they offered proof of the defendants' view of urban industrial society as a ticking bomb.

Some openly said as much. Two days after the executions, the Reverend H. W. Thomas delivered a sermon in McVicker's Theater in which he stated that no event since the Civil War had "produced such profound and long-continued interest and excitement as have been felt over the Haymarket tragedy in this city." May 4, 1886, and November 11, 1887, the dates of the bombing and of the hangings, were "historic days in the life of our city," he reflected, not because of the "terrible deaths" with which they were now associated, but because "they occurred in free America and in a time of peace." The events of Haymarket were significant also because "they were not the results of immediate passions" or "the deeds of common murderers or highway robbers . . . but the studied and organized resistance of otherwise temperate and industrious men to the laws of the State and of the country; and an effort by intimidation and violence to redress certain supposed or real wrongs." The "apprehensive concern" surrounding Haymarket was based in "the feeling and the fact that it is one phase, and the worst phase, of a widespread discontent upon the part of millions of the poorer people of this and other countries."[45] Even those who refused to accept the anarchists' definitions of such key terms as "liberty" and "order," as well as of "foreign," "manly," and "natural," sensed that Haymarket detached all these terms from stable meanings. If it required such an assertion of the power of the state to demonstrate that these terms meant what the prosecution, speaking in behalf of the public, said they did, perhaps the real lesson was that such definitions had no stable and inherent truth or reality behind them and instead rested only on the ability of one group in society to enforce a meaning and thus unnaturally create the conditions of urban society.

Given the tension surrounding the executions and all the significance so many people loaded on them, the actual carrying out of the death sentence may have seemed disappointing. If so, those who had most zealously demanded the rope did not admit it. Their immediate response was to declare that the hangings had in fact done what they were supposed to accomplish. John Bonfield's brother James, a police detective who had arrested Spies and Schwab after the bombing, predicted that there would not be another red flag in Chicago for fifty years. Captain Schaack bragged that "there will be a big crowd of Anarchists on their way back to Europe in the coming few weeks," though in his eagerness to drum up support to continue his witch-hunt, he dismissed the idea that the trial had closed the book on the repression of radical dissent in the city. "I tell you," he told the *Daily News*, "the anarchist business in Chicago has only commenced, and before it is through with we will have them all in jail, hung, or driven out of the city." In his memoirs, Lyman Abbott called Haymarket a "tragic" event that had still "served a useful purpose" in that it "put an end to the International in America and awakened the complacent and self-satisfied nation to the existing perils."[46] The reaction of many who had opposed the sentence, if not the guilty verdict, was pessimism about what the executions boded for Chicago and the nation. Among those most deeply discouraged were many individuals who had worked for clemency but who were as repelled by the anarchists' politics and histrionics as they were by the irregularities of the trial. Joseph Gruenhut, a socialist who served in Mayor Harrison's administration, regretted that the Haymarket bomb "not only killed the eight-hour movement, but forced us to espouse the cause of men who have been and some of whom still are our most bitter enemies.[47]

Almost immediately champions of the police and of the anarchists claimed a ceremonial space and a time of their own from which to proclaim their version of what had happened. The supporters of the hangings held their ceremonies near the site of the bombing, where in May of 1889 the son of Mathias Degan unveiled a heroic statue of a Chicago policeman with his hand raised commanding peace. Paid for by grateful Chicago businessmen, the statue was dedicated in the city's name "to her defenders in the riot." The friends of the anarchists would remember their cause in November, on the anniversary of their deaths. They would usually gather around the graves at Waldheim, where on June 25, 1893, Albert Parsons, Jr., unveiled the memorial to the fallen heroes. A hooded female figure of justice and liberty glares defiantly into the distance. She holds her right arm firmly across her chest while with her left hand she reaches back and down to place a wreath on the brow of a nude male figure fallen at her feet.

The day after this latter dedication, Illinois governor John Peter Altgeld, noting that "several thousand merchants, bankers, judges, lawyers and other prominent citizens of Chicago" had urged executive clemency for Fielden, Schwab, and Neebe, and, having reviewed the case exhaustively, decided that reducing the sentences was not enough. While condemning anarchy and defending the soundness of American institutions, Altgeld, who as a Chicago attorney and as a colleague of Gary on the Superior Court of Cook County (he was elected in the fall of 1886 and resigned in July of 1891) had played no public role in the clemency movement, concluded that the eight men were found guilty in an unfair trial. In Altgeld's long and detailed opinion the bomb was probably the work of a single person provoked less by anarchist rhetoric than by the authorities and their agents. Citing the raid on the furniture workers in 1877 and the behavior of the police during the 1885 street railway strike, Altgeld declared in what must be one of the angriest of American state papers, "Captain Bonfield is the man who is really responsible for the death of the police officers." The governor refused to discuss directly charges that Judge Gary had been prejudiced, though he dismissed the conspiracy argument and curtly observed that criticisms of Gary "seem to be sustained by the record."[48] He granted Fielden, Neebe, and Schwab an absolute pardon, an action which drew harsh criticism from most newspaper editors and other social leaders. While the pardon of the surviving defendants provided an acknowledgment by the highest official in the state that the anarchists' version of the drama of Haymarket, and the language they used to describe it, was in substantial part correct, the unpopularity of the governor's action indicated that the issue was still far from settled in the public mind. The pardon became one more document in the continuing controversy, not a resolution of it. The *Chicago Tribune* read the victory of Republican nominees, including Judge Gary, in the fall elections as the casting of Altgeld "into outermost political darkness . . . with his mob of Socialists, Anarchists, single-taxers, and office-holding louts at his heels."[49]

As doubts about the conduct of the trial grew and support for persecution of alleged radicals subsided in the early 1890s, partly because of corruption and recriminations in the Police Department involving several principals in the case, including Bonfield and Schaack, the public discussion of what had happened and its relevance to contemporary Chicago life continued.[50] With some impatience, Jane Addams recalled the time as "a period of propaganda as over against constructive social effort," of "marching and carrying banners" and stating principles rather than taking effective social action. But she also noted that after "the first period of repressive measures" resulting from Haymarket had closed, "the city had reached the conclusion that the only cure for the acts of anarchy was free speech and an open discussion of the ills of which the opponents of government complained." Addams remembered in particular "[g]reat open meetings" in the recital hall of the new Auditorium Building, presided over by such prominent individuals as the public-spirited Chicago banker Lyman Gage, an advocate of clemency in 1887, who was later a key figure in making the Columbian Exposition a reality and secretary of the treasury under

McKinley. On the same podium was an anarchist associate of the convicted men. "One cannot imagine such meetings being held in Chicago today," Addams wrote from the perspective of 1910, "nor that such a man should be encouraged to raise his voice in a public assemblage presided over by a leading banker. It is hard to tell just what change has come over our philosophy or over the minds of those citizens who were then convinced that if these conferences had been established earlier, the Haymarket riot and all its sensational results might have been avoided."[51]

In fact, serious-minded observers had earlier openly raised the question of whether repression, however necessary, was the best answer to the instability of urban order revealed by Haymarket, and whether the system required some substantial reforms if society was to avoid the disaster of class war. While the Reverend Dr. Robert Collyer, now in a New York pulpit, regretfully approved the hangings as an effective method of stamping out the "plague" of anarchism, he asserted the dictum that the worker "must be lifted to a higher order of life," and that "the barriers between employed and employer must be broken down and the working classes educated." The editors of *Harper's Weekly* concurred with both parts of this argument, commenting that, while there was no excuse for crime, "Relief of circumstances often opens the way to spiritual regeneration, and it is useless to reason with a starving man, or to suppose that drunkenness may not be diminished by diminishing temptation." Lyman Abbott maintained that even if Haymarket quelled the radical movement in America, it also "demanded of the reformers that . . . they direct their thoughts to a study of the question of how the evils could be cured and the perils averted."[52] The solution, like the evils, would have to be systemic, involving a remaking of the modern metropolis that would free it of bombs without having to resort to troops and executioners.

Some hopefully saw the city as its own corrective. "The massing of these immense populations makes them far more pliable, far more susceptible to progressive influence, to enlightenment, and to improvement," wrote Universalist minister J. Coleman Adams in the *Forum*, listing urban institutions such as newspapers, clubs, lecture halls, political meetings, and "the old, time-honored, and thoroughly proved Anglo-Saxon principle of self-government" as agents of this enlightenment and improvement. What was needed was sympathy and understanding, with the more privileged and responsible members of society taking the first step not by building armories but by reaching out across the classes. Advice like this found listeners in some surprising places. In the summer of 1890, Judge Gary's daughter Fannie took the place of a female operative in a tailor shop so that the young woman might have a two-week vacation.[53]

By this time others had called for more ambitious local programs to counter the catastrophic tendencies of city life. Speaking in the Union Park New Jerusalem Church less than two weeks after the bombing, the Reverend C. C. Bonney equated anarchy with religious infidelity and attacked the "intelligent and cultivated people of this country," as some had done at the time of the fire, for allowing "the dangerous classes of the great cities to hold the balance of political power," which is what had turned places like Chicago literally and figuratively into firetraps and bombs. One solution was to get the states to assume control of local government "until the corruptions and imbecilities of municipal politics shall have been reasonably well removed." But the more important current agenda, which Bonney called a "sacred and imperative duty," was to make sure that every family in the community be taught "in its own familiar language, whatever that might be, the objects of our free government, and that its supreme purpose is the elevation, the prosperity and the happiness, not of a favored class, but of the whole body of the people; and that those grand results can be secured in only one way, the way of industry, virtue, sobriety, obedience to law, and conformity to the principles of Christian civilization." In his post-execution sermon at McVicker's Theater, H. W. Thomas maintained that "those who have grown rich should do more in providing places of entertainment and instruction—halls, art-galleries, reading-rooms, and churches for the poor." This reprised the post-fire arguments that the establishment of institutions of culture was critical to social control.[54]

Seven years before Bonney and Thomas delivered their remarks, one of Chicago's most prominent citizens, a man who had witnessed the havoc of the fire and the violence of 1877 and who was determined that the anarchists must be ferreted out and hanged, had begun an extraordinary effort to find the kind of solution to social disorder that the two clergymen advocated. George Pullman's model community just south of Chicago seemed to many to provide the kind of bold and clear, humane and constructive answer to the conflicts of urban life that Haymarket so vividly revealed. If the town of Pullman was based on at least a partial concession to the anarchists' contention that the city was the source of its own disorder, and that generosity was perhaps a better form of social control than the club and the scaffold, it still seemed to guarantee that, with some adjustments, the working class might be successfully reconstructed within the values and hierarchies of the current order. In light of all the antagonism and alarm of which Haymarket was as much result as cause, it is little wonder that this experiment in urban industrial living on the edge of the embattled city attracted as much hopeful attention as it did, and that its own dramatic undoing was in many respects even more distressing than the fire and the bomb.

Part Three

NINE

Taming the Urban Beast

In the late afternoon of June 22, 1893, George Mortimer Pullman stood proudly before a gathering of 250 distinguished onlookers, as his daughter Florence, then twenty-four, and his son George, Jr., a few days short of eighteen, "drew aside the silken folds" of an American flag that draped a statue their father had commissioned. This work of art commemorated the most famous event in Chicago's frontier history, the Fort Dearborn massacre of August 15, 1812, a catastrophe that, well before the fire, had been integrated into the larger legend of the city's indomitability. The complex bronze memorial group, depicting settlers in a death struggle with Potawatomi Indians, was Pullman's gift to the Chicago Historical Society, in trust for the city. It was placed a hundred feet due east of the so-called "Massacre Tree," an old cottonwood that was the only remaining landmark of the spot where the Indians surprised these pioneers as they fled the fort on the Chicago River for safer outposts to the east. The site was of special personal interest to George M. Pullman because it was now the location of his mansion on elegant Prairie Avenue, where his family had lived since 1876 in prestigious proximity to other leading Chicago families, including the Fields, the Dexters, and the McCormicks. Immediately following the unveiling, Pullman was thus able to host a reception on his well-groomed lawn.

Those in attendance, including ex-president Benjamin Harrison, recognized the occasion as having contemporary as well as historical significance. In elevated language that with minor variations would have been appropriate at the dedication of the Haymarket police statue four years earlier, Chicago Historical Society president Edward G.

Mason accepted the "noble gift" by noting that the memorial honored "the trials and the sorrows of those who suffered here in the cause of civilization." Ignoring the fact that the Potawatomi had inhabited the area long before the white settlers arrived, Mason stated that the tragedy the monument marked "was in reality one which nerved men's arms and fired their hearts to the efforts which rescued this region from the invader and the barbarian." The real purpose of the ceremonies, however, was less to talk of victories over Indians or any other "invaders" or "barbarians" than to celebrate the remarkable distance Chicago had come in the very short time since the fire. The guest list published in the papers and in a special pamphlet prepared for the occasion singled out numerous luminaries of that disaster, including several members of the board of the Relief and Aid Society and such stalwarts as Charles C. P. Holden, the Common Council president who had summoned the city's leaders into action while Chicago was still burning, and John G. Shortall, the real estate man who had impressed at gunpoint two prisoners from the Courthouse to help him salvage a set of property records. Among the artifacts enclosed in the time capsule in the statue's base were pictures of the fire, as well as current histories, directories, and guides to the city and to the dazzling World's Columbian Exposition that was now successfully underway in Jackson Park, and which that very day set a new daily attendance record of 127,272.[1]

Probably few in this fancy crowd were much aware that the anarchist memorial in Waldheim Cemetery would be dedicated only three days later, even if several may have known that Governor Altgeld was seriously considering repudiating the verdict of the Haymarket trial. What no one in attendance could even imagine was that in the near future two of Pullman's honored guests, General Nelson A. Miles, who since 1890 had occupied Philip Sheridan's old position as commander of the Division of the Missouri, and Melville W. Fuller, Chief Justice of the Supreme Court of the United States, would play important roles in a national railroad strike that would begin with a dispute between Pullman and his employees, Miles by commanding the federal troops sent to break the strike and Fuller by joining his colleagues in ruling that the government had the authority to send them. Labor strife was far from the minds of the members of this group as they enjoyed the refreshments and celebrated the civic achievement of Chicago.

What they all knew was that the gathering was a graceful opportunity for an aging captain of industry at the height of his success to honor the city that he had helped build and that had brought him fame and fortune. Pullman, born in western New York in 1831, had been a clerk in a country store and a cabinetmaker before settling in Chicago in 1859. Like so many other ambitious newcomers, his career quickly merged with that of the rising young urban center. "Rising" is a particularly fitting word here, for Pullman, who had done similar work when the Erie Canal was widened, made his first money in Chicago coordinating teams of workers with jackscrews who together lifted and moved small and large buildings, as the city literally raised its grade to overcome the problems posed by its swampy site. He then devoted himself mainly to the design of an improved railroad car before leaving by stagecoach in June of 1860 for Colorado and the boom mining town of Central City, where he ran a general store, an ore refinery, and related businesses. In the spring of 1863, he returned to Chicago, where he hired a substitute to serve in the Union army and entered into a series of partnerships devoted to refining the sleeping-car project. He received a patent for his soon-to-be-famous hinged berths in 1864 and incorporated the Pullman Palace Car Company in 1867.[2]

George Pullman and Chicago had grown to greatness together, and their reputations were intertwined. For more than a quarter of a century, Pullman's signature railroad cars had been spreading his and Chicago's glory all across the nation and into Europe. Six years before the unveiling ceremony, a *London Times* reporter observed, "The development of the sleeping-car project, which is the history of a busy life, shows the possibilities of the Great West, both in the effect of the growth of a city and a business in the expansion of a man, and the influence of a man in building a city."[3] As treasurer of the Relief and Aid Society at the time of the fire, president of the Young Men's Christian Association just after this disaster, vice president of the Law and Order League following the railroad strike of 1877, and as a backer of Captain Schaack's investigations and of the Haymarket verdict, he had been involved in Chicago public life during the city's most serious moments of crisis. In the early 1880s, General Sheridan located his headquarters—now occupied by General Miles—on the fourth floor of the new Pullman Building on the northwest corner of Michigan Avenue and Adams Street. As an officer and founding member of the Commercial Club, and as one of the business leaders most responsible for winning Chicago's right to host the world's fair and guaranteeing its fiscal solidity, Pullman had every reason to share in this moment of civic glory when, as ex-President Harrison said in brief remarks at the dedication, Chicago was "exalted. . . , lifted up to a pinnacle that brings upon her the vision of the world."[4]

In his own eyes, and in the opinion of most Americans, however, George Pullman's greatest contribution to his city and his time was not the fair or perhaps even his railroad cars, but the model town he had constructed in Chicago for his works and his workers. From the time of the groundbreaking in May of 1880 on an expanse of open prairie some fourteen miles south of central Chicago, the model town appeared to be a masterful response to the upheavals that beset the modern city in the same period that witnessed such events as the railroad strike of 1877 and the Haymarket bombing. It seemed to demonstrate how a complex industrial society, without making a concession to critics of the current system, might avoid the apparently inevitable economic and human costs of urban disorder. But embedded in the Pullman "idea" and all the praise it received were some basic assumptions about workers and urban culture that revealed a darker side of this undertaking. Even a brief examination of the extensive contemporary discussions of why and how the town of Pullman offered a solution to the potentially explosive problem of capital and labor reveals that most commentators, as was implicitly the case in the fire literature and explicitly in analyses of Haymarket, assumed that the problem was not one of capital *and* labor, but of labor alone. From this point of view, one of the most encouraging aspects of Pullman was the way it worked a transformation on employees who lived there. Praise for the Pullman resident-operative was thus frequently inseparable from a critique of the "typical" worker. Likewise, many of the plaudits for the town itself contained strong criticism of Chicago and all it represented. While most observers in the years before the strike either did not see or purposely overlooked the more repressive aspects of this social experiment, a few perceptive critics did point out those flaws within the town's form of urban order that subsequently proved to be its undoing.

The Model Town

In a feature article published in 1884, *Scientific American* proclaimed that "the building of the city of Pullman, and the success which has marked the scope of the enterprise, represents much more than the making of a great industrial city in a wilderness in a short period of time."[5] This unique community, designed by Solon S. Beman and landscaped by Nathan Barrett according to George Pullman's governing conception, was not within the city limits of Chicago, but in the adjoining town of Hyde Park. Nor was it a municipality in the ordinary sense, but a large parcel of private property owned and maintained by the company under the direction of one of its employees, the town agent. The *Scientific American* article measured it as two miles long and one mile wide, though George Pullman owned more adjacent land.

A visitor would disembark at the charming Illinois Central station and gaze east over man-made Lake Vista to the Pullman factories. There, on prominent display behind a glass wall in a building eighty feet square and sixty feet high, was the same majestic 350-ton, 2400-horsepower Corliss engine that had been the central exhibit of the power of modernity at the Centennial Exposition in Philadelphia in 1876. Pullman had purchased it for $130,000 and had it taken apart and shipped in thirty-five railway cars to his town, where it was reassembled and placed in operation on a platform of stone and brick set on an oak and walnut floor. Its huge drive shaft, nine inches in diameter and six hundred feet long, ran through a tunnel under the shops and drove the entire works. Twelve years before she helped dedicate the Fort Dearborn statue, young Florence Pullman, her father's favorite of his four children, pushed the button that started the engine. Nothing could have better dramatized the fact that the country had moved into an age of prodigious productive energy whose unprecedented scale seemed matched only by its ease of control.

Just south of the manufacturing area, on the other side of a broad landscaped boulevard, which, like the town's sole hotel, was named after Florence, was the residential section of the town. This occupied 150 acres, and it included tenements, flats, and single-family homes that rented from $4.50 to over $100 a month. These were situated on handsome streets named after pioneers of the industrial age: Morse, Watt, Whitney, Bessemer, Stephenson, and Fulton. The residences featured modern conveniences such as gas, water, indoor plumbing, sewerage, and regular garbage removal—amenities that were, like the well-paved streets and sidewalks of Pullman, far from commonplace in workers' neighborhoods in Chicago. Since the town was meant to be complete in itself, Beman also designed a fourteen-room school, a firehouse, a railroad station, stables, the hotel (with the only bar in Pullman), parks and playing fields, the Arcade, and Market Hall. The Arcade was a massive structure containing retail stores, the Pullman Bank, meeting rooms, a subscription library, and a splendid mahogany-and-gilt theater done up with Moorish motifs and seating up to a thousand. Market Hall was another multipurpose structure that provided stalls for the sale of groceries and a large second-floor meeting room. A block south of the Hotel Florence, architect Beman placed the Greenstone Church, which could accommodate up to six hundred congregants. It was dedicated in 1882 and was built with the distinctly colored material that gave it its name and which made it stand out against the red brick that dominated Pullman's staidly eclectic architecture. All these buildings and grounds were not only owned but maintained by the company.

By 1884, the town included more than 1,400 tenements and flats, and by July of the following year its population was over 8,600. In addition to the trademark olive green sleeping coaches bearing the Pullman name in gold, the company manufactured, operated, and maintained dining and luxury day cars that were attached to passenger trains. The cars usually remained the property of the company (it also made freight cars and streetcars, which it sold outright), and passengers paid a surcharge to ride and sleep in the Pullmans, which were staffed by the Negro porters who were as synonymous with the company's service as its tasteful decor and comfortable seats and beds. The superior comfort, convenience, and luxury of the Palace Cars appealed greatly to businessmen and middle-class pleasure travelers (a wealthy few had their own cars made to order) for whom long railroad journeys along America's rapidly expanding railroad routes had been a trial. By the time the Fort Dearborn statue was dedicated in 1893, the population of the town had reached about 12,000, of whom more than 6,000 were among the company's 15,000 employees, and the company was operating 2,512 sleeping, parlor, and dining cars that carried almost 5,200,000 passengers close to two hundred million miles a year.

Well before the ascendancy of the manufacturing techniques associated with Taylorism, Pullman paid special attention to efficiency of operation. Constructing a central works enabled him to consolidate his heretofore scattered operations while building housing that would attract and keep the large specialized labor force required to manufacture the cars. But the forethought behind the design went a good deal further than that. The raw materials that entered the fully integrated factory were transformed into luxury railroad cars with an eye on minimizing wasted time, materials, and labor. Apparently useless and hazardous wood shavings from the carpentry shops were removed by fans to fuel the boilers that powered the Corliss engine, whose exhaust water filled Lake Vista. The dredging of nearby Lake Calumet that made it deep enough for shipping yielded the hard blue clay that laborers baked into the millions of bricks used to build the town. In the winter the company harvested ice from the lake for local residents and for passengers in its dining cars. Among the many machines driven by the Corliss engine was a pump that delivered the town's sewage from a 300,000-gallon cistern to a farm three miles away, providing fertilizer for vegetables that were sold, among other places, back in Pullman.[6]

George Pullman belongs at the forefront of modern corporate leaders not only because of the way he revolutionized an industry and offered an alternative urban industrial order, but also because of his realization that public opinion, like rolling stock, could be manufactured. He saw that his ideas and his Palace Cars might mutually market each other. Even before Pullman consolidated his operations in the model town, he was aware of the value of seizing certain opportunities to sell his product. He arranged special demonstration trips, from a few miles to across the continent, on which he would show off the advantages of his cars to reporters, business leaders, and elected officials. He put his newest and grandest creations—including his own personal coach, built in 1877 and valued as high as $50,000—at the disposal of presidents and other prominent figures. He displayed two of his newest cars at the same 1876 Centennial Exposition from which he purchased the Corliss engine.[7] As the model town evolved, Pullman continued to be an exceptionally sophisticated publicist, missing no chance to create occasions to use the town to advertise itself, the company, and the conception behind both. The ceremonies marking the groundbreaking and the dedication of major components of the works or of the town were, like the unveiling of the Fort Dearborn statue, aimed at celebrating the experiment and its creator's genius, and at being widely reported. Pullman paid as much attention to how an outsider would experience his town as he did to the organization of the shops. With this in mind, Beman placed the local railroad station in such a way that the visitor's first impression of Pullman would be most favorable. This was strikingly different from most new arrivals' view of Chicago, which was also usually first seen as one approached on a train but which often produced conflicted thoughts and emotions that were disturbing and disheartening.[8]

The inaugural use of the station was to receive the guests conveyed to the town in Pullman's personal car to be on hand as Florence Pullman started the Corliss engine. On other occasions, company officials, sometimes Pullman himself, escorted delegations of visitors around the splendors of his creation, these tours often to be covered by reporters. An 1882 story titled "Visit to the Eighth Wonder of the World, the New City of Pullman," told of how a group of St. Louis and Cincinnati businessmen, along with twenty-five of the sixty members of the Commercial Club, were hosted to a "dainty breakfast" at the Hotel Florence by the proud founder. Pullman soon became a tourist attraction, with special excursion trains to the site, and by 1893 sixty-two trains stopped in Pullman daily. Even passengers who did not get off pressed against the windows for a glimpse. One overenthusiastic reporter even suggested that this industrial town might become a vacation resort.[9]

The central theme of the company's many presentations of itself was that the town of Pullman was the answer to the pressing questions of the time. This was certainly the message of the corporate history prepared for public consumption at the time of the Columbian Exposition. The author was probably Duane Doty, the tireless company executive who also served for a time as town agent as well as in several other capacities. He and his wife, who published her own volume on the model town the same year, were Pullman's most enthusiastic spokespersons.

"The Pullman idea in particular, that money could be safely invested in an elaboration of the utilitarian into the artistic and beautiful," Doty asserted, "was a startling departure." The company had proved wrong all those who thought that Americans were not interested in anything "which in the slightest degree stepped over the baldest utility into the boundaries of the ornamental." Beauty, in fact, was practical, "having an incitive energy of its own, capable in its way of being turned to account as a force in the production of results, just as is the force of the steam engine itself." The cars and the town were linked by this notion, which was celebrated by Doty and others as the key to their common success: "The same organic solidity of structure, the same faith in the intrinsic commercial value of the beautiful, which entered into the one entered into the other."[10] The Pullman attitude toward the treatment of workers, the company claimed, was equally practical. It was not that employers could afford to treat employees this way—they could not afford to treat them any other way. Traditional thinking about minimizing labor costs and ignoring working and living conditions was bad business. George Pullman had the shrewdest understanding of machines, money, and men.

To make the case convincing for stockholders and the world, it was important for Pullman to demonstrate that his system not only paid off in higher productivity, which might be difficult to prove, but also that the rentals on the dwellings and retail space he built to attract and keep labor themselves produced a good return on investment. He felt obligated to show the financial community that it was not a starry-eyed humanitarianism but a hardheaded bottom-line mentality that was behind his decision to build quality housing rather than consign workers to unhealthy and unattractive dwellings. Early in the town's life, Pullman said that he expected to prove "that these favorable and healthful conditions, comfortable homes and widening opportunities, can be secured for laborers at the same time that a reasonable per cent. and permanency of investment is secured for investors." He continued, "Capital will not invest in sentiment nor for sentimental considerations for the laboring classes. But let it once be proved that enterprises of this kind are safe and profitable and we shall see great manufacturing corporations developing similar enterprises, and thus a new era will be introduced into the history of labor."[11]

The Hope of Pullman

As energetic as the company was in showing itself off, virtually all of the early commentary on the town by outsiders made, if anything, even greater claims for Pullman's achievement than he himself did, indicating how eager the public was to see the experiment as an effective alternative to contemporary social and economic dysfunction and disruption. Visitors and observers through the 1880s and early 1890s rushed to profess themselves true believers and declare the experiment a success. To the author of the 1884 article in *Scientific American,* Pullman signaled a new age and a new kind of urban dispensation that marked the triumph of modernization. The founder's "design" was "to build a city in which, as far as possible, all that would promote the health, comfort, and convenience of a large working population would be conserved, and"—equally important—"many of the evils to which they are ordinarily exposed made impossible." The whole enterprise was managed, like any solid corporation, on "thoroughly sound business principles, looking for a moderate and sure return on the capital invested." The magazine illustrated its report with a bird's-eye view of the town seen from the west, with Lake Calumet in the background, the works in the center, the hotel and housing to the right. In the foreground was a charming bucolic scene that was completely fanciful. Several refined urban figures, some sporting parasols, drive carriages, or stroll through fictive woods. Nature and industry, man and machine, progress and prosperity, wealth and commonwealth, are perfectly integrated, without any hint of social tension.[12]

Those within the company and without who spoke and wrote about Pullman were, above all, fond of referring to the Pullman "idea." The most important thing to understand here is the imaginative appeal, at the time, of talking about an industrial center in terms of any "ideas" besides power, profit, competition—and conflict. While most business leaders were distracted by day-to-day interests, and while most cities did not seem to grow or evolve so much as lurch uncertainly from crisis to crisis, George Pullman (so the popular understanding went) had been thinking in the boldest and most farsighted terms. He had reflected on all the struggle and strife in Chicago and the nation from the 1860s on and had concluded that the key was to act systematically and holistically. In an article revealingly titled "A Western Utopia" that appeared early in 1883, the Boston-based *Christian Register* described the power of the "central idea" felt everywhere in the town of Pullman, which seemed nothing less than a triumph of mind over matter. This idea "looms up in the great water tower, it beats in the Corliss engine, it rises in the church spire, shines from the windows of the workmen's houses, is felt in the clean, neat streets; in short, it is articulated in every joint of the great enterprise." After inspecting the workshops several years later, the French economist Paul de Rousiers remarked, "One feels that some brain of superior intelligence, backed by a long technical experience, has thought out every possible detail."[13]

Had this intelligence devoted itself merely to the production of railroad cars, however, its achievements would not have been noteworthy. To most commentators, Pullman's most significant accomplishment was that he had engaged the thorniest social, economic, and moral problems of the age, and through the comprehensive Pullman "idea" had apparently solved them all. In an age regretfully resigned to the notion that blight, poverty, and social disorder were perhaps the unavoidable price of progress and profit, the Pullman Company had demonstrated that beauty and utility, good works and solid returns, far from being mutually exclusive, could go hand-in-hand. The Pullman experiment dared to claim that the pursuit of aesthetic and humane values need not suffer amidst the drive for material progress, that parks and gardens were as "efficient" as the Corliss engine, and that attention to living and working conditions was sound fiscal as well as social policy.

Pullman seemed to fulfill the primary cultural standards of morality and beauty, as well as productivity. An early article on the town commented, "[I]f the projectors of Pullman can show that comfort, cleanliness and taste in a manufacturing village can be made commercially profitable, they will rank hereafter as among the greatest of public benefactors." A story published a decade later indicated that this now had been proved. The Pullman idea was not a fantasy, but the "highest humanity and philanthropy" and "the solid foundation of business." The company had reconciled so many supposedly fundamental oppositions that it raised the question of whether they had ever actually existed in the first place:

> It [Pullman] is, in fact, philanthropy made practical; humanity, founded on business principles; sobriety, art, music, clean living, refined homes, self-respecting independence of character without paternalism; a vindication of the theory that there is an economical value in beauty, and that the workingman is capable of appreciating and wisely using the highest ministries of art and beauty.

"This city," the author observed two years before the dedication of the Fort Dearborn statue, "will be Mr. Pullman's monument."[14]

To Americans in the 1880s, the greatest promise Pullman's city offered, however, was that it seemed to show a way in which violent confrontations between capital and labor could be avoided. In its publicity, his company claimed that, just as the Pullman Palace Car "solved the problem of long continuous railway journeys," the town, "along new lines, gives a hope of bettering the relations of capital and labor," offering proof that a large-scale, modern, and yet humane and harmonious industrial community could be constructed.[15] Others agreed. The

Christian Register spoke of Pullman as "a fresh illustration of the identity of interest which subsists between capital and labor and the mutual advantage which comes from recognizing it." Reviewing the town's illustrious history after nine years, *Frank Leslie's* cited Pullman as an example of community harmony and order to be followed elsewhere. The Pullman experiment proved what could be achieved "by kindly and liberal consideration in furtherance of the welfare of the industrial classes," and perhaps soon "all great employing corporations will realize more or less profoundly, that the true solution of all troubles of capital and labor lies in the application of the principles upon which Pullman is built."[16]

Nearly all commentators focused on Pullman in terms of what it meant to the future of class relations. In 1882, when the resident population was barely 2,000, an article in the *Western Manufacturer* (reprinted in the *Railroad Gazette*) spoke hopefully of "the relation of capital and labor" as a "problem to be solved by this grand Pullman enterprise." Pullman was the wise capitalist's answer to the rising tide of attacks on the current economic system. "No agitator in view of the provisions that have been made here for the amelioration of the condition of the laborer—to minister to his comfort and add to his enjoyment, and at the same time furnish the means for his intellectual improvement—can prate about an irresistible conflict between capital and labor," the article proclaimed. "Even communism must here be dumb and hide its Gorgon head in shame."[17] George Pullman had demonstrated that the anarchists were completely wrong: the ideal urban setting was one designed from the bottom up and controlled from the top down. The power of concentrated capital, correctly exercised, could be society's salvation.

As several observers pointed out, Pullman was superior to other cities primarily because of the way it had developed. Once again, the distinction here was that the town, like every other aspect of the corporate operation, was based on an *idea*. As he had been a pioneer in railroad travel and in the development of a complex, integrated manufacturing enterprise, George Pullman was at the forefront of city planning and in applying corporate management procedures to living as well as working conditions. "Pullman is a creation," one reporter explained two years after the groundbreaking, "every building is part of a pre-arranged plan, and it is this which gives interest to the enterprise." Visitors noted in particular two closely related results from all this planning that distinguished the city George Pullman made from the one he had found when he moved to Chicago. While these visitors differed in the extent to which they believed that the architecture of Pullman was aesthetically appealing, they concurred on the related and more significant point—in this period when the term "dirty" was so loaded—that it was *clean.* Virtually no description of Pullman, whether generated by the company or by an outsider, failed to mention its system of sewerage and drainage that was installed before its streets and buildings were constructed. Every laudatory report on the model town favorably compared its sanitary conditions with those of the typical industrial city, usually singling out Chicago. "Although as yet exclusively a manufacturing town," the journalist who spoke of the "pre-arranged plan" declared, "[Pullman] is a model of good order and neatness; there is no dirt, nor is there a suspicion of any nuisance."[18]

Pullman, in short, was not only clean; more important, it was *orderly.*[19] As a result of the same kind of planning that went into the construction of railroad cars and the sewage and drainage system, the town seemed to be a kind of flawless deistic world that, once set in motion by George Pullman, regulated itself. "There are no court houses, no saloons, no jails, and only one policeman," *Scientific American* marveled. The *Pall Mall Gazette* said almost the same thing in deeming Pullman "An American Utopia," pointing out, "There are no policemen or constables, no justice's court, no aldermen, no public functionaries of any description." The apparent absence of visible authority ironically made Pullman sound like the kind of society that the anarchists envisioned, with the one enormous difference that what enabled this polity to run without a government was the total authority of George Pullman, who lived on Prairie Avenue and worked primarily in downtown Chicago. The social peace of Pullman, which the *Pall Mall Gazette* related to its exclusion of "dirt," was the best evidence so far of the wisdom behind his exercise of this power: "[A]s no breach of the peace has ever occurred, Mr. Pullman's benevolent despotism has a very clean record." One reader of the *Arcade Mercantile Journal* was even moved to compose a poem to this "[q]ueenly city" that was located "Away from pitfalls, ever alluring, / Far from gilded markets of sin," so that "Crime and consorts stalk not therein." The poem further described Pullman as a "Mecca" for the "laboring man," before concluding:

> A master hand truly has modeled
> The bread-winners' haven fair.
> Thousands of tongues unanimous voice
> Glad recognition of one man's power.[20]

Keynotes

Of all the positive responses to Pullman in its early years, two in particular stand out as expressions of all the hopes invested in the town by

voices of informed and respectable public opinion. The occasion for
the first was the dedication of the library in the Arcade Building, which
took place in the theater on April 11, 1883, three months after the Arcade itself was dedicated with great fanfare. At such events, carefully
chosen speakers would explicate the significance of the social experiment, and the keynote address on this occasion was delivered by the
Reverend David Swing, a close friend of George Pullman and one of
the most influential ministers among Chicago's well-to-do as well as
one of the most popular clergymen in the city.[21] The contemporary urban social context, Swing argued, was troubling, which gave the Pullman experiment "an interest above and beyond that of railcars and
wheels" that was "related to the question of how cities should be built
and in general how man should live." This was a question, Swing explained, that great minds from Plato to Robert Owen had pondered.
Like those who applauded the Pullman "idea," Swing maintained that
the town "illustrates the value of thought and taste in the building of a
city or village." But he went beyond the praise of Pullman's efficiencies
to argue that the town's design addressed the issues of spirit and character that were such a concern at the time of the fire. Swing saw the
town's "material symmetry" as "only the outward emblem of a moral
unity among the inhabitants." In this respect it was not only superior to
Chicago but also to such failed communitarian experiments as Brook
Farm and New Harmony, since it embodied not "abstract philosophy
or socialism," as they did, but "common sense of the highest and best
order," based on "industry, sobriety, economy." The challenge facing
thoughtful and responsible citizens was to follow the Pullman example
in redeeming the mistakes of the past. Swing scorned those wealthy individuals who, unlike Pullman, squandered their money ostentatiously
on luxury and show, or who invested it in government bonds rather
than in improved housing. He insisted, however—as Pullman himself
always did—that "four per cent cottages" were not only a "nobler" investment than bonds, but just as sound and practical. Swing remade
the related point that beauty was a good investment, no more costly to
create in the first place than the deformity that characterized most
American cities, and much more promising for a better return in the
long run.

Swing concluded with one of the period's fullest expositions on the
liabilities of "dirt," which consisted of a pastiche of ideas whose overall
point was to celebrate Pullman as the age's best answer to typical urban
disunity, diseconomy, disorder, and disaster. Few, if any, of the attempts by the contending sides in the Haymarket trial and after to argue
that nature, cleanliness, and order were on their side were as pointed as
Swing's little sermon:

The man who first said "Cheap as dirt" should have been slain for corrupting the public. The public needed no persuading in that direction. "Dirt is expensive." It will not bring the money and happiness cleanliness and beauty will bring. A thing of beauty is not only a joy forever, but it is a perpetual income. All harmony, and symmetry, and unity are conservative. If the wheel of a car or locomotive does not run truely the axle heats, and will, if let alone, burn up the train. Nature hates discords. When the wheels of a city government run falsely the car of progress must stop. The harmony of this town will be its source of wealth, and health, and happiness.

In Swing's analysis, cleanliness and beauty were so dependent on order and control that the two sets of terms were interchangeable, and these values constituted the basis of all prosperity and happiness, two more terms that merged into all the others. Though this town was unquestionably the work of man, it was in accord with the laws of nature, which "hates discords" and loves the harmony, symmetry, and unity of Pullman, and is, at its heart, "conservative." Other cities should now look to the town that manufactured the Palace Cars for a vision of the ideal urban social order blessed by natural law and the God who decreed it. Comparing the dedication of this library in a factory town to the consecration of a church, Swing launched into an appeal for America's urban centers to be born again in the image of Pullman. "What a country shall we have," he mused, "when such an example shall be imitated in all parts of the land!"[22]

Perhaps the most powerful expression of the hope of Pullman was the far more objective endorsement the town received in the mid-1880s from a contingent of the directors of state departments of labor statistics. This group constituted one of the more impressive of the emerging national organizations of professional social scientists, managers, and bureaucrats whose influence in the shaping of society through their role in business and government was rapidly growing. Meeting in St. Louis for their second annual national convention, they decided that Pullman, "one of the most attractive experiments of the age seeking to harmonize the interests of labor and capital," was of sufficient interest to merit a personal investigation. In September a delegation spent three days in the town conducting their own independent scrutiny of "all the economic, sanitary, industrial, moral, and social conditions of the city," and shortly after they issued a report. Its key author was Carroll Wright, chief of the bureau of labor statistics in Massachusetts, and soon to be appointed the first United States commissioner of labor.[23]

While it was centrally interested in the needs of labor, the report unquestionably pondered these needs from the vantage of a nation irreversibly committed to large-scale private industry. It expressed a palpable sense of relief that the Pullman experiment seemed to make it possible to be optimistic about the labor question in this context. The report methodically assessed Pullman's founding and site plan, its system of drainage and sewerage, its buildings and industries, and its wages, living conditions, and health and safety. Committed to the modern notion that any informed analysis and successful reform must be based not on sentiment and abstraction but on careful observation and measurement, Wright and the other members of his delegation checked the diameter of sewer pipes and tried to quantify the town's cultural level, breaking the population down by religion as well as nationality and counting the number of books (30,000), and pianos (75) in all the households. They noted some failures (e.g., the unrented Greenstone Church) and friction between company and workers, and they expressed concern about the absence of private home ownership and a profit-sharing plan. Here, too, however, they looked at matters in large part from the point of view of the company, worrying that the town's lack of economic diversification would leave its stockholders doubly vulnerable in case of a downturn in its business, since they would stand to lose not only its manufacturing revenues but also rental income.

For the most part, however, these experts spoke in superlatives. The town's attention to "artistic effect" did not at all conflict with its dedication to "the strictest business principles." The works and shops were "kept in the neatest possible order." Health conditions were "unequaled by those in any city of the world." The Pullman experiment was to even "the most casual observer . . . rare enough to be remarkable, and good enough to be commendable." More careful scrutiny revealed "that its excellence was by no means superficial, that it is not only as good as it looks, but better, and that every promise has been made more than good." The delegation's two favorite words, however, were "scientific," to describe the conception and building of Pullman, and "perfect," which it applied to the drainage of the site, the ventilation of the sewers, the disability insurance plan, and, most important, the cleanliness and order throughout. This town was, indeed, close to being the industrial Eden or utopia that less expert observers declared it to be, a happy hive almost completely lacking in disease, crime, drunkenness, and pauperism, where only policemen and doctors would fail to find full employment.[24]

The language of the almost magical hygienic transformation and purification Pullman performed on all kinds of "dirt" appeared throughout the report. "Where the sewage water leaves the drains it is as clear and sparkling as spring water, and laborers often drink it," Wright and the others explained, adding, "All waste products at Pullman are carefully utilized, being transformed by vital chemistry into luxuriant vegetable forms." Through his noble enterprise, Pullman himself had "furnished a desert with wells of living water that all may come and drink through all time." If the rents were somewhat higher than in Chicago, they were still reasonable and well worth it, for one had to keep in mind that worker housing in Chicago "would be in a narrow street or alley, while in Pullman it is on a broad avenue where no garbage is allowed to collect," and "where beauty, order, and cleanliness prevail, and fresh air abounds." The commissioners' evaluation ended with a summary of all the expectations loaded on the model town by a worried age. This experiment offered the best prospects of profits and what the commissioners called "self-respect and self-culture." If it put the wage-earner in a "'gilded cage,'" they noted, "we must congratulate him on its being so handsomely gilded; the average workman does not have his cage gilded." Besides, the report reminded the reader, "all men are circumscribed by the conditions with which they surround themselves, and imprisoned by the daily duties of life." The Pullman example deserved imitation. "Let the model manufactory and the industrial community of Pullman city be commended as they deserve for whatever they are or what they promise to be," the commissioners concluded. "Let them be held up to the manufacturers and employers of men throughout the country as worthy of their emulation."[25]

In many ways, George Pullman did provide industrial America with an example worthy of emulation. His consolidation of his several shops into a central location that served the entire country recognized and facilitated the development of a national economy and transportation system. His Palace Cars revolutionized railroad travel, and his model town unquestionably was a daring experiment in city planning. The achievements revealed an ability to understand and take advantage of the possibilities of large-scale integrated systems in an urbanizing America linked together by railroads. Although his primary motive in building Pullman was to gather a stable, skilled labor force in an efficient manufacturing enterprise, he did treat his workers and their families better—in many respects, far better—than did other manufacturers with similar needs, apparently proving that the interests of labor and capital were not necessarily opposed to each other.

Some of the town's objectionable aspects, which few visitors noted in any case, seemed either to have good reason behind them or were mitigated by compensating practices and policies. If residential leases could be terminated on ten days' notice and the company monitored the living habits of residents, much as it used "spotters" to make sure that employees in the works and porters on the trains followed work rules, this was only another form of quality control that benefited the community as a whole as well as the company's customers. Likewise, if it screened the occupants of commercial spaces as carefully as it selected the works that appeared on the library's shelves and the theater's stage, this kept out brothels, gambling houses, saloons, and "low" forms of amusement and entertainment. True, George Pullman did not give his tenants and operatives a voice or any kind of ownership in his town or his company, but he did promote those who served him well and in some instances helped them get established on their own outside the company. If he was fixated on cleanliness and order in his railroad cars and his town to a degree that revealed an almost compulsive obsession with "dirt," it is only fair to keep in mind that he was participating in the nineteenth century's best scientific efforts, which were both socially conservative as well as reformist, to root out the sources of disease to which concentrated and shifting populations, whether in railroad cars or in cities, were prone.[26]

The Remaking of the American Working Class

There is little question, however, that Pullman received as much attention as it did not simply because of its integrated factory or its worker housing or its hygiene, but because it seemed a way to avoid the kind of catastrophic conflict between employers and workers that produced such awful calamities as the Haymarket bomb. In his history of Chicago, published in 1892, Joseph Kirkland immediately followed his chapter on Haymarket with one of the most gushing descriptions of the model town. He ended by holding out the prospect that Pullman offered the key to future social prosperity and harmony. "The historian is not the prophet," Kirkland admitted, "but it may be said without undue presumption that if—*if* the path in front of Pullman proves as fair to the foot as its vista appears to the eye, then the enterprise sounds the keynote for the full and final chorus of concord between labor and capital. In that case its founder has, single-handed, built the enduring monument of the passing XIXth century; a pyramid, the broad, deep ground-course whereof is human nature, while its sun-lit cap-stone is peace."[27]

Most visitors to Pullman agreed that it was important for everyone's sake to look out for the well-being of the worker, but that the purpose of this benevolence was to assure labor's loyalty and worth to the industrial order as it was constituted. As Stanley Buder observes, few of the many visitors to Pullman solicited the operatives' views.[28] To those who wished to see the model town as the solution to class conflict, the core question was how to manage a large population of workers whose values and habits were assumed to be inferior to those of their bosses and to the middle-class readers of the many analyses of the town that appeared in the press. Pullman's answer was an aggressive early experiment in urban environmentalism in which the worker would be indirectly transformed through direct control of his immediate surroundings. The assumption was that this carefully ordered and administered town raised workers to a higher level of being, and to the realization that what was good for capital was good for them. The worker benefited from this transformation, which was not a matter of manipulation and coercion, but of education and uplift.

Some claimed that Pullman was simply applying the same psychology to his workers as he had to his customers. To those who believed that the tasteful decor and attentive service offered by Pullman's cars would be wasted on the boorish American railroad passenger, the company responded that these features in fact encouraged polite and seemly behavior. The "same instinct" which made people "conform their habits to elegant surroundings in homes" would make them behave well in the Pullman car.[29] But it was evident that Pullman and most commentators believed that the town would do more than inspire proper behavior. The unified solution that was the Pullman idea would change the very nature of the worker in moral and aesthetic, as well as economic, terms. He would become more upstanding and more attractive, and, in the process, more tractable and thus more productive. Looking back just after the strike on his twenty years of service with the company, Pullman's second vice-president, Thomas Wickes, recalled, "It was the hope and belief of the management that the character of the buildings and houses and streets at Pullman, and the order in which they are kept, would raise the standard of desire of working people for such surroundings; and that such surroundings would improve their character as citizens, and the quality of their work."[30] In other words, the Pullman system would produce better workers as well as better railroad cars.

These hopes and beliefs were not rationalizations prompted by the strike but part of company ideology that from the outset was based in some of the same kinds of beliefs about the civilizing potentials of culture that were expressed in the fire literature. In 1882 George Pullman described the almost miraculous change that took place in "the poorer and more improvident families moving their old, shabby and untidy household effects into these nice new flats." At first, he admitted, he felt "sick at heart" at the apparent failure of the new setting to alter the workers' inbred slovenly habits. But after six months he took a tour of the flats and "was greatly encouraged and delighted" to discover how families "had improved in general appearance and mode of life. Evidently they were striving to make their homes correspond to their surroundings, and if able to do nothing more to beautify them, they at least kept them cleaner and planted flowers in their windows." The resident superintendent at the time pointed out how common this sort of improvement was. Where once an operative "would lounge around his doorstep in the evening, unkempt, unshaven, in his shirt sleeves and stocking feet, smoking his pipe, his untidy wife and children around him," he "might now be seen" entirely changed "for the better, both in appearance and demeanor."[31] The dirty worker had come clean.

In the corporate history it prepared in 1893, the company again stressed this point, maintaining that all the effort "to surround the workingmen in Pullman with such influences as would tend to bring out the highest and best there was in them" had beneficently developed "a distinct type—distinct in appearance, in tidiness of dress, in fact in all the external indications of self-respect." This self-respect was proportional to the extent to which the workers had adopted respectable middle-class habits and values. The Pullman worker, like the Pullman car, was readily identifiable as superior: "Not only as compared with the majority of men in similar walks of life do they show in their clearer complexions and brighter eyes the sanitary effects of the cleanliness and abundance of pure air and sunlight in which they live, but there is in their bearing and personal demeanor what seems to be a distinct reflection of the general atmosphere of order and artistic taste which permeates the entire town." The company even maintained that this superiority was measurable, that "a representative gathering of Pullman workmen would be quite forty per cent. better in evidences of thrift and refinement, and in all the outward indications of a wholesome habit of life, than would a representative gathering of any corresponding group of workingmen which could be assembled elsewhere in the country."[32]

Mrs. Doty's book made even grander claims for the success of the Pullman experiment in solving the labor problem. The town was nothing less than "the most remarkable business enterprise of the age, or of any age," of special interest to "all students of social science, . . . political economists, capitalists, philanthropists, engineers, sanitarians, artists, and men of science" because of its success in putting the workingman "on a higher plane, and plac[ing] about him conditions which are better than he could have hoped for if unaided." This achievement was in turn part of a cosmic plan in which labor was "not only bettered" but given "a dignity which it did not before possess." Pullman had done no less than accelerate the evolutionary process, and he had done so through peaceful means, not violent competition. "The history of civilization," Mrs. Doty declared, "exhibits a steady growth and progress of the masses of the human race to higher levels, and in showing to the

world that the interests of capital can be amply provided for while operatives, more largely than ever before, are made sharers in the results of
good work, an example has been set here which exerts and will exert a
beneficial influence in myriads of ways."[33]

Professional advocates for the improvement of the worker concurred, often implying that the culture of labor was inherently debased
and repeatedly identifying the laborer's adoption of the habits of indus-
triousness and discipline with being "civilized," and even with spiritual
rebirth. In a section of their report titled "Moral Influence," Carroll
Wright and his team of experts agreed with others who contended that
the surroundings of Pullman were exercising a "silent educational influence" on the worker. Since operatives "could turn nowhere without
meeting order, they naturally began to make comparisons, and such
comparisons have resulted in setting their own houses to rights." Living
in the town of Pullman made workers into "better men," and so this
city was "a permanent benefaction." To do what Pullman had undertaken was "to carry the world, so far as such men can reach it, to a
higher level in civilization." Helen Starrett was more effusive in describing workers' first uneasy reactions to Pullman: "They feel at first
as strange and unfamiliar and uncomfortable as they would if suddenly
transported to heaven. . . . But it is cheering to learn that already the
improving and educating influences of such surroundings are beginning to be apparent."[34] The attitudes behind this language reveal how
much the design of the model town, for all its dedication to modern
beliefs in industrial production and environmentalism, was also rooted
in the same traditional Protestant evangelical imaginative framework
that inspired the talk of purification at the time of the fire. To Pullman,
as to many other leading Chicago businessmen, the worker existed in a
"fallen" condition of improvidence, intemperance, and uncleanli-
ness.[35] The worker's "salvation" could best be achieved by his development of those personal characteristics that George Pullman defined as
valuable and worthy, and which living in his town would best inculcate.

Various visitors singled out for special scorn those members of the
working class who would not be reconstructed by this new environment. Any resistance to the elevating climate of Pullman, and to the
changes that it would work in them, was nothing less than perverse.
Pointing out that Pullman was under no obligation to have undertaken
this "conspicuous example . . . of the nobler uses of great wealth," the
Wright report sympathized with the founder's feelings of disappoint-
ment when workers "who had been in the habit of living in a filthy, shiftless way" in city tenements did not appreciate their surroundings. A St.
Louis paper observed that "brutes" must go elsewhere, and cited the
case of an Irish policeman "with the choicest brogue," who "had as

lively an appreciation of the meaning of this latest and most wonderful flower of civilization as a hog wallowing in a mud hole." This boor was "disgusted" by "the decency and quiet of the place." The objections of such a person only certified the value of Pullman. The policeman's unhappiness, like that of radical agitators, was dismissed by categorizing him as a foreign and subhuman savage outside the pale of progressive society. "Doubtless born in a bog and raised upon a diet of sour milk and potatoes, he had as little enjoyment of the comfortable dwellings, the green clover-carpeted and flower-scented lawns, the general air of thrift as a Digger Indian." After offering the common observation that Pullman had elevated the character and behavior of its residents ("Both the health and the *morale* of the town are exceptional; and the oral tone of the workmen has constantly improved under the agreeable surroundings"), Charles Dudley Warner responded sarcastically to criticism of the company's control of living and working conditions with a variation on Carroll Wright's gilded-cage remark: "Those who prefer the kind of independence that gives them filthy homes and demoralizing associations seem to like to live elsewhere."[36]

The good news from Pullman was that workers who preferred such independence to the gilded cage were rare exceptions or unreconstructibles not worth saving. The key assumption regarding the "good" worker was that he could be "civilized." If, as his tendency to be duped by political and labor organizers indicated, he did not always know that he was wisest to trust his employer, it was partly because most employers did not realize that with care and foresight the worker could be refashioned into productive respectability. George Pullman had demonstrated that anyone who worked for him was as susceptible to being "refined" into an efficient operative and good citizen as the raw materials that entered his shops were to being turned into a beautiful and practical Palace Car. He had made his first money in Chicago raising buildings out of the muck. Now he was figuratively doing the same thing in uplifting the worker.

Reinventing the City

Even more remarkable than the attack on the worker that underlay this thinking was the implicit notion that the best thing to do with the industrial city was to abandon it and start all over again with an integrated master plan. According to the logic of the Pullman idea, taking the worker out of cities like Chicago would remove the causes of social and economic disorder. The city was a degraded and degrading environment where beauty and utility, good works and profit, capital and labor could never be reconciled, and where fire, filth, and ferment perhaps could never be avoided. Most, though certainly not all, of the worried commentary on the fire and Haymarket had viewed the city as a physically, economically, and morally sound community endangered by outsiders who would destroy and defile it. By contrast, the praise of Pullman more often conceded that, while the age demanded concentrations of capital and labor typical of cities, the need for efficiency, profit, beauty, and humane social relations required a new and different kind of setting whose success would be measured by the extent to which it was *not* like the modern American city.

Pullman himself was quite candid on this issue. Once he attracted "the best class of mechanics," he wanted to protect them from the city, which he seemed to regard as an animate evil force. By establishing his town on undeveloped private land outside of Chicago and by excluding what he called all "baneful influences," he would enable the community to achieve "the greatest measure of success" as a social as well as financial enterprise. He found plenty of support for this position. In its account of the annual stockholders meeting of 1885, the *Chicago Inter-Ocean* noted, "It is fair to assume that the gradual increase in savings is, in some degree, attributable to the absence of saloons and other debasing influences, and the general healthful and moral surroundings of the place." As another reporter explained, Pullman was "expected to be an exact counterpart in miniature of the great cities, except that in its appointments it is a vast improvement, and by virtue of its regulations is free from many city temptations and vices."³⁷ It was this kind of environment, where "dirt" was either kept out in the first place, removed through regular garbage pickups, or transformed into fertilizer, that the worker would himself be reformed to intellectual and spiritual, as well as physical, cleanliness. Nothing could contaminate this city, and this city would contaminate no one.

Similar criticism of the modern industrial metropolis as an almost hopeless center of distress and disorder infused the report of the state commissioners of labor. To accomplish his dream, they explained, Pullman had to "leave the great cities for many reasons," for "[h]e wished above all things to remove his workmen from the close quarters of a great city" to a place where they would have good air, water, and drainage, and "where they would be free, so far as it lies in the power of management to keep them free, from the many seductive influences of a great town." In contrast to Pullman, the "average village or city" was unhealthy and chaotic, a "haphazard conglomeration of odds and ends in the way of buildings, whose inartistic forms, defective construction, and inconvenient arrangements are supplemented by such drainage and sewerage systems as can be utilized." What most characterized cities was dirt, "the accumulated filth of years."³⁸ Richard Ely noted with some consternation that some of the workers' wives had to be weaned away from the dark alleys of Chicago to dwell in the sunshine and flowers of Pullman. He then added with some satisfaction, "But they are learning to do it." Ely was particularly pleased to report the high approval of Pullman by the mothers in the town, "one of whom exclaimed to the writer, in speaking of Chicago: 'I just hate the ugly old city.'"[39] "Ugly" and "old" Chicago was barely fifty years "old" at this time and, given the fire and settlement patterns, it was highly likely that the housing this woman had left was less "old" than that. Like "dirty," however, "age" was as much a moral and aesthetic category as a physical attribute.

The anti-urban bias in much of the publicity and praise for Pullman was sharpest in the explicit representation of the city of Chicago as antithetical to the budding Pullman idea. Pullman's "bright beds of flowers and green velvety stretches of lawns," its parks and trees and vistas and homes, all "bright and wholesome and filled with pure air and light," made it a place unlike Chicago, since "all that is ugly, and discordant, and demoralizing, is eliminated, and all that inspires to self-respect, to thrift and to cleanliness of person and thought is generously provided." By 1893, the company was calling the town, which was, after all, a center of heavy industry that no longer enjoyed what limited isolation it once had from metropolitan Chicago, "a bright and radiant little island in the midst of the great tumultuous sea of Chicago's population; a restful oasis in the wearying brick-and-mortar waste of an enormous city." The great threat was that the city would engulf the town: "Already the advance waves of Chicago's swelling tide of population are lapping [Pullman's] edges and encircling its borders."[40] It was a moral duty to preserve this oasis and replicate its success elsewhere in the urban "waste" land.

The most troubling aspect of the praise of Pullman as a model of social planning was the way in which it revealed a willingness to suspend some of the individual liberties that supposedly defined American society. While the Pullman idea was based on a belief in the operative's capacity for improvement, this improvement was to take place in a setting completely controlled by George Pullman. The company continued to argue even after the strike that this was the only way to assure a stable, healthy, and productive urban order. Defending the policy of refusing to sell any of its land, second vice president Wickes maintained that company ownership of all "public" space and every home was the foundation of the beauty, cleanliness, and civility of the town, which "could only be accomplished under a single control of plan and expenditure, which would have failed if a single lot had been sold."[41] Those who recommended that the Pullman idea be applied more widely seemed to have missed the way the company restricted the free enterprise of which George Pullman was supposedly a champion, that he had tried to remove the possibility that urban life could be contested by the bold but simple measure of making all the space his.

In his remarks at the library dedication, for example, David Swing expressed regret that Chicago resembled "a modern woman's crazy quilt." Its growth had followed a disheartening "law of chaos," in which "the saloon became as welcome as the schoolhouse." The want of plan had proved to be "an expensive fact," one that "has made the work of destruction as constant as that of construction." Chicago was hardly exceptional in this regard. According to Swing, "It stands for all the great cities of the land." Without acknowledging the antidemocratic implications of what he was saying, Swing argued that the success of Pullman suggested that cities should be governed by a kind of trusteeship of the "best" men, which, like the Reverend Goodspeed's vision of utopia in his fire history, sounded like an institutionalization of the temporary powers assumed by the Relief and Aid Society in 1871. "Could Chicago have foreseen itself and have passed into the hands of some master-mind or building committee or corporation in 1835, it would now surpass in neatness, and wealth, and beauty Paris or Brussels," Swing maintained, overlooking the fact that what he saw as the admirable qualities of these European cities were based on the exercise of imperial power.[42]

Paternalism and Role Models

The adjective most often applied to the Pullman system and its founder was "paternalistic," but George Pullman and his spokesmen rejected this term. They were quick to point out that Pullman treated employees neither like children nor as objects of philanthropy since workers sold their labor to the company and rented housing on strict business terms, and were free to come and go as they wished. The company's disclaimers were correct, but not exactly for the reasons offered. Pullman's attitude toward his workers put a gap between himself and them too wide and deep for their relationship to be called paternalistic without important qualifications. Building a safe and healthy living and working environment was a good investment for the company's stockholders (including, above all others, George Pullman himself), to whom he believed he owed his primary familial responsibility.[43]

What paternalistic feelings George Pullman harbored were mainly directed toward his town, his brainchild. In an assessment both sympathetic and shrewd, Jane Addams explained that as the town developed "it became a source of pride and an exponent of power" for Pullman "that he cared most for when it gave him a glow of benevolence."[44] It was the source of his continuing wealth, but it was also something more personal than that, and he dressed it up with lakes and parks as much or more to show himself off to the world as to benefit his workers. He gave its main boulevard and its showplace hotel, where no operative could afford to sleep or eat and drink, the same name as his most beloved off-spring. As far as his workers were concerned, he may have desired, like a good parent, that they adopt the "right" values, but this meant that he wanted them to act in such a way that they would be worthy of his town and further burnish its glory. In a time when "manhood" was such an important issue, he treated his workers like "children" in the sense that he did not wish to acknowledge them as adults. He and his representatives repeatedly claimed that he would sell his workers land and housing when what Charles Dudley Warner called "the full evolution of the Pullman idea" came to pass, when "laboring people will voluntarily do . . . what they have been here induced to accept." But this would never happen even if they did everything he expected of them, because it would have meant some sacrifice of corporate control. As a class, the worker-children would never be ready.[45]

One can see this attitude expressed most clearly in the discussion of the actual children of workers in Pullman. The salutary environment of the town, George Pullman was sure, would work toward the "continued elevation and improvement" not merely of his operatives, "but of their children growing up about them." When Richard Ely spoke about the longer-term positive effect of all the aesthetic considerations in the design of the town, he predicted that the atmosphere of Pullman was "only the beginning of an education of the highest faculties, and better things will be seen in the children." And the same article that described Pullman as encouraging workers to "lift themselves to nobler manhood and womanhood" argued that living in the town would also "bring to their children higher conceptions of life."[46] The message in all these remarks was that the children living in Pullman, who were presumably more malleable and tractable than their elders, would instinctively forsake their parents' inferior values and habits for those of the town. They would be educated and elevated in a way that would make them more useful employees and citizens than their mothers and fathers. This arrangement was perhaps paternalistic to the extent that the company was taking responsibility for their upbringing, but it was doing so by displacing their natural paternity and inducing them to deny their own heritage as inferior to that chosen for them by the distant master, George Pullman.[47]

In trying to understand his outlook on the culture of workers and of cities, it is helpful to examine some of the imaginative models for

Pullman's social thought in the years when he was deciding to build his town. While sailing to England in 1872, the year after the fire, Pullman "read and then reread" English author Charles Reade's novel, *Put Yourself in His Place* (1870), which, according to Florence Pullman, "had considerable influence" in her father's life.[48] Its subject was the state of labor in a blighted industrial city called Hillsborough, supposedly based on Sheffield, England, which Pullman visited on his journey. It is crowded with slums that "seem to have battled in the air, and stuck wherever they tumbled down dead out of the mêlée." And "worst of all," it is "pockmarked with public-houses, and bristles with high round chimneys" in chaotic array.[49] The novel takes its title from the pet phrase of a reform-minded physician named Amboyne, who believes that the key to social harmony lies in one's ability to see the world through the eyes of others.

What no doubt made the novel of special interest to Pullman was Reade's attack both on the indifference of manufacturers to the dangerous working environment in their factories and on the destructive arrogance of organized labor. Dr. Amboyne enlists the forward-looking protagonist, Henry Little, in his scrutiny of working conditions, and an "Extract from Henry Little's 'Report' " is appended to the book. This document includes detailed recommendations of what changes are needed to reform the industrial policies and practices which Reade felt jeopardized England's economic future. Reade reserved his harshest criticisms, however, for unions. They are constantly engaged in "rattening," a cowardly strategy of sabotage and terrorism aimed at labor-saving technology and at innovative individuals like Henry, who dare to raise productivity and quality standards. To some extent workers' actions are depicted as understandable responses to employers' abuses, but Reade fiercely condemns labor leaders' opposition to anything that might weaken their control of the workplace and of their members. Owners must choose between going out of business immediately or submitting to unreasonable terms that will probably break them eventually. Union leaders fight even improvements in worker safety because they fear that these will depress wages by keeping more men healthy and able to work. They thus do their constituents real harm as well as contribute to England's decline in the world market.

A man like Pullman would have been drawn to the novel's criticism of the industrial city and of those social forces and institutions— especially organized labor, of which he was always suspicious—that threatened the businessman's control of his company and, by extension, the whole economic order. What would have attracted him most of all, however, was the portrayal of Henry Little, with whom he might understandably have felt a close kinship. Here was a man of genius and vision, a natural gentleman of a modern type whose superiority to other men lay in his ability to combine a craftsman's skill, an inventor's imagination, and an entrepreneur's boldness to remake the world around him for the better. Pullman believed that he, like Henry Little, was out to build not just the best railroad cars in the world but also a finer human race. Early in the book we meet a grinder who is the descendant of generations in his craft. He has a "degenerate face . . . more canine than human," and is particularly resistant to Henry's cleansing and uplifting ideas.[50] He is the type who himself must be reconstructed in Henry's ideal factory, which George Pullman would soon make real just outside Chicago.

The most powerful appeal of *Put Yourself in His Place* to George Pullman may well have been that it enabled him to see himself as coming into a fallen industrial world as a savior and an outsider. Through his achievements in the model town he would prove himself a true aristocrat, a genuine man among pretenders, just the sort of individual to whom the reform and redemption of an unproductive and disordered society should be entrusted. For all their talk about how he understood the conditions of his time, however, Pullman and his supporters did not realize or admit that he was hardly a lone skilled craftsman-inventor like Little, but a wealthy and famous corporate leader complicit in constructing the complex industrial urban world that he was supposedly remaking.[51] Perhaps because he was so enveloped by praise, much of it generated by his own tireless public relations machinery, George Pullman was not able to do what Reade's title asked and understand how his town looked through the eyes of a worker, and so he could never perceive fully what it meant that within a supposedly democratic republic a single industrialist could build a city where the only word that counted was his.

Dark Features

Even in its early years, Pullman's industrial utopia had its critics. In some cases their motives and their information were somewhat suspect. In 1883 the *Chicago Herald,* the most vocal anti-Pullman paper at the time, ran a series of stories, some factually questionable, on nepotism and housing abuses in the model town. In one of them the *Herald* dubbed Pullman a "pseudo-philanthropist." Three years later it characterized his company as "a corporation without a soul," a charge repeated by the *Philadelphia Evening Bulletin,* which listed several unfair practices and predicted the town's demise. By 1888 the *Herald* regularly referred to George Pullman as "the Duke" because of what it saw as his aristocratic pretensions and his desire for absolute power. "About the only difference between slavery at Pullman and what it was down South before the war," a worker supposedly told a reporter, "is that there the owners took care of their slaves when they were sick and here they don't."[52]

A few years earlier, this particular charge had come from a far less "respectable" voice. In December of 1884, Albert Parsons, Samuel Fielden, and August Spies addressed a meeting called by the International Working People's Association just outside the model town. "What is Pullman," Parsons asked, "but a plantation, a penitentiary, a slave-pen, where 4,000 men come and go at the beck and call of one man?" Parsons and Michael Schwab were back the following fall, when a reduction in wages led to strike talk. The *Tribune* reported that Parsons's audience included eight hundred Pullman workers, and that for over an hour he "howled forth his denunciations of capitalists and monopolists in his usual Lake-front style" before passing out copies of the *Alarm*. "His reference to dynamite, the poor man's weapon, was loudly cheered," the *Tribune* noted. The company was sufficiently disturbed by this meeting to have a spokesman dismiss its significance. The most important outcome of the gathering may have been to spur George Pullman to contribute seven months later to Police Captain Michael Schaack's persecution of "subversives."[53]

By far the most damaging criticism of Pullman prior to the strike of 1894 appeared several months before Parsons's harangue, however, and in one of the most distinguished forums in the country. In 1884 *Harper's New Monthly Magazine* had asked Richard Ely to write an article on the town. Ely, at that point an assistant professor of economics at Johns Hopkins, decided to combine his research with his honeymoon, and he and his wife checked into the Hotel Florence for a ten-day visit at the beginning of October, shortly after the departure of Carroll Wright and his colleagues. "Pullman: A Social Study," extensively illustrated with maps of the town, exterior and interior views of major buildings, and floor designs of the dwellings, appeared the following February.[54]

Ely began by observing that all the current political agitation in western industrial countries reflected the truth that "[t]he pretty dream of a perfect, natural order of things brought about by the free play of unrestrained social forces has vanished." Pullman's "social experimentation on a vast scale" demanded attention precisely because of the "eager interest in social and economic facts" that was provoking discussion across the political spectrum about the need to regulate "the unrestrained action of existing economic forces." The model town raised several important questions that needed to be answered: "Is Pullman a success from a social standpoint? Is it worthy of imitation? Is it likely to inaugurate a new era in society? If only a partial success, what are its bright features and what its dark features?"[55]

What attracted most attention at the time and since were Ely's comments on the "dark features," but in fact he began by joining in the prevalent praise for the "sagacious foresight" behind the town's integrated design, its recognition of "the *commercial value of beauty,*" its approach to the problem of the "diffusion of the benefits of concentrated wealth among wealth-creators," its attention to hygiene and the well-being of injured and disabled employees, and its efforts at education and uplift. Speaking with the same superior tone that characterized most commentary on Pullman, Ely noted with approval the enthusiasm of the wife of a worker for her new surroundings: "Pullman had taught her better things than she formerly knew, and thus it is becoming a great school, elevating laborers to a higher plane of wholesome living." He endorsed the action of a town official who sent plants to a woman who managed a particularly well-kept house, since "the effects of systematic persistence in little acts of kind thoughtfulness like these is seen in the diffusion of a spirit of mutual helpfulness, and in frequent attempts to give practical, even if imperfect, expressions to the truth of the brotherhood of man." Ely judged such gestures as essential to the long-term effort of using culture to improve the quality of workers as a class. One sign of this improvement was the art works, mainly prints and engravings, he saw on the walls of some workers' homes. If the taste was not up to the standards of "a highly developed aestheticism," one had to keep in mind that this was "only the beginning of an education of the highest faculties."[56]

"In the way of material comforts and beautiful surroundings," Ely observed in perhaps his most condescending statement, "Pullman probably offers to the majority of its residents quite as much as they are in a position to enjoy, and in many cases even more." Several of the flaws he found in the town were relatively minor in relation to its high aspirations and considerable achievements, and several of these shortcomings were not vital to the basic character of the experiment. There was a "needless air of secrecy" that made it difficult for him to obtain reliable statistics for his article; the diversity of the architecture, even if it was better than in the typical city, was still "not all that could be desired," so that the overall impression was not pleasing but "monotonous, and rather wearying to the eye"; and the living conditions of the unskilled workers who made up a quarter of the labor force were crowded and dreary, if still "vastly better than the poorer class of New York tenements."[57]

In the last few pages of the article, however, Ely's comments turned sharply negative, as he enumerated the "unpleasant features of social life" in Pullman that "are soon noticed by the careful observer." These included bad middle-management rife with favoritism, which discouraged good work and led to high turnover and "an all-pervading feeling of insecurity." Unlike virtually every other evaluator, Ely evidently took the trouble to interview residents and employees, and he found operatives who complained of their lack of a close identification with the town and who described living in Pullman as "camping out." But, worst of all, and most corrosive to the establishment of a genuine community, was the completeness of Pullman's control of the lives of its workers and residents, next to which, Ely said, the power of Bismarck in Germany was "utterly insignificant." The destructive psychological effect of this situation was palpable, no matter how good George Pullman's intentions or even his actions were: "Whether the power be exercised rightfully or wrongfully, it is there all the same, and every man, woman, and child is completely at its mercy, and it can be avoided only by emigration."

In Ely's opinion, Pullman was a city that paid a very high cost in human rights for its beauty and order. It was dangerously lacking in any newspaper or other independent political or moral voice, including from the pulpit. Ely remarked on the chilling fear felt by residents, especially men, that kept them from saying what was on their minds, lest they be reported. This was not the showplace that the company wanted the world to see, but a "sad spectacle," a "population of eight thousand souls where not one single person dare speak out openly his opinion about the town in which he lives. One feels that one is mingling with a dependent, servile people." Ely decried the unwillingness of the company to give the workers a financial interest in the town or an opportunity for self-government that would form the basis of a stable social order far better than would the policy of total control from above. "The citizen is surrounded by constant restraint and restriction, and everything is done for him, nothing by him," Ely wrote. This caused the repression of "any marked individuality." To Ely, the town of Pullman remade urban workers not into finer citizens in a better community, but into dehumanized industrial products in a place with no community at all except a manufactured one. As he described it, "Everything tends to stamp upon residents, as upon the town, the character expressed in 'machine-made.'"[58]

Ely's conclusion, to put it in some of the same key terms in which Haymarket was discussed, was that the social order of Pullman was foreign, unmanly, and unnatural. Remarking on how little the residents controlled the governance of their lives, he wrote, "The people of the place had no more to say about it than a resident of Kamtchatka." The "facts of the case" led to the unavoidable conclusion "that the idea of

Pullman is un-American." The best name for the policies that un-
manned the workers in the town was not paternalism but "benevolent,
well-wishing feudalism," and what was really needed was greater democracy. The Pullman experiment was anything but worthy of imitation, since it stood for, the town's marriage of beauty and utility
notwithstanding, "[t]he establishment of the most absolute power of
capital, and the repression of all freedom." Even if the company was
well-meaning, there could be no assurances that it would always be benevolent. It was anything but progressive in its orientation, or educative
and uplifting in its most significant results, since the unlimited power
and perpetual dependence on which it was based unnaturally "de-
grades the dependent, corrupts the morals of the superior, and finally
that is done unblushingly in the light which was once scarcely allowed
in a dark corner. This is the history of a large share of the degeneracy of
manners and morals in public and private life."

Ely closed on this note of concern, raising the question of whether
one of the most troubling signs of the times evidenced in Pullman was,
as the anarchists were claiming, the forging of "new bonds of dependence." He asked his readers, using the same metaphor as did Carroll
Wright and Charles Dudley Warner in expressing their approval of the
model town, "Are we not frequently trying to offer the gilded cage as a
substitute for personal liberty?" His concluding thought was that both
capitalism and its radical critics had become overly materialistic and
had lost sight of the effect of materialism on "the formation of character" to such an extent that "the impassioned pleas for liberty which
moved Americans mightily one hundred years ago fall to-day on the ear
as something strange and ridiculous." He ended with one last sobering
rhetorical question: "Have we reason to be pleased with the direction in
which the current is setting?"[59]

The criticism in the second half of Ely's article was all the more powerful because it went well beyond the faults of Pullman to express concern about the wide and enthusiastic response that the town had so far
received. Reflecting on chaos and control a year before the Haymarket
bomb, Ely wondered out loud whether the price many Americans were
willing to pay for a clean and orderly nation was the sacrifice of those
very principles and values that gave the United States its identity. Attractive as it might seem to middle-class Americans and perhaps to
some workers alarmed at the problem of labor and the disorderly propensities of American city life, Pullman was in many senses a captive
territory whose example could not be followed without the risk of the
country becoming estranged from itself.

Ely's article provoked other commentary early in 1885 that questioned the Pullman experiment. The *New York Sun* called George

Pullman "a philanthropic despot" and contended that the failure of the town was "inevitable from the start" since Americans cherished liberty over material things. "People want to regulate their own lives," the *Sun* observed, "and they enjoy freedom even more than they do Wilton carpets, and velvety lawns, and scientific drainage with a despot, even a philanthropic despot, to mark out their path for them." The *Nation* picked up on Ely's remarks on the "foreignness" of Pullman, commenting that the town was "alien from the republic in which it exists. . . . It can no more become the social unit of the future than the national character can become Asiatic, a compound of tyranny and torpor." Similarly, the "natural" values that Pullman violated went back even further than the founding of the nation, to the formation of the Anglo-Saxon character. Undertaken "without regard to the underlying principles of our nationality bred into the race by a thousand years of ever-increasing popular liberty," the Pullman experiment was "one of the strikingly characteristic phenomena of the machine-making age." It promised anything but long-term social stability since it depended on "the complete autocracy of corporate wealth" and the beneficence of this lone, powerful individual, not the cooperative effort of an entire people.[60]

The strongly positive response to Pullman continued to dominate commentary on the town, however. Charles Dudley Warner's upbeat report on Pullman was published in the pages of *Harper's* more than three years after Ely's article appeared there, which was a year after the Haymarket executions, and Warner responded directly to the criticism of the company's total ownership and regulation of living conditions in the town with the same defenses that had been offered before. Given the alternatives, it apparently struck many that it was acceptable to build new cities where control of all property was in the hands of an autocratic captain of industry, and where the workers were put not so much in a cage of gold but one made of regulations and drainage pipes in which they "could turn nowhere without meeting order." To follow Pullman's lead, after all, would avoid what a St. Louis paper in 1882 called "the beaten paths of ugliness."[61] It would, in short, avoid building another Chicago, where chaos seemed to be inevitable.

TEN

Putting Pullman in Its Place

The Search for a New Urban Order

The model town was an exceptional combination of corporate enterprise and urban planning that was extraordinary in the thoroughness of
the original design, its scale and complexity, and the amount of notice it
received. But the building of Pullman was neither a unique or unprecedented development. Carroll Wright and Richard Ely were among
many observers who compared it to several similar projects in other industrial nations and across the United States.[1] It also belonged to a rich
American tradition of antebellum mill villages, plantations, company
towns, and communitarian experiments, and it was one of several pioneering "satellite cities" devoted to manufacturing that were emerging near major metropolitan centers.[2] Nor were the kinds of comments
Pullman received something new or isolated. The discontent and dissatisfaction with modern industrial life that lay behind all the attention
paid to Pullman were part of a continuing discussion of urbanization
and social disorder that began in Europe in the eighteenth century.
When American analyses of mechanization and urbanization appeared
in substantial numbers in the decades before the Civil War, they joined
a large body of works by a variety of figures from William Blake to Karl
Marx, many of whom had their followers in the United States.

By the time George Pullman broke ground in Hyde Park, however,
the nature of this discontent and dissatisfaction had become particularly intense. The feeling that something was fundamentally wrong
with the disorderly and unstable culture of the Chicagos of the world
explains the high level of interest in the town and the fact that many
others were prompted to ponder how the alarming tendencies of urban
industrial life might be corrected and the promise of the city realized.[3]

Several authors expressed their ideas in articles and books that attracted a wide public interest. Most of these works were written with cities like Chicago expressly in mind. A few individuals or their followers, like Pullman, were able to see their thoughts put into action, and some of the most notable of other contemporary efforts to maintain or establish an acceptable and attractive urban order were also located in Chicago. Each of these plans and projects, including the model town, is most richly understood in relation to the others, and together they reveal a great deal about how Americans understood city life at the end of the nineteenth century.

In spite of their many real differences, there is a notable overlap in these different reform efforts relating to urban order and disorder. Along with George Pullman, their framers and backers presented proposals that they believed would reconcile individual self-interest and the common good without violence, though they sometimes warned that adopting their proposals was America's last best hope for avoiding social apocalypse. While many political leaders, businessmen, reformers, and commentators often stated that what they wanted to do was realize the promise of urban life, they found it hard to think of the city as it was except as a problematic center of disorder. They also frequently expressed the belief that the causes of disorder were within the system as currently constituted, and mainly in the cataclysmic American city. They implicitly or explicitly declared that the country's urban centers desperately needed to be reformed, possibly even abandoned, if the future of the true America that they threatened was to be assured. While they claimed to be realistic and forward-looking in their thinking, their solutions frequently evaded rather than confronted contemporary reality not, as the fire literature had done, by an escape into the future, but by a retreat into the past.

Rediscovering America

The period between the founding of Pullman and the strike against it witnessed the publication of a remarkable number of social critiques and cataclysmic warnings—and combinations of both.[4] The broad range of the most closely argued analyses is suggested by two prominent and popular works from the mid-1880s, the Reverend Josiah Strong's *Our Country* (1885) and Laurence Gronlund's *The Cooperative Commonwealth* (1884). The purpose of the former, which was published under the auspices of the American Home Missionary Society, was to express "the imperative need . . . for the evangelization of the land," while the latter was among the earliest book-length popularizations in the United States of Marxist ideas.[5] Most discussions of contemporary social ills that found a significant audience fell within the poles of thought defined by Strong and Gronlund, though they frequently included elements of both men's thinking, linking a sometimes strongly xenophobic summons to moral rearmament with a call for fundamental reforms in the structure of society. Three books from the period belong in a category all their own, however, because of the interest stirred by their visions of what John L. Thomas terms an "alternative America" that would redirect the unhappy course of social change.[6] While neither strikingly original, remarkably profound, nor particularly well-written, Henry George's *Progress and Poverty* (1879), Edward Bellamy's *Looking Backward* (1888), and Henry Demarest Lloyd's *Wealth Against Commonwealth* (1894) individually and collectively evoked such a broad response because their authors, like George Pullman, seemed to address the problems of the age simply, boldly, and comprehensively.

Despite their many distinctive qualities, several important elements linked these authors to each other and to the development of reform thinking in the last two decades of the century.[7] George, Bellamy, and Lloyd, along with Gronlund and even Strong, shared a suspicion of the traditional economic rationalizations of free enterprise, believing that these were used to justify a society that was based on selfishness and perilously divided into rich and poor.[8] While George and Bellamy in particular were, like Gronlund, quick to distance themselves from anarchism (*Looking Backward* suggests that the anarchists were secret agents of monopoly hired to turn the public against reform), they argued along with Spies and Parsons (and Strong) that the current system was social dynamite. They claimed to appeal to the best, rather than the worst, in the individual spirit, in ways that would foster human community and encourage in all citizens a belief in the value to all of universal education and training, productive labor, and social service.

The rise of powerful industries like the Pullman Company might at first seem to be the main source of the "progress" that George believed inevitably produced poverty, the constant social strife that Bellamy described as the defining condition of his time, and the "wealth" that Lloyd argued was at war with commonwealth, but significant aspects of the thinking of these men resembled the Pullman idea.[9] Along with the founder of the model town, they approached the complex social conditions of their time with programs which, they claimed, joined the practical and the ideal in a way that would assure a prosperous society free of conflict and the threat of social revolution. With the possible exception of Lloyd, these authors shared the patronizing assumption of Pullman and his supporters that the worker needed to be improved by being educated in middle-class values.[10] In presenting their ideas,

George, Bellamy, and Lloyd also expressed some of the same reservations about urban life as did those who admired Pullman, and their vision of the reformed city closely resembled some of the hopes that surrounded the model town.[11]

From the outset, *Progress and Poverty* virtually equated the historical movement toward urbanization with the fall of man. "In the United States it is clear," George maintained in a tone as righteous as Josiah Strong's, "that squalor and misery, and the vices and crimes that spring from them, everywhere increase as the village grows into the city, and the march of development brings the advantages of the improved methods of production and exchange." Shortly before this, he observed, "Where the conditions to which material progress everywhere tends are most fully realized—that is to say, where population is densest, wealth greatest, and the machinery of production and exchange most highly developed—we find the deepest poverty, the sharpest struggle for existence, and the most of enforced idleness." The worst specific problems he cited were mainly ones identified with cities:

> the social maladjustments that force society to spend millions on charity and which condemn large classes to poverty and vice. . . . The potential earnings of the labor thus going to waste, the cost of the reckless, improvident and idle habits thus generated; the pecuniary loss . . . suggested by the appalling statistics of mortality, and especially infant mortality, among the poorer classes; the waste indicated by the gin palaces or low groggeries which increase as poverty deepens; the damage done by the vermin of society that are bred of poverty and destitution—the thieves, beggars, and tramps; the cost of guarding society against them. . . .

His critique of America's uncontrolled development, prompted by the social conflict of the 1870s, was also unmistakably urban-centered in its vivid evocation of a society where every "advance" was accompanied by further social division and the increased likelihood of class violence. "The 'tramp' comes with the locomotive," he warned, "and almshouses and prisons are as surely the marks of 'material progress' as are costly dwellings, rich warehouses, and magnificent churches. Upon streets lighted with gas and patrolled by uniformed policemen, beggars wait for the passer-by, and in the shadow of the college, and library, and museum, are gathering the more hideous Huns and fiercer Vandals of whom Macaulay prophesied."[12]

George's book received a modest response at first, but then took off, selling two million copies by 1905. Other books and pamphlets he authored added another three million to this count.[13] Among these works was *Social Problems* (1883), some of the most ominous passages of which were quoted or paraphrased by Strong in *Our Country*. Three years before Haymarket, George warned of the vulnerability of urban life to acts of terrorism by enemies of the current order. The strategic deployment of "a little nitroglycerin" could disrupt the water supply and "make a great city uninhabitable," he advised, while "the blowing up of a few railroad bridges and tunnels would bring famine quicker than the wall of circumvallation that Titus drew around Jerusalem," and "the pumping of atmospheric air into the gas-mains, and the application of a match, would tear up every street and level every house."[14] The more basic urban social problem that concerned George as much as the threat of isolated acts of sabotage was a second paradox that he saw accompanying the primary one of progress and poverty: the density and interdependence of the urban population weakened rather than encouraged the development of real human community.

George worried that cities in his own country were following the example of London, where "dwellers in one house do not know those in the next; the tenants of adjoining rooms are utter strangers to each other." The consequence of this was a terrifying social precariousness. "Let civil conflict break or paralyze the authority that preserves order," he maintained, expressing some of the same fears that accompanied the paranoid rumors of criminal behavior at the time of the fire, "and the vast population would become a terror-stricken mob, without point of rally or principle of cohesion, and your London would be sacked and burned by an army of thieves." George rejected any exceptionalist argument that America might be spared: "What is true of London is true of New York, and in the same measure true of the many cities whose hundreds of thousands are steadily growing toward millions." The most dangerous source of unrest was not the unkempt malcontent muttering anarchy into his lager, but the structure of urban society itself. George's comments provide perhaps the period's fullest exposition of the idea of the inherent instability of the city:

These vast aggregations of humanity, where he who seeks isolation may find it more truly than in the desert; where wealth and poverty touch and jostle; where one revels and another starves within a few feet of each other, yet separated by as great a gulf as that fixed between Dives in Hell and Lazarus in Abraham's bosom—they are centers and types of our civilization. Let jar or shock dislocate the complex and delicate organization, let the policeman's club be thrown down or wrested from him, and the fountains of the great deep are opened, and quicker than ever before chaos comes again. Strong as it may seem, our civilization is evolving destructive forces. Not desert and forest, but city slums and country roadsides are nursing the barbarians who may be to the new what Hun and Vandal were to the old.[15]

George claimed that the Single Tax would cure these problems by creating the incentives and disincentives that would disperse the urban population into happy and productive smaller settlements whose citizens would live in harmony with each other and nature, where every man and woman, unfettered by the disadvantages built into the current order, would prosper in proportion to his or her own efforts. They would all dwell in a country where revenue generated by the tax on land would not have to be spent on social control, and would instead be devoted to "public baths, museums, libraries, gardens, lecture rooms, music and dancing halls, theaters, universities, technical schools, shooting galleries, play grounds, gymnasiums, etc." In Henry George's brave new world, "[h]eat, light, and motive power, as well as water, might be conducted through our streets at public expense; our roads be lined with fruit trees; discoverers and inventors rewarded, scientific investigations supported; and in a thousand ways the public revenues made to foster efforts for the public benefit." George Pullman might strongly disagree on how all this would be made possible, but he would offer few arguments on the specific details and overall organization of George's urban vision.[16]

The Haymarket bombing was one of the several outbreaks of labor strife that were critical to crystallizing *Looking Backward* in Edward Bellamy's mind.[17] While Bellamy was not the first reformer of his era to turn to utopian fiction to express and disseminate his ideas, his novel became a pathbreaking literary phenomenon, selling nearly a million copies and spurring dozens of similar books in the next decade and remaining steadily in print to this day.[18] When the story opens in 1887, well-to-do Bostonian Julian West is exasperated by strikes in the trades that have delayed the building of his new home. Public life in the divided city is an "impending social cataclysm," a wasteful, warlike series of crises that, we later learn, economists, with a sense of resignation and defeat, compare to such unavoidable natural catastrophes as droughts and hurricanes: "It only remained to endure them as necessary evils, and when they had passed over to build up again the shattered structure of industry, as dwellers in an earthquake country keep on rebuilding their cities on the same site." The credit system that supposedly holds society together is in reality "a material which an accident might at any moment turn into an explosive."[19]

The unsettled city has made West into an insomniac who must resort to a special subterranean chamber and mesmerism to find rest. These measures work all too well, and Bellamy's hero one evening falls into a sleep that lasts 113 years, from which he awakens to discover a Boston very different from his own and which resembles George's ideal urban center:

At my feet lay a great city. Miles of broad streets, shaded by trees and lined with fine buildings, for the most part not in continuous blocks but set in larger or smaller inclosures, stretched in every direction. Every quarter contained large open squares filled with trees, among which statues glistened and fountains flashed in the late afternoon sun. Public buildings of a colossal size and an architectural grandeur unparalleled in my day raised their stately piles on every side.[20]

It also resembles George Pullman's model town, and in more than a physical sense. While the reader never sees the machinery of productivity in *Looking Backward* or the workers in the industrial army, what allows the whole system to function is the kind of sophisticated organization of labor and life in which Pullman was an innovator. What has made the Boston of 2000 possible, West learns, was the unanimous acceptance of the giant industrial corporation as a social model. Indeed, in *Looking Backward* the labor problem has been solved through the peaceful evolution of private trusts into "a single syndicate representing the people, to be conducted in the common interest for the common profit." In other words, something very much like the Pullman plan was adopted by the nation as a whole, which became "the one great business corporation in which all other corporations were absorbed, . . . the one capitalist in the place of all other capitalists, the sole employer, the final monopoly in the profits and economies of which all citizens shared."[21]

If private ownership has been abolished in this world, other features of the Pullman experiment have not. The answer to urban disorder is not just efficient factories and shops, humane and sensible housing, and attractive fountains and parks, but a tightly bound integration of public and private life in which the individual demonstrates his or her value by fitting in and serving the larger order. Each person's performance is carefully monitored under the watchful eye of officials, who are highly visible counterparts of the incognito "spotters" of the Pullman Company. More significantly, Bellamy's ideal world is governed by distinguished veterans of the industrial army, who are very similar to a board of directors of a giant corporation like the Pullman Company or of an organization like the Relief and Aid Society, a group of wise and powerful men dedicated to making sure that the masses are behaving according to an elite's vision of useful labor. This elite's central task is to maximize productive output and minimize disorder in modern urban industrial life.

In many respects Henry Demarest Lloyd possessed the most open-spirited social vision of the three men, the one most idealistically committed to the transcendence of class division and the restoration of the human family. The national railroad strike of 1877 convinced him that

America was in the grip of plutocratic greed that would destroy it. But he was critical of the ideas of George and Bellamy as cure-alls, and he was more willing to devote himself fully to broad-based political movements.[22] From his groundbreaking articles (starting with "The Story of a Great Monopoly," which appeared in the *Atlantic Monthly* in 1881 and became the basis of *Wealth Against Commonwealth*), Lloyd presented detailed indictments of corporate power. He charged that the Standard Oil Company, through secret agreements with the railroads, unfairly crushed smaller competitors by making it impossible for them to ship their product. Monopolistic corporations cynically sang the praises of free enterprise as they exploited their control of vital industries to sack and pillage the country. The state of America's cities was an indication of the extent of the problem. In the fourth paragraph of *Wealth Against Commonwealth*, hard by his central assertion that "Liberty produces wealth, and wealth destroys liberty," Lloyd included cities (along with "factories, monopolies, fortunes, which are our empires") among "the obesities of an age gluttonous beyond its powers of digestion."[23]

"If our civilization is destroyed, as Macaulay predicted," Lloyd himself prophesied, "it will not be by his barbarians from below. Our barbarians come from above."[24] But in 1881 Lloyd did not consider George Pullman one of these new barbarians. In fact, a few months after his first article on Standard Oil appeared in the *Atlantic*, he prepared an unpublished piece on Pullman that differed very little from the company's own publicity.[25] Lloyd's Pullman manuscript marveled at the limitless possibilities of Chicago's growth and praised the sleeping-car manufacturer for having "irretrievably committed himself" to making his model town "the flower of his achievements in the field of human endeavor." The article was full of dazzling statistics about the power of the Corliss engine, the scale of the capital investment, and the dimensions of the water tower and the shops. It described the housing as modern and scientific, the grounds and works as safe and attractive, the overall site plan as efficient and convenient.

"Pullman," Lloyd concluded, "is one of the half dozen noted places in the world where brains have been mixed with the mortar from the foundations to the roofs, and where the self-interest of the capitalist has been something shrewder than selfishness of the ordinary type." By bold planning and by daring to offer his workers so much, its founder had his pick of the best men, whom he could then mold into a productive and loyal work force in a place where "the troublesome disputes between capital and labor [could be] avoided."[26] Along with Pullman, George, and Bellamy, however, Lloyd expressed doubt whether these or other "troublesome disputes" that were characteristic of the time could be avoided in the typical American industrial city, and whether it was not a matter of necessity to construct some alternative social order. "A really human life is impossible in our cities," he lamented near the close of *Wealth Against Commonwealth*. While Lloyd by this time would have disagreed with Pullman's basic premise that the enlightened use of corporate wealth could, without interference, preclude all "interpositions" to social and economic success, he, too, suspected that it was necessary to abandon the old city and start anew to achieve a stable and attractive urban order. If America's cities could somehow be constructed all over again, however, it was essential to escape "the old self-interest" that currently dominated them. As for his own city, he added, "Chicago was rebuilt wrong after the fire."[27]

A major novel by one of the most well known authors of the period serves as an intriguing, if anything but conclusive, additional piece of imaginative evidence in the effort to put Pullman in its cultural place amidst the period's collective meditation on modern industrial order. Despite Mark Twain's unmistakably idiosyncratic vision, his *A Connecticut Yankee in King Arthur's Court* (1889) is part of the same milieu as *Put Yourself in His Place*, *Progress and Poverty*, *Looking Backward*, and the town of Pullman.[28] The career of protagonist Hank Morgan recalls that of George Pullman and offers an interesting counterpoint to the experiences of Charles Reade's Henry Little. This son of a blacksmith has risen to head superintendent of an enormous arms factory in Hartford on the strength of his personality and technological aptitude. Finding himself transported back in time much as Julian West travels ahead, he discovers that King Arthur's Camelot has even more opportunities for a man with his assurance and expertise than Gilded Age Chicago had for George Pullman.

Twain's personal writings show his increasing sympathy with the cause of labor and the oppressed through the 1880s, as well as his enthusiasm even for the excesses of the French Revolution as an antidote to the tyranny of wealth, privilege, and superstition masquerading as religion.[29] *A Connecticut Yankee*, however, seems to support some important elements of the Pullman idea. Henry Nash Smith is correct in saying that Hank Morgan "is a vernacular hero but also a capitalist hero." Like Pullman, Hank creates an alternative industrial world where he is Sir Boss, running a tightly organized system that radiates along lines of force emanating from his own inventive and ambitious mind. Smith argues that one of Twain's key innovations was "his deliberate abandonment of the genteel perspective," but this abandonment is hardly complete.[30] Hank may not be exactly genteel, but he keeps his distance from most of the population and expresses his contempt for all but a few. One of his initiatives—turning his bravest knights into sandwich men on horseback who bear snappy slogans advertising soap and toothbrushes—is a sanitation project that would have pleased Pullman. Among the "several wholesome purposes" of this particular enterprise "in view toward the civilizing and uplifting of this nation," Hank explains in a passage reminiscent of the praise lavished on the model town's hygiene and the condemnation of the anarchists as dirty, are the undermining of knight-errantry and also, "without creating suspicion or exciting alarm," the introduction of "a rudimentary cleanliness among the nobility," which then "would work down to the people, if the priests could be kept quiet."[31]

Hank sets up a new industrial order under Camelot's nose, as Pullman seemed to do just outside Chicago, though he keeps his hidden from the public view rather than publicizing it as Pullman did. Here he builds his own schools and churches, and in time he erects a corporate-progressive dream of order close to that of Bellamy: a thousand trained men overseen by fifty brilliant experts. Wary of the established church and the nobility, he sends out his own spotters, whom he calls "confidential agents," to bring him intelligence. His plan is to reform things gradually, "turning on my light one-candle-power at a time," waiting for the moment he can "flood the midnight world with intolerable light." Having routed knight-errantry and discredited Merlin, Hank feels confident enough to turn the lights on full and reform England completely, bringing universal prosperity by establishing colleges and schools, encouraging literature and journalism, instituting political democracy, equalizing taxation, abolishing slavery, and introducing the telegraph, telephone, phonograph, typewriter, sewing machine, and every other manner of nineteenth-century innovations, including steamboats and trains. He secretly plans to set up a "go-as-you-please" Protestantism, which resembles Pullman's Universalism, in its place, and he hopes eventually to displace the monarchy with a bloodless revolution that will make him the first president. In the meantime, he recalls, "I was getting ready to send out an expedition to discover America."[32]

The most crucial and Pullman-like element of Hank's program of reform and revolution is his plan for training those few individuals he finds who are both intelligent and independent-minded enough to be the experts who can fulfill his vision. He directs his confidential agents to comb the country secretly for those people with the most potential. He sends these recruits to what he describes as "my colony," a "Factory" (Hank supplies the capital F) "where I'm going to turn groping and grubbing automata in *men*." Hank's Man-Factory recalls the remarks of commentators on Pullman describing how the model town would be the mechanism to realize the potential in the common worker. The observation that Pullman would have an especially beneficial effect on the workers' children, who, by living and going to school in the town, would avoid the handicap of being indoctrinated in their parents' culture, finds a haunting echo in Twain's novel. When events begin to turn against his hero, the only allies Hank can now trust are the fifty-two teenage boys who "have been under our training from seven to ten years" and "have had no acquaintance with the Church's terrors." The boys are the sole sure bet in the task of education and uplift, and only because they came under Hank's paternalistic sway early enough.[33]

What complicates the discussion of parallels, of course, is that Twain's novel ends in a bloodbath. Hank's own model town suffers a far worse cataclysm than any fire, bomb, or strike. The ending does not come as a total surprise, however, because of a few foreshadowing remarks throughout the novel, but also because of Hank's persistent fondness, which links him to the anarchists, for guns and explosives as instruments of self-defense, personal empowerment, and radical reform. Halfway through the book, he observes that "all revolutions that will succeed must *begin* in blood, whatever may answer afterward. If history teaches anything, it teaches that." Not much later, when two knights threaten him and Arthur as they travel through the kingdom incognito, Hank expertly dispatches them and their mounts with a homemade dynamite bomb very much like the one used in the Haymarket. Hank describes the blast with appreciative detachment as "a neat thing, very neat and pretty to see." He hints that cataclysmic destruction is an inevitable concomitant of progress when he calls the nineteenth-century civilization that he secretly assembles in Arthurian England "as substantial a fact as any serene volcano, standing innocent with its smokeless summit in the blue sky and giving no sign of the rising hell in its bowels." The immediate cause of this hell finally breaking loose is one of Hank's "modern improvements," the stock exchange where Launcelot angers other knights through his manipulation of railroad shares, provoking his victims into exposing his affair with the queen, which soon leads to open war.

The underlying cause of conflict, however, is Hank's systematic program of enlightenment, since it threatens deeply entrenched interests whose influence over the people must be overcome if any meaningful change is to be instituted. In Reade's *Put Yourself in His Place,* the great villain was corrupt labor leaders, while in Twain's novel it is the church. The problem is far greater in *A Connecticut Yankee* because the enemy's hold is wider, deeper, and more long-standing, and because Twain despairs far more than Reade does of mankind's ability to overcome its tendencies toward self-enslavement and barbarism. The church takes advantage of the confusion caused by the scandal in the monarchy to

issue the Interdict, the "fearful disaster" that reinforces the supersti-
tions that empower it in the people's minds and puts out the electric
light of Hank's new industrial and social order. "My dream of a Republic is to *be* a dream, and so remain," Hank gloomily concludes, and con-
soles himself in an orgy of revenge.[34] The serene volcano erupts
completely out of control, with Hank's explosion of all the "civilization-
factories" and his mass slaughter of the enemy in the Battle of the Sand-
Belt with a "red terror" of land mines, Gatling guns, flood, and electro-
cution. The failure of Hank's more noble ideas, and, indeed, of any
ideas, to survive the carnage, has very grim implications about the direction of "progress." Particularly troubling to the modern reader is
Hank's confusion of ends and means; no project of constructive reform
seems to absorb his imagination so thoroughly as the technical details
behind his deadly weaponry.[35]

As an indirect commentary on the Pullman experiment, and as part
of the same far-ranging cultural context of urban disorder and belief, *A
Connecticut Yankee* finally warns about the dangers of an inflexible and
unquestioning faith in any method or system, be it the lies perpetuated
by established authorities like the pope and the king or wholesale reforms such as those instituted by Hank Morgan. Twain was concerned
in this novel, as were few contemporary social analysts, with the incalculable and inexplicable element of human perversity in history, which
became a major theme in his late work. There was, he argued, some
dark element in the human spirit, in the social order, and in "civilization" that constantly threatened to push day into night, democracy into
feudalism, benevolence into tyranny, happy prosperity and progress
into catastrophe.

Recreating Chicago

The clearest evidence that different proposals for remaking modernity
captured the imaginations of many Americans was not just the number
of books that were sold, but the way the more popular works became
the inspiration for political and social action. *Progress and Poverty*
launched the Single Tax movement, and *Looking Backward* became the
sacred founding text of over 150 Nationalist Clubs from coast to coast.
George came close to being elected mayor of New York in 1886, while
Henry Lloyd tried to rally the support of workers and farmers to the
national People's Party. Bellamy, who for reasons of health and inclination was less fully engaged in politics than George and Lloyd were, still
provided financial and vocal support for the Nationalist Clubs, the
People's Party, and various reform publications. The three men and
their followers combined forces on several occasions, though the differ-

ences in their personalities and priorities sometimes put them at cross-purposes. In a few instances, Single Taxers and Nationalists even tried to construct model towns of their own, though these were usually in far more remote locations than Pullman, were much more modest in size and capitalization, and were based in a traditional communitarian idealism that was expressly opposed to modern corporate capitalism.[36] More relevant to the task of understanding the imaginative context of the model town, however, are three other very different undertakings that were near or in Chicago and that, like Pullman, in very different ways tried to control and even civilize the disorderly city.

The first of these made no bones about the fact that it was based in the belief that urban order could be assured through armed force. In the mid-1880s, several Chicago businessmen, led by members of the Commercial Club, lobbied the federal government for the establishment of a local garrison. What they were asking for was a permanent installation of troops of the kind that had been summoned temporarily to protect the city following the fire and during the railroad strike. The Haymarket bombing convinced them that their proposal was a matter of urgency. They were aided considerably by the appointment to the Senate of one of their number, Charles B. Farwell, who had chaired the emotional meeting of civic leaders in the Moody and Sankey Tabernacle in the anxious July days of 1877. By March of 1887 Congress approved the requisite legislation, and a site in Highwood, about thirty miles north of downtown Chicago, was chosen by June. The first troops arrived in the fall, and the official installation was, probably not coincidentally, November 11, 1887, the day of the Haymarket executions. The following February the fort, staffed with soldiers transferred from Fort Douglas in Utah, was named for the members of the Commercial Club's old friend Phil Sheridan, who died a few months later. Situated far from both the country's borders and its vanishing Indian frontier, Fort Sheridan was built to defend Chicago and America from "internal insurrection." The inescapable "idea" behind its construction was that the way to prevent urban disorder was not by improving the masses but by having ready at hand a powerful and effective organization of well-armed professional keepers of order.[37]

When Jane Addams and Ellen Gates Starr moved in September of 1889 into the "hospitable old house" that Charles J. Hull had built in the West Division in 1856, they were just as concerned about the state of urban society as were the businessmen who secured Fort Sheridan, but they had a very different conception of the best way to head off social cataclysm. They chose this location because they believed that what had happened to the Hull home and its neighborhood in three decades demonstrated the problems posed by urban growth and change. This once gracious residence now found itself wedged between a saloon and an undertaker. The Haymarket was about ten blocks up Halsted, the site of the O'Leary barn a few blocks to the southeast. Over the years the house had first been converted by the Little Sisters of the Poor into a home for the aged and then occupied by a secondhand furniture store. Most recently it provided offices and storerooms for a factory just behind it. As Addams explained, her immediate neighbors were three or four colonies of newer immigrants from southern and eastern Europe who crowded into the polyglot nineteenth ward. Of the 50,000 residents in the ward, she claimed, only a seventh had been registered for the 1888 presidential election, and these votes were in the pocket of the local saloon-keepers. The area and its population, in short, were exactly what the whole range of contemporary social analysts believed had to be made over.

As pioneers in the settlement house movement, which directed middle-class energies back into the city that others were ready to abandon, Addams and Starr were hardly free of cultural blind spots, but they were dedicated to the idea that the urban social order was something of immense human value and could be better held together with mutual understanding than by force. The settlement, Addams explained in 1892, was "an experimental effort to aid in the solution of the social and industrial problems which are engendered by the modern conditions of life in a great city." Sounding like George and Lloyd, she added that it was "an attempt to relieve, at the same time, the over-accumulation at one end of society and the destitution at the other" that were the main causes of urban distress.[38] Addams thought that what she called the "social organism" had tragically "broken down through large districts of our cities." She was as troubled about the consequences of this breakdown for people of her own privileged background as she was for recent immigrants, and her move to Hull-House was motivated by what she believed was a widely shared malaise among people like her that was based in a sense of uselessness and disconnection. Where George Pullman maintained a physical and psychological distance from his operatives, Addams likened the settlement to "the big brother whose mere presence on the play-ground protects the little one from bullies." At the time she made this remark, however, she would not have listed Pullman as one of the bullies. In *Twenty Years at Hull-House,* published sixteen years after the Pullman strike (and thirteen years after Pullman's death), she spoke of "his genuine pride and pleasure in the model town he had built with so much care."[39] And while Hull-House was an institution so different from Pullman that comparing them is difficult, some of Addams's methods in working against the dislocations that made normal urban life potentially explosive were an inner-city version of what Pullman was trying to do on the outskirts of Chicago.

Hull-House, like Pullman, developed into a fully integrated (if not as fully preplanned) community. The settlement soon extended over thirteen buildings, including its own versions of the theater, club-rooms, school, library, and playgrounds that Solon Beman assembled in a more orderly, architecturally integrated, and hierarchically regulated fashion. Addams also expressed concern about the special dangers to a healthy urban order posed by such "baneful influences" as the saloons, the brothels, and the cheap and sensational theatrical productions that George Pullman would never allow on the stage of the Arcade Theater. If the Hull-House organizers respected far more than did Pullman or most other urban planners the culture of laborers and immigrants, they still shared some aspects of Pullman's belief that the way to develop and maintain a productive and harmonious citizenry was to promote education and uplift among the working class.[40]

The most elaborate attempt in Chicago to recreate and redefine the city and urban culture, however, was neither the fort nor the settlement house, but the World's Columbian Exposition that ran from May to October, 1893. While Pullman knew that the increase in travel which the exposition would generate promised him additional business no matter where it was located, his civic-mindedness and the unequaled opportunity to show off his model town made him one of the leading proponents of locating the fair in Chicago. When in 1889 Chicago was vying with other cities to be designated as the fair site, the Pullman Company subscribed $100,000 in stock (later doubled) to guarantee the project, and he offered a piece of his land near the town for the fair site. Although the location eventually selected was Jackson Park, about seven miles north of his town, George Pullman's high expectations for the fair, as a boon to both his city and his company, were fulfilled. The first Baedeker guide to America, published in anticipation of the rise in tourism spurred by the exposition, advised visitors to Chicago to tour Pullman, and many of them did. Those who could not see the town itself could still view the company's impressive display in Louis Sullivan's Transportation Building. There, in a prime location near the main entrance, was a plaster of paris scale model of Pullman. Nearby, in an equally prominent position in the enormous annex that held two-and-a-half miles of track on which were mounted railroad cars from Europe and America, was a selection of the company's luxury coaches. The *Chicago Tribune* judged these cars the best in the building. "Of the material benefits to humanity which [Pullman's] labor has wrought," the *Tribune* declared, "the palatial train of World's Fair cars is the expression. It has spoken to the multitudes who have examined it during the season more eloquently than words, and has been Mr. Pullman's silent though effective eulogist."[41]

In sponsoring the fair, Pullman's brethren among Chicago's commercial leaders were trying to construct a businessman's utopia that demonstrated how splendid a world could be built and managed by a small group of enlightened executives who were given complete authority. Like the model town, the Columbian Exposition, with its comprehensive and carefully landscaped grounds designed by Frederick Law Olmsted (who had reported on "Chicago in Ruins" in the *Nation* in 1871), its brilliantly "clean" and white neoclassical Court of Honor created by leading architects under the supervision of Daniel Burnham, and its emphasis on industrial and technological achievement and display, presented to those who paid the fifty-cent admission charge a harmonious and sanitized urban order (many remarked on the fair's "perfect" system of waste removal).[42] For good measure, the Columbian Guards, bedecked in splendid uniforms decorated with fancy braid and broad epaulets, were supplemented by a secret service department under John Bonfield, the former police inspector, who in June of 1893 had been blamed by Governor John Altgeld for the Haymarket riot seven years earlier.[43]

Merely attending the fair was, like living in Pullman or riding on a Pullman Palace Car, an "uplifting" experience that taught the value of middle-class habits of decorum and self-improvement. Architect Henry Van Brunt, who designed the Electricity Building, sang the praises of the exposition in the *Atlantic Monthly*, proclaiming (as many did of Pullman) that "the carefully provided vistas cannot fail . . . to have their due effect upon the mind, and leave upon it an indelible impression of unity and order." He pointed out that the fair offered a special education for the student of architecture in "the virtues of repose and self-repression." In the opinion of Van Brunt, the individual exhibits and the exposition as a whole thus blessed and bettered all who experienced them by offering them "a higher standard by which to measure their own shortcomings and deficiencies." Speaking of these fairgoers much as visitors to Pullman and its founder discussed the town's working-class residents, Van Brunt assured his readers, "They will be suddenly confronted by new ideals and inspired by higher ambitions; they will find in themselves qualities hitherto unsuspected, capacities for happiness and powers of production hitherto unknown."[44] Not only individuals, but whole cities, starting with Chicago, could measure their shortcomings and deficiencies by comparison with this lofty example, and might then improve themselves accordingly by following its lead.

Whether the pristine urban paradise of the exposition was in fact a practical model was an open question. Some of the most effusive descriptions were enraptured recollections of the world's fair experience as a temporary interlude that offered a glimpse of a dream city that was, unfortunately, beyond the reach of the "real" world.[45] Architecture critic Montgomery Schuyler intruded into such musings with a more down-to-earth criticism of the fair's lack of a vital and meaningful connection to urban reality, calling its design "holiday building" and "occasional architecture," a "success of unity, and a success of magnitude," but "also and very eminently a success of illusion." Schuyler's critique of the "fairy" city as being "foreign" to the real America recalled Richard Ely's much harsher remarks on Pullman's alien political culture. "It is essential to the illusion of a fairy city that it should not be an American city of the nineteenth century," Schuyler explained, adding, "Arcadian architecture is one thing and American architecture is another."[46]

The fair did seem to show, however, that the utopian thinking of the preceding years was within the realm of possibility. Accounts of the exposition were often almost indistinguishable from Bellamy's vision of the Boston of 2000 in *Looking Backward*, which was published five years before the fair opened. Bellamy's description of the great store Julian West visits, with its "majestic life-size group of statuary, the central figure of which was a female ideal of Plenty," was a fantasy many believed that they actually experienced while touring the Court of Honor.[47] The exposition served in turn as a forum and an inspiration for further reflection on the prospects for the future. In conjunction with the fair, several conventions of different religious, social, and intellectual groups were held in the new Art Institute of Chicago across Michigan Avenue from the downtown headquarters of the Pullman Company, on the same location that had been occupied by the Inter-State Exposition Building.

The fair likewise had a lasting influence on public architecture and on the City Beautiful movement. The popular success of the World's Columbian Exposition helped inspire a series of major city-reconstruction plans, including those Burnham was asked to prepare over the next several years for Washington, Cleveland, San Francisco, and Chicago. The Chicago Plan of 1909 was commissioned by the Commercial Club, which wanted him to extend his (and their) triumph at the fair to the city at large. But others with very different political and social outlooks also drew inspiration from the White City. The Columbian Exposition seems to have served as a remarkably flexible model, not only reassuring men like Pullman that the world they were making was sound, but also even encouraging those with more critical views that major reforms were possible. William Dean Howells, by this time a critic of the destructive effects of capitalist competition, remarked that the White City was one of the happiest places in the country "perhaps because the place is so little American in the accepted sense," but he also expressed the hope that the fair might instruct the world in the value of those cities that were the result of "a design, the effect of a principle, and not the straggling and shapeless accretion of accident." Eugene Victor Debs praised the "lofty ideal" of the exposition for its "healthful influences . . . upon the national character."[48] Few saw the irony and cultural anxiety in the desire to recuperate American urban life by reconstructing it in such "alien" forms.

Looking Backward

The most revealing of all the thoughts on urban order and disorder that the fair inspired in its own time were expressed by Henry Demarest Lloyd. Lloyd was among those reformers the fair most profoundly moved. He was the secretary of the program committee of the World's Labor Congress, to which he invited, according to Thomas, "Single Taxers, Fabians, Christian Socialists, and communitarians of all stripes, who debated proposals on slum clearance and social insurance, public ownership and binding arbitration, child labor laws and direct democracy." Jane Addams recalled that "[o]f the remarkable congresses held in connection with the World's Fair, perhaps those inaugurated by the advocates of [a] single tax exceeded all others in vital enthusiasm." Lloyd also asked Edward Bellamy to come, but he was too ill to attend.[49] The spirit of the fair affected Lloyd so deeply that he was moved to try his own hand at utopian speculation. The result was a popular talk that he later published. In "No Mean City," Lloyd invited his listeners and readers to consider a post-exposition "history" of the evolution of Chicago looking back from a point late in the twentieth century. As Lloyd hopefully imagined it, this history began with the closing of the fair and the dismantling of all the exhibition buildings. Then miraculously transpired a mass secular conversion with strong Christian overtones (as the essay's title suggested) that resembled the mechanism of change in *Looking Backward.* It was "a deep and sudden vision of what had been the soul of the Dream City" that came "into the minds of the people as by the dropping of scales from their eyes." They now fully recognized for the first time that "[t]hey had created a new beauty that would be radiant in the memory of mankind," and that would liberate them from "smoke and whir, dinners, sleep and dollars," from destructive and disheartening competition with their fellow-man. "Under this new inspiration, the people rose spontaneously against the destruction of the World's Fair City, and demanded that it be rebuilt."[50]

Designed by the greatest artists and architects, the rebuilt fair was as splendid as the original exposition, but it was made to last and be lived in, not just visited over one long summer. It was more of an environmentalist's dream than even the Columbian Exposition's sponsors ever imagined. In this earthly paradise of Christian democracy the Liberty Bell was rehung and throughout the day rang out its message, "A new commandment I give unto you, that ye love one another." Here rich and poor gathered to marshal their labor and their resources, overcoming their "meannesses, shortages, hatreds" in their dedication to the common good. "While they were thus engaged," Lloyd explained, "the spiritual secret of the power that was in them became revealed to the people." In this setting, "Violence of speech, destruction of life and property,illegal riots by the people, and legal riots by the police and military got to be obsolete."[51] In short, movements like anarchism and social cataclysms like those that took place in 1877 and 1886 simply disappeared in a self-regulating social order. This was accompanied by advances in sexual equality and in commerce, both of which further improved the moral tone of society without diminishing in any way its productive capabilities. Compulsory school ages were raised, child labor was banned, and working conditions became safe and humane. Armed with figures supplied by political scientists and statisticians that proved the social and economic benefits of putting everyone to work, society effectively solved the labor problem by buying tracts of land for cooperative colonies to retrain the unemployed.

Lloyd's colonies shared some important features not only with the proposals of *Progress and Poverty* and *Looking Backward,* but also with Pullman. "Every feature of the experiments" was to be "planned by experts—from the selection of the site to the division of employments." Cleanliness and order were to be their leading features, for in them "[a] scheme of life was platted in which were embodied all the latest and best results of sanitary, industrial, and artistic experience here and in Europe." As was true in the model town, cleanliness was next to godliness. The river "was held as sacred by the sanitary engineers as by the landscape architects. Not one drop of sewage was ever to be allowed to soil its waters and banks or to be discharged by it upon the luckless people living beyond." Around every house was a garden, and all citizens were given occupations "for which they were fitted." Lest one fear that there was something repressive about this community, Lloyd pointed out that "[t]he very tramps ran over each other for a chance to live the life possible there." Completely won over by the spirit of the place, all its residents worked harder than they ever did before. In the new social order of "No Mean City," labor was not degrading, but a "badge of honor" that made life "bright, happy, beautiful, and rich for all."

The inevitable occurred when Chicago was finally "annexed to its offspring No Mean City," population twenty million. The old city, "now regarded as a horror and an injury to the health, morals, and artistic sensibilities of the people," was legally condemned. The mistakes of the urban past were thus corrected by obliterating Chicago and rebuilding from scratch. It was replaced by "a great Court of Honor," modeled on that of the exposition. The river and lake were restored to "their original purity and beauty," the soil "ploughed and disinfected, and sown with aromatic plants," and the old downtown turned into a great park of universities, theaters, libraries, meeting-halls, coliseums for sports and public festivals, and temples of every religion on earth—into residential Pullman writ large. "The world had seen many great cities, but here for the first time it saw a good city—good enough for human beings to be born in, to live in, and to die in."[52] To clear the way for this urban elysium, Chicago was ceremonially razed on October 9, 1971, the centennial of the fire.

Lloyd's "No Mean City" thus ended on a note that explicitly recalled the fire literature's emphasis on renewal and that rejected the carnage and despair of *A Connecticut Yankee* and of urban dystopias like Ignatius Donnelly's *Caesar's Column* (1890). Lloyd seemed to accept the premise that Chicago was a locus of uncontrollable filth and inhuman destructiveness that could best be dealt with by not dealing with it at all. The wisest course of action would be to remove every trace of the city with a purifying fire that was perhaps not so different from the uncontrolled self-destruction that reigned at the end of Twain's and Donnelly's novels, and then to start over under the care of enlightened experts whose leadership was universally agreed to in some beatific moment of revelation and universal acceptance of the ideals of Christian brotherhood in the form of efficient cooperative enterprise. Meaningful reform takes place when Chicago finally chokes on its own foulness and dies, put out of its misery with a planned catastrophe. Its salvation depends upon its destruction.

Lloyd should have known by this time that his vision was not going to come true, that Chicago was not going to wither away in the shadow of some paradise on its periphery, but would itself continue to expand while drawing population from the countryside and incorporating other towns. All he needed to do was see what had happened to Pullman. Five years earlier, far from absorbing the residents of an abandoned Chicago, the "radiant little island" that was the model town was itself legally swallowed through popular referendum by "Chicago's swelling tide." This election followed a national trend in which citizens in smaller municipalities adjoining cities, eager for better government services and other resources of major urban centers, chose to become part of a larger metropolis. Hyde Park was one of several towns neighboring Chicago that voted to be annexed at this time.

It is not clear to what extent George Pullman perceived that his experiment's success and fame had encouraged the nearby population growth and economic development that, with or without actual legal annexation to Chicago, had already effectively made his town part of the city. He strongly opposed the annexation movement, not only because he believed his own town's services were better than those in the city and that he could get more favorable rates on water and property taxes from Hyde Park, but also because in a more personal and symbolic sense the merger threatened the purity of his namesake town as a separate and superior community administered by an enlightened corporation rather than by mere politicians. He had managed to get Pullman exempted when Hyde Park first approved annexation in 1887, but this vote was voided and another election that included the model town was set for June of 1889. Even though by this time Hyde Park's government was less friendly than it had been previously to company interests, Pullman continued to resist union with Chicago, and he sponsored an anti-annexation rally in the Arcade Theater. While better than three-fourths of the votes cast in Pullman itself were negative, the measure passed.[53]

A few local reporters used the annexation debate to attack George Pullman personally and to focus on discontent in his town. Their stories contradicted all the commentary that offered Pullman as an example of how to avoid the catastrophe that otherwise threatened the American city and the nation as a whole. The *Chicago Evening Journal* reported early in 1888, for example, that "Sir George Pullman, unlimited potentate of the little kingdom in the southern end of Hyde Park," would be "grieved and shocked" to learn that many of his "subjects, discontented with the rigor of his rule, and the consequent hardship of their lot," were eager to vote for annexation. "Tired of the pomp and circumstance of royalty," the story continued, "the inhabitants pine for the democratic simplicity of a city like Chicago."[54]

For all of the "realistic" claims of the popular social reformers of Pullman's era (in the opening chapter of *Wealth Against Commonwealth* Lloyd called his book "a venture in realism in the world of realities"), most of them shared with Pullman a nostalgia for a simpler time that saw the modern city as the principle of social disorder, the site and source of the potential disaster that would end all hopeful dreams of an

American future. Josiah Strong expressed both his sense of alarm and his program for reform in specifically evangelical Christian terms that, however much they dealt with contemporary conditions, equated the conditions of modernity—and cities in particular—with catastrophe. His plan for urban redemption hinged on Christ's intervention in human affairs, which were beyond salvation by other means. Recalling Shelley's comparison of London to hell, he reminded his readers that "the city redeemed is, in the vision of the revelator, the symbol of *heaven*—heaven on earth—the Kingdom fully come."[55] George, Bellamy, and Lloyd likewise offered proposals driven by a desire to establish what John L. Thomas calls (in specific reference to George) "a transpolitical and transhistorical realm of social harmony" that was less trenchant social analysis than a yearning for the restoration of an order that never was and never could be.[56] Essential to this yearning was the desire for the sudden miraculous emergence of a social consensus, a kind of universal simultaneous secular epiphany, that would somehow overcome all political and social conflict and provide the intellectual and spiritual impulse behind the physical redistribution of the urban population and the complete makeover of the cityscape—whether as Strong's Coming Kingdom, Gronlund's Cooperative Commonwealth, George's Single Tax economy, Bellamy's Boston in the year 2000, Burnham's Court of Honor and Chicago Plan, or Lloyd's "No Mean City"—and at once solve all the problems of physical and moral disorder posed by modern urban culture.

How much did George Pullman and those whose favorable notice his experiment attracted share this vision and desire? Pullman never moved out of dirty Chicago (though he spent significant portions of his time either traveling on business or at his vacation homes in New Jersey and the Thousand Islands), and if he tried to build a city that was as pastoral and village-like as possible, one must keep in mind that the real heart of his model town was not the Arcade or the dwellings but an immense factory that was based (as was the Columbian Exposition) in an economic and social order that had forever superseded the Jeffersonian ideal of a nation of small producers. But Pullman apparently believed that modernity could still be encompassed and expressed through the creation of an ordered community loyal to the "old" values of morality and self-help, even if these values had to be imposed from above, and even if his achievements in following these values had helped create a world in which his extraordinary personal success would be harder rather than easier for one of his resident-operatives to replicate.

To the extent that his social order was paternalistic and, as some critics charged, feudal, Pullman looked further backward than did Strong, George, Bellamy, Lloyd, and others who wished to restore the country to itself. The model town demonstrated his conviction that order was not to be found in modern America but had to be artificially made, and that perhaps the best way to confront the future was to use the immense resources of his corporation to try to fit his mighty modern industrial machine into his idealized vision of the past. The Pullman "idea" was ultimately rejected by his workers, and his model town, designed as a showcase for a more harmonious future, soon became the period's most notorious source of the disorder it was trying to transcend.

ELEVEN

Making Sense of the Age

"The Pullman strike," Jane Addams recollected in *Twenty Years at Hull-House*, "afforded much illumination to many Chicago people. Before it, there had been nothing in my experience to reveal that distinct cleavage of society, which a general strike at least momentarily affords." She described it elsewhere in literary terms as "a drama which epitomized and, at the same time, challenged the code of social ethics under which we live, for a quick series of unusual events had dispelled the good nature which in happier times envelopes the ugliness of the industrial situation." She most regretted "the sharp division into class lines, with the resultant distrust and bitterness." Addams recalled also how much the strike entered public consciousness on a personal level. "Every public-spirited citizen in Chicago during that summer," Addams explained, "felt the stress and perplexity of the situation and asked himself, 'How far am I responsible for this social disorder?'"[1]

If Addams perhaps overestimated the readiness of her fellow citizens to consider their own responsibility for the bitter feelings and class conflict that surrounded the Pullman strike, she was correct in her perception that many serious-minded people in Chicago and across the nation shared "the stress and perplexity of the situation" and tried to explain what it meant. Like the Great Chicago Fire and the Haymarket bombing before it, the Pullman strike became a major topic for analysis in itself and in relation to historical change in America, especially that change most fully represented in city life. The discussion of the strike soon opened into a consideration of the nature of the present, particularly the American urban present, at the close of the nineteenth century, that revealed a tension between old and new bases of conceptualizing modern reality.

On the one hand, many of the terms that were used to characterize the individuals, groups, and ideas that seemed to be determining events, and the interpretive narratives that were offered to explain these events, had been in the cultural imagination for some time. The understanding of Haymarket heavily influenced the analyses of the Pullman strike, just as concerns expressed in the fire literature and in commentaries on the railroad strike of 1877 shaped the view of what had happened at Haymarket. Once again different spokespersons tried to win public support for their opinions by claiming that they represented the real America. And, as before, they maintained that what the opposition said was the reverse of the truth, and that ideas, methods, goals, and leaders of the other side promoted disorder and disaster. All of this gives much of the debate over the meaning of Pullman a certain familiar quality that reveals the staying power of certain ideas and forms of expression in the discussion of urban disorder in post–Civil War America. On the other hand, some questioned the old terms and categories in light of the fact that they no longer seemed to apply to what appeared to be a new kind of social order.

A Walkout in Utopia

The Pullman strike was really not one strike but two, a small walkout limited to company employees and a nation-wide sympathetic boycott by members of the American Railway Union of trains pulling Pullman cars. The first was rooted in long-standing discontents with the company, but its immediate cause was the Panic of 1893. The international economic downturn that began in the spring was delayed locally by the Columbian Exposition, but it soon descended on Chicago in full force. The closing of the exposition and the continuing flow of newcomers into the city in a time of general depression created massive unemployment. Without food, shelter, or hope of income, by mid-November people were taking meals at soup kitchens and sleeping on the hard stone stairways and floors of City Hall and, as in 1873, police stations. "The homeless, the hungry, cried aloud, and the peace of the city was disturbed," wrote one reporter, who compared a visit to City Hall to "a walk through a potter's field of unburied dead."[2] While officials tried to discount the problem by claiming that these homeless were part of a semipermanent population of tramps and vagrants, there were reports of respectably dressed men exchanging three hours of sweeping for a bed and food in a lodging house.

The employees of the Pullman Company faced tough times as the demand for the products they manufactured dropped off. The flow of praise for the model town as immune to all the conflict and upsets suffered elsewhere continued into the spring of 1894, but negative reports appeared more frequently in the Chicago newspapers.[3] The company's visibility, not to mention its reputation for being the answer to the problems that beset capital and labor, made its difficulties a compelling subject, especially for those journalists who were already skeptical about the Pullman idea. "Great destitution and suffering prevails in Pullman," the *Chicago Times* declared in early December of 1893, contending that the "sullen gloom" that "envelope[d] the whole town" was born not so much of poverty but "of bitterness and a feeling of resentment at what is openly called the slavery imposed by the conditions of employment by the Pullman company." Like Richard Ely, the *Times* maintained that the company's housing policies and prices made for a shifting and resentful population. What stability there was in the community derived not from the imposed system of social control, but from the workers' loyalty to each other. "If it were not for some conservative influences in the community and a certain fraternity in suffering and neighborliness in bonds which prompt deeds of genuine charity and benevolence," the *Times* said, "the town would be ripe for any violence."[4]

The *Times*'s anti-Pullman articles contained a few exaggerations, but they were not far from the mark in describing conditions in the town. In response to a drop in orders, the company had begun to cut wages in August of 1893, and the number of employees fell from 4,500 to 1,100 between July and November. Pullman's decision to take new contracts even at a loss raised employment to 3,100 by April of 1894, but this was done by spreading work and with a continuing decline in pay. Insisting that the administration of the factories had no connection to the housing, the company refused to reduce rents. Unable to make ends meet, employees protested and organized. There had been strike actions or threats of strikes by workers in different trades since the early 1880s, but none of the actions were of significant breadth and duration.[5] By the spring of 1894, company operatives across the trades had combined under the auspices of the American Railway Union, which had been founded in Chicago only a year before but which now boasted 150,000 members nationwide and was fresh from a major victory in a strike against the Great Northern Railroad.

A committee of workers met with Pullman executive Thomas Wickes in company headquarters on Michigan Avenue in early May to ask for adjustments in wages and rents and to complain about the practices of shop foremen. Accompanied by George Howard, vice president of the American Railway Union, they spoke again with Wickes and with other representatives of the company two days later. George Pullman joined this second meeting after it began, but neither he nor his subordinates promised any substantial relief. The chances of reaching an accord diminished when the company, after promising no reprisals, fired three workers who were on the committee. This quickly led to a strike on May 11. As the lines were drawn in this "industrial war," the rhetoric on all sides became more confrontational. American Railway Union president Eugene Victor Debs proclaimed, "The whole country is in an inflammable condition."[6]

More reports of the severe hardships experienced by unemployed Pullman workers soon appeared in the press. The *Chicago Mail* ran a story subtitled "Grim Want in the Model Town" whose lead paragraph began with the word "Starvation," the first letter of which was held by a skeleton. In June, the American Railway Union membership assembled in Chicago for its national convention and expressed its support for the Pullman strikers, but Wickes refused to see a delegation made up of company employees and union representatives. Several distinguished individuals and organizations dedicated to conciliation, notably the Chicago Civic Federation, joined labor leaders in appealing to the company to submit the dispute to arbitration, but Pullman management, which was always aggressively anti-union, kept restating that they had "nothing to arbitrate." Even the *Tribune* was to complain about the stubbornness of George Pullman, whose response to the situation was to leave town, and later to order his house put under guard, his servants evacuated, and his best plate locked away in a vault in the Pullman Building. The deteriorating situation quickly produced the "stress and perplexity" among Chicagoans that Jane Addams recalled. In a sermon that was reprinted in several papers, the Reverend David Swing admitted that "there is something annoying in a time when nobody seems to know the cause and effect."[7]

On June 20 the American Railway Union informed the Pullman Company that beginning June 26 its members would no longer handle trains that included Pullman cars. In response to this threat, the General Managers Association of the twenty-four railroads serving Chicago met on June 25 to plan tactics. They empowered John M. Egan to direct their strategy, which was based on the argument that the boycott was an illegal and unjustified violation of contract.[8] At first, the American Railway Union was very successful and appeared to have the upper hand. "NOT A WHEEL TURNS IN THE WEST," crowed the *Chicago Times,* which also predicted "the biggest tie-up in all history."[9] But the federal government was more than ready to take management's side. Attorney General Richard Olney, a Boston corporate lawyer who had represented and served on the boards of several leading railroads, maintained that the boycott obstructed interstate commerce and the United States mail, and on July 2 the United States Circuit Court issued an exceptionally broad injunction, restraining, commanding, and enjoining Debs, his union, and "all other persons combining and conspiring with them" from interfering or encouraging anyone else to interfere with railroad traffic.

President Grover Cleveland ordered troops into Chicago from Fort Sheridan, over the objections of Governor Altgeld and Chicago mayor John P. Hopkins, who was, coincidentally, a former Pullman employee who had risen quickly in the company and in George Pullman's esteem until the two of them had a falling out.[10] In a talk on the strike he gave at Princeton ten years later that was also published in *McClure's*, Cleveland sounded like those who had spoken against the Haymarket accused when he called the Pullman strike a "conspiracy" that "immensely increased executive anxiety and foreboded the most calamitous and far-reaching consequences."[11] The soldiers arrived just after midnight on Independence Day, 1894. Their commander, General Nelson Miles, summoned more troops from posts in Michigan, Kansas, and Nebraska, and within a week there were almost 2,000 army regulars in the city, many of them living in an encampment of tents pitched on the lakefront near the Pullman Building.[12] For the third time in a little more than twenty years, Chicago was under military occupation.

While Altgeld continued to protest against this federal intervention and Debs counseled against physical confrontation, violence broke out in several areas throughout the city, leading to the shooting of two rioters and the destruction of over 700 cars at the Panhandle yards in South Chicago. The language used to describe the scene in the streets recalled the vividly overwritten descriptions of the mob during the Chicago fire:

> From this moving mass of shouting rioters squads of a dozen or two departed, running toward the yards with fire brands in their hands. They looked in the gloaming like specters, their lighted torches bobbing about like will-o'-the-wisps. Soon from all parts of the yard flames shot up and billows of fire rolled over the cars, covering them with the red glow of destruction. The spectacle was a grand one. . . . Before the cars were fired those filled with any cargoes were looted. . . . The people were bold, shameless, and eager in their robbery. . . . It was pandemonium let loose, the fire leaping along for miles and the men and women dancing with frenzy. It was a mad scene where riot became wanton and men and women became drunk on their excesses.[13]

As in 1877, the violence was in all likelihood not the work of union leaders, who posted their own guards to protect the Pullman factories, but of thrill-seeking troublemakers, unemployed and otherwise discontented workers with no direct connection to the strike or the boycott, and individuals resentful of the power of the railroads. The anti-union journalists were still not ready to make distinctions between vandals and strikers, however. Most newspapers called the boycott an un-provoked war not on the Pullman Company or even the railroads, which had no disputes with the Pullman operatives, but against the basis of the social order. Debs answered that "the struggle with the Pullman company has developed into a contest between the producing classes and the money power of the country." He blamed hostile editors and publishers for "manufacturing a sentiment against this strike and against the men connected with it." In his eyes, "Peace and order were fatal to the railroad corporations. Violence was as necessary to them as peace was to the employes," and he accused them of hiring people to incite rioting.[14]

On July 7 a mob tried to obstruct a train at 49th and Loomis that was being protected by the state militia. They pelted the soldiers with stones, provoking a bayonet charge and a series of encounters that left several people on both sides wounded and four more rioters dead. The same day General Miles and the federal marshal decided to despatch mail trains from six major depots. The military presence, the arrest of Debs and other leaders for contempt, the breakdown of communications between strike committees throughout the country, the lack of support from other national unions (notably the American Federation of Labor and the Knights of Labor), the adamant stance of the Pullman Company, the unified will and power of the General Managers Association, and the general ebbing of the riot fever together caused the American Railway Union boycott to collapse.[15] By July 10 the militia had broken a blockade of trains in the stockyards, and within a few days the union was totally beaten. On July 18, with the battle won, Attorney General Olney ordered the army to evacuate.

Convicted of contempt, Debs served six months in the McHenry County jail in rural Woodstock, where his reading supposedly included *Looking Backward* and *The Cooperative Commonwealth*. Debs later stated that the whole experience was crucial in his conversion to social-ism. "[I]n the gleam of every bayonet and the flash of every rifle *the class struggle was revealed* [emphasis his]," he recalled, claiming that the strike had been won until "detectives, thugs and murderers were equipped with badge and bludgeon and turned loose," backed by the press and the "'lawful' authorities of the federal government."[16] De-spite the efforts of several prominent attorneys, including Clarence Darrow and the distinguished former Illinois senator Lyman Trumbull (now in his eighties), both of whom had advised Governor Altgeld the year before in his decision to issue the Haymarket pardon, the Supreme

Court unanimously upheld the federal government, handing down its decision in May of 1895. As prescribed by law, President Cleveland appointed a three-member Strike Commission to investigate what had happened. The commission was headed by United States Commissioner of Labor Statistics Carroll D. Wright, who had led the 1884 Pullman tour by state labor commissioners. In mid-August the commission began taking testimony. It heard from over a hundred witnesses on both sides, including Debs and Pullman.[17]

The panel went beyond the events of June and July to investigate the underlying causes of the original strike against the Pullman Company. If George Pullman and the railway managers expected vindication for themselves and the same kind of condemnation of labor organizers that had come out of the Haymarket trial, they were badly disappointed. The tone of the official findings by these sober experts was appropriately restrained, but the message was sharp and clear. George Pullman's policies had left his workers "without local attachments or any interested responsibility in the town, its business, tenements, or surroundings." His grand design, far from offering a model for a sound social order, had torn the whole country apart. The commissioners criticized the Pullman Company's refusal to arbitrate, saying that they were "impressed with the belief, by the evidence and by the attendant circumstances as disclosed, that a different policy would have prevented the loss of life and great loss of property and wages occasioned by the strike." They recommended the establishment of a permanent United States Strike Commission and other actions to prevent economic disputes from turning into social disorders. "REPORT IS A ROAST," the *Chicago Tribune* snapped angrily.[18]

Strike Talk

In most important ways the lines of argument between the contesting parties in the Pullman strike followed very similar patterns to those that had shaped the discussion of earlier disorders. The Pullman Company, the railroad managers, and the federal government, with the support of the editors of most newspapers and periodicals, discussed labor's actions as a deliberately managed assault on the social and economic well-being of the country. Regardless of the policies of the company, they viewed the boycott as a conspiracy to shut down interstate commerce, which made it one of the greatest threats to the nation in the history of the republic. Such a dangerous situation more than justified the deployment of federal troops and the prosecution of Debs. What legitimate grievances the worker felt were minimal, or unavoidable in such hard times. In an article published in the *Forum, Railway Age* editor Harry Perry Robinson called the report of the Strike Commission "a public calamity" because it did not wholeheartedly endorse the government's suppression of the union's lawless action. "It is probably safe to say," Robinson wrote, "that in no civilized country in this century, not actually in the throes of war or open insurrection," had society been so "disorganized" as it was in America at the time of the strike. With human life held "cheap" and authority "incompetent," he added, "The social fabric seemed to be measurably near to dissolution, and the country was not far from the verge of anarchy."[19]

Two arguments that the anti-Debs forces made repeated the old claim that the current social and economic system, while under the most fearsome attack, was fundamentally healthy and not in need of profound reform. Both of these arguments, and several closely related ones, were clearly influenced by the memory of Haymarket. The first argument was the good worker/bad leader (or bad union) explanation of the current disorders, which held that the great majority of American working people were industrious and upstanding citizens who had been "duped" by "pestilential professional agitators" like Debs.[20] Since such agitators were cowards and troublemakers who would wage war on society, the government acted wisely and justly when it treated them harshly. Faced with social disturbances so large in number and so widespread that it was very hard to attribute them to a small core of agitators, commentators tried, as they had following Haymarket, to see these disorders not as indications of deep flaws in the state of things but as "natural" dislocations that necessarily accompanied healthy growth, dangerous only insofar as opportunists would exploit them for their own conniving purposes. "In the face of individual or collective demonstrations which threaten to disturb the equilibrium of society," read an editorial in the *Chautauquan,* "it is well to remember that surface movements of greater or less degrees of aggravation are the natural accompaniment of the march of civilization and rarely interfere with the hidden undercurrents which advance largely in perfect accord with the measured trend of social progress."[21]

The second argument was simply to accuse labor leaders like Debs and their most prominent supporters, including Governor Altgeld, of being anarchists. The words "anarchist," "anarchy," and "anarchism" were everywhere in the discussion of the Pullman strike. Critics of organized labor resorted to these terms to brand any critic of the current order as the same kind of conspirator and "out-and-out destructionist" who hurled the Haymarket bomb. A typical story from the *Washington Chronicle* of July 1 carried the headline, "Anarchy Rampant Over Half the Nation" and then asserted, "Anarchists *hate* all who have saved or made property."[22] Equating anarchism with terrorism, and then using this definition to label every sort of resistance to the status quo as anarchistic, set a rhetorical backfire whose purpose was to preclude a serious discussion of difficult issues regarding the structure of American society that might lead in undesirable directions. To call a strike anarchistic was to isolate it as the source of, and not the response to, current troubles, and to dismiss it as senseless. It was not something to be discussed or debated or reflected upon, but a hostile undertaking by an unprincipled enemy who had to be destroyed.

Hence the attractiveness of discussing current events once more in relation to the Civil War, even though by this time almost thirty years had passed since Lee's surrender. Business and government leaders took the position that labor had ultimately assaulted not Pullman or the railroads but "the people." *Railway Age* deemed the boycott "an unprovoked war on the public."[23] The armed clashes between rioters, police, militia, and deputies seemed to provide proof that the journal was hardly speaking figuratively. Advocates of bringing the regular army to Chicago, like those who welcomed military intervention following the fire and again during the railroad strike of 1877, pointed out the parallels between the present situation and the battle for the Union a generation earlier. An article on Cleveland's proclamation of federal intervention stated approvingly, "There had been nothing like it since Lincoln's call for volunteers after the firing on Fort Sumter."[24] While photographs of post-fire Chicago evoked those of ravaged southern cities after the Civil War, pictures of military campsites in the city during the strike recalled images of the Union army tenting for the night and of Lincoln meeting in the field with his generals.

But critics of Debs and the strike mainly wanted to make the same point that the Haymarket prosecutors advanced, that this war was being waged against a "foreign" force. Even if Debs was born in the Indiana heartland, he was attacking everything that America stood for. The extraordinary amount of name-calling during the Pullman strike promoted this idea. Dubbing Debs a dictator, despot, or designing demagogue made for a nice bit of alliteration that tied the union leader to "foreign" political systems inimical to the United States. It was a small step to say, as the *Chicago Tribune* did in an editorial a few days before the federal troops arrived, that Debs and American Railway Union vice president Howard had "set up a coup d'etat." The same editorial judged them "autocrats, who have established an *imperium in imperio*," and stated that "[n]o despot ever conducted himself with more brazen and insolent defiance of popular rights than this man Debs, who, seeking for some pretext to make war upon society, found it in this Pullman strike. . . . Louis Napoleon after his coup d'état never ruled France like that."[25] This turned the union's attacks on the plutocratic power of

Pullman and the railroad barons back against labor leaders, justifying in the name of liberty, democracy, and freedom the repression of Debs and his cause. In mounting their defense in the court of public opinion, the strike leaders and their supporters tried to undermine their enemies' arguments by relying on the same strategy of reversal the Haymarket defendants had used. According to Debs, it was George Pullman, the railway managers, and President Cleveland who were the true organizers of disorder, while labor leaders who convened in Chicago in July to discuss the strike described Pullman the town as a "pharisaical paradise" and Pullman the man as "a public enemy." Samuel Gompers decried the dissemination of the false idea that corporations "stand for law and order, and that those opposing them represent lawlessness and anarchy."[26] In a sermon delivered ten days after the walkout began, William Carwardine, the most outspoken prolabor clergyman in Pullman and author of his own book on the strike, urged those in authority to deal with social wrongs honestly and constructively. Rooting out anarchy was justified "in time of awful peril," he advised, "But do not call all 'strikers' anarchists." Shortly after the walkout began, Carwardine contended that it was the actions of corporations like the Pullman Company that were "hurrying the Nation to the Niagara of industrial revolution" and to "the slaughterhouse of anarchy."[27]

To Debs and his allies, George Pullman was the one who was truly "foreign" to the spirit of the country since his aristocratic attitudes destabilized democratic America. This kind of criticism had surfaced a few years earlier, when the opposition press dubbed him "the Duke." In the figurative language of his opponents, Pullman was now also likened to Richard III in his deceitful plotting. A switchman and union activist named William Burns bemoaned "[t]he prostitution of the government—founded on the blood of our forefathers—by the organized capital of this country, of which the greater part is foreign gold." Carwardine revived Ely's assessment of a decade earlier in calling the model town "a hollow mockery and a sham. . . . the most un-American of all American cities: it belongs to the map of Europe." In his book he argued that in all of Pullman there was nothing that could be called a home "in the American sense of the word." The town was "a civilized relic of European serfdom," over which George Pullman was "the King," as inaccessible to any of his employees as the czar was to his subjects.[28]

Here again different parties claimed that their position represented the true spirit of the nation. The Haymarket accused traced their ideas and actions back to Thomas Jefferson, Patrick Henry, and John Brown. In an article in the *Arena,* Walter Blackburn Harte now compared the strike to the Boston Tea Party as an apparent assault on property that was actually a blow for liberty. Turning to the present, he warned, "The bayonets and repeating rifles, the 'gatling gun' injunctions of plutocracy and the howling dervishes of the plutocratic press-gang have obtained *order;* but the moral questions of this conflict will arise again, and will never down until either they are settled or human reason flickers out into night." Having asserted that *they* were on the side of the "real" America, the union advocates were more than willing to accept the characterization of the current crisis as a war to save the republic. Debs described the strike as "a contest between the producing classes and the money power of the country."[29]

After the Supreme Court upheld his conviction, he again attacked the corporations, "which by the use of money could debauch justice, and, by playing the part of incendiary, bring to their aid the military power of the government." He claimed, with more alliteration, that "this solidified mass of venality, venom and vengeance constituted the foe against which the American Railway Union fought Labor's greatest battle for humanity." In response to critics who maintained that the strikers had mounted a "rebellion" and "insurrection" as threatening as the Civil War, labor spokesmen revived the argument the anarchists had made in calling their cause the liberation of a subject people from bondage. Burns asserted that the Pullman workers were in fact "reduced to a condition of slavery beneath that of the black slave of the South," who was at least provided with food and shelter while "the white slave of Pullman was forced to work for wages entirely inadequate to furnish a sufficient amount of food to keep body and soul together."[30]

The characterization of Pullman and the railroads as foreign enemies and slaveholders readily merged with two other polemical patterns that had special importance to labor leaders, union members, and their sympathizers as they tried to explain how America had been betrayed and suborned by Pullman's company town, with the backing of the government. The first was the complaint, which had been voiced since before Haymarket, that the nation had been taken over by "soulless corporations." America had lost the sense of human community that had always been vital to democracy. Soon after the walkout, for example, the *Chicago Times* accused Pullman the reputed philanthropist of being nothing more than "the head of a great and soulless corporation." Debs tried to attach this accusation to his strike-as-liberation argument when he claimed that, just before his death, Abraham Lincoln predicted the current conflict between the "money power" and the "producing classes." Debs fancifully asserted that in the transcendent moment of his triumph and martyrdom, Lincoln was granted a tragic vision into the unpromised land of a new slavery in which "free" workers were forced to mortgage "their bodies and souls, as well as their children's, to that heartless corporation." It was this vision, Debs contended, which "gave the great emancipator his gloomiest forebodings."[31]

More powerful and pointed than the assault on the corporations as soulless was the accusation that they violated the worker's manhood, the only thing he could truly claim as his own and on which the integrity of the country was based. The implications of Pullman for the ideal of manhood had been argued throughout the town's history, particularly in the discussions of the positive and negative effects of Pullman's control of living and working conditions. A Pullman operative supposedly told the *Chicago Herald* that he agonized through a sleepless night over the choice between giving in to company pressures to vote Republican or following his conscience to vote Democratic, thereby putting his job and his family at risk. "The next day," he reported sadly, "I went up and surrendered my manhood and I haven't been free since." In *Tenure and Toil; or, Land, Labor and Capital* (1888), another of the several books from the period that proposed how to correct the injustices of a social order that consisted of "the toiling millions and the scheming few," John Gibbons devoted two chapters to the abuse of labor practiced in Pullman. Gibbons maintained that Pullman had institutionalized "under a new form, the degrading relation of lord and vassal, which is utterly abhorrent to the advanced humanity of the age, and utterly subversive of every correct principle of true manhood and true womanhood."[32]

While critics of the strike advised the workers that they were abandoning their manly obligations by causing their families to suffer, union leaders forcefully responded by describing the strike and the boycott as brave and selfless actions undertaken by responsible men. Gompers tied the union cause to the same manly virtues that had brought the republic into being: "It is something not yet fully understood how thoroughly organized labor stands as the sturdy pioneer of all the hopes of the masses for justice and humane conditions, of their aspirations for a nobler manhood resultant from an equality of opportunities." Testifying before the Strike Commission, he bitterly attacked the "present industrial and commercial system" as the cause of the rise in the number and intensity of strikes. Gompers told the commission, "I regard the strikes as the sign that the people are not yet willing to surrender every spark of their manhood and their honor and their independence."[33]

Eugene Victor Debs, whose sensitivity to social oppression was virtually innate (he was named after Eugène Sue and Victor Hugo) and was easily equal to that of the Haymarket accused, was, like them, par-

ticularly drawn to the manhood issue. In one of his first speeches to the
Pullman workers after the walkout, he told them that he was opposed to
strikes, except "when the only alternative to a strike is the sacrifice of
manhood." He later explained how the boycott, far from threatening
disaster, was what would save the country from the true catastrophe of
accepting "degrading or enslaving conditions." Only the worker's resistance would accomplish the social progress that was the town of
Pullman's ostensible purpose but to which it was actually opposed. "It
seems to me," Debs testified, "if it were not for that resistance to degrading conditions, the tendency of our whole civilization would be
downward; after a while we would reach the point where there would
be no resistance, and slavery would ensue." Ten years after the strike,
Debs still contended that what the railroads had been afraid of in 1894
was not any specific demands so much as the fear of the workingman
asserting himself against plutocratic power. He maintained that the
railway corporations "would rather have destroyed their property and
seen Chicago perish than see the American Railway Union triumphant
in as noble a cause as ever prompted sympathetic, manly men to action
in this world."[34]

No doubt part of the angry reaction to the strike report from supporters of the railroads arose because the commissioners accepted
some of the assertions made by Debs and Gompers. Wright and his
colleagues ascribed to the union members the traits that the city's elite
had long claimed for itself in times of crisis. The report commended the
"dignified, manly, and conservative conduct" of the workers "in the
midst of excitement and threatened starvation," calling them "worthy
of the highest type of American citizenship." Looking for an explanation of why the workers were dissatisfied with the model town, the
panel suggested, "Men, as a rule, even when employees, prefer independence to paternalism."[35] This observation revealed how closely
connected all the references to foreignness, slavery, soullessness, and
manliness were to the continuing discussion of paternalism at Pullman.
In spite of all the talk over the years about education and uplift, and
George Pullman's own remark to the delegation of employees whom he
met with two days before the strike that he regarded them as his children, the official company line during and after the strike, as it had been
before, was to deny that it was paternalistic. "No paternalism has ever
been in the plan," Second Vice President Wickes told the strike commissioners.[36] Others pointed out, as proof that Pullman did not control
his employees, how often they voted for candidates he opposed.

Obviously aware of the charge of paternalism, Pullman answered it
indirectly through his close friend, the Reverend Charles H. Eaton,
who prepared an article on "Pullman and Paternalism" for the Decem-

ber 1894 issue of the *American Journal of Politics*. Speaking for the founder, Eaton rejected the contention that the town was either paternalistic or, as was also often charged, feudalistic. He argued that the company respected the "fundamental rights" of the workingman, who was free to choose his home and sell his labor where and how he pleased. Pullman helped increase the worker's wealth and "social importance" by giving him nothing for free and encouraging his independence. Even in defending Pullman against the charge of paternalism, however, Eaton repeated the defense of the company's ownership of the housing as the reason why Pullman's social and moral condition was so superior to that of nearby Kensington. "The promiscuous character of the workingmen at Pullman, as in other manufacturing towns," Eaton concluded, "makes an effective supervision of the houses impossible except under a central and complete control." Evidently he had little faith in the workingman's ability to make the best use of his "fundamental rights."[37]

Few really doubted that George Pullman was paternalistic. The more pressing and divisive questions were whether the paternalism he practiced was beneficial to his employees, and whether paternalism of any sort was an effective and sound basis for an urban industrial social order. Even well after the strike began and Pullman came under fire from all sides for his aloofness from his workers, his enmity toward unions, and his unwillingness to arbitrate, the approving reports of his paternalistic benevolence continued. Their authors assumed that they were thinking only of the workers' own good in endorsing the organization of the model town. "It is immediately apparent to the visitor at Pullman," read one article that appeared just after the troops withdrew in mid-July, "that the men, women, and children of the place are well cared for, and surrounded with those things which create the comforts of this life." The source of the recent troubles could not possibly be the social plan of "this new Arcadian village," and it was "not reasonable to believe that any of Mr. Pullman's workmen could have been found in the mob that threatened the town." If George Pullman was at fault at all, the author wondered, maybe it was because he had treated his operatives too well.[38]

Speaking from firsthand experience as a Methodist minister in Pullman, Carwardine denied that George Pullman had been a good "parent" to his workers. The luxurious furnishings of the library did not spread culture and education but reminded the worker of his inferior caste. There was no place for operatives to congregate and talk, which was one reason they patronized the Kensington saloons. The rent of the Greenstone Church was beyond the means of a congregation of workers, showing that the company put the worship of profit ahead of that of God and Christ. Even the celebrated housing was bad. Except for the part of town around the Hotel Florence, which was designed mainly with the visiting public in mind, Pullman was "crowded and unwholesome." The monotony of the dwellings made them resemble soldiers' barracks, and, to make matters worse, the high rents forced hundreds of families to take in boarders. These conditions undermined the supposed high moral standards of the town. And hanging over it all was the fact "that you are made to feel at every turn the presence of the corporation."[39] The Strike Commission was especially critical of Pullman's refusal to deal with the unions, which Wright and his associates saw as one more instance of his insistence on maintaining a strict social and economic hierarchy in which he had the only say in any matter of importance. "This position secures all the advantage of the concentration of capital, ability, power, and control for the company in its labor dealings," the commissioners observed, "and deprives the employees of any such advantage or protection as a labor union might afford."[40]

Deeply alarmed about threats to their skills, their families, and their manliness, labor leaders saw Pullman's policies as paternalism of a particularly insidious kind that was destructive to the American idea of citizenship as it was to manhood. George Pullman not only treated them as children but also rendered them impotent, reducing his employees to docile drones serviceable to the company but of little use to themselves. Using more guarded language, the Strike Commission reached a similar conclusion. It found a fatal disjuncture at the root of the failure of this model community. Pullman claimed that he wanted his workers to better themselves, but he could not recognize that adults prefer independence. What made matters worse was that the kind of paternalism Pullman practiced was divorced from the concept of family. He never trusted his children-employees enough to create a stable, functioning community. Had he really considered his operatives as being related to him as citizens and workers, he would have been more generous in sharing the company's considerable reserves with them, recognizing that these resources were in significant part created by the operatives. His employees would have in turn remained loyal to him because of his generosity and concern. By putting what he saw as the interests of the company and the stockholders ahead of the employees, Pullman the one-time skilled worker inevitably alienated the very people whose labor was the basis of his wealth.

The Lessons of the Strike

In both 1871 and 1886, a number of commentators had spoken of the "lessons" of the fire and the bomb, but now this noun seemed to be in the title of virtually every interpretation of what had happened: "The Lessons of the Recent Civil Disorders," "Some Lessons of the Great Strike," "The Lesson of the Recent Strike," "Pullman and Its Lessons," and (in response to this last article) "Pullman and Its Real Lessons."[41] The amount of disagreement on just what the lessons of the strike were was far greater than it had been on the burning and bombing of Chicago, reflecting the different nature of this event but, more significantly, the ways in which the public mind had become divided. After their visit to Pullman in 1884, Carroll Wright and the other heads of state bureaus of labor statistics had been impressed with the ways this social experiment seemed to be ahead of its time, but now Wright and his fellow commissioners concluded that the Pullman Company was "behind the age."[42] The commissioners ignored important complications, however, if they assumed that all observant and reasonable individuals would agree on what "the age" was. The conflicting analyses of the strike reflected a larger lack of consensus on the nature of the times and on what should be done to avoid such disruptions in the future.

These disagreements were present everywhere in the discussion of what Americans took to be the most important current events in their own country and abroad. The pages of the periodical press in 1894 were full of articles about many other lockouts and strikes besides the one centered at Pullman, as well as about bombings and assassinations (notably the fatal stabbing of French president Sadi Carnot by an Italian anarchist in late June), immigrants and political corruption, tramps and crime, hard times and soft currency, and the threat and promise of socialists, Nationalists, Single Taxers, and other reformers. The turmoil that preoccupied public attention led to some sober reflections on what the future might hold. "Are Our Moral Standards Shifting?" Albert B. Hart asked in the title of a *Forum* essay reviewing the events of 1894, in which he traced a regression toward the dominance of force rather than the rule of law in human affairs. The Fourth of July issue of the same journal featured an article by Harvard's longtime president, Charles W. Eliot, the most noted educator in the country, titled "Some Reasons Why the American Republic May Endure," but, as the wording of his title suggested, Eliot's optimism was decidedly qualified.[43]

In offering their explanations and proposals for the strike and the age, many commentators on all sides called for a reassertion of older values that had somehow become forgotten amid the conflict and hard feeling that seemed to accompany social change. With capital and labor at such an impasse, those who spoke of reconciliation commonly appealed to the nobler impulses of all parties, which usually meant the transcendent spirit of Christian brotherhood of the kind that had supposedly responded so magnificently to earlier crises such as the Chicago fire. T. Burke Grant commented in "Pullman and Its Lessons" that he was not taking sides in the Pullman strike by suggesting that "it will be shown that the exercise of a little Christian feeling on the part of Mr. Pullman would have averted the scenes that shocked the people at Chicago, and brought the nation itself up to the very gates of hostility between the federal and state powers, and, therefore, in the presence of the tumult that existed, within measurable distance of civil war."[44] As might be anticipated, those who advanced this argument included socially aware ministers like William Carwardine.

Few clergymen were as politically engaged as William T. Stead, the Anglican minister and editor who visited Chicago for several months beginning in 1893 in order to attend the congress on religion held in conjunction with the Columbian Exposition, and who quickly became very involved in the Chicago reform community in which Henry Demarest Lloyd was an important member.[45] In *If Christ Came to Chicago!*, his fervent exposé of the social and moral failings of the city that was written before the walkout, Stead specifically indicted George Pullman, Marshall Field, and meatpacker Philip Armour—whom he sarcastically said were viewed as "the manifest expression of the best conception of the will of God"—for perpetuating the chaotic and destructive economic "warfare of their time." He singled out the town of Pullman for a biting, extended critique.[46] In a second book, written in response to the Pullman strike, Stead blamed "the whole of the catastrophe" on George Pullman's refusal to submit to arbitration, comparing the state of the city to that of a Chicago armory that had recently suffered a fire. Those inside had died in agony because the fire department had been unable to penetrate the urban fortress's massive gates. This "grim and horrible experience . . . resembles only too closely," he wrote, "the miserable tragedy at which civilisation is now assisting in the city of Chicago."[47]

Stead filled his articles and books with carefully researched details about the suffering in America's cities, and then called for a collective spiritual conversion to avoid the damnation and destruction of the kind prophesied by figures like Ignatius Donnelly. The whole social system required salvation, since the heedless power of massed capital was inherently immoral and labor was "disorganised, undisciplined, and irreligious," adjectives which to his mind were inseparable. Workers were doomed "to writhe helpless for some time longer beneath the ironshod heel of Capital" until the moment when they would "get religion," which Stead defined in secular terms as accepting the sacrifices involved in paying dues and obeying union leaders. If they did not choose this course, "they [would] remain as they are at present, a hopeless, helpless, blaspheming, writhing crowd, whose only plan of campaign is reliance upon the sporadic violence of excited mobs when confronted by the organized forces of the existing order." At the height of the strike, Stead found more objectionable than the violence "the utter paralysis of public and moral authority" amidst which the church was notable by its absence. From his vantage as an Englishman and man of the cloth, Stead asked if the separation of church and state in the United States did not deprive Americans of a critical force "which will assert the eternal law of righteousness and justice and brotherhood in all the affairs of men."[48]

Stead's views were shared both by preachers of different varieties of the Social Gospel and by reformers (the most well-known would be Upton Sinclair) who claimed that what some called socialism was simply the teachings of Christ expressed in contemporary terms. The one pro-union novel explicitly based on the strike, Nico Bech-Mayer's *A Story from Pullmantown* (1894), made such an argument. The story centers on a South Dakota family named Wright, who came to Chicago to see the World's Columbian Exposition and stayed to open a store in Pullman.[49] Pullman himself is dubbed Mr. Hoard, and Bech-Mayer emphasizes his detachment from the workers (he visits the factory once a year) and their resulting hatred of him as an indication of the "selfishness, greed and lawlessness of monopoly, and of its disregard for human life." In contrast, the workers' organizing themselves into a union is a humane and heroic task that is described as a sacred mission of salvation and redemption that provides the only real community available to them.[50]

Opponents of organized labor found it harder to justify their position persuasively in terms of established Christian ideals, but several tried. One of the most chilling comments to come out of the strike was South Carolina elder statesman Wade Hampton's observation, which he was not alone in voicing, that while "[e]very humane man" must sympathize with poorly paid workers, no legislation or other "earthly power" could "rectify the immutable law by which the gifts of fortune are distributed with an unequal hand." Arguing against federal regula- tion of economic life, Hampton maintained that it was the part of the holy order of things that the world's wealth was divided unequally.[51] Other conservative critics of the strike and of reform argued more effectively, however, that the attempt to analyze conditions in terms of morality and similar abstractions and ideals was one of the causes of the current conflict. Claiming that they were not so much partisan as realistic, various spokesmen both within and outside the business community maintained that the only way to understand what had happened was to keep in mind the venerable tenets not of Christian ethics but of classical economics, which social reformers and activists forgot only at the nation's peril. Railroad managers contended that the recent labor problems could be simply explained in terms of the law of supply and demand, a timeless and sacred axiom that no amount of tampering with the system could alter. In support of their position, they might have cited no less imposing an authority than Social Darwinist and defender of the status quo William Graham Sumner, son of a railroad worker himself and an Episcopal clergyman before assuming the first chair in political and social science at Yale. In the year of Haymarket, Sumner had published an essay dismissing the notion that there was any other principle relevant to the setting of wages than the iron law the managers cited.[52]

Rethinking Disorder

Nevertheless, several individuals suggested that the first step in mastering the cataclysmic tendencies of the age was to reconceptualize the issue of social order and disorder in a way that brought ideas more effectively to bear on experience and the apparent directions of change. While so much of the discussion of the Pullman strike, as well as of pre-strike Pullman, was imaginatively and rhetorically backward-looking, the national conflict that centered in the model town encouraged more Americans to conclude—even if this contradicted other beliefs to which they nonetheless adhered—that a new and different order had developed, a completely interdependent system with a new power balance and new rules. Or, perhaps, an imbalance and lack of rules. This viewpoint was present in the analyses of the fire that spoke of the importance of Chicago to the national economy and the insistence by the Haymarket defendants that technology, massed capital, and urbanization had made America a qualitatively different country than it once had been. By the time of the Pullman strike, this recognition extended into official public policy put into practice by the president and backed by the Supreme Court.

The Pullman strike was a groundbreaking event in the history of federal intervention in labor disputes.[53] Speaking for the court in *In re Debs,* Associate Justice David J. Brewer maintained that there was in this modern age the possibility of "wrongs" that "are such as affect the public at large, and are in respect of matters which by the Constitution are entrusted to the care of the Nation, and concerning which the Nation owes the duty to all the citizens of securing to them their common rights." The president could use "[t]he strong arm of the national government . . . to brush away all obstructions" to interstate commerce and the mails. "The entire strength of the nation," Brewer held, "may be used to enforce in any part of the land the full and free exercise of all national powers and the security of all rights entrusted by the Constitution to its care." The case at hand involved "vast interests . . . not merely of the city of Chicago and the State of Illinois, but all of the States, and the general confusion into which the interstate commerce of the country was thrown."[54] Far from restoring the ideal village community as a model for the future, the town of Pullman had proved that the entire nation was now an interconnected whole. Thinking of the city as separate from the country, or Chicago from America, was unrealistic and impossible. As the *Nation* had remarked at the time of the fire, the Happy Valley was a thing of the past—if it had ever existed at all.

Some tried to explain in more detail how the causes of the current disorders were inseparable from the country's transition to new social, political, and economic circumstances. An article contemporary with the strike called for new approaches to the study of the problem of disorder. W. L. Sheldon began his essay, "The Place of the Labor Leader," by observing, "It has struck me that in the cause of social science we ought to make a study of the labor leaders as a class of men by themselves. They are coming to be a kind of *institution* in the modern world. They are certainly a recognized factor with which the business community is obliged to deal."[55] Critics of the "Debs Insurrection" meanwhile blamed current problems on the recent development of large-scale combinations of workers that they claimed interfered with the individual worker's freedom to decide his terms of employment, threatened sacred rights of property, and terrorized the public. As they and others of similar opinions had done in 1871 and 1877, they recommended a bigger army, citing the superior job done by professional soldiers in keeping the peace. A few days before the troops marched into Chicago in 1894, Captain Charles Bird King, a veteran of the Civil War and the Indian campaigns and a well-known author whose works included a group of military romances with such titles as *The Colonel's Daughter, A War-Time Wooing,* and *Under Fire,* published an article rebutting the remarks another literary soldier, General Lew Wallace, had made recently at the Naval Academy. Wallace had predicted that with the end of the Indian wars and the expansion of American interests overseas, the army would diminish in importance and the navy would be America's key military force. King countered that the navy could not effectively respond to the kind of "internecine war" that was going on in

America. "Will the navy meet the mobs in the coal regions, the rioters on the railways?" he inquired of his readers.[56]

Union leaders explained that the growth of their organizations was a natural and necessary response to the rise of enormous corporations, like the Pullman Company, that destroyed the social fabric. Since the railroads had been permitted to combine to reduce wages, the workers could unite to resist these reductions, Debs told the Strike Commission, and if a strike ensued it was as much the fault of organized management as it was of organized labor. And if labor had lost the strike, it was only because the federal government had thrown its massive power behind the railroads. It would be far better to implement a whole new system in which the government owned such corporations rather than continue to endure the current one, in which the corporations owned the government. Debs's great personal discovery was that the strike had been a political struggle as much or more than it had been an economic one, and he and many of his followers soon traded the American Railway Union for the Socialist Party as the best means of achieving the workers' goals.[57] To the extent that the attorney general and the courts refused to acknowledge this, Debs contended, they were allying themselves with capital in denying reality and participating in the spread of disorder by refusing to acknowledge how much things had changed. Debs offered his own version of August Spies's comparison of contemporary social unrest to a subterranean fire, testifying to the Strike Commission that corporate power "might as well try to stop Niagara with a feather as to crush the spirit of organization in this country."[58] Prolabor journalist John Swinton explained that a "new state of things" was arising out of mechanization, the massing of capital under the control of "shrewd and rapacious individuals or syndicates," increased immigration, more women in the work force, and lack of access to land. Until the workers took command of the country by an organized use of the ballot to create a truly new government, the abuses of "the wild beast, capitalism," would be uncontrolled and major strikes would continue.[59]

This argument called for reform measures ranging from voluntary arbitration to public ownership of key industries, first and foremost the railroads. Samuel Gompers attacked the government's perversely pro-business application of its powers to regulate interstate commerce and what he saw as the disingenuous invocation of fundamental rights and principles of liberty and property in defense of large corporations. Corporate power, which by its very nature was antagonistic to these rights and principles, was something the country's founders had never anticipated. "Do what you will, declaim as you may," he wrote, "industrial and commercial development cannot be confined within the limits of laws enacted to fit past decades the theories of which are sought to be applied to modern conditions."[60] Without making specific recommendations for remedies, the Strike Commission concurred. The commissioners advised that the public good demanded greater government regulation of the "quasi-public corporations" that had become dominating forces in a new America. They also chastised the courts for "poring over the law reports of antiquity in order to construe conspiracy out of labor unions," and charged large employers with obstructing progress "by perverting and misapplying the law of supply and demand, and who, while insisting upon individualism for workmen, demand that they shall be let alone to combine as they please and that society and all its forces shall protect them in their resulting contentions." Carroll Wright emphasized this point in a paper he presented late in 1894 to the seventh annual meeting of the American Economic Association. Calling the Chicago strike an "an epochal event in the labor movement and the industrial development of the country," Wright maintained that if the federal power to regulate commerce led to government control of business, "it will be because of a great necessity existing for such control, and good citizens should have no fear." Though he was opposed in principle to intervention, he was concerned that it might be the only way to avoid disastrous disorders. In any case, it was wrong for corporations to demand regulation of unions while insisting on no restrictions for themselves, for "[t]he dictates of the highest patriotism again demand that there be consistency in these matters."[61]

Not all professedly "modern" thinkers called for greater government activism, on whatever side. In his noted essay, "The Absurd Effort to Make the World Over," which was published the year of the strike, William Graham Sumner agreed that the rapid advance of industrial development had transformed the country, but he dismissed the proposals of would-be reformers because he believed that they lacked an accurate understanding of the age. "Nine-tenths of the socialistic and semi-socialistic, and sentimental or ethical, suggestions by which we are overwhelmed come from failure to understand the phenomena of the industrial organization and its expansion," he declared, and this failure caused "the turmoil of heterogeneous and antagonistic social whims and speculations in which we live." In belittling all attempts "to make the world over," he also rejected the idea that the present was a dramatically cataclysmic period anywhere but in the deluded popular mind. It was best for all to recognize, through the kind of "objective" study he championed, the advantages and disadvantages of an era of industrial organization and learn to deal with them. The modern concentration of capital had in fact brought a net increase in productivity and comfort. All the talk about wage-slavery and capitalistic tyranny was wrongheaded and beside the point. Corporate wealth was only the latest form of power, and there was no concrete proof that it had been abused or that it was somehow in conflict with "democracy," an idea that was still itself in a trial period. No individual could transcend or "order" the age.

To Sumner, change could be brought about only by "the great discoveries and inventions, the new reactions inside the social organism, and the changes in the earth itself on account of changes in the cosmical forces." Men could watch and participate in the course of change, but they could not manage or guide it. "That is why it is the greatest folly of which a man can be capable," Sumner advised, "to sit down with a slate and pencil to plan out a new social world." Sumner the tough-minded realist thus bolstered the conservative position from the point of view of the emerging social science in which he was a leader, though his criticisms would also seem to apply to "visionary" capitalists like George Pullman who tried to construct new industrial worlds when they should have stuck to making railroad cars. He specifically praised the "captain of industry," however, for his "executive and administrative skill, power to command, courage, and fortitude," all of which enabled him to prevail in the new and changing conditions.[62]

Thorstein Veblen, in an essay on Coxey's Army, speculated in a different direction, trying to predict the shape of this change. What he saw potentially developing out of the current unrest was a tremendously significant shift in the public mind. The new attitudes he saw unfolding involved a movement from "the civil republic of the nineteenth century" toward "the industrial republic of the socialists, with the gradual submergence of private initiative under the rising claims of industrial solidarity." While he believed that it was unlikely that this new attitude would attract the support of a majority of the American people, Veblen saw as momentous the tacit acceptance of a view of the nation as "a single industrial organism, whose integration is advancing day by day, regardless of any traditional or conventional boundary lines or demarcations, whether between classes or between localities." It was easy to dismiss Coxeyism, but not the fact that "advancing 'industrial integration' has gone far enough to obtrude itself as a vital fact upon the consciousness of an appreciable fraction of the common people of the country."[63] Even some of the railroad managers and the federal officials who did most to break the strike seemed to recognize this. Their success in dealing with the Pullman boycott encouraged further collectivism and reduction in competition under more centralized corporate control, but it also included a greater respect for organized labor. Richard Olney himself argued less than two months after the Pullman strike, in relation to a case in which workers were ordered to quit a

union or be fired, "Whatever else may remain for the future to determine, it must now be regarded as substantially settled that the mass of
wage-earners can no longer be dealt with by capital as so many isolated
units."[64]

A Modern Lear

Much of the eloquence of Jane Addams's analysis of the Pullman strike
derived from her evocation of enduring values, but she also suggested
that it was time to find modern principles on which to build a stable
and healthy urban order that responded constructively to contemporary social conditions. As she explained in *Twenty Years at Hull-
House*, her experience of the conflict was direct and personal, and the
details remained vivid in her mind long after. She recalled the troops
camped near the Post Office, the white ribbons worn by members of
the Hull-House community to mark their sympathy with the strikers,
and the arguments over who was setting fire to the railroad cars. She
sadly remembered how the boycott prevented other members of the
family from reaching Addams's dying sister before she passed away,
and the broken life of a skilled worker she knew who had been blacklisted because of the strike and so became an example of "the wretched
human waste such a strike implies." As a member of the Chicago Civic
Federation and the Citizens' Arbitration Committee, Addams had
tried unsuccessfully to coax Pullman toward a peaceful negotiated settlement that was fair to all sides. As she explained in her testimony before the Strike Commission, she investigated conditions at Pullman
firsthand and then went to see company officials in the futile hope of
getting the company to consent to arbitration at least on the rental
charges. Looking back on events over fifteen years later, she observed
that the strike "demonstrated how often the outcome of far-reaching
industrial disturbances is dependent upon the personal will of the employer or the temperament of a strike leader," and is influenced "by
poignant domestic situations, by the troubled consciences of the minority directors, by the suffering women and children, by the keen excitement of the struggle, by the religious scruples sternly suppressed
but occasionally asserting themselves, now on one side and now on the
other, and by that undefined psychology of the crowd which we understand so little."[65]

Her response at the time of the strike was typical of her whole career:
in her principled and pragmatic manner, she tried to make sense of it all
for herself and for others in the hope of healing the damage that had
been caused and avoiding such divisions in the future. "It seemed to me
unendurable," she explained, "not to make some effort to gather to-

gether the social implications of the failure of this benevolent employer and its relation to the demand for a more democratic administration of industry." The result of this effort was a talk that she gave to the Chicago Woman's Club and the Twentieth Century Club of Boston, among other audiences. In "A Modern Lear," as in so many of Addams's writings, she tried to draw on the lessons of great literature, in this case Shakespeare, to find a relevant social message for the present. Pullman was not dissimilar from many other employers who felt a certain fatherly duty toward his employees, Addams argued, but his power and his riches made him a king of sorts, so he "projected this ideal more magnificently than the others."[66]

Addams then analyzed the misunderstandings that undermined the good intentions of both capital and labor. She compared Pullman to Lear in his well-meant but misguided refusal to give his workers any voice in shaping their lives. He originally built the town to provide his employees with the best surroundings, but that "[a]s it developed it became a source of pride and an exponent of power, that he cared most for when it gave him a glow of benevolence." In his self-absorption and willful ignorance, he "lost the faculty of affectionate interpretation," refusing to see that his workers, like Cordelia, had developed a character of their own. Pullman also "demanded a sign" of loyalty, but his policies assured that "[h]e and his employes had no mutual interest in a common cause." "His conception of goodness for them had been cleanliness, decency of living, and above all, thrift and temperance," but he would not acknowledge that they were genuinely caught up in newer and larger issues of industrial organization whose importance he wanted to deny.[67]

In Addams's analysis, at the heart of this misunderstanding was Pullman's inability to recognize how the world had changed in his lifetime, let alone how much he himself had brought that change about. He also failed to see or to recognize the emptiness of some of the "truths" to which he had resorted so many times in defense of his actions and attitudes. "He stood throughout pleading for the individual virtues, those which had distinguished the model workman of his youth, which had enabled him and so many of his contemporaries to rise in life, when 'rising in life' was urged upon every promising boy as the goal of his efforts." But he had no sense of "the higher fellowship and life of association into which [his workers] were plunged" by the immense concentrations of capital and labor in the urban industrial order. Instead of bridging the social and economic divisions created by his own achievements and trying to understand his workers' attempt, in which they resembled Cordelia, to define a meaningful place for themselves in this new and larger collectivity of the industrial city, he had demanded that they accept his control over their lives. By insisting on the rightness of his thinking, and by using his power to enforce his position, Pullman only irreversibly alienated them. "He felt himself right from the *commercial* standpoint, and could not see the situation from the *social* standpoint." Convinced that he was the one who had been cruelly wronged by his "thankless" children to whom he had offered so much, he hardened his position and retreated to his summer home on the Jersey shore, his own personal heath. "[W]hile the interior of his country was racked with a strife which he alone might have arbitrated, [Pullman] lived out within himself the tragedy of King Lear." The consequences for his psyche were sadly predictable, Addams explained, with her characteristic ability to grasp and express the key point: "The shock of disaster upon egotism is apt to produce self-pity."[68]

The workers, like Cordelia, were themselves not innocent of the charge of self-absorption, and Addams hoped that they would not forget the importance of the old bonds of common affection and community in working out some new social dispensation, which would require compromise. For American society as a whole, the "lesson" of the Pullman strike was that the divided social classes in this age of big cities and giant corporations now more than ever had to "put yourself in his place" and acknowledge each other's hopes and needs. The Pullman idea that the workers needed to be elevated according to standards set by their employers was wrong, and thus unacceptable as the basis of a stable social order, even if the intentions behind it were in some measure benevolent. The effective reformer would be the one who realized that even in as complex a social organism as the industrial city, a sound community must be based on the consensual participation of all the people involved and on an understanding of the need and desire of all to shape their world and their lives within it. The "progress" of society working by this principle might be slower and less dramatic than the advances that the much-publicized building of Pullman seemed to represent, but it would be more substantial and stable.[69]

Addams was trying to talk positively about the possibilities of modern urban community at a time when so many others could discuss it only in terms of disorder. She found it hard to get listeners. She tried to publish her thoughts in the *Forum,* the *North American Review,* the *Century,* and the *Atlantic Monthly,* but all turned down her plea for mutual understanding and social harmony as too controversial. Apparently their audiences were better prepared to deal with the idea that the city was catastrophically out of control than with the notion that it was necessary to work harder to understand the shape of change. Henry Demarest Lloyd told Addams that it might be possible to "to depersonalize" her article, and thus get it into print, but she rejected this advice.

She finally published it in the journal *Survey*—almost two decades after the strike.[70]

The Future of Urban America

While they often differed on just what the sources of the strike were, many Americans agreed amidst the distress that the city itself was at the heart of the problem. "Chicago is a vast metropolis, the center of an activity and growth unprecedented in history, and combining all that this implies," the Strike Commission observed in language that could have come from the time of the fire or of Haymarket. "Its lawless elements are at present augmented by shiftless adventurers and criminals attracted to it by the Exposition and impecuniously stranded in its midst. In the mobs were also actively present many of a certain class of objectionable foreigners who are being precipitated upon us by unrestricted immigration." Given all these conditions, "No more dangerous place for such a strike could have been chosen."[71] Unless some way was found to control it, the city would catch fire and explode again and again. The Chicago strike made many wonder once again whether urban culture itself was an "alien" threat. When the *North American Review* in its issue of August 1894 published the analyses of the strike by General Miles, Wade Hampton, Harry Robinson, and Samuel Gompers, all but Gompers predictably saw the workers' actions as an attack on American rights and values. During the strike, Miles was disappointed that his request for permission to open fire on the rioters had been denied, and he hired agents to spy on union meetings. While he had at first opposed the deployment of troops in Chicago, he soon asked for reinforcements and sided with the General Managers Association in resisting the withdrawal of the troops, exaggerating the dangerous condition of the city in order to justify his request. His reports to his superiors compared Chicago to Paris in 1790 and 1791, telling of all kinds of plots by anarchists, communists, and foreigners.[72]

In his *North American Review* article, Miles revealed his nativist and anti-urban prejudices when he described what had happened in the city of Chicago as ultimately threatening the destruction of the ideal small town, which to his mind was the true America. "If the property of a corporation or company in which the laboring men, the capitalists, the widows and orphans, the savings banks, properties in which any or all our people are interested, cannot be respected and protected," he wrote, "then the cottage, the hamlet, and the little personal property of the humblest citizen is in jeopardy, liable at the moment to be confiscated, seized, or destroyed by any traveling band of tramps." As far as Miles was concerned, the country faced a choice between "anarchy, secret conclaves, unwritten law, mob violence, and universal chaos," all of which he associated with Chicago, "or the supremacy of law, the maintenance of good order, universal peace, absolute security of life and property, the rights of personal liberty, all under the shadow and folds of 'Old Glory,'" which waved most proudly over the villages of the republic.[73] Opponents of Debs and the union expressed similar anti-urban sentiments when, in yet another instance of the continuing influence of Haymarket, they pushed their discussion of enemies and foreignness into an opposition between the "clean" and "dirty." George Pullman had tried to sanitize the city and the worker, and this strike was the thanks he received for all his trouble. Several newspaper reporters lumped all union members with the rabble that made up the destructive mob as one noisome and irredeemable mass. To emphasize the point further, they also repeatedly referred to the drunkenness of the rioters in Chicago and specifically mentioned Debs's personal problems with alcohol.[74]

The artist Frederic Remington mounted perhaps the most extended and prominently placed attacks on the strikers and Chicago as both foreign and filthy. In a series of articles he wrote and illustrated for *Harper's Weekly,* Remington, best known for his celebrations of manly action on battlefields of the open plains, depicted the unfolding events from the point of view of the regular soldier sent to quell this urban uprising.[75] Remington was struck by the incongruity of the Seventh Cavalry camped "right in the middle of civilization . . . right on the scene of the great Fair." What he wanted to communicate to his readers above all in his first article was how these brave and disciplined troops, which he took to embody all that was best about America, responded to what they perceived as threats to the country—and how little they cared for Chicago. This no-nonsense outfit, he reported, "has fifty copper cylinders in its belt, and its old campaign hat on, and there are things in Chicago it doesn't like, and if you want the recreated spirit of Homer you ought to hear a Seventh Cavalry trooper tell what he thinks of Chicago's mob."

The soldiers, according to the stridently xenophobic Remington, felt angry at being restrained from advancing on "the malodorous crowd of anarchist foreign trash" that worked against the cause of those honest workers with whom the soldiers were brothers in spirit. Using language remarkable for its manic focus on the evils of strikers and the city, Remington was especially eager to contrast the soldiers with the agitators. Regarding the first, he maintained that "a cleaner, decenter lot of young fellows can't be found anywhere." This whole conflict was mere police work that insulted their dignity and professionalism. They were trained warriors who much preferred to fight wild Indians than be made to clean up the city, which he described as "a seething mass of smells, stale beer, and bad language." In his next article in the series, Remington claimed that "decent people of Chicago" were receptive to the troops, whose "presence alone keeps the social scum from rising to the top." Sounding like those who at earlier moments of crisis, including the fire, had called for a reassertion of a lapsed moral authority to correct the challenge to all that was right and true raised by a debased democratic process, he condemned the "conscienceless politicians" who had encouraged this "scum" and "vermin" to think that they could take over the country. The only problem now was that the soldiers, unlike the vigilantes who supposedly cleansed the city of incendiaries, were not allowed to shoot a few rioters and put an early end to the nonsense. In the article that described the departure of troops from the city after the strike was broken, Remington took some comfort in the fact that while there would not be many soldiers stationed at Fort Sheridan (which, he said, should be expanded), even these few would be "enough to uphold the law, and if Chicago wants to make a Sumter of this fort there is plenty of material left in the country to make an Appomattox of Chicago."

Remington's cultural critique was clear even if his geographical juxtapositions were not: Chicago as a political and social entity was inimical to the nation, not just a tinderbox or a bomb but the source and location of everything that put the country at risk. Breaking the Pullman strike reasserted the will of the *real* America, and provided perhaps the last chance to save Chicago and the country. Whether America's cities could or should be reclaimed, or simply set afire as was Atlanta in the Civil War (or as Lloyd would have it in "No Mean City") was a good question. Remington's remarks on the departure of the soldiers from Chicago left little doubt that he believed that it was an enemy enclave. "As the column cleared the city and got into the United States of America proper," he wrote, "it was saluted by the waving of flags and cheers, which was quite a relief after being in the midst of a hostile population for so long."[76]

Captain Charles King wrote one of the small group of novels based on the Pullman strike, and he developed several of Remington's ideas about the city and American character. In the course of the love plot of *A Tame Surrender: A Story of the Pullman Strike* (1894), King condemned mobs, union leaders, immigrants, slumdwellers, and politicians (he was especially hard on Altgeld) for their responsibility in creating the disorders of the Pullman strike. He extolled the valor of the troops, who were ever "[c]alm, grim, and silent, conscious of their power, merciful in their strength, superb in their disdain of insult, their contempt of danger, their indifference to absolute outrage." They represented the true spirit of the nation, as they "coolly held that misguided, drink-crazed, demagogue-excited mob at bay, reopening railways, protecting trains, escorting Federal officials, forcing passage after passage through the turbulent streets, until the fury of the populace wore itself out against the rock of their iron discipline, and one after another the last of the rioters slunk to their holes, unharmed by even one avenging shot." Repeatedly the soldiers held their ground as "almost the sole bulwark between the great city and absolute anarchy." At one of the several melodramatic climaxes in the book, the cavalry, instead of arriving in the nick of time at some remote outpost under siege, rides into this city of more than a million residents to rescue the good citizens from their fellow Chicagoans.[77]

Both those who believed that organized labor or some loosely defined urban "other" must be suppressed and those who argued that the grip of capital must be broken seemed to concur that the best thing to do with the city was to remake it, or at least reduce its influence on the rest of the country. Most suggestions on how to do this in one way or another involved programs to slow or even reverse the movement of population to America's urban centers, whether from rural America or abroad. Besides restricting immigration, one of the most popular "solutions" offered at the time of the strike was the old proposal that the discontented and unstable urban population should be sent out onto the vast bosom of the American countryside, where, in harmony with the land, these unproductive and disorderly city-dwellers would be transformed into solid and responsible citizens. The Reverend David Swing was especially emphatic on this issue. "All the great cities seem to be united to make all law ridiculous," he warned, virtually accusing these cities themselves of somehow committing the crime of conspiracy. Swing pointed to the widespread corruption and disruption that marked urban life, which he tied to the exhaustion of local resources and lack of jobs. "The American paradise is at last overrun," he reflected sadly. "We have no more work." It was folly to allow any more immigrants into the cities, especially when such immigrants had few skills and devoted their meager resources to drink, with the result that "the saloon and death" now overwhelmed such republican institutions as "the school-house and the church." As for the present surplus population, there was work "if they will turn from the city to the farm."[78] Swedish Evangelical Lutheran Church minister Henry O. Lindeblad advised the Strike Commission that "one of the best remedies against all strikes . . . will be for the people to move out into the country and cultivate the land. There are too many people in the city."[79]

Several other social leaders expressed virtually the same sentiments. Together their recommendations revealed a pro-country, anti-city consensus that seemed to transcend other sharp differences. After decrying the "anarchy, secret conclaves, unwritten law, mob violence, and universal chaos" that he attributed to the socialism he saw festering in places like Chicago, General Miles declared, "There has been too much concentration in the cities." He followed this with the most explicit of his endorsements of the American pastoral ideal as the proper basis of the community: "More of our people should get out into the country, into the pure air and among the birds, flowers, and green fields, where they may cultivate the ground; for really all wealth comes from the ground, directly or indirectly." With restriction of immigration and some attention to irrigation of the arid western states and territories that General Miles's troops had conquered, there would be plenty of land available for "our intelligent, self-respecting, industrious population."[80]

Wade Hampton, too, found hope that America's open spaces would save it from the travails of other industrial nations, "for with our boundless and fertile acres now lying waste, every prudent man can acquire a home at a small cost, and a landowner is rarely an anarchist or a socialist." Hampton did not note that his advocacy of a stable society based on personal home ownership coincided with the views of Henry George and implicitly criticized George Pullman, who refused to allow residents of his town to own their homes. Historian Goldwin Smith, in an unfavorable review of Stead's *If Christ Came to Chicago!*, asserted that American cities to which the English reformer paid so much attention were in fact an aberration. Admitting that excesses of materialism, corruption, and other social evils were prevalent in these places, Smith advised Stead to visit a country town for a few years if he wished to see "an adequate measure of the habits of the American people, or of the sinews and safeguards of the American commonwealth." Stead himself argued in his book that the "healthy natural community" was "that of a small country town or village in which every one knows his neighbor, and where all the necessary ingredients for a happy, intelligent and public-spirited municipal life exist in due proportion."[81]

Some recommended such measures as redoubling the efforts of such organizations as the Children's Aid Society, which by this time had placed about 90,000 city children in country homes. To others, the current situation seemed to demand the more radical initiative of subsidized colonization of the kind called for in John Gibbons's *Tenure and Toil*, which appeared in a second edition in 1894 with a new introduction that maintained that the "deplorable scenes witnessed in the course of the recent conflicts between capital and labor" verified the fears expressed in the first edition and made the book even more timely. The Reverend Francis G. Peabody, Plummer Professor of Christian

Morals at Harvard and a popular and widely respected pioneer in social ethics in America who was sympathetic to labor, also found the rate of urban growth alarming. Referring to the problems of poverty in New York, which he called a "monstrous and unnatural . . . aggregation of humanity," Peabody stated that the agencies of charity and relief could be effective only if the population stayed constant, "but the complicating and, sometimes, the heartbreaking aspect of city charity is the constant inrush of immigration, foreign and native, as though a city were a whirlpool which drew into itself all the floating fragments of unattached humanity." His answer was a program very much like that Gibbons recommended, which would promote "the development of an efflux" to counteract the urban influx.[82]

The dangerous nature of the American city was perhaps the one major point on which contending principals in the Pullman strike could agree. In building his self-contained model town in Hyde Park, George Pullman was seeking to fashion a healthy industrial community in the image of a thriving village. While attacking the abuses of massed capital, Eugene Victor Debs expressed some of the same anti-urban biases of his most passionate enemies. In a 1902 essay titled "What's the Matter With Chicago," he approached the city with as much suspicion and anger as any antilabor polemicist. Debs, however, attributed the faults of Chicago not to unions, foreigners, or corrupt politicians, but to the fact that its main purpose was to make money rather than to provide a decent place for its citizens to live. From its first moment of settlement, Chicago was "unfit for human habitation," a swamp prone to dirt, disease, and darkness. "Look at some of her filthy streets in the heart of the city," Debs advised, "chronically torn up, the sunlight obscured, the air polluted, the water contaminated, every fountain and stream designed to bless the race poisoned at its source—and you need not wonder what ails Chicago, nor will you escape the conclusion that the case is chronic and that the present city will never recover from the fatal malady."

In Debs's opinion, this problem was a condition that applied to all dimensions of Chicago life and, beyond that, to modern urban culture everywhere: "What is true of Chicago physically is emphasized in her social, moral and physical aspects, and this applies to every commercial metropolis in the civilized world." As he, along with many others, so often did in his assessment of contemporary conditions, Debs here found the meaning he wanted in the language of disaster, speaking of the "reeking corruption" of cities that flowed like "lava tides" of "social anarchy" and "social disease." "Regeneration," he maintained, using a term much favored three decades earlier in discussions of the fire's effect on Chicago, "will only come with depopulation—when Socialism has relieved the congestion and released the people and they spread out

over the country and live close to the grass." A few years before he
wrote this essay, he had endorsed the colonization movement, even so-
liciting financial support from, of all people, John D. Rockefeller, to establish "a co-operative commonwealth" with "no class distinctions"
instead of "the present cruel, immoral and decadent system."[83]

This continuing idealization of the country as the locus of the nation's soul and health, along with an attack on the city as the main
source of disorder and dislocation, colored a wide range of partisan political rhetoric and more dispassionate social and historical analysis
contemporary with the strike, including some of the period's most
noted assessments of American life. Ironically, a few of the most famous formulations of these ideas were presented in the city of Chicago.
Virtually two years to the day after the federal troops arrived to rescue
America from the Pullman strike, William Jennings Bryan delivered his
legendary "Cross of Gold" speech at the 1896 Democratic National
Convention in the Chicago Coliseum. To Bryan, rural America was the
only true source of national vitality. In one of the most stirring passages
of this oration, Bryan proposed a simple experiment that would prove
his point: "Burn down your cities and leave our farms, and your cities
will spring up again as if by magic; but destroy our farms and the grass
will grow in the streets of every city in the country."[84]

Bryan and all of those who advocated sending the urban population
to the country may have been troubled, however, by the fact that for
some time other serious cultural analysts were maintaining that Americans had virtually exhausted the resources of usable open land that were
the source of the nation's physical and spiritual strength. "The general
intelligence, the general comfort, the active invention, the power of ad-
aptation and assimilation, the free, independent spirit, the energy and
hopefulness that have marked our people," Henry George stated in
Progress and Poverty, "are not causes, but results—they have sprung
from unfenced land." Part of the urgency of George's social argument,
picked up by Josiah Strong and others, rested in the fear that the end of
the availability of inexpensive and productive land for new settlement
would only accelerate the urban "progress" that was directly related to
poverty, degradation, and disorder. George remained deeply concerned about the social consequences of what he believed was the inevitable increase in urban population resulting from the diminishing
supply of promising rural land. America, he warned in *Social Problems,*
was "very soon to lose one of the most important conditions under
which our civilization has been developing—that possibility of expansion over virgin soil that has given scope and freedom to American life,
and relieved social pressure in the most progressive European nations."
Some of the unfortunate social "tendencies" of the time that were

"harmless" as long as the safety valve of open land existed now "may become most dangerous." In what can be read as a prophecy of Haymarket, George explained, "Gunpowder does not explode until it is confined." You may rest your hand on the slowly ascending jaw of a hydraulic press. It will only gently raise it. But wait a moment till it meets resistance!"[85]

Speaking in Chicago a year before the Pullman strike, the young University of Wisconsin historian Frederick Jackson Turner developed some very similar ideas in his paper, "The Significance of the Frontier in American History," that subsequently had in its own way as wide an imaginative influence as the writings of Henry George. Turner came to the city to speak at the World's Congress of Historians and Historical Students, one of the many such "congresses" of the world's fair summer.[86] The historical point of departure for Turner's presentation was what he saw as the fact, revealed by the 1890 census, that the American frontier, the most important source of the development of democratic institutions and the American character, had for all practical purposes ceased to exist. The closing of the frontier did not, strictly speaking, eliminate the possibility of the dispersal of the urban population that many advocated, but the inevitable conclusion was that further concentration—i.e., urbanization—was an inescapable trend. While Turner celebrated the importance of the West in the development of America, his assertion, which was open to question, that the frontier was now effectively closed undercut any last lingering claims for American exceptionalism. Turner, who was not a critic of cities, did not himself use the language of catastrophe in describing this irreversible course of events, but his talk was distinctly elegiac, expressing a romantic vision of the transcendent "significance" of the open lands of the West.[87]

The conclusion that Turner did not draw but which others did was that the challenges of urban culture in America, especially given the end of the availability of open land, made it the most important and troubling "frontier" in America as the twentieth century approached. In September of 1894, while people like Swing were calling for a movement of people out of the city for their and its own good, an article on the new Chicago drainage canal reported with approval that the work on the massive project had gone on through all the "panic and social disorder" of the past year. It was a good thing, too, for this bold engineering achievement would be badly needed by the swelling urban population. After all, the article explained, "The West of the pioneers is gone. Its good lands are privately owned. The westward wave of population has passed. Future increase will develop that latent resources passed over in the rush."[88]

Anyone living in Chicago did not need to hear Turner or meditate by the side of the drainage canal to understand that the future of the nation had shifted from the open lands to such contested sites as the lake front, the Hull-House neighborhood, the stockyards, the railroad crossings, and the model industrial town of Pullman, and that here the nature of American institutions and of the American character would be determined. All they had to do was note that most of the authors of the anti-urban commentaries they read themselves lived in cities, that the Chicago of the strike had more than three times the population of the Chicago of the fire, and that many of its new citizens had come on one-way tickets from the same countryside to which the urban population was supposedly to be dispersed. Or they could observe that the army regulars had been pulled off the prairies and plains, which no longer needed their protection, and sent to the city, which evidently did. Pullman's own *Arcade Mercantile Journal* concluded in a front-page story in 1890 that industrialization and the railroad seemed "destined to render the entire population of the country practically urban in character." It was on the densely populated but far from "settled" urban frontier that the future would be played out.[89] Any hope for a reversal of this trend was destined to lead to discouragement, for it ignored the social and economic incentives that had brought people to the cities in the first place and would continue to draw them there in the years ahead. Trying to get them to go back was not just a matter of moving bodies but of fighting history.

Farewell to the White City

Often to their credit, Chicago's leaders kept looking for other ways to construct an urban future free of the distress that some felt was inevitable. As events in Pullman demonstrated, these efforts could produce disappointing results, and even some of the successes offered strong evidence that the task of creating a stable urban order would prove very difficult. Few cases were more instructive than the denouement of the World's Columbian Exposition. The fair's directors had set aside special days to celebrate certain holidays or honor particular countries, organizations, or causes (and to raise attendance). The grandest moment of all was reserved for Chicago Day, which was appropriately set for October 9, 1893, twenty-two years after the fire and three weeks before the exposition was to close. In honor of the occasion, newspapers prepared special editions that in the best booster spirit contrasted the Chicago of yesterday with the bigger and better Chicago of today. The *Tribune* illustrations glorifying the new Chicago included a scene of the bustling commercial activity in the Haymarket, now complete with the police statue. The paper printed Whittier's verses on the great con-flagration and the reminiscences of several firemen who fought the blaze. An editorial titled "What the Day Means" explained that the commemoration was not a celebration of the catastrophe, which would have been "in shockingly bad taste," but an effort "to glorify all that has been done since then." In the years since the fire, noted a related arti-cle, "Chicago has passed from the position of a mere receiving point for the produce of a limited area to that of a metropolitan city." That the world's attention was now as focused on Chicago in her triumph as in her tragedy was impressively proved by the fact that several hundred thousand visitors jammed the city's railroad stations and hotels so that they could join proud local citizens in setting an all-time single-day at-tendance record of 716,881.

What they witnessed did not disappoint them. The festivities began with a "monster concert" to "Welcome the World in Music in Song," followed by a "Grand Reunion of the States," a pageant enacted by an enormous cast of "youths and maidens." This was succeeded by "Chi-cago in Her Growth Welcoming the World," consisting of eight floats representing different significant historical moments, one of which was titled "Chicago Prostrate." The festivities culminated with what was described as the "Most Gorgeous Display of Fireworks Ever Seen in America—Forming in Its Entirety the Most Significant and Grandest Spectacle of Modern Times." The *Tribune* correctly predicted the morning of the great day that "a larger audience will gather along the lake-front east of the Manufactures Building tonight to see the burning of Chicago than that which witnessed the original performance twenty-two years ago."[90]

But the uninvited and unwanted guest of disorder was to have the last word on the exposition. As the fair wound down, the news-papers devoted their attention not only to Marshall Field's pledge of $1,000,000 (and George Pullman's promise of another $100,000) to convert the Fine Arts Building into a permanent museum (now the Museum of Science and Industry), but also to such continuing con-flicts as the political enmity between Governor Altgeld and Judge Gary. The last scheduled special day before closing was October 28, when Mayor Carter Harrison, now in his fifth term, hosted the largest collec-tion of mayors ever assembled at ceremonies that honored America's cities. Harrison, who had helped lead Chicago through the railroad strike and the Haymarket bombing, proudly ended his welcoming re-marks to this group with a tribute to the Chicago "that never could con-ceive what it wouldn't attempt, and yet has found nothing that it could not achieve." It was the last public speech he would utter. Harrison went home to take a nap, from which he was aroused by a visit from another kind of representative figure of the age, a disappointed (and sadly demented) office-seeker, who shot him dead with three bullets from point-blank range.

The assassin, Eugene Patrick Prendergast, fled the scene but almost immediately surrendered at the Desplaines Street police station, from which Inspector John Bonfield had marched his men on the Haymarket rally. Prendergast soon found himself in a cell in the Chicago Avenue station that had once been occupied by Louis Lingg and which was now, as then, watched over by Michael Schaack. The Haymarket connections continued, as William Black participated in Prendergast's unsuccessful defense. The convicted assassin was hanged on July 13, 1894. Clarence Darrow, who headed a last-minute appeal for Prendergast's life, then almost immediately took up the case of Eugene Victor Debs, who, shortly after the execution, was temporarily held in the assassin's cell in the Cook County Jail. The directors of the fair lowered all flags to half-mast and canceled the closing ceremonies. The exposition quietly shut its gates on October 30.[91]

The fairgrounds, which, like Pullman, had been designed to present a finer urban alternative to places like Chicago, and which had inspired Americans to believe that such an alternative was possible, seemed to fall prey in a most dramatic fashion to the same kind of ills that beset the modern city. Early in 1894 a fire, possibly caused by a member of Chicago's depression homeless, consumed much of the Court of Honor and drew a vast crowd that oohed and aahed as flaming chunks of fair fell into the icy lagoon. In May the remaining exhibition halls were sold to the Columbian Exposition Salvage Company, but on the evening of July 5, with the troops confronting rioters throughout the city, another blaze of unknown origin destroyed virtually all that was left of what had been the heart of the fair before the salvage company could claim it. It was a far more impressive reenactment of 1871 than had been the fireworks display on Chicago Day. As during the original conflagration, firemen could only watch helplessly as fiery brands jumped from one colossal White City building to another, which, since they were temporary structures with stage-set facades made mainly of wood, cloth, and plaster, burned "like tinder." The last moments of the lofty Administration Building at the head of the Court of Honor recalled the final collapse of the bell tower in the Courthouse at the time of the Great Fire: "There was a sort of shifting motion around the base of the dome and then the monster dream in gold and white tottered, stool still for an instant, and then shut up as if it were a huge accordion." The final group of doomed statuary that tumbled off the Administration Building before the building itself gave way represented "Fire Uncontrolled."

The fair's unscheduled fiery grand finale attracted a generously estimated 100,000 spectators, who judged it without irony as an aesthetic success and a "glorious ending" to the exposition. They were described by a reporter as "good-natured" and "leisurely," settling themselves into comfortable vantage points from which they "quietly gazed upon the magnificent destruction much as they gazed at the fireworks displays last summer." There was little excitement, and "[e]very one was satisfied with the spectacle." The only cheer came with the fall the huge Manufactures and Liberal Arts Building, which evoked one long collective sigh from the assembled masses, "in the midst of which the clear, bell-like voice of a girl could be heard: 'O, it's all over.'"[92]

Illustrations of the fair on fire competed for space in newspapers and magazines with drawings of mobs attacking locomotives trying to break the boycott. The juxtaposed images in the papers could only have contributed to a most disorienting sense that events and cultural categories were collapsing into one another. The purpose of the exposition was to demonstrate how far Chicago had come since the fire, but with the Court of Honor aflame and federal troops from the plains riding in on trains to save the city from those who lived there, the distance and direction of progress were hard to calculate. In his poem *The Vanishing Fair*, published as a book, H. H. Van Meter tried to make some positive sense of this latest disaster in the same way city boosters had done after the fire, by finding in the ruins of the exposition some evidence of redemption and renewal. He mourned the destruction of the exposition but insisted that its message of beauty would never be forgotten. He also engaged in some only slightly veiled criticism of Pullman in asserting that the city would "Rise to greater grander good"

> When no more with martial measure
>   Troops shall tramp with heavy tread
> Where the miser hoards his treasure
> And mad misery hides her head.

> When no more Wants [*sic*] frenzied minions
> Shall break forth with blood and flame,
> Cursing men who count their millions
> Covering all with sin and shame.[93]

Like many others at this time, Van Meter faced the future by looking backward, not only by employing stilted diction but also by implying that somehow the shining memory of the transcendent beauty of the fair would magically lead America toward some kind of politico-religious transcendence of all these worldly troubles. William and Charles Ottman's illustrations and "embellishments" that accompanied the poem undercut and confused its message, for they mixed images of the devastated fairgrounds with renderings of such subjects as the landings of Columbus and the Pilgrims, the Liberty Bell, troops defending trains from strikers, scenes of the exposition in all its glory, and winged angels appearing to biblical shepherds. Their choice of styles for these illustrations ranged from detailed photographs of the fire damage to late Victorian kitsch. Trying desperately to contain disorder and imaginatively find some positive meaning in it, this peculiar book was itself out of control.

But Van Meter's basic impulse was laudable, since it was important to try to come to terms with such distressing events, as it had been many times since 1871. He also correctly noted that the city's future had not been catastrophically cut off by the fire or any other event, and that there was no reason to believe that it would not again "arise." There were, however, some "lessons" that he ignored. The city and the nation may have been right to examine and celebrate how far they had come, but not—as the fair, the town of Pullman, and many critics as well as defenders of the social order did—by turning their backs on the city and looking out over the lake or across the hinterland for some new discoverer-deliverer who would enable them to start anew. As Jane Addams suggested, what was needed was a fuller understanding of the proper meaning of progress in a modern urban world, and a recognition that the emergence of such a world was the result of growth and change, and not of catastrophe.

EPILOGUE

As the century turned, there certainly were signs that people were responding to urban change differently than they had before. This period has proved very difficult to define, as scholars continue to disagree about the meaning of terms—most notably "progressive" and "modern"—commonly used to characterize and discuss it.[1] One can still speak usefully, however, of general trends in the thinking of middle- and upper-class Americans, all of which were closely connected to their reflections on the challenges presented by urban experience. These include above all a faith in the value of rational analysis and organization (whether in industrial corporations, government agencies, labor unions, whole neighborhoods, or even entire cities), but also a recognition of instability and change as conditions of life, to be understood better in terms of process rather than of order and disorder.

Both this faith and this recognition were expressed in a multitude of different permutations and in many kinds of discourse, from the abstract to the particular. In his brilliant if idiosyncratic account of the difficult emergence of a twentieth-century sensibility, the cranky patrician Henry Adams characterized this development as a movement from "unity" to "multiplicity" that progressed faster with each succeeding generation. More and more was happening in less and less time, and any theory of history would have to deal with the brave new discovery that chaos was the law of nature, order the dream of man. The modern age demanded "a new social mind." Past experience perhaps justified some guarded confidence that the mind would not now fail, but, as Adams put it, "it would need to jump." More than twenty years earlier, in *Social Problems*, the simultaneously forward-and-backward-looking Henry George had similarly observed, "As society develops, a higher and higher degree of . . . social intelligence is required, for the relation of individuals to each other becomes more intimate and important, and the increasing complexity of the social organization brings liability to new dangers."[2]

Speaking on the level of practical philosophy and effective action, other early modern intellectuals, led by figures such as William James and John Dewey, argued not only for the unavoidability of social complexity, conflict, and disorder, but even for their essential value to a vigorous imagination and a meaningful existence. Some of James's reflections directly joined the period's discussion of urban disorder. In his inspirational essay "What Makes a Life Significant," first published in 1899, he spoke of his reaction to a summer stay at the Assembly Grounds at Lake Chautauqua in western New York, which was, coincidentally, very near George Pullman's boyhood home. His description of Chautauqua's perfect order and wondrous array of mental, physical, and spiritual culture and kindness sounds like a realization of all the utopian hopes of the time. At first James was totally charmed. Having intended only to take a brief look, he lingered a week, "held spellbound by the charm and ease of everything, by the middle-class paradise, without a sin, without a victim, without a blot, without a tear." But once he did leave, James found himself "quite unexpectedly and involuntarily" relieved to get out, longing "for something primordial and savage, even though it were as bad as an Armenian massacre, to set the balance straight again." This hygienic world of soda-water fountains, bicycle paths, religious services, and popular lectures was "too tame," its culture "too second-rate," its goodness "too uninspiring." One could never achieve "the higher sort of contentment" in such a place, because it was lacking "the element that gives to the wicked outer world all its moral style, expressiveness and picturesqueness,—the element of precipitousness, so to call it, of strength and strenuousness, intensity and danger."[3]

James's essay is open to the criticism that he aestheticizes the struggles of life, especially among the working classes. It is in this respect perhaps not so different from the tributes to the fire as a great occasion for the human spirit and a civic blessing in disguise. What is noteworthy, however, is James's richer sense of both the inevitability and the possibilities of disorder. He certainly would not have wanted anyone to burn down Chicago, throw the Haymarket bomb, or precipitate a national railroad strike in order to make life interesting and significant (though when, during a visit to Stanford in 1906, the sixty-five-year-old James was shaken from his bed by the San Francisco earthquake, he greeted its "overpowering dramatic convincingness" with "glee and admiration" and took a train into the city to view the catastrophe for himself).[4] But his remarks reveal that one did not have to feel displaced, disadvantaged, or discontented in order to greet the "precipitousness" of life with at least some sense of its value. Much of the vocabulary of the formative period of modernism is based in the attempt to capture and express this value, and it does so by taking the power, dynamism, vital energy, and even the danger of the disorderly city as its subject.

Schooled by events in the late nineteenth century, progressive reformers approached the disruptions of urban life not as causeless and intractable aberrations but as systemic problems that grew out of the current order and could be successfully dealt with by disciplined scrutiny that would suggest effective measures. If some of these reformers envisioned a future not very different from the world that George Pullman tried to build, where a more powerful if "enlightened" state (or large companies) successfully managed the complex endeavors of society at the possible expense of individual freedom, others agreed with Dewey, who argued that the best hope for society was the encouragement of practical democracy.[5] As time went on, those who shared this outlook would say that one had to accept and even encourage a certain amount of real or apparent disorder and social chaos because of their inherent worth, as well as inevitability, in a vibrant urban culture, and also as the best way to avoid truly cataclysmic events like the Haymarket bomb or the Pullman strike.

Disorder Revisited

Particularly revealing of the persistent ambivalence toward urban disorder is the continuing cultural history of the fire, Haymarket, and the town of Pullman. Visitors to Chicago at the time of the Columbian Exposition and for several years after could visit Isaac N. Reed's and Howard H. Gross's Cyclorama Building on Michigan Avenue and view "the most elaborate and expensive work of art ever created in the history of the world," a colossal (fifty feet high and four hundred feet long) rendering of the fire that transformed civic destruction into an aesthetic and educational experience, complete with an accompanying booklet that included a fire memoir written by the Reverend David Swing.[6] As the years went by, the fire continued to belong to the future, not the past. By the time of the semicentennial observance in 1921, October 9 had come to be noted as Fire and Accident Prevention Day. For this special anniversary, the Chicago Historical Society regathered veterans of the disaster to share their reminiscences. The Chicago Association of Commerce meanwhile planned a much more ambitious program that showed little interest in remembering the fire itself. The association's preliminary announcement of its plans focused exclusively on the "unprecedented growth, the development of great industries, and the realization of vast material as well as cultural progress" since the flames were doused. In explaining the object of its commemoration ceremonies, the association declared: "It is desirable that the coming anniversary shall be the starting point of a great civic awakening and definite program for the rebuilding of the 'Chicago of Tomorrow'—that the next fifty years—even greater in accomplishment than the past—shall round out a century of unparalleled achievement." To emphasize the point, the announcement continued, "It is intended that the observance shall inspire pride and purpose; that it shall look forward rather than backward; that it shall be practical and constructive,—reflecting a high resolve that the coming years shall be years of realization of Chicago's splendid possibilities."

The 1921 commemoration included a number of other events typical of the period: large meetings conducted by civic and patriotic organizations, ceremonies in schools, special sermons in churches, athletic events, a "No Accident Week," a special songbook, and an "Americanization demonstration" devoted to the "Re-dedication of Chicago" that drew over six thousand people to a reception in Grant Park for 648 "newly made citizens." What these naturalized Americans, especially those who came from war-ravaged Europe, thought of their adopted city that took such pride in its devastation is hard to guess. Featured in the official semicentennial poster was a militant maiden who represented the spirit of Chicago. She stood in her winged helmet overlooking the ruins of the old city, Chicago's official motto "I Will" emblazoned in capital letters across her breastplate, her long and lithe right arm pointing over the bustling modern skyline to an even better tomorrow. The motto for the celebration, printed on the poster, was "UNDAUNTED—WE BUILD." The most ambitious component of the semicentennial, one that recalled the Chicago Day ceremonies at the World's Columbian Exposition, was a "historically correct" festival play staged in Humboldt Park and organized by the Bureau of Parks, Playground, and Beaches. "[V]ividly dramatized" by a cast of 2,500 people, and "augmented by a chorus of 500 voices with an orchestra of 100 pieces," it was attended by an audience estimated at 50,000, even though the weather was unfavorable. This dramatic performance, *The Seven Fires,* was subtitled *A Masque of Chicago,* and it wedded one more time the city's moral and statistical progress in a highly stylized narrative of Chicago's past as the prelude to glories yet to come.[7]

All the pageantry, civic meetings, and Americanization ceremonies at the time of the fiftieth anniversary of the destruction of the city had hardly anything to do with the fire at all, except as an occasion to reaffirm the faith of the Association of Commerce in the material progress of the city. The *Masque of Chicago* was not an isolated event, but one of many contemporary urban civic pageants. Ceremonies of this kind were more in the progressive spirit and less directly coercive than the policies of the Relief and Aid Society after the fire or the comprehensive control of life and work in Pullman, but their goals were in important ways quite similar, since they hoped to educate and uplift the mass of city-dwellers to a unified urban ideal defined by an elite and middle-class vision.[8]

The struggle over the cultural memory of Haymarket, both in itself and as a key to understanding modern city life, reveals how urban culture has resisted the establishment of such a unified view of social reality and the meaning of order. The pluralistic city was and would continue to be contested space, imaginatively as well as in many other ways. Those who had argued for clemency on the grounds that executing the anarchists would make martyrs of them were proved right, as Haymarket quickly took a central place in the culture of many different labor, radical, and immigrant groups throughout the world, who honored the defendants in books, pamphlets, posters, rallies, pageants, and songs. Writing in 1898, Eugene Victor Debs, no longer concerned about being associated with the convicted anarchists, called the trial "a plot, satanic in all its conception, to wreak vengeance upon defenseless men, who . . . were found guilty of exercising the inalienable right of free speech in the interest of the toiling and groaning masses." Ten years later, Frank Harris published *The Bomb,* a novel narrated by the alleged bomb-thrower, Rudolph Schnaubelt, and full of inaccuracies. Several twentieth-century poets, including Edgar Lee Masters and Kenneth Rexroth, devoted verse to the Haymarket tragedy. As recently as 1970, a group honoring the struggles of the eight-hour movement modeled the call for one of its meetings directly on the circular that summoned workingmen to the Haymarket on the evening of May 4, 1886.[9] To this day, Haymarket is ritualistically recalled when labor strife or other conflicts with civil authority are perceived to be class-based. The monument at Waldheim (now Forest Home) Cemetery has become over time an unofficial shrine of dissent, the final resting place chosen by several of America's most well-known radicals, including Voltairine de Cleyre, Elizabeth Gurley Flynn, William Z. Foster, and Emma Goldman.[10]

Haymarket has hardly been the cultural property of outsiders and dissenters alone, however, since to many it has been a reminder of the sacrifices required to preserve law and order. In 1901 the surviving policemen who marched on the rally fifteen years earlier incorporated the

Veterans of the Haymarket Riot, which they devoted to "Good Fellow-ship and Fraternal Feeling," as well as to keeping alive the memory of their bravery and that of their fallen brothers. Four years later they presented a special citation to Judge Gary, "remembering back to the dark days of May the 4th in 1886." Well into the 1960s, representatives of civic groups and descendants of Haymarket police veterans, joined by an honor guard that included an officer in period dress, would pose proudly for photographers beside the police statue in May.[11] The travails of this statue are an indication of the high level of feeling that has continued to surround Haymarket. It was repeatedly moved, defaced, and damaged over the years. In October of 1969, someone placed a powerful explosive between the statue's legs that blew it apart. It was restored, but was blown up a second time a year later, again in protest against government policies at home and abroad. Repaired once more, it eventually retreated to its current, and presumably safe, home in a locked interior courtyard in the Chicago police training academy.[12]

In spite of Governor Altgeld's pardon and much progress in the area of social and economic justice, Haymarket set a pattern for the repression of real and imagined subversives at times of cultural crisis, and for the discrediting of philosophical anarchism and other radical critiques of the state as wild-eyed terrorism preached by crazy, lazy, dirty, and dangerous "aliens." In respect to urban culture in particular, Haymarket contributed to the popular conception of the city as a place that one enters expecting unpleasant confrontations and anonymous acts of meaningless violence, which, for all their apparent unnaturalness, are perhaps more authentic than the civility which the ideal of urbanity preaches. Advocates of radical ideas of almost every conceivable political stripe still invoke the bombing, trial, and executions to advance their own causes. Outside the Chicago Historical Society on the day its Haymarket centennial exhibition opened, a group called Chicago Anarchists United distributed a leaflet titled "Tell the Truth About Haymarket," charging that the Illinois Labor History Society and the "so-called" Haymarket Centennial Committee, using corporate grants "and serving the same system that murdered our fellow workers in 1887," distorted the truth by portraying the martyred men as "misunderstood liberals" and even praising business leaders and police. Another leafleteer meanwhile urged that the occasion be dedicated to attacking "the Zionist connection to apartheid, Naziism, Central America, and the atomic bomb."[13]

By this time Chicago had an African-American mayor, Harold Washington, who had run against "the system," and in official public memory the centennial's entire purpose was to honor workers, unions, and free speech. In his proclamation of the Haymarket Centennial,

Washington pledged the city to a commemoration of "the movement towards the eight-hour day, union rights, civil rights, human rights," and to the remembrance of the "tragic miscarriage of justice which claimed the lives of four labor activists." The poster that included the proclamation spoke of "the vicious frameup" of 1886 and listed a schedule of events marking "A celebration of the history and culture of working people." August Spies's last words, shouted from the gallows and inscribed on the Waldheim monument, had been confirmed: "The time will come when our silence will be more powerful than the voices you strangle today."[14]

In Pullman, the acrimony of the strike left bitterness on all sides. In July of 1897, three years after the federal government had broken the strike, the few remaining activists of the American Railway Union, meeting in Chicago, dissolved their organization and established the Social Democracy of America. The members of the new party's executive board had served time at Woodstock with Debs, who became the Socialists' national standard-bearer for a generation.[15] The strike weakened the health of George Pullman, who died of heart failure in the autumn of 1897. In his will, he treated his wife, his two daughters, and his siblings generously, and he designated special bequests to a dozen local cultural and charitable institutions, including the Chicago Historical Society and the Relief and Aid Society. The strike evidently did not discourage his interest in educating and uplifting the children of workers, at least within their class, for his largest institutional gift was $1,200,000 to erect and endow a manual-training school.

But Pullman, who had been both admired and attacked for his paternalism, died disappointed in his inability to direct the lives of his own twin sons as he wished. He left each a relatively small allowance of three thousand dollars a year since "neither . . . has developed such a sense of responsibility as in my judgment is requisite for the wise use of large properties and considerable sums of money." Wary of bodysnatchers, as well as of old enemies or terrorists whose animosity toward George Pullman might continue beyond his death, his family placed his body in a specially fortified burial vault, which the *Tribune* described as "impregnable to the attack of vandals with picks or even dynamite itself." The neoclassical monument on the family plot in Graceland Cemetery, which Pullman had purchased only a few months earlier, was Solon Beman's last commission for his long-time patron.[16]

Although the company was "victorious" in the strike, the social experiment that was once the most promising, and always the most interesting, feature of Pullman soon began to unravel. The year after George Pullman's death, the state of Illinois won a suit in which it challenged the legality of the model town, contending that the corporate charter restricted the company to manufacturing railroad cars. The company soon divested itself of the property and buildings not devoted to industry, and this extraordinary social experiment became another industrial neighborhood on the endless South Side of the second biggest city in America. The corporation continued to prosper over the next several decades, but then went into decline with the rise of travel by highway and by air. Lake Vista, the charming railroad station, the playing fields, and some of the street names (including Florence Boulevard) are now long gone. What remains of the shuttered works awaits restoration as a state historic district, while the residential section enjoys a modest revival, thanks to long-time residents with strong attachments, newer arrivals seeking appealing and affordable housing, and historical preservationists. There are guidebooks and house walks for modern tourists, who can refresh themselves in the dining room of the Hotel Florence after viewing the hotel's small group of historical exhibits, including the room on the second floor that was always kept ready for the founder.

The passing of the sleeping-car magnate and the breakup of his model town were representative events, signaling the passing of his generation of elite leadership and of their vision of urban order and social control. Despite the ability of George Pullman and his peers to write the history of the fire from their point of view, to hang the Haymarket anarchists, and to put down the Pullman strike, their view of what constituted an orderly city was cast aside as impractical, undesirable, or politically impossible by the next generation, even if several of their ideas were adapted by the more paternalistic progressive reformers. At the same time, the imaginative appeal of Chicago that had attracted people and public attention had also begun to wane. Chicago's eminence had peaked by the mid-1890s, and it would no longer command as much fascination, excitement, and concern as it had in the turbulent quarter century between the fire and the strike.

If it lost its special status as a center of the nation's uncertain reflections on the nature and meaning of urban life, the intellectual transformations that were based in the series of spectacular traumas that beset Chicago in the late nineteenth century became an essential part of the way Americans think about cities. This is evident in the patterns of imaginative response to urban disorders extending from the San Francisco earthquake and fire of 1906 to the Los Angeles riot and earthquake of the 1990s, and, more significantly, in the way Americans talk about city life in "ordinary" circumstances. The integration of the idea of disorder into the view of the city is so pervasive that it is now unremarkable. To say that the city is "a disaster" is an offhand expression, as is the description of any of its elements, from public transportation to the quality of education, as "catastrophic." Such terminology expresses a view of urban experience in which the disorderly and even the disastrous are taken to be at a rising but somehow still always "normal" level. While many Americans through the twentieth century have continued to pursue the promise of city life, including its qualities of variety, vitality, and culture, as well as its economic opportunities, more and more of those who have had a choice have sought the social order of the suburbs. At this writing the picture is confused, both by the sense that certain conditions, most notably the level of violence, have become unacceptable, but also that many of the problems of social distress traditionally associated with cities are pervasive everywhere. Urban disorder, whose central theme is the breaking of imaginative frames, has in many ways become the frame itself.

NOTES

CHAPTER ONE

1. "Haymarket" is comprehensively used here to refer to the rally that took place on the evening of May 4, 1886; the bombing and riot that occurred at the end of that rally which caused the death of seven policemen (an eighth died of bomb-related injuries considerably later); and the subsequent trial and execution of those held responsible.

2. It is possible to overemphasize the significance of the Haymarket bombing and trial in relation to the history of labor organization, radical protest, industrialization, immigration, and urbanization in which it took place. Bruce C. Nelson points out that much of the attention devoted to the trial has ignored other important developments. Inside the courtroom, Nelson argues, "a judicially foreshortened cast of accused conspirators moved inexorably toward the gallows. While dramatic, the process under investigation was legal, not historical: neither judge, prosecutor, nor jury was interested in the origins or development of the political movement led by the Martyrs, only in the conviction and execution of criminals." *Beyond the Martyrs: A Social History of Chicago's Anarchists, 1870–1900* (New Brunswick: Rutgers University Press, 1988), pp. 2–3. It is precisely the purpose of this study to analyze how and why the bombing and trial seized the public imagination as they did and to understand their significance in the evolution of the way Americans thought about the modern city.

3. Paul Boyer, *Urban Masses and Moral Order in America, 1820–1920* (Cambridge: Harvard University Press, 1978), p. 131; Richard T. Ely, "Pullman: A Social Study," *Harper's New Monthly Magazine* 70 (February 1885), 453.

4. *Harper's Weekly* 38 (7 July 1894), 627.

5. Eric H. Monkkonen, *America Becomes Urban: The Development of U.S. Cities and Towns, 1780–1980* (Berkeley: University of California Press, 1980), p. 70.

6. At the same time the total population of the country not quite doubled, growing from almost forty million to nearly seventy-six million.

7. United States Department of Commerce, Bureau of the Census, *Historical Statistics of the United States, Colonial Times to 1970* (White Plains, N.Y.: Kraus International Publications), vol. 1, pp. 11–12; Department of the Interior, Census Office, *Report of the Population of the United States at the Eleventh Census: 1890*, Part I (Washington, D.C.: Government Printing Office, 1895), pp. lxv–lxvi.

8. Wesley G. Skogan, *Chicago Since 1840: A Time-Series Data Handbook* (Urbana, Ill.: University of Illinois Institute of Government and Public Affairs, 1976), pp. 18–19; *Report of the Population at the Eleventh Census*, pp. lxvi–lxvii. While the percentage increase of some new midwestern and western urban centers, notably Minneapolis-St. Paul, Omaha, and Denver, was higher, Chicago's absolute growth was unmatched during the 1880s. At 596,665, it surpassed its nearer competitor, New York City, by almost 290,000.

9. This is one of the organizing themes of William Cronon's *Nature's Metropolis: Chicago and the Great West* (New York: W. W. Norton, 1991). See especially pp. 91, 283–84, 307. Of Chicago as an unprecedented kind of mercantile nexus, Cronon writes: "The lessons of the urban market were about *newness*. The merchandise one could buy was new, the way one bought it was new, the life one could live with it was new. Buying from the city meant participating in the progress of the age. It meant becoming modern" (p. 318).

10. Pauly explains, "Because Chicago was the most rapidly expanding city of the industrial age, the fire there offered a perfect occasion for reflections on the state of American society." "The Great Chicago Fire as a National Event," *American Quarterly* 36 (1984), 673. This is a central point of this essay and of Ross Miller's *American Apocalypse: The Great Fire and the Myth of Chicago* (Chicago: University of Chicago Press, 1990). Mainly because of the wider interest in human drama than in isolated natural destruction, city fires have generally attracted more immediate and sustained attention in this country than have rural fires, except, as Stephen J. Pyne points out, when the latter endanger settled areas, as in present-day southern California. The Great Chicago Fire was much smaller in scale than the rural fire that broke out at virtually the same time and destroyed Peshtigo, Wisconsin, and nearby settlements, causing a greater loss of life (1,500 people) than any fire in United States history, but the Peshtigo disaster, while still relatively well-known locally, has had nothing approaching the imaginative dimensions of the destruction of Chicago. On rural fire, including some comparisons with urban fire, see Pyne, *Fire in America: A Cultural History of Wildland and Rural Fire* (Princeton: Princeton University Press, 1982); and Margaret Hindle Hazen and Robert M. Hazen, *Keepers of the Flame: The Role of Fire in American Culture* (Princeton: Princeton University Press, 1992), pp. 75, 78.

11. Mary Douglas, *Purity and Danger. An Analysis of the Concepts of Pollution and Taboo* (London: Ark Paperbacks, 1984; originally published by Routledge and Kegan Paul, 1966), p. 4. Douglas explains further: "In a chaos of shifting impressions, each of us constructs a stable world in which objects have recognisable shapes, are located in depth, and have permanence. In perceiving we

are building, taking some cues and rejecting others. The most acceptable cues are those which fit most easily into the pattern that is being built up. Ambiguous ones tend to be treated as if they harmonised with the rest of the pattern. Discordant ones tend to be rejected. If they are accepted the structure of assumptions has to be modified" (p. 36). On the inherently conservative notions of the concept of order, and the preoccupation with cultural disorder in social thought from the late eighteenth century to the present, see also Leon Bramson, *The Political Context of Sociology* (Princeton, N.J.: Princeton University Press, 1961), p. 26. The leading study of concepts of order and disorder in the American setting in the late nineteenth and early twentieth centuries remains Robert H. Wiebe's *The Search for Order, 1877–1920* (New York: Hill and Wang, 1967). Wiebe speaks specifically about the challenge posed by the distinctive culture and institutions of the city and by urban-centered conflict and unrest. See also Richard Sennett, *The Uses of Disorder: Personal Identity and City Life* (New York: Alfred A. Knopf, 1970).

12. Alan Trachtenberg makes a related point in his study of the nation in this period: "From Appomattox to White City . . . controversies over the meaning of America symbolized struggles over reality, over the power to define as well as control it." *The Incorporation of America: Culture and Society in the Gilded Age* (New York: Hill and Wang, 1982), p. 8.

13. I purposely do not draw sharp distinctions between areas of belief (e.g., religious, economic, political) since I think that making such distinctions has, as Murray G. Murphey has written, "no epistemological warrant," and that "all belief systems have the function of giving order and stability to experience." Murphey, "The Place of Beliefs in Modern Culture," in John Higham and Paul K. Conkin, eds., *New Directions in American Intellectual History* (Baltimore: The Johns Hopkins University Press, 1979), pp. 152–53.

14. For a thoughtful analysis of the desire to find such a consensus, see Sacvan Bercovitch, "The Ritual of Consensus," in *The Rites of Assent: Transformations in the Symbolic Construction of America* (New York: Routledge, 1993), pp. 29–67.

15. Burton J. Bledstein, *The Culture of Professionalism: The Middle Class and the Development of Higher Education in America* (New York: W. W. Norton, 1976), p. 322.

16. While this book focuses on those who wished to maintain the established order, one important cultural strain in this period involves the attraction, even among those in enviable positions in the culture, of disorder and heroic violence, usually out of a profound sense of discontent with the moral and spiritual torpor of the dominant culture and a growing sense of the restrictions of organized modern life. Hence the eagerness with which some northern intellectuals greeted the Civil War, and the cultivation of heroic violence and the martial spirit by a cultural elite, in the decades that followed. On these developments, see George Fredrickson, *The Inner Civil War: Northern Intellectuals and the Crisis of the Union* (New York: Harper & Row, 1965); and T. J. Jackson Lears, *No Place of Grace: Antimodernism and the Transformation of American Culture, 1880–1920* (New York: Pantheon Books, 1981).

In her discussion of the centrality of the Civil War to postwar cultural patterns, Anne C. Rose argues that middle-class Americans of the late nineteenth century were romantics in "their search for intense experience" and, more strictly, in the way they "approached society with questions raised by problems with faith." She sees them as being engaged in a search for transcendence in "an expansive, horizontal world that invited the expression of human potential," so that "they grasped the promise of the Civil War as a field, a cultural as well as physical space, for recasting ideals." Rose adds: "To the extent that the Victorians' relentless search for meaning in secular activities finally achieved resolution, it was the Civil War, conceived as a struggle over profound issues, that convinced them that human effort even without clear supernatural references still had value." *Victorian America and the Civil War* (New York: Cambridge University Press, 1992), pp. 4–5. See also Chapter 6, "Victorian America and the Civil War," pp. 235–55.

17. Writing of parades, for example, Susan G. Davis describes them as "public dramas of social relations," in which "performers define who can be a social actor and what subjects and ideas are available for communication and consideration." She maintains that such "public dramas" were one of the most powerful expressive means available to working people, though by no means to this portion of the population alone. She points out that strike parades—a combination of parade and demonstration—in antebellum Philadelphia "served to recruit members, gather moral force, propagate a point of view, and threaten retribution to opponents and betrayers." Davis adds, however, that "[n]ot until the labor movement gathered mass strength after the Civil War would strikers and unionists be able to begin to define more fully how they would represent class conflict in public." *Parades and Power: Street Theatre in Nineteenth-Century Philadelphia* (Philadelphia: Temple University Press, 1986), pp. 6, 115, 152. See also Sean Wilentz, *Chants Democratic: New York City and the Rise of the American Working Class, 1788–1850* (New York: Oxford University Press, 1984), and Mary P. Ryan, *Women in Public: Between Banners and Ballots, 1825–1880* (Baltimore: The Johns Hopkins University Press, 1990).

18. Bledstein, *The Culture of Professionalism*, p. 72. On the growth of the American book industry in this period, see John Tebbel, *A History of Book Publishing in the United States*, vol. 2: *The Expansion of an Industry, 1865–1919* (New York: R. R. Bowker, 1975).

19. Gunther Barth, *City People: The Rise of Modern City Culture in Nineteenth-Century America* (New York: Oxford University Press, 1980), pp. 58–59. On the nature and importance of the urban daily, see Chapter 3, "Metropolitan Press," pp. 48–109. John F. Kasson, *Rudeness and Civility: Manners in Nineteenth-Century Urban America* (New York: Hill and Wang, 1990), pp. 70–71.

20. Trachtenberg, *The Incorporation of America*, p. 8; Hayden White, "Introduction: Tropology, Discourse, and the Modes of Human Consciousness," in *Tropics of Discourse: Essays in Cultural Criticism* (Baltimore: The Johns Hopkins University Press, 1978), pp. 3, 5; Carl S. Smith, "Urban Disorder and the Shape of Belief: The San Francisco Earthquake and Fire," *Yale Review* 74 (November 1984), 79–80.

21. John E. Toews, "Intellectual History after the Linguistic Turn: The Au-

tonomy of Meaning and the Irreducibility of Experience," *American Historical Review* 92 (1987), 883. Toews is here discussing the work of Roger Chartier and Dominick LaCapra in the course of this long review article on the "linguistic turn" toward the study of meaning in intellectual history over the last decade, which itself has become a subject of continuing discussion.

22. Mary Douglas observes: "Granted that disorder spoils pattern; it also provides the materials of pattern. Order implies restriction; from all possible materials, a limited selection has been made and from all possible relations a limited set has been used. So disorder by implication is unlimited, no pattern has been realised in it, but its potential for patterning is indefinite. This is why, though we seek to create order, we do not simply condemn disorder. We recognise that it is destructive to existing patterns; also that it has potentiality. It symbolises both danger and power." *Purity and Danger*, p. 94.

23. Citing Clifford Geertz and Edward Shils, Lynn Hunt speaks similarly of the cultural frames, master fictions, and cosmic cultural presuppositions that hold reality together for individuals. *Politics, Culture, and Class in the French Revolution* (Berkeley: University of California Press, 1984), p. 87. The three main subjects treated in this book became what Geertz calls, in the essay Hunt notes, "concentrated loci of serious acts," since "they consist in the point or points in a society where its leading ideas come together with its leading institutions to create an arena in which the events that most vitally affect its members' lives take place." "Centers, Kings, and Charisma: Reflections on the Symbolics of Power," in Joseph Ben-David and Terry Nichols Clark, eds., *Culture and Its Creators: Essays in Honor of Edward Shils* (Chicago: University of Chicago Press, 1977), p. 151. See also Murphey, "The Place of Beliefs in Modern Culture," pp. 153-54.

24. Notable exceptions include the Haymarket anarchists and a few union leaders such as Eugene Victor Debs and Samuel Gompers, though in their backgrounds, their careers as organizers and publicists and small businessmen, their language, and their personal habits, these individuals could be classified as being as middle-class as many they opposed. These men (with some qualified exceptions) were not workers in the sense that they performed manual labor for wages. One should quickly note, though, how difficult it is to speak simply of "workers" as a single group in this time when labor's search for union and identity was complicated by many different kinds of workers often viewing each other warily in class terms, and when union leaders and organizers were frequently at odds with their supposed constituents. Nonetheless, as Stuart M. Blumin observes, recent labor scholarship indicates that most American manual workers "inhabited a social, moral, and ideological world that was different from and even antagonistic to that of the professionals and businessmen who came to be called the middle class. These workers were, and knew they were, of another social order." *The Emergence of the Middle Class: Social Experience in the American City, 1760-1900* (New York: Cambridge University Press, 1989), p. 3. On Gompers and class consciousness, see p. 251.

25. Frederic Cople Jaher, *The Urban Establishment: Upper Strata in Boston, New York, Charleston, Chicago, and Los Angeles* (Urbana: University of Illinois Press, 1982), p. 456; Rima Lunin Schultz, "The Businessman's Role in Western

Settlement: The Entrepreneurial Frontier, Chicago, 1833–1872," (Ph.D diss., Boston University, 1985), Chapter 10: "The New Business Elite," pp. 243–68. Jaher presents a detailed profile of this generation of Chicago's elite in pp. 472–539. For a discussion of the remarkable similarity of background of many leading members of this group, see James Gilbert, *Perfect Cities: Chicago's Utopias of 1893* (Chicago: University of Chicago Press, 1991), pp. 37–39.

26. Bledstein, *The Culture of Professionalism*, pp. 31, 54; Daniel Walker Howe, "Victorian Culture in America," in Howe, ed., *Victorian America* (Philadelphia: University of Pennsylvania Press, 1976), p. 18. On the individual internalization of the values of order, see also Bledstein, pp. 214–15. For excellent discussions of the development of codified rules of manners and other forms of social ritual in relation to the emerging cultural order of nineteenth-century middle-class America, see Karen Halttunen, *Confidence Men and Painted Women: A Study of Middle-class Culture in America, 1830–1870* (New Haven: Yale University Press, 1983), and Kasson, *Rudeness and Civility*.

27. Richard L. Bushman argues that while the divide between the middle class and the upper classes had perhaps become less marked than before, the difference between the middle class and the lower orders (which mainly consisted of the social categories of workers and recent immigrants) was more visible and inflexible. *The Refinement of America: Persons, Houses, Cities* (New York: Alfred A. Knopf, 1992), p. xv. Bushman's book ends at mid-century, but the trends he traces continued. Blumin also sees the decades before the Civil War as critical to class formation, asserting that, in his judgment, "a middle class was not fully formed before the war, and that developments of the postwar period—most notably, widening differences between the worlds of nonmanual and manual work, the expansion of middle-class suburbanization, and the resumption and expansion of social and economic conflict that was phrased in class terms—contributed to the further articulation of the American middle class." *The Emergence of the Middle Class*, p. 13. See also Chapter 8, "White-Collar Worlds—The Postbellum Middle Class," pp. 258–97.

28. In regard to the development of a distinctive class consciousness among workers in the late nineteenth century, David Montgomery writes, "Although the personal bondings of families, migrant groups, young wage-earning women, craftsmen, strikers, voters, and rioters defined people's loyalties in different and often conflicting ways, all attachments were rooted in the shared presumption that individualism was appropriate only for the prosperous and wellborn." *The Fall of the House of Labor: The Workplace, the State, and American Labor Activism, 1865–1925* (New York: Cambridge University Press, 1987), p. 2. The lengthy and complex history that Montgomery provides follows the mainly unsuccessful battle of workers in this period to control the terms of work, policy agendas, and public opinion. One of the significant achievements of large entrepreneurs was to convince many middle-class Americans that the organization of workers against employers was opposed to everything for which the country stood.

29. One can argue that a disaster like the Chicago fire was not natural but man-made since, by building the city the way they did and then failing to take adequate precautions, Chicagoans "invited" disaster. In addition, different so-

cieties may react to the same kind of event in different ways, and even within a particular society where and when such an event occurs are crucial to how it is perceived and processed. But, generally speaking, disorders linked to fires or metereological or geological conditions are generally classified as natural, and, while they are often followed by some doubt and blame, usually also become a positive rallying point, at least for a brief time, for the societies in which they take place. Disorders that derive from internal conflict are more apt to be followed by continued division and recrimination. Depending on the circumstances, technological disasters may lead in either direction. Indeed, it is rare to find any kind of disorder whose imaginative, social, and political dimensions are not mixed. The general issue of natural versus man-made is related in complex ways, as my discussion in the body of this book reveals, to the question of whether disorder was something that happened to, or was in the nature of, cities.

30. Throughout I have included in the notes some biographical information on many of the individuals I mention (especially Chicagoans) who are probably no longer recognizable to most readers, on the assumption that knowing who they were will help in better understanding them, their remarks, and their times.

CHAPTER TWO

1. Chicago's first significant fire destroyed eighteen buildings in the fledgling town in October of 1839. Other large fires struck the city in 1868 and 1870. Fires have been a significant force in shaping the history of virtually every American urban center (and of cities throughout the world). Boston suffered major conflagrations in 1676, 1679, and 1711, and its downtown was almost completed destroyed in 1760. Most leading American cities had switched from volunteer fire brigades to professional departments by the 1860s. David R. Goldfield and Blaine A. Brownell, *Urban America: From Downtown to No Town* (Boston: Houghton Mifflin, 1979), pp. 82–83, 176–77; Monkkonen, *America Becomes Urban*, Chapter 4, "The Emerging Service City: Fighting Fire and Crime," pp. 89–110; Hazen and Hazen, *Keepers of the Flame*, pp. 70–75. For a survey of fires in Chicago in the years just before the "great conflagration," see A. T. Andreas, *History of Chicago. From the Earliest Period to the Present Time,* vol. 2: *From 1857 Until the Fire of 1871* (Chicago: A. T. Andreas Company, 1885), pp. 99–102.

2. Andreas, *History of Chicago,* vol. 2, p. 708.

3. For a discussion of the Courthouse in the context of the Chicago's early ambitions, see Daniel Bluestone, *Constructing Chicago* (New Haven: Yale University Press, 1991), pp. 154–57.

4. This description of the fire relies most heavily on H. A. Musham, "The Great Chicago Fire, October 8–10, 1871," *Papers in Illinois History and Transactions for the Year 1940* (Springfield, Ill.: The Illinois State Historical Society, 1941), pp. 69–149 (see n. 6 below). For more recent popular accounts, see Robert Cromie, *The Great Chicago Fire* (New York: McGraw-Hill, 1958); and Herman Kogan and Robert Cromie, *The Great Fire: Chicago 1871* (New York: G. P. Putnam's Sons, 1971). The latter is heavily illustrated. The records of the

Fire Department's official inquiry into the fire, including the O'Learys' testimony, are in the Archives and Manuscripts collections of the Chicago Historical Society. The inquiry was conducted from late November into early December of 1871.

5. *Eleventh Annual Report of the Board of Public Works to the Common Council of the City of Chicago, for the Municipal, Fiscal Year Ending March 31, 1872* (Chicago: D. & C. H. Blakeley, 1872), pp. 3–7; *Report of the Chicago Relief and Aid Society of Disbursement of Contributions for the Sufferers by the Chicago Fire* (Cambridge, Mass.: The Riverside Press, 1874), pp. 10–11 (hereafter *Report of the Chicago Relief and Aid Society*); Andreas, *History of Chicago*, vol. 2, pp. 764, 767; Elias Colbert and Everett Chamberlin, *Chicago and the Great Conflagration* (Cincinnati: C. F. Vent, 1871), p. 390. Chicago in 1871 occupied about thirty-six square miles encompassing 534 miles of streets (eighty-eight paved, fifty-seven constructed of wooden blocks), 561 miles of sidewalks (virtually all wooden), and 6,555 gas lamps. Musham, "The Great Chicago Fire," p. 74.

6. Musham, "The Great Chicago Fire," p. 69. Musham, a military architect and research engineer, was the son of W. H. Musham, former city fire marshal. The elder Musham was born in Chicago in 1839 and in his years on the force fought, as the foreman of a company, not only the Great Chicago Fire but also, as a young volunteer, the terrible fire of 1857.

7. The largest collection of such fire narratives is in the Archives and Manuscripts Department of the Chicago Historical Society (hereafter CHS Fire Narratives), whose members and employees made several efforts in the years following the fire to encourage eyewitnesses to record their experiences. Some accounts, including several not deposited in this collection, were published in newspapers or privately printed, and many have been gathered into fire histories and printed collections, including Andreas's section on the fire in the second volume of his *History of Chicago;* Mabel McIlvaine, ed., *Reminiscences of Chicago During the Great Fire* (Chicago: The Lakeside Press, 1915); and Paul M. Angle, ed., *The Great Chicago Fire* (Chicago: The Chicago Historical Society, 1946). The text of McIlvaine's collection, whose contents were published earlier in Andreas and other sources, is reproduced in David Lowe, ed., *The Great Chicago Fire* (New York: Dover Publications, 1979), which also contains an excellent selection of illustrations and post-fire photographs.

8. See in particular the accounts of the London fire in *The Diary of Samuel Pepys*, ed. Robert Latham and William Matthews, vol. 7: 1666 (Berkeley: University of California Press, 1966), pp. 267–79; and *The Diary of John Evelyn*, ed. E. S. de Beer, vol. 3 (Oxford: The Clarendon Press, 1955), pp. 450–62. There are several parallels between the London and Chicago fires, which struck at analogous moments in each city's history. Both occurred in centers of rising commercial empire shortly after the resolution of civil war. The fire of London had a similar humble origin (in a bakery in Pudding Lane), burned nearly as many buildings, left as many homeless, and was followed by a comparable rapid program of rebuilding, though the vision behind London's reconstruction, unlike Chicago's, was dominated by one man, Christopher Wren. See Walter George Bell, *The Great Fire of London in 1666* (London: John Lane, 1920).

9. Andreas, *History of Chicago*, vol. 3: *From the Fire of 1871 Until 1885* (Chi-

cago: A. T. Andreas Company, 1886), p. 151; McGovern, *Daniel Trentworthy: A Tale of the Great Fire of Chicago* (Chicago: Rand, McNally, 1889), p. 191. McGovern, who was twenty-one at the time of the fire, had worked as typesetter, proofreader, and night editor at the *Tribune*. He later became the leading editorial writer of the *Chicago Herald* and then editor of the *Illustrated World's Fair*, a publication devoted to news of the Columbian Exposition. He also published poetry and other fiction.

10. This book was published in several different editions. Colbert came to Chicago in 1857 from England and worked on the *Chicago News* before joining the *Times* and, in 1863, the *Tribune*, where, at the time of the fire, he was commercial editor. He was a prolific writer on many topics concerning local trade and history, but his great passion was astronomy. He followed the early progress of the fire through a telescope he kept on the roof of the *Tribune* building. See Andreas, *History of Chicago*, vol. 2, p. 494; and Lloyd Wendt, *Chicago Tribune: The Rise of a Great American Newspaper* (Chicago: Rand McNally, 1979), p. 234. Colbert's writings also included a history of Chicago. Chamberlin's paper was the *Times*.

11. Roe (1838-88) was a former Civil War chaplain who in 1871 was serving the congregation of the Presbyterian Church of Highland Falls, New York. Excited by news reports of the fire, he hurried to inspect Chicago firsthand. This experience inspired him to write his novel, which was serialized in the *New York Evangelist*. His manuscript was rejected by two book publishers, however, before it hit the jackpot for the New York house of Dodd, Mead, which had only been founded in 1870. Roe went on to write other successful romances of a similar nature and retired from the ministry. See John Tebbel, *A History of Book Publishing in the United States*, vol. 2, pp. 228-29.

12. James D. Montague, *The Fire Bugs of Chicago* (New York: Frank Tousey, 1897), p. 13; Carl S. Smith, "Fearsome Fiction and the Windy City; or, Chicago in the Dime Novel," *Chicago History* 7 (Spring 1978), 2-11. With every claim of truthful and thrilling eyewitness accounts, authors and editors and publishers fought with each other for the attention—and money—of readers. This competition was reflected in the headlines, title pages, and advertising copy of different works, which told how they were to be read and in what context (today the phrase might be "market niche") their producers tried to place them. Pastor O. A. Burgess of the Second Christian Church of Chicago described his reflections on the disaster as a "homily," titled *The Late Chicago Fire* (Indianapolis: W. H. Drapier, 1871), while several others promised more secular "lessons of the fire" along with "graphic accounts" and "comprehensive histories of the great disasters of all time." In their endpapers or back covers, many of the books indicated the extent to which such works were also vying with other forms of popular literature that spoke to current concerns. Ornum and Company's pulp history of the disaster hawked the company's whole line of "fifteen-cent romances," including *The Mysteries of the Night; or, the Freaks and Fortunes of a News Boy*, as well as its "ten cent song and joke books" with such titles as the *Fenian Martyrs Cushla Gal Machre Songster*. The fire story also had to contend for prime space within the boundaries of some publications. The same newspapers that reported the Chicago fire discussed the undoing of the

Tweed Ring in New York and the terrible rural fire of the same date in Peshtigo, Wisconsin.

13. Musham, "The Great Chicago Fire," p. 69. One of the contemporary accounts similarly observed: "The detailed history of the Chicago fire will never be written, because there is an almost inconceivable mass of details that can never be gathered—many that can never be known, because their principal actors fell before the advance of the enemy they were striving to repulse—and even if all could be readily obtained, their voluminousness would prevent publication in any but a book of the most extraordinary size." Frank Luzerne, *The Lost City! Drama of the Fire-Fiend!—or—Chicago, As It Was, and As It Is! and Its Glorious Future!* (New York: Wells, 1872), p. 66. This book had an alternate main title, which was *Through the Flames and Beyond*.

14. Mayer and Wade, *Chicago: Growth of a Metropolis* (Chicago: University of Chicago Press, 1969), p. 107. The original Waud sketches are in the Prints and Photographs collections of the Chicago Historical Society. McGovern, *Daniel Trentworthy*, p. 223.

15. *Report of the Chicago Relief and Aid Society*, pp. 8–9, 15.

16. Luzerne, *The Lost City!*, p. 65.

17. Subcategories include the brief and straightforward observation: "It was simply indescribable in its terrible grandeur" (Horace White, in McIlvaine, *Reminiscences of Chicago During the Great Fire*, p. 63).

The reflection on literary limits: "The sensations conveyed to the spectator of this unparalleled event, either through the eye, the ear, or other senses or sympathies, can not be adequately described, and any attempt to do it but shows the poverty of language" (Colbert and Chamberlin, *Chicago and the Great Conflagration*, p. 211).

The claim of sensory overload: "All intelligent persons that witnessed the burning of Chicago are prepared to testify that nothing is more indescribable than a great conflagration. Nothing is more bewildering, exciting, electrifying, astounding and weirdly stupendous. It is a spectacle that forces into activity all the emotions of the heart, but benumbs judgement and disconcerts action" (Luzerne, *The Lost City!*, p. 65).

The prayer for genius: "What can be said to adequately, or even to approximately, describe the grand catastrophe in any one of its innumerable characteristics? Where is the mind that can measure the pecuniary loss, the millions consumed, and the other millions just blossoming, and whose fruition was only a question of time? Who is there that can measure the beauty of form, the strength of construction, the exquisiteness of detail that have been annihilated in the architectural cataclism [*sic*] of fire that has rolled over our beautiful city? Where is there the artist-writer whose soul can be taken in, and whose hand can even outline, the awful horror, the immeasurable sublimity of the hurricane of destruction that tore through our city for a night and a day? Who is there, alas, who can go below these material facts and comprehend and estimate the mass of hopes, of happiness, of household ties, of family loves that were shriveled and consumed by this fire like bits of tissue paper flung into a thrice-heated furnace?" (*Chicago Times* [18 October 1871]).

18. *Report of the Chicago Relief and Aid Society*, p. 8; *The Greatest Calamity of*

Modern Times. An Account of the Burning of Chicago. Compiled by Special Eye-Witnesses, Being An Interesting and Graphic Narrative of That Appalling Catastrophe (Toronto: Richardson & Punchard, 1871), p. 45.

19. Ross Miller writes of the authors of the instant histories in particular that they articulated "a seemingly objective account that gave people a way to view a common experience. Instant history is now a common phenomenon; a population comes to learn how it feels by reading about itself." *American Apocalypse*, pp. 25–26. Residents and visitors through the rest of the nineteenth century would increasingly describe phenomenally busy and rapidly changing Chicago in terms of its indescribability. See Carl S. Smith, *Chicago and the American Literary Imagination, 1880–1920* (Chicago: University of Chicago Press, 1984), pp. 1–3.

20. Richard D. Brown, *Knowledge Is Power: The Diffusion of Information in Early America, 1700–1865* (New York: Oxford University Press, 1989), especially Chapter 10, "The Dynamics of Contagious Diffusion: The Battles of Lexington and Concord, George Washington's Death, and the Assassination of President Lincoln, 1775–1865," pp. 245–67. Chicago's first telegraph connection to another city—Milwaukee—was established by early 1848, with the link to the East opened by April of the same year. Chicago was hooked up to San Francisco in October of 1861 and became the center for the transmission of information back and forth across a national telegraph network spun out of over 50,000 miles of wire. Five years later the transatlantic cable made Europe directly accessible. See Bessie Louise Pierce, *A History of Chicago*, vol. 2; *From Town to City, 1848–1871* (New York: Alfred A. Knopf, 1940), pp. 173–74. On the developing national network of cities and of news and information dissemination in the years before the fire, see Allan Pred, *Urban Growth and City-System in the United States, 1840–1860* (Cambridge, Mass.: Harvard University Press, 1980); Richard A. Schwarzlose, *The Nation's Newsbrokers*, 2 vols. (Evanston: Northwestern University Press, 1989–90); Cronon, *Nature's Metropolis*, p. 121; Daniel J. Czitrom, *Media and the American Mind: From Morse to McLuhan* (Chapel Hill: University of North Carolina Press, 1982), Chapter 1, " 'Lightning Lines' and the Birth of Modern Communication, 1838–1900," pp. 3–29; Cecilia Tichi, *Shifting Gears: Technology, Literature, Culture in Modernist America* (Chapel Hill: University of North Carolina Press, 1987), p. 45; and Brown. Schwarzlose (vol. 2, pp. 70–71) discusses the efforts of the Western Associated Press's William Henry Smith, aided by Western Union's Anson Stager, to send continuous, accurate reports on the fire to the rest of the country. On the news of the Chicago fire in relation to the creation of national unity, see Pauly, "The Great Chicago Fire as a National Event." Reports of Civil War battles (including Lee's surrender) and the assassination of Lincoln were also quickly disseminated, although these reports, which predated the postwar expansion of transportation and communications systems, including the completion of the transcontinental railroad and the transatlantic cable, did not spread as widely and as rapidly as the news of the fire.

21. A recent example of a far-flung audience knowing more than those nearby about a disaster is the 1989 San Francisco earthquake, which interrupted the local supply of electricity (and the World Series), so that people in

the Bay Area could not see the television reports that were broadcast virtually everywhere else to many who had originally tuned in to see a baseball game.

22. Memoir of Sara Maria Seymour Blair, CHS Fire Narratives. This was prepared in 1921.

23. The mass-produced books on the fire were themselves made physically possible and financially practical by such technological advances as high-speed presses, the introduction of groundwood pulp paper, and the continuing development of a rail-distribution system serving a readership concentrated in Chicago and other rapidly growing cities. The more inexpensive fire histories appeared near the outset of what John Tebbel has described as "the enormous flood of cheap books, both in paperback and hardcovers, which washed over America in a tidal wave beginning in the 1870s." Tebbel, *A History of Book Publishing in the United States*, pp. 481-83. The all-encompassing titles of the fire histories, such as George L. Barclay's eighty-page softcover volume, *The Great Fire of Chicago! Being a Concise Account of the Origin, Progress, and Conclusion of this Terrible Fire, The Greatest the Civilized World Has Ever Known, Burning a District of 60 Miles of Buildings, or 100 Miles If Placed Side by Side. Thrilling Accounts! Wonderful Escapes!! Interesting Anecdotes!*, published in Philadelphia in 1871, evoked the stacked tiers of attention-arresting headlines atop the frenzied accounts of the fire in the dailies. Not just the titles but much of the contents of the fire histories were very similar to the stories in the newspapers. Indeed, they were sometimes identical, since the authors of these books freely borrowed wholesale from newspapers and each other, with and without acknowledgment.

Among the most interesting "homemade" varieties of fire literature were the scrapbooks that many individuals compiled. In one now in the library of the Chicago Historical Society, newspaper and magazine articles are carefully pasted into a catalogue the pages of which are completely covered with clippings cut in such a way that in many instances there is no indication of where they were taken from. The stories carry the reader haphazardly through an unpredictable succession of grand descriptions and small anecdotes, creating the feeling of reading yet another published fire history hastily compiled from whatever sources were at hand.

24. On the rich and complex relationship of late nineteenth-century Chicago to the cities of the East and the hinterland to the West, see Cronon, *Nature's Metropolis*. On the flow of news in and out of Chicago in relation to the emergence of a "new market geography," see in particular pp. 121-22, 332-33.

25. *Nation* 13 (12 October 1871), 233. Pauly notes how people milled around telegraph offices, eager for more news: "As a widely reported event, the fire demonstrated that news could create for Americans a commonly available simulation of national life. Nationally disseminated telegraphic news reports could bind all Americans instantaneously to a common experience." "The Great Chicago Fire as a National Event," p. 682. On the importance of the forms of mass communication, particularly newspapers, to the development of a shared national consciousness, see Benedict Anderson, *Imagined Communities: Reflections on the Origin and Spread of Nationalism* (London: Verso, 1983), especially pp. 37-40.

26. Some of the more colorful styles include the formally poetic: "The Genius of speculation had o'erspread the whole land with his wings . . ." (Colbert and Chamberlin, *Chicago and the Great Conflagration*, p. 94).

The biblical: "There was a general hope and prayer for rain, but it came not. The sky was of brass, and the south wind was heated. . . ." (Alfred L. Sewell, *The Great Calamity! Scenes, Incidents, and Lessons of the Great Chicago Fire of the 8th and 9th of October, 1871* [Alfred L. Sewell, 1871], p. 2).

The eclectically mythological: "Here [in the crush of people of all classes to escape the burning South Division through one of the Chicago River tunnels] the Graces and Gorgons met, Euphrosyne, Aglaia and Thalia, hand in hand with Stheno, Euryale and Medusa, seeking the poor boon of life at the utter sacrifice of all those weak conventialisms, that only a few short hours ago were thought to be the sole object and aim of existence. Here Pudicitia mingled her tears with the Lady Godivas and Cyprian nymphs; and here Mercurius joined Oedipus in supplicating the triple throne of Clotho, Lachesis and Atropos." (Luzerne, *The Lost City!*, p. 78).

And the explicitly apocalyptic: "The brute creation was crazed. The horses, maddened by heat and noise, and irritated by falling sparks, neighed and screamed with affright and anger, and reared and kicked, and bit each other, or stood with drooping tails, and rigid legs, ears laid back and eyes wild with amazement, shivering as if with cold. The dogs ran wildly hither and thither, snuffing eagerly at every one, and occasionally sitting down on their haunches to howl dismally. When there was a lull in the fire, far-away dogs could be heard barking, and cocks crowing at the unwonted light. Cats ran along ridge-poles in the bright glare, and came pattering into the street with dropsical tails. Great brown rats with bead-like eyes were ferreted out from under the sidewalks by the flames, and scurried hither and thither along the streets, kicked at, trampled upon, hunted down. Flocks of beautiful pigeons, so plentiful in the city, wheeled into the air aimlessly, circled blindly once or twice, and were drawn into the maw of the fiery hell raging beneath" (*Chicago Evening Post* [18 October 1871], p. 2). The *Evening Post* excerpt comes from a particularly memorable full-page account that originally appeared the day before and was reprinted because of what the paper called the "universal demand for extra copies." Andreas quoted from it extensively in his fire history.

27. Luzerne, *The Lost City!*, p. 89.

28. *The Ruined City; or, The Horrors of Chicago* (New York: Ornum, 1871), p. 9.

29. *Chicago Times* (18 October 1871), pp. 1–2; Andreas, *History of Chicago*, vol. 2, p. 724; Colbert and Chamberlin, *Chicago and the Great Conflagration*, p. 195. Most conflicted were the voices in the 1874 report of the Relief and Aid Society. The bulk of the report consisted of page after page outlining the Society's methods of operation, accompanied by lengthy tables of fine print that presented a week-by-week statistical audit of everything that could be enumerated, from the total of families fed to the number of pecks of turnips and pairs of men's socks distributed. But when the report described the fire itself and the tasks facing the Society in the aftermath of the disaster, it abandoned the dry language of bureaucratic accounting for an elevated style the Society's mem-

bers apparently felt was more appropriate to their lofty mission: "Bread was to be furnished to the hungry, and raiment to the insufficiently clad; hope needed a resurrection in the hearts of the despondent, the bereaved needed the ministries of consolation, the sick required the nurse and the physician, the homeless were to be sheltered, the dying were to be proffered the offices of religion, and the dead granted the last ceremonial and service that man renders to his fellow." Elsewhere, the report counted the funds sent to Chicago down to the last penny, then spoke of how the relief "touched" the "heart of mankind . . . with a sense of brotherhood, so lyric that poets will sing of it; so unique that historians will record it; and so divine that philosophy will treasure it as the first memorable proof, that the race, of all lands and creeds, has advanced beyond the forms of civic and religious limitation, and henceforth, in its march toward a final and perfect civilization will unite its sentiments and endeavors wherever man is to be pitied, or his sufferings assuaged." *Report of the Chicago Relief and Aid Society,* pp. 115, 24.

    30. In discussing contemporary speculation over the fire's cause and significance, John J. Pauly, citing the work of Charles Rosenberg in *The Cholera Years,* notes that "[w]ars, fires, floods, and epidemics in the United States had for some time lent themselves to debates between providential and scientific styles of interpretation," but he observes that "it would be misleading to reduce the debate over the fire's cause to one more example of a long-standing conflict between rational analysts and fanatic mythologizers." He correctly points out that most Americans adopted elements of both arguments, and that their real interest was less in the conflict between religion and science than "the tendencies of American society in a turbulent time," especially since "Chicago itself had become a well-known symbol of American progress and expansion." Pauly, "The Great Chicago Fire as National Event," p. 671. On the mixture of romance and realism in urban writing, see Donald Fanger, *Dostoyevsky and Romantic Realism: A Study of Dostoyevsky in Relation to Balzac, Dickens, and Gogol* (Cambridge: Harvard University Press, 1965).

    31. *Harper's Weekly* 15 (28 October 1871), 1002; James W. Sheahan and George T. Upton, *The Great Conflagration* (Chicago: Union Publishing Company, 1871), p. 75. Sheahan was an editor at the *Tribune.* Upton also worked on that paper's editorial staff, and he wrote several works on music and composers. The full title of their book, which is one of the most substantial instant histories, is *The Great Conflagration. Chicago: Its Past, Present and Future. Embracing a Detailed Narrative of the Great Conflagration in the North, South, and West Divisions: Origin, Progress and Results of the Fire. Prominent Buildings Burned, Character of Buildings, Losses and Insurance, Graphic Description of the Flames, Scenes and Incidents, Loss of Life, the Flight of the People. Also, a Condensed History of Chicago, Its Population, Growth and Great Public Works. And a Statement of All the Great Fires of the World.*

    Colbert and Chamberlin extended the fire-as-battle conceit for several pages. In their book we see the left column of the fire "attack" all buildings to the west of LaSalle Street, accomplishing its "mission" well, while the right column resourcefully discovers "a large area of wooden buildings on which to ration and arm itself for its march of destruction." Soon after we learn that the fire "swept down upon" the Bigelow House and "assaulted the noble *Tribune* build-ing," proving itself an "enemy" that was "wily as well as strong" as it "threw a red-hot brick wall upon the building's weaker side" before it finally "conquered and destroyed" the structure later in the evening. Then it "marched on and laid waste Book-sellers' Row," "fell upon" Field, Leiter & Company's magnificent department store of Massachusetts marble, and "deployed to the right," de-stroying churches and homes on Wabash and Michigan Avenues. Before long it "effected a foothold" in the North Division and seemed to go right for the wa-terworks, "as if the terrible marauder had, with deadly strategy, thrown out a swifter brand than all others to cut off the only reliance of his victims, the water-supply." Yet insatiable, it "organized an advance" against the grain elevators near the river and began "scores of separate irruptions . . . in unexpected places." Colbert and Chamberlin, *Chicago and the Great Conflagration,* pp. 208–11.

32. White, in McIlvaine, *Reminiscences of Chicago During the Great Fire,* p. 60. The *Chicago Evening Post* likewise commented: "To describe this fire in its details through the North Division would be utterly impossible. It was like a battle, where all was din, smoke, confusion and turmoil." The Reverend Henry Ward Beecher admitted in his "Lecture Room Talk" of October 13, "I am ut-terly unable to take in the calamity of Chicago. As it is in the case of mountains when first seen, I cannot adjust my sight to take it in. It was so during the war." *Chicago Evening Post* (18 October 1871), p. 2; Beecher, quoted in Colbert and Chamberlin, *Chicago and the Great Conflagration,* p. 523. White's remarks are from a letter to Murat Halstead, editor of the *Cincinnati Commercial,* which was published in Halstead's paper. After winning a struggle for editorial control with Joseph Medill, who owned a large interest in the *Tribune,* White had estab-lished a politically independent (and antitariff) outlook at the staunchly Re-publican paper. Along with Halstead and Whitelaw Reid, he was a leader in the Liberal Republican movement and instrumental in Horace Greeley's presiden-tial campaign of 1872. Late in 1874 White retired and Medill assumed a con-trolling interest in the *Tribune.* Wendt, *Chicago Tribune,* esp. Chapter 11, pp. 229–51.

33. See, for example, stanzas 235 to 244 of Dryden's *Annus Mirabilis,* whose subject is the London fire and England's foreign wars. Stanza 235 reads:

> To every nobler portion of the Town,
> The curling billows roul their restless Tyde:
> In parties now they straggle up and down,
> As Armies, unoppos'd, for prey divide.

The Works of John Dryden, vol. 1, *Poems 1649–1680,* ed. Edward Niles Hooker and H. T. Swedenberg, Jr. (Berkeley: University of California Press, 1956), p. 95.

34. On the outpouring of books about the war in the Gilded Age, see Thomas C. Leonard, *Above the Battle: War-Making in America from Appomattox to Versailles* (New York: Oxford University Press, 1978), Chapter 1, "The En-during and Forgotten War," pp. 7–39.

35. Quoted in Sheahan and Upton, *The Great Conflagration,* p. 295. How-

ever much citizens in other cities may have taken some satisfaction in the misfortune of such a formidable commercial rival as Chicago, there were relatively
few expressions of this sentiment. Miller and Pauly discuss the association of
the fire, the relief, and the rebuilding with the war and the mythology of democratic unity.

CHAPTER THREE

1. Fredrickson, *The Inner Civil War;* Rose, *Victorian America and the Civil
War;* and James H. Moorhead, *American Apocalypse: Yankee Protestants and the
Civil War, 1860–1869* (New Haven: Yale University Press, 1978).

2. H. R. Hobart, "The Flight for Life," in *The Lakeside Memorial of the
Burning of Chicago, A.D. 1871,* p. 40. See n. 8.

3. Pierce, *A History of Chicago,* vol. 2, pp. 432–35.

4. Moody quoted in Colbert and Chamberlin, *Chicago and the Great Conflagration,* p. 522. Moody's comments may also have reflected Cincinnati's dis-
pleasure at being surpassed by Chicago as a commercial competitor. Letters of
William H. Carter (15 October 1871) and Francis William Test (13 October
1871), CHS Fire Narratives.

5. [Edgar John Goodspeed], *The Great Fires in Chicago and the West . . . by a
Chicago Clergyman* (Chicago: T. W. Goodspeed, 1871), p. 55; *Report of the Chicago Relief and Aid Society,* pp. 15, 21. The proclamations of Mayor Mason have
been reprinted in many different accounts of the fire. The setting aside of a special day of repentance was another aspect of the history of the fire with many
precedents. On the fast day declared following "the late dreadfull Conflagration" in London in 1666, for example, see *The Diary of John Evelyn,* p. 464.
Goodspeed, minister of the Second Baptist Church, made fire literature a personal industry. He brought out in quick succession a series of revised and expanded instant histories, beginning with a seventy-eight-page pamphlet titled
Earth's Holocaust, soon followed by *The Great Fires in Chicago and the West,*
which ran an additional forty pages. With his *History of the Great Fires in Chicago
and the West,* which, like the other two, was published before the end of 1871, he
was up to 667 pages, and its full title alone was a paragraph long. John J. Flinn,
in his history of the Chicago police, published sixteen years after the fire, agreed
with those who saw a moral dimension to the disaster. "Water or fire, a deluge
or a conflagration, was necessary," he conceded, "in order that the careless,
reckless, godless inhabitants of the young Western metropolis should be
brought to their senses." Flinn, *History of the Chicago Police from the Settlement of
the Community to the Present Time Under Authority of the Mayor and Superintendent of the Force* (Chicago: The Police Book Fund, 1887), p. 123. Flinn came to
America in the mid-1860s at the age of fourteen from his native Ireland. Arriving in Chicago in 1875, he worked for several newspapers before going into
business for himself as the author of several books, including a series of guides
to Chicago, a compilation of biographies of leading citizens, and a few volumes
devoted to the World's Columbian Exposition.

6. *Chicago Weekly Post* (26 October 1871), p. 1; Townsend cited in Sheahan
and Upton, *The Great Conflagration,* pp. 361–63.

7. Sewell went on, "Whether Chicago has been punished and humbled on

account of her pride, or brought low because of her presumptuousness; or whether the divine purpose of her destruction was to teach man that 'riches have wings and will fly away,' and that it is far better and wiser for him to lay up for himself 'treasures in heaven,' instead of storing them here where moth may eat, and rust corrupt, or fire destroy them, is too deep a question for us to solve." He added that Chicago was in any case no prouder or more presumptuous or iniquitous than any other cities. Sewell, *The Great Calamity*, p. 77. On Sewell as the author of the first fire history, see Andreas, *History of Chicago*, vol. 2, p. 759; and Joseph Kirkland, *The Story of Chicago* (Chicago: Dibble Publishing Company, 1892), vol. 1, p. 306.

8. N. S. Emerson, "The Stricken City," in Luzerne, *The Lost City!*, pp. 117–18; Andrew Shuman, "One Year After," in *Lakeside Monthly* 8 (October 1872), 246–47. This was the first essay in a fire anniversary issue of the *Lakeside Monthly*, which was the leading literary magazine published in Chicago and the Northwest. It had previously devoted its January 1872 issue to articles on the fire by well-known local authors. This issue was also published in book form, handsomely bound in red leather with gold engraving and titled *The Lakeside Memorial of the Burning of Chicago, A.D. 1871* (Chicago: The University Publishing Company, 1872).

9. This narrative squared with a general middle-class outlook toward apparently undeserved personal misfortune. "Mid-Victorians believed that worldly reversals were tests of will, commitment, and endurance. A fall now and then would eventually prove to have been 'fortunate,' when one looked back from the heights after the long race upward." Bledstein, *The Culture of Professionalism*, p. 113. See also p. 147 on the relationship of character, faith, and meaning.

10. William S. Walker, cited in Andreas, *History of Chicago*, vol. 2, p. 727. Walker's account appeared earlier in *The Lakeside Memorial of the Burning of Chicago*.

11. Mary Ann Hubbard, *Family Memories* (privately printed, 1912), p. 127. Mrs. Hubbard (1820–1909) had come to Chicago from Massachusetts in 1836, traveling almost two weeks by steamer, riverboat, railroad, canalboat, sidewheeler, and stage. Her husband, Gurdon S. Hubbard, had arrived in 1818, when he was sixteen, as a fur buyer for John Jacob Astor. He subsequently invested in real estate in Chicago and became involved in a variety of businesses, including the city's earliest ventures in meatpacking. The Hubbards had lived since 1857 in a North Division "country" home on whose grounds were a conservatory and a large garden. The Cleveland narrative is in the Fire Narratives Collection of the Chicago Historical Society, and also appears in Andreas, McIlvaine, and Lowe. Cleveland was a major figure in the development of the city's park system in the late nineteenth century. Olmsted, "Chicago in Distress," *Nation* 13 (9 November 1871), 303.

There are many more comments of this kind. Aurelia King, wife of wholesale clothing merchant Henry King (who was president of the Relief and Aid Society in the early 1870s), wrote on October 21, "We are all cheerful and hopeful. I have seen only one complainer, and that was a millionaire," while James W. Milner, in a letter composed a week earlier, was long and eloquent on

the city's calmness and resolution. He observed, in part, "The general sentiment and feeling of the people, is an honor to humanity. The business men are
cool and cheerful. A quiet determination to accept the situation, and steadily
weather it through to better times, is the prevailing feeling. There is no whining,
no 'Black Friday' hair tearing, and insanity, but a grand manliness of feeling."
CHS Fire Narratives. Elsewhere in her generally upbeat letter of October 21,
King confessed, "[B]ut I can't help mourning over my household goods, the
dear things that can never be replaced, my books, the gifts of dear friends, the
treasured locks of hair, my Mother's Bible, relics of my little daughter Fanny,
my wedding dress, and a thousand things I had saved for my children." William
Alvin Bartlett later proudly observed in an essay titled "What Remains," "That
night, when the social and the civil framework were [sic] shattered, bloody riot
and chaotic lawbreaking did not seize our masses. Calmness, earnest resignation and heroism stood out to dignify destruction." Bartlett, "What Remains,"
Lakeside Memorial of the Burning of Chicago, p. 83.

    12. As Michael Barkun points out, this heightened sense of community
transcends local cultural conditions and is linked to a universal millennial impulse. "One of the curious ambiguities of disaster," Barkun writes, "is that,
while it is by definition a form of intense deprivation, it produces feelings of
well-being that sometimes verge on euphoria. This is often referred to as *disaster
utopia.*" *Disaster and the Millennium* (New Haven: Yale University Press, 1974),
p. 163.

    13. Letter of Emma Hambleton (10 October 1871), CHS Fire Narratives;
Goodspeed, *The Great Fires in Chicago and the West*, p. 21; Colbert and
Chamberlin, *Chicago and the Great Conflagration*, pp. 364, 450-51. One of the
anonymous pulp histories, "prepared and written by a journalist," concluded
by maintaining that the people of Chicago "will emerge from the ordeal purified, and with manly zeal, endeavor to accomplish the labor before them; the
sons of these men, too, will work; they will forget the club and gambling rooms,
and haunt the busy marts of commerce and the counting-house; the pampered,
petted—yet tender and loving—daughter of the stricken, will forsake the fashionable milliner and the fascinating watering place—one and all remembering
that, notwithstanding worldly prosperity and goodly possessions, the words of
the poet will stand true to the end:—

> 'Tis only noble to be good;
> Kind hearts are more than coronets,
> And simple faith than Norman blood."

*The Doomed City, Chicago During an Appalling Ordeal. The Fire Demon's Carni-
val. The Conflagrations in West, South and North Divisions. Graphic Sketches from
the Scene of the Disaster* (Detroit: The Michigan News Company, 1871), p. 54.

    14. Roe, *Barriers Burned Away* (New York: Grosset and Dunlap, nd.),
p. 419. This is one of several reprints of the Dodd and Mead edition of 1872.

    15. Letter of James W. Milner, CHS Fire Narratives.

    16. On Collyer, see Colbert and Chamberlin, *Chicago and the Great Confla-
gration*, pp. 268, 404-5. In this first post-fire gathering, Collyer confessed that it
was still too soon for him "to find some altitude of soul, some height of moral

sentiment, from which I might look down and thank God for overshadowing us with this great sorrow," but a month later he told Edward Everett Hale's Boston congregation that he had recanted: "Now I take it all back just as Job did" (*The Great Conflagration*, p. 314).

17. Colbert and Chamberlin, *Chicago and the Great Conflagration*, p. 462.

18. The original painting was given to the Chicago Historical Society but was itself lost in a fire. Several lithographs were produced that differed from the original in making the identification of the two clothed figures with England and America more explicit and in taking care to drape the genitals of the recumbent Chicago. A. T. Andreas reproduced a lithograph version of the Armitage painting as the frontispiece illustration of the second volume of his *History of Chicago*. On such representations of women in America, with particular application to the period 1876 to 1918, but with much relevance to the period before, see Martha Banta, *Imaging American Women: Idea and Ideals in Cultural History* (New York: Columbia University Press, 1987).

19. *New York Tribune* (26 October 1871), p. 4. For a wedding illustration, see Luzerne, *The Lost City!*, p. 165. Variations on these kinds of wedding stories appear often in the wake of natural disasters. In its coverage of the blizzard of the late winter of 1993 that paralyzed much of the eastern portion of the country, the *Chicago Tribune* of March 15 carried the feature, " 'The wedding nobody would forget': giant storm can't delay wedded bliss."

20. Mrs. Martha J. Lamb, *Spicy* (New York: D. Appleton, 1873).

21. Roe, *Barriers Burned Away*, p. 439. The Ludolph gallery may have been modeled on downtown establishments like Brand's Temple of Art and Mosher's Art Gallery, which served the budding aesthetic aspirations of Chicago citizens (Kogan and Cromie, *The Great Fire*, p. 27). The linking of external and internal cataclysms, and of secular and spiritual urban renewal, is another convention of urban disaster literature. The irreverent saloonkeeper Blackie Norton, as played by Clark Gable in MGM's *San Francisco* (1936), which is justifiably renowned for its special effects in recreating the 1906 earthquake, turns to Christianity following the disaster (with the help of a two-fisted priest played by Spencer Tracy) and, having finally and indisputably won the heart of pious songbird Jeanette MacDonald, strides hand-in-hand with her and a host of other San Franciscans back into the ruined city as they all sing "The Battle Hymn of the Republic," which soon blends into the film's spirited theme song, "San Francisco." In a final touch of movie magic, the San Francisco that was fades into a long shot of the rebuilt twentieth-century city.

22. Lamb, *Spicy*, p. 164; Whittier, from Colbert and Chamberlin, *Chicago and the Great Conflagration*, p. 524. Pauly points out how the press served as a symbolic domain in which the fire could be seen as melting away day-to-day differences based on hard political and economic problems, and, in the process, created at least the appearance of consensus, stability, unity, and progress without sacrifice of traditional values. "For one blazing moment Americans seemed to discover in the Chicago Fire a symbol of all they hoped for—a world in which progress and piety could coexist and in which all groups could cooperate in a common mission." "The Great Chicago Fire as a National Event," pp. 682–83.

23. "The Silver Lining of the Cloud," p. 1002; Andrew Shuman, "The

Burnt-Out People, and What Was Done for Them," *Lakeside Memorial of the Burning of Chicago*, pp. 49–50.

24. *New York Herald*, quoted in *The Ruined City*, p. 23.

25. Colbert and Chamberlin, *Chicago and the Great Conflagration*, pp. 408, 515, 523.

26. "The Silver Lining in the Cloud," p. 1002; *Report of the Chicago Relief and Aid Society*, p. 115; Bret Harte, "Chicago," in Sheahan and Upton, *The Great Conflagration*, p. 364; William Bross, *History of Chicago* (Chicago: Jansen, McClurg, 1876), p. 97. Andreas accurately described Bross as "one of those early and prominent residents of Chicago, who has grown with the city's growth," calling him "the father of commercial journalism in Chicago, that feature of the daily press which has done more than all else to attract the solid wealth and enterprise of other localities to this city." Born in New Jersey in 1814, "Deacon" Bross settled in Chicago in 1848 and soon became a major figure in both journalism and Republican politics, indefatigably dedicating himself to the promoting of Chicago's prospects. Andreas, *History of Chicago*, vol. 2, pp. 492–93.

27. *Report of the Chicago Relief and Aid Society*, p. 6; Olmsted, "Chicago in Distress," pp. 304–5; *Chicago Inter-Ocean* (10 October 1872), p. 3.

28. Ross Miller, *American Apocalypse*, p. 49. Cronon discusses the conventions of booster thought and its combination of fantasy and serious theorizing in regard to frontier economic growth in *Nature's Metropolis*, pp. 33–34. As he points out, much work has been done in this field by Charles N. Glaab, David Hamer, and others. On early boosterism in Chicago, see also Carl Abbott, *Boosters and Businessmen: Popular Economic Thought and Urban Growth in the Antebellum Middle West* (Westport, Conn.: Greenwood Press, 1981), Chapter 5, "Chicago: The Preeminent Wonder of the Nineteenth Century," pp. 126–47. Wright (1815–74) made a fortune in the boom market of the mid-1830s, which he lost in the Panic of 1837 (in the same year he built Chicago's first schoolhouse at his own expense). Undeterred, he founded *The Prairie Farmer* in 1840, and in this and other publications continued to extol the potential of Chicago and its hinterland for the rest of his life. In 1861 he predicted that Chicago's population would reach a million—almost ten times the count in 1860—within twenty-five years. Andreas, *History of Chicago*, vol. 2, p. 573; Lloyd Lewis, *John S. Wright: Prophet of the Prairies* (Chicago: Prairie Farmer, 1941).

29. John S. Wright, *Chicago: Past, Present, Future. Relations to the Great Interior, and to the Continent* (Chicago: Horton and Leonard, 1868), pp. 249, 25. Mayer and Wade are among many who retell the Wright story, in *Chicago: Growth of a Metropolis*, p. 117.

30. William Bross, *History of Chicago*, p. 96; *New York Tribune* (14 October 1871), p. 1.

31. *Chicago Tribune* (11 October 1871), p. 2. Both Joseph Medill and Horace White have been credited with writing this editorial. Wendt, *Chicago Tribune*, pp. 236–37.

32. George F. Root, "From the Ruins Our City Shall Rise" (Chicago: Root and Cady, 1871). Wendt states that the *Tribune* editorial was the source of Root's title. *Chicago Tribune*, p. 237. Root's other fire songs included "Passing

Through the Fire," and they joined a medley of inspirational dirges prompted by the calamity, such as James R. Murray's "Pity the Homeless, or Burnt Out." As the rebuilding of the city progressed, the rhetoric of righteous battle and inevitable resurrection marched right along with it. A year after the fire, Andrew Shuman ("One Year After," p. 242) likened recently completed buildings to "newly uniformed soldiers," while "like young, half-grown recruits preparing to join their ranks, are those new structures which are rising day by day beside them." The passage concluded: "What a noble army of architectural creation already occupies the late battle-field of fiery terrors! What a still nobler army, standing in immense regiments, imposing, ponderous, and grand to look upon, will, ere another twelvemonth, cover this wide area of late desolation." Olmsted ("Chicago in Distress," p. 304) used the imagery of a battle at sea: "Chicago, in short, is under jury masts, and yet carries her ensign union down, but she answers her helm, lays her course, is making fair headway, and her crew, though on short allowance and sore tried, is thoroughly sober and knows its stations."

33. *Chicago Evening Post* (18 October 1871), p. 2; N. S. Emerson, "Call for Help for Chicago," in Luzerne, *The Lost City!*, p. 199.

34. Likewise, descriptions of the first tentative inspections of the ruins compared the experience to a descent into the underworld. See Miller, *American Apocalypse*, p. 93.

35. Frank Jellinek, *The Paris Commune of 1871* (New York: Grosset and Dunlap, 1965); Steward Edwards, *The Paris Commune, 1871* (Chicago: Quadrangle Books, 1971); and Robert Tombs, *The War Against Paris* (Cambridge: Cambridge University Press, 1981).

36. "Paris and Chicago," quoted in Sheahan and Upton, *The Great Conflagration*, p. 367. Alfred Sewell described the post-fire chaos as "worse than Paris during the German siege or the mob-reign of the Commune," while the *Chicago Evening Post* reported that the use of explosives to stop the fire "reminded one of the booming of heavy siege guns," making it seem as if "the [C]ommune and the reign of terror were being realized in the very heart of the Garden City of the West." Sewell, *The Great Calamity*, p. 32; *Chicago Evening Post* (18 October 1871), p. 2. In his comparison of the ruins of Chicago with those of the Civil War, Miller also includes photographs of the devastation of Paris. *American Apocalypse*, pp. 94–95. Cecilia Tichi offers a similarly suggestive comparison of stereographs of the damages caused by the Galveston hurricane of 1900 and by the Homestead strike of 1892. See *Shifting Gears*, p. 48.

37. This anonymous figure, "one of the prime movers in this fiendish work," revealed that the organization had its start "during the troublous times that preceded the election of Louis Napoleon to the Presidency of France." Luzerne explained, "It is the startling theory that a secret organization conceived and matured the diabolical plot for the destruction of the city, and sent their agents here to execute it." Luzerne, *The Lost City!*, pp. 185–86, 189. Karen Sawislak indicates that the confession first appeared in the *Chicago Times* on October 23. Sawislak analyzes this invention of an international terrorist network and the angry denial of it in the pages of the German-language *Illinois Staats-Zeitung*, describing this story and the harsh treatment of Mrs. O'Leary

in the press as appealing to ethnic and class fears. See Sawislak, "Smoldering City: Class, Ethnicity, and Politics in Chicago At the Time of the Great Fire, 1867–1874" (Ph.D diss., Yale University, 1990), pp. 40, 43. These rumors may have been based on similar stories of female incendiaries, or *pétroleuses,* on the loose in Paris during the Commune. See Gay L. Gullickson, "The Unruly Woman of the Paris Commune," in Dorothy O. Helly and Susan M. Reverby, eds., *Gendered Domains: Rethinking Private and Public in Women's History* (Ithaca, N.Y.: Cornell University Press, 1991), pp. 135–53. See also n. 56 below.

38. Letter of Cassius Milton Wicker (15 October 1871), CHS Fire Narratives; *Chicago Evening Journal* (9 October 1871), p. 2; *Galena Daily Gazette* (10 October 1871), p. 1; "Chicago in Ashes," *Harper's Weekly* 15 (28 October 1871), 1010. At the time of the fire, Wicker was assistant general freight agent of the Chicago and Northwestern Railroad. The following June he married Augusta French, eldest daughter of former Illinois governor Augustus French. The *New York Tribune* similarly reported that several local career criminals (including Aaron and Munday) were among those shot or hanged "while plundering in Chicago," explaining, "They, with many other of their class, left for Chicago as soon as news of the conflagration was received here, trusting to reap a rich harvest, amid the confusion consequent on the appalling catastrophe." The talk of thieves holding high carnival attempted the isolate the implications of the crime spree by implying that it was a momentary lapse after which normality would be restored. The term "carnival," as M. M. Bakhtin has argued, suggests "temporary liberation from the prevailing truth and from the established order," acceptable because this order contains this liberation without fundamental disturbance. *Rabelais and His World* (Bloomington: Indiana University Press, 1984), p. 10.

39. *The Greatest Calamity of Modern Times,* p. 27.

40. *New York Tribune* (13 October 1871), p. 2; *Chicago Evening Post* (18 October 1871), p. 2. The racially mixed nature of the mob described here increased its terrors. The accuracy of the report is questionable. There were fewer than 3,600 blacks in Chicago in 1870, or slightly more than 1 percent of the population. Pierce, *A History of Chicago,* vol. 3: *The Rise of a Modern City, 1871–1893* (New York: Alfred A. Knopf, 1957), p. 48. "The conflagration," Sawislak writes ("Smoldering City," pp. 30–31), "brought the people of Chicago face-to-face with an elemental force—and with each other. With the disaster's graphic revelation of Chicagoans' moral behavior and material standings, the stuff of popular fiction was literalized in a sudden, shocking reality." Ross Miller adds, "To the city's respectable citizenry, Chicago seemed to erupt during the fire. Long-buried and suppressed forces bubbled up from the overheated ground. As fearful as the flames was the potential human threat." *American Apocalypse,* pp. 46–47.

41. Such fears were not new. Richard Bushman cites Philip Hone's revulsion at "the miserable wretches who prowled about the ruins" of a fire in Manhattan in 1835, turning into beasts from drinking the alcohol they found. "At least in the imaginations of the wealthy gentility," Bushman writes, "this horde of discontented back-street barbarians threatened to invade the genteel city whenever suffering or disaster stirred them." *The Refinement of America,* p. 366.

42. This illustration appeared in the November 4, 1871, issue of *Every Saturday*.

43. Chicago's foreign-born population comprised half of the city's residents by 1850, and while this percentage gradually decreased to 48.35 percent in 1870 and 40.7 percent in 1880 (where it remained for the next decade), the percentage of Chicagoans who were either immigrants or who were children of at least one foreign-born parent was just under 80 percent by 1890. In 1870 17.73 percent of the city's residents had been born in Germany, 13.37 percent in Ireland. The 1890 census was the first to note the number of people who were native-born residents with at least one parent who was an immigrant. Pierce, *A History of Chicago*, vol. 3, pp. 21, 515–16; Skogan, *Chicago Since 1840*, pp. 15, 19.

44. Colbert and Chamberlin, *Chicago and the Great Conflagration*, p. 223; Frank Gilbert, "Commercial and Public Institutions," in *The Lakeside Memorial of the Burning of Chicago*, p. 71.

45. Luzerne, *The Lost City!*, p. 121. In one of the few expressions of sympathy for the condition of working people after the fire, a survivor wrote to his parents, "We can't tell yet what effect this will have upon labour and wages and the price of provisions but we are inclined to think it will be a bad job for the labouring classes." Letter of H. Hartley (10 October 1871), CHS Fire Narratives. Sawislak asserts that the fire literature did single out Mrs. O'Leary for class-motivated attacks. "But it is important to recognize that the story of Mrs. O'Leary's cow," she writes, "while on one level merely picaresque media creation, at the time represented vilification fraught with specific meaning: in the popular press, Mrs. O'Leary became an easy target for anti-Irish, anti-working class, and anti-woman invective" ("Smoldering City," p. 38). The *Chicago Times*, while not naming Mrs. O'Leary specifically or accusing her of setting the fire deliberately, described her as a welfare cheat who, "when cut off, vowed revenge." *Chicago Times* (18 October 1871), p. 1. On the mistreatment of the beleaguered Kate O'Leary in the popular press, see Perry R. Duis and Glen E. Holt, "Kate O'Leary's Sad Burden," *Chicago* 27 (October 1978), 220–24.

In perhaps the freest retelling of the O'Leary legend, the Twentieth Century-Fox film *In Old Chicago* (1938), Kate O'Leary (played by Alice Brady, who won the Academy Award for Best Supporting Actress) is aged about twenty years and divested of her first name, her husband, and some of her children, as she is transformed into the spirited widow Molly O'Leary, who runs a successful hand laundry that caters to Chicago's best. To her dismay, one of her sons (Tyrone Power) becomes an unprincipled saloon owner, but another (Don Ameche) is an idealistic attorney who is elected mayor, though he does not realize that he owes his victory to his brother's cynical scheming. In any case, the centerpiece of his program is to level the firetrap neighborhood controlled by gamblers and political operators like his brother. He dies valiantly in the fire, trying to save Chicago, when, after bravely lighting the fuse on an explosive set by General Sheridan's men, he is wounded by a bullet from the gun of a corrupt political opponent and then, unable to get away, is crushed by a collapsing building. Hearing this sad news from her now morally awakened saloonkeeper son as they, joined by his sweet-souled dance-hall queen beloved (Alice Faye), find refuge in the lake, Molly proudly rededicates the family to the building of a new and better Chicago. In this narrative, with conventions of plot shared with a long list of disaster stories (including Roe's *Barriers Burned Away* and the film *San Francisco*), Hollywood turned immigrants like Molly, who keeps a comfortable and respectable home, into upwardly mobile champions of undoing the corruption and blight that they have helped cause. Kate O'Leary did have a son who, well after the fire, became a gambling and political boss in the stockyards district, but the historical accuracy of the film is mainly limited to the facts that there was a Chicago fire and there was an O'Leary family.

46. Hubbard, *Family Memories,* pp. 126, 136. The fire histories contained similar episodes of individuals preying on each other in the panic, and several of the personal narratives mention "lost" clothes or other property of the well-to-do turning up in the possession of members of the lower classes. Mrs. Mary Emily Blatchford, who fled from the fire to her aunt's home in Evanston, later ransomed for a dollar a box that contained her wedding dress, which was worn by Mrs. Blatchford's daughter at her wedding, and by Mary Emily Blatchford again on her golden anniversary. M. E. and E. W. Blatchford, *Memories of the Chicago Fire* (n.p., n.d.).

47. William S. Walker, "Description of the Great Fire," in *The Lakeside Memorial of the Burning of Chicago,* pp. 31–32.

48. Burton J. Bledstein notes that "science as an attitude for professional discipline required inner control and an individual respect for rules, proven experience, and a system of hygienic laws concerned with such personal habits as diet, bathing, sex, dress, work, and recreation. Typically, middle-class Americans with professional pretensions translated the moral cause of temperance into a scientific truth for successful living." *The Culture of Professionalism,* pp. 90–91.

49. Exactly how much objectionable behavior can be attributed to the fire is very hard to reconstruct. Perry Duis points out, however, that the same railroad system that brought the relief trains in did make it easier for criminals (as well as reporters) to get to the city. "Whose City? Public and Private Places in Nineteenth-Century Chicago," *Chicago History* 12 (Spring 1983), 14.

50. In an uncharacteristic moment of authorial restraint, Frank Luzerne framed the terrorist's "confession" with the disclaimer that he offered it "without the expression of any opinion as to its authenticity," admitting that it seemed to be "utterly romantic and improbable." Olmsted told of "respectable citizens who hold to the opinion that the fire was started and spread systematically by incendiaries," and that he had spoken with one person, "lately from Paris, who is sure that it was part of a general war upon property," but he then dismissed the story outright: "Numerous alleged facts are cited to sustain this view, but I believe them generally to be delusions growing out of the common excitement, or accidental coincidence." Luzerne, *The Lost City!,* p. 186; Olmsted, "Chicago in Distress," p. 303. Flinn added, "Exaggerated reports of disorder, tumult, riot, loss of life, lynchings, etc., were sent out by excited or unscrupulous newspaper correspondents for a week after the fire. The truth is, the people, while panic-stricken at first, very soon regained their composure and went about making the best of it, attending to their own business, and look-

ing neither to the right nor to the left, but to the future, which looked bleak enough before the ashes cooled." *History of the Chicago Police*, p. 129.

51. Similar rumors of foreign incendiaries circulated in London in 1666. See *The Diary of Samuel Pepys*, p. 275, and *The Diary of John Evelyn*, p. 462.

52. The Matthews memoir is in a file of miscellaneous clippings and typescripts pertaining to the fire in the library of the Chicago Historical Society. This was probably written well after the fire, at which time Matthews was a bookkeeper for the Board of Trade firm of Jones and Raymond.

53. Robin Einhorn points out that some of the support in the mid-1850s for a powerful, uniformed, centralized police force in Chicago was aimed at controlling transients who were thought to embody virtually all of the city's crime problem. *Property Rules: Political Economy in Chicago, 1833–1872* (Chicago: University of Chicago Press, 1991), p. 148. On the widespread concern with the large number of recently arrived single men in the city thought to be in danger of falling prey to the temptations of urban life, see Boyer, *Urban Masses and Moral Order in America*, pp. 109–10.

54. There has been a rise in scholarly interest in this literature in recent years. Stuart M. Blumin offers an excellent overview in his recent edition of Foster's writing, *New York by Gas-light and Other Urban Sketches by George G. Foster* (Berkeley: University of California Press, 1990), pp. 1–61. See also Blumin, *The Emergence of the Middle Class*, p. 286; and Kasson, *Rudeness and Civility*, pp. 74–80. Note that much of this literature had to do not with crimes directly against property, but with vice, mainly gambling and prostitution, and some of it, including the work of Lippard and Foster, attacked the moral hypocrisy of America's urban social and political elite as a betrayal of American cherished ideals. Virtually all of the fire literature sides with the comfortable classes and treats the working poor with suspicion. For the broader literary context, see David S. Reynolds, *Beneath the American Renaissance: The Subversive Imagination in the Age of Emerson and Melville* (Cambridge, Mass.: Harvard University Press, 1988), esp. chapters 6 and 7, pp. 169–224.

55. Luzerne, *The Lost City!*, p. 187.

56. Barclay, *The Great Fire of Chicago!*, p. 32. A few pages later, Barclay wrote of a thief who evaded the police, only to be set upon by a crowd that "without waiting for even the summary practice of the lamppost, tore him, it is said, literally limb from limb" (p. 41). Note that even Barclay avoided absolutely vouching for the account with the phrase "it is said."

It is possible that the anecdotes and illustrations of the Chicago arsonists derive from images of figures hanged on lampposts going back to the French Revolution, and, as noted earlier, from the stories—also largely unsubstantiated—of the *pétroleuses* who supposedly were mainly responsible for the burning of Paris in 1871 and who, as Gay L. Gullickson writes, "came to represent the crimes of the Commune" even though they were "almost entirely a figment of the government's and the conservative press's imagination." Hundreds of alleged Communard women were arrested for lighting the fires (although the actual perpetrators were mainly male) and other crimes, and several were executed or sent to penal colonies. Gullickson argues that the conservative imagination devised the *pétroleuse* to express its fears of social revolution, here represented as the "unruly woman" whose rejection of woman's traditional role and bearing implicitly threatened the whole social order. Gullickson, "The Unruly Woman of the Paris Commune," pp. 135–53. In depictions of the French Revolution, the figure on the lamppost is not a revolutionary brought to justice but a victim of the social upheaval. See also Neil Hertz, "Medusa's Head: Male Hysteria under Political Pressure," *Representations* 4 (1983), 27–28. Gullickson cites Hertz in her essay.

57. Letter of Phillip C. Morgan (11 October 1871), CHS Fire Narratives (the emphasis is Morgan's); *The Greatest Calamity of Modern Times*, p. 27. The *New York Tribune* coldly observed that "we can shoot old women for pumping petroleum if we are Parisians, and we can resurrect them in back alleys if we live in Chicago." *New York Tribune* (13 October 1871), p. 2.

58. Walker, "Description of the Chicago Fire," p. 28; *Chicago Times* (18 October 1871), p. 1; Andreas, *History of Chicago*, vol. 2, p. 725.

59. Andreas, *History of Chicago*, vol. 2, p. 725.

60. Closer to actuality were two other accounts of the release that appeared in several places. The first told of how A. H. Miller, owner of a handsome four-story building across from the Courthouse that was the home of his well-known jewelry store, simply handed his doomed wares to surprised ex-prisoners as they hurried to find refuge. The prisoners also figured in one of the heroic legends of the fire, real estate man John G. Shortall's quick-thinking rescue of records from his office near the Courthouse. Since the city's documents and those of every other similar firm were lost to the flames, the files from Shortall's firm were thought to be the only documentary proof of ownership of property that survived the evening. With the assistance of associates and a borrowed pistol that he kept cocked, Shortall commandeered a wagon that he and the others filled; they then "recruited" two prisoners to help him manage the overloaded vehicle as it pulled away. But both the Miller and the Shortall narratives, and especially the prisoners' unthreatening role in them, received much less attention than the dangers supposedly posed by the escaped demons.

The fullest version of the Miller story is his widow's privately published *Reminiscences of the Chicago Fire* (n.p., n.d.), which was written at the urging of her friends. Mrs. Miller's *Reminiscences* is one of the few memoirs, certainly one of the very few published, that depict the fire as the source of sustained personal misfortune. John G. Shortall's personal recollection is in the Chicago Historical Society Fire Narratives, and is reprinted, with a flattering photographic portrait, in Joseph Kirkland's *The Story of Chicago*, vol. 1, pp. 310–15.

61. Flinn, *History of the Chicago Police*, pp. 136–37.

62. Pierce, *A History of Chicago*, vol. 2, pp. 433–34. See also Flinn, *History of the Chicago Police*, pp. 82–83.

63. Colbert and Chamberlin, *Chicago and the Great Conflagration*, p. 223.

64. Shuman, "The Burnt-Out People, and What Was Done for Them," p. 43.

65. Andreas, *History of Chicago*, vol. 2, pp. 754–55. What he calls "the recurrent turn of mind" in which "what would seem to be a political threat" is represented "as if it were a sexual threat" is the subject of Neil Hertz's essay,

"Medusa's Head" (see n. 56). The narratives of the transgressions that supposedly took place on the Sands are a good example of the "explicit linking of what is politically dangerous to feelings of sexual horror and fascination." "Medusa's Head," p. 32. See also the descriptions of the forced democracy of other refugee communities, such as the one on the prairie west of the city: "There was the same contrast of classes—Mr. McCormick, the millionaire of the reaper trade, and other north-side nabobs, herding promiscuously with the humblest laborer, the lowest vagabond, and the meanest harlot." Colbert and Chamberlin, *Chicago and the Great Conflagration*, p. 268.

66. Paul Boyer describes the decades before the war as "a time of almost continuous disorder and turbulence among the urban poor." *Urban Masses and Moral Order in America*, p. 69. The richest discussion of perhaps the most notorious nineteenth-century outbreak of mob action, in relation to the broader urban social and political order, is Iver Bernstein's *The New York City Draft Riots: Their Significance for American Society and Politics in the Age of the Civil War* (New York: Oxford University Press, 1990). Of social analyses contemporary with the Chicago fire, the outstanding example is New York reformer Charles Loring Brace's *The Dangerous Classes of New York, and Twenty Years' Work Among Them*, which first appeared in 1872. Brace's book was mainly based on his experiences with the American-born children of immigrants, whose antisocial and often criminal behavior he saw as the result of terrible environmental conditions. His attitude toward these disadvantaged and disaffected city youth was sympathetic—he deemed them "our *enfants perdus*" and devoted himself to improving their lot and thereby encouraging them to lead productive lives— but his description of the potential dangers of such "roughs" to moral and genteel society was as vivid as in the more sensational and fear-mongering literature of the fire: "Let but Law lift its hand from them for a season, or let the civilizing influences of American life fail to reach them, and, if the opportunity offered, we should see an explosion from this class which might leave this city in ashes and blood." *The Dangerous Classes of New York*, 3d ed. (New York: Wynkoop and Hallenbeck, 1880), pp. 27, 29.

67. Roe, *Barriers Burned Away*, pp. 392, 401, 407–8, 414–15, 420.

68. D. H. Wheeler, "Political Economy of the Fire," in *The Lakeside Memorial of the Burning of Chicago*, p. 99. David Hilton Wheeler was professor of English Literature and History at Northwestern University, which he also served as librarian and president *ad interim* from 1867 to 1869. Having worked in Lincoln's Iowa campaign in 1860, he was rewarded with the consulship in Genoa. He also reported from Italy for both the *New York Tribune* and *Chicago Tribune* (some have called him America's first foreign correspondent) before taking the position at Northwestern.

CHAPTER FOUR

1. Andreas, *History of Chicago*, vol. 2, pp. 769, 775; Paul Andrew Hutton, *Phil Sheridan and His Army* (Lincoln: University of Nebraska Press, 1985), pp. 117, 153.

2. Andreas, *History of Chicago*, vol. 2, pp. 764, 769.

3. The best source of information on the work of the Society during the fire

is the 1874 report. The outstanding modern analysis of this work is in Karen L. Sawislak's "Smoldering City," especially pp. 81–156. See also Sawislak, "Relief, Aid, and Order: Class, Gender, and the Definition of Community in the Aftermath of Chicago's Great Fire," *Journal of Urban History* 20 (1993), 3–18; Otto M. Nelson, "The Chicago Relief and Aid Society, 1850–1874," *Journal of the Illinois State Historical Society* 59 (1966), 48–66; and Timothy J. Naylor, "Responding to the Fire: The Work of the Chicago Relief and Aid Society," *Science and Society* 39 (Winter 1975–76), 450–64. An excellent study of the Society's efforts in relation to the history of cultural philanthropy in Chicago is Chapter 3 of Kathleen D. McCarthy's *Noblesse Oblige: Charity and Cultural Philanthropy in Chicago, 1849–1929* (Chicago: University of Chicago Press, 1982), pp. 53–72. For an uncritical view, see Elisabeth Kimbell, " 'We Could Not Do without the Chicago Fire . . . ,' " *Chicago History* 1 (Fall 1971), pp. 220–31. The records of the Society are in the Manuscripts and Archives Department of the Chicago Historical Society, in the collection of the United Charities of Chicago, which was formed in 1909 when the Chicago Relief and Aid Society joined with the Bureau of Charities, which had been organized from several other welfare agencies in 1894 in response to the Panic of 1893. On the many other organizations involved in relief, see Sawislak, "Smoldering City," pp. 143–50. Sawislak maintains that most of the other groups were different from the Relief and Aid Society in their emphasis on reinforcing community ties rather than molding individual conduct. In regard to the Society and the prevention of smallpox, see *Report of the Chicago Relief and Aid Society*, pp. 215–16. Inoculation was required of those expecting material assistance.

4. *Report of the Chicago Relief and Aid Society*, p. 440.

5. Ginzberg traces these trends in *Women and the Work of Benevolence: Morality, Politics, and Class in the Nineteenth-Century United States* (New Haven: Yale University Press, 1990). See in particular Chapter 6, " 'The Moral Eye of the State,' " pp. 174–213. Ginzberg's main concern in this book is, at its title implies, the efforts of women and issues of gender, but she places these in the context of the broader history of the work of benevolence, examining the diminishment in practice of the importance of the idea of women's separate sphere of morality and sentiment and the increasing influence of class considerations. Writing specifically in regard to the work of the Charity Organization Societies that were formed out of dissatisfaction with the task of relief during the depression of the mid-1870s, she maintains that these organizations' "emphasis on science and business helped transform the discourse over benevolence from one about gender to one about class at a time of growing conservatism and class awareness on the part of the Protestant middle and upper-middle classes" (p. 198). See also Blumin, *The Emergence of the Middle Class*, Chapter 6, "Coming to Order: Voluntary Associations and the Organization of Social Life and Consciousness," pp. 192–229.

6. Boyer, "Building Character Among the Urban Poor: The Charity Organization Movement," Chapter 10 of *Urban Masses and Moral Order in America*, pp. 143–61. Sawislak states that the kind of class monitoring practiced by the Society was pioneered by New York's Association for Improving the Condition of the Poor, founded a few years earlier, which "offered an alternative to what

its managers viewed as the disorganized and overly sentimental practices of earlier urban charities" ("Smoldering City," pp. 112–13). For more on the Association for Improving the Condition of the Poor, see *Urban Masses and Moral Order in America*, pp. 88–89.

7. Nelson, "The Chicago Relief and Aid Society, 1850–1874"; *Annual Report of the Chicago Relief and Aid Society, for the year ending October 31st, 1871* (Chicago: J. M. W. Jones, 1871); *Third Annual Report of the Chicago Relief and Aid Society* (Chicago: Guildbert and Clissold, 1870), pp. 4, 6, 8.

8. *Report of the Chicago Relief and Aid Society*, pp. 141, 142. There are dozens of application forms and letters of recommendation in the archives of the Society in the Chicago Historical Society. Sawislak analyzes the play *Relief: A Humorous Drama* that was published in 1872, which satirized the work of the Ladies' Christian Union, an auxiliary group to the Relief and Aid Society composed of the wives and female relatives of the Society's members, and which, in spite of many assertions to the contrary, "makes it plain that the Relief and Aid vision of what was best for Chicago was not universally accepted." She singles out for special notice a scene in which two Irish women masterfully manipulate two condescending and self-congratulatory female visitors. "Smoldering city," pp. 139–42. Sawislak discusses the Society's assumption—which explained its denial of aid to several obviously deserving sufferers who were not so clever—"that poverty and distress would be, to some degree, a natural part of every worker's life" (p. 137). Interestingly enough, Aurelia King, whose husband was president of the Relief and Aid Society, confessed in a letter to a potential donor, "In so large a work as the present Chicago Relief there must of course be some donations misapplied. Mr. King feels this, and I thought perhaps it might please your Society to send their supplies where they would reach some of the sufferer's [*sic*] directly. I only suggest this, but you may think it better for you to send to the general fund." Letter of Aurelia King, CHS Fire Narratives.

9. Sawislak, "Smoldering City," p. 106.

10. On the evolution of Chicago's elite, see Jaher, *The Urban Establishment*, pp. 453–575. Dexter, who turned thirty-eight in the year of the fire (at this time Field was thirty-six, Pullman forty, and King forty-three), was born and raised in Michigan, where he worked in the lumber business. He came to Chicago in 1865 and was admitted to the bar the following year. His major client was the Chicago, Burlington & Quincy Railroad. Dexter used his position as attorney for the Michigan Central Railroad to make a train available to King when the fire threatened his warehouse. King credited Dexter's fast thinking with saving his company $100,000 worth of stock and enabling him to resume business quickly after the fire. Andreas, *History of Chicago*, vol. 3, p. 721. One member of the executive committee, attorney Julius Rosenthal, was Jewish.

11. McCarthy, *Noblesse Oblige*, pp. 56–68; Schultz, "The Businessman's Role in Western Settlement: The Entrepreneurial Frontier, Chicago, 1833–1872," pp. 243–68; Einhorn, *Property Rules*, pp. 226–27, 233–35. McCarthy points out that the trustees of the Society saw its assistance to the unemployed and burned-out at least partly as a form of self-protection, and that they distributed much of their resources to existing voluntary organizations, whose policies they could then control. McCarthy, *Noblesse Oblige*, pp. 68–70.

12. Jon C. Teaford, *The Unheralded Triumph: City Government in America* (Baltimore: The Johns Hopkins University Press, 1984), pp. 187–88; Theda Skocpol, *Protecting Soldiers and Mothers: The Political Origins of Social Policy in the United States* (Cambridge: The Belknap Press of Harvard University Press, 1992), p. 95. Skocpol, like Ginzberg, cites in particular the work of Charity Organization Societies in the late 1870s, which was very similar to that of the Relief and Aid Society.

13. Sawislak, "Smoldering City," p. 113.

14. *Report of the Chicago Relief and Aid Society*, p. 6. On the conflicting and incomplete information behind the appointment of the Society, see "Smoldering City," pp. 101–107.

15. Blatchford's father had been the first ordained Protestant pastor in Chicago, and he himself had been treasurer of the Northwestern branch of the Sanitary Commission during the war. He later became president of the board of trustees of the Newberry Library. Inspired by a sign that read "Food for Chicago" that he saw in Fort Wayne, he bought a bushel basket and set out to fill it with provisions for his city. On learning Blatchford's purpose, the vendor donated as much as Blatchford could carry with him. Once he arrived, Blatchford learned that Ulmenheim, the family home, and the ten elms that gave it its name, had been destroyed by the fire, and that his family had found safe refuge. M. E. and E. W. Blatchford, *Memories of the Chicago Fire*, pp. 25, 42–43. The memoirs of Mr. and Mrs. Blatchford were prepared for their children, but were published to help raise money for the Chicago Historical Society.

16. Sydney Howard Gay, "Chicago and the Relief Committee," in *The Lakeside Memorial of the Burning of Chicago*, pp. 105–8. In some places Gay's first name is spelled Sidney. Joseph Kirkland's *The Story of Chicago* (vol. 1, p. 342) names Gay as the author of the 1874 report.

17. *Chicago Tribune* article (written by the paper's London correspondent) quoted in Sheahan and Upton, *The Great Conflagration*, pp. 322–26; Olmsted, "Chicago in Distress," pp. 304–5. *Harper's Weekly* directly tied the relief work in Chicago to the fight against crooked politics in New York as one united effort of purification and reform: "The land is answering the young man's question, 'Who is my neighbor?' as the Master himself answered it; and no American had ever more right to be proud of his country than at the moment when it is soothing the suffering of Chicago and correcting the corruption of New York." "The Silver Lining of the Cloud," p. 1002.

18. Rose, *Victorian America and the Civil War*, p. 231. On political corruption in Chicago at the time of the fire, see Pierce, *A History of Chicago*, vol. 2, pp. 297–99; and Einhorn, *Property Rules*, pp. 232–33.

19. Sawislak surveys the criticisms of the Society (143ff.) and calls the suspicion of Chicago's elected officials "dubiously overwrought" and based in elite fears of the working class. She cites criticisms of the work of the Society by Holden. See "Smoldering City," pp. 105, 153–54. Timothy J. Naylor maintains that a substantial part of the motivation of the Society's leading members was the desire "to restore the base of their power and wealth." He continues, "The Society recognized that the disorderly behavior of the poor during the fire portended the undermining of society in ways more fundamental than the physical

destruction of the city; its leaders were determined not to allow this disorder to act as a catalyst for basic social change" ("Responding to the Fire," p. 452). While Sawislak agrees with Naylor's revisionist account of the work of the Relief and Aid Society, she points out that he fails to note that the Society was one of many charitable organizations in the city and that it was the object of some attacks while it was conducting the work of relief. She also criticizes Naylor for failing to put in historical perspective the Society's principles and procedures. On Dexter and tariff reform, see Pierce, *A History of Chicago*, vol. 3, pp. 16-17.

According to Teaford, the exaggerated and largely unjustified middle-class suspicion of city councils and party politicians was the dominant trend in late nineteenth-century urban politics, as was a tension between mayors like Mason, who had ties to the business community, and aldermen with a power base in neighborhood and immigrant communities. While such a "heterogeneous polyarchy" functioned reasonably well, Teaford argues, it lacked an ideology to bolster it. He further maintains, "The 'failure' of the American city was a matter of subjective perception and not objective fact. Many middle-class Americans of the late nineteenth century simply refused to view a municipality governed by ward-heeling Irish politicians as worthy of praise." He observes, however, that the one area in which municipal government was least effective was in the sensitive matter of social control and the enforcement of middle-class codes of morality (*The Unheralded Triumph*, pp. 10, 218, 280).

20. Gibbs followed this up with another order three days later reminding Society workers that there were several thousand men and boys "whose families we are feeding" who were about to get paid enough to meet their own food and fuel costs. "Be sure that every such family is known in your District, and reported at the office, so that no more supplies be given to it," Gibbs advised, warning that the Society's supplies were dwindling "at a *fearful* rate." He cited sacred authority in justification of this order: "If any men, boys or women are not working, apply St. Paul's Rule: 'If any man among you will not *work*, neither let him *eat*.'" *Report of the Chicago Relief and Aid Society*, pp. 273, 158. The order of October 27 was not included in the 1874 report. A copy of it is in the broadsides collection of the Chicago Historical Society. Sawislak argues that the Relief and Aid Society's zealous concern about the dangers of benevolence actually penalized honest workers whose assistance was suspended as soon as they found work but before they were actually paid. Sawislak and Naylor also explain that the Society further regulated labor by monitoring the issuing of railroad passes out of the city to workers whose skills would be needed in rebuilding Chicago.

21. *Report of the Chicago Relief and Aid Society*, pp. 184-89. A few of these structures, much renovated, still stand.

22. *Report of the Chicago Relief and Aid Society*, p. 189. Anna Higginson, herself a victim of the fire, believed that in some ways she was better off than the Ogdens. "I think Mrs. O. feels worse, living in her elegant, untouched house, than we do who are altogether homeless—& I do not wonder at it," she wrote, "as they live in fear of their lives, with their house watched day and night by policemen." Letter of Anna E. Higginson (10 November 1871), CHS Fire Nar-

ratives. Mrs. Higginson preceded this with a lighter thought: "Washington Park is full of the barracks built by the city for the houseless poor—& they are the only neighbors Mrs. Ogden has within a mile. One of the men whom we employed for a day told Charlie that, 'they had not many neighbors but, they were very select!'—meaning the Ogdens!" Sawislak (p. 123, n. 94) cites other evidence of the tension caused by this situation, including an anxious letter by Mrs. Ogden's niece and the demand by Herman Raster, editor of the German-language *Staats-Zeitung*, for General Sheridan to confiscate the Ogden mansion and use it to shelter the homeless. Raster specifically feared that to do otherwise would be interpreted as a sign of the arrogant dominance of "rich Yankeedom," and he warned that a resentful fire victim might try to set the house on fire.

23. *Report of the Chicago Relief and Aid Society*, pp. 196–201; Sawislak, "Smoldering City," pp. 88–93, 130–38. Sawislak explains how the German immigrant community was particularly badly served by the Society. As does Naylor, she argues that the handling of the special relief grants, which the Society claimed got people back to work and off the charity rolls, demonstrated blatant class prejudice and a desire to perpetuate pre-fire social divisions. Special Relief aid also provided funding and furniture to help open boarding houses and the distribution of 5,299 sewing machines, purchased at half-price in a special arrangement with their manufacturers, to "worthy and industrious sewing women." According to Robert Cromie, The Ladies' Relief Society was organized October 19 at the Dexter home "to find those in need who were too proud to apply, and to help them with a minimum of embarrassment." *The Great Chicago Fire*, p. 264.

24. *Report of the Chicago Relief and Aid Society*, pp. 196, 198–99. The unexpected and, to some people, unseemly appearance of the well-to-do in the relief lines was a topic of discussion in some of the letters written after the fire. Ellis Chesbrough, the civil engineer who had supervised the construction of the new waterworks, advised his son at Harvard, "Do not say anything about it to Dyer, but we hear that his sister Mrs. Loving has actually been to the 'Relief' for clothing.—However a good many other ladies as respectable as she have done this same thing.—I fear that in some cases, respectable people have gone for aid, who ought to wait a little while for their friends to come forward; but some folks seem to give way to despair almost immediately." Letter of Ellis Chesbrough (21 October 1871), CHS Fire Narratives. In the same letter where she described the barracks opposite the Ogden mansion, Anna Higginson told a friend of how standing in line for relief could have quite the opposite effect of humiliation in some people's eyes: "You may imagine how I felt on meeting Mrs. [Isaac] Arnold coming from the Relief Society with a bundle of clothing for Mr. Arnold; though I think she felt rather uplifted by the necessity, appearing somewhat in the character of a martyr—& when Dr. Rylance [J. H. Rylance, the recently retired minister of the St. James Episcopal Church, which included many prominent North Side families] went to see her & seizing her hands with one of his characteristic gushes, exclaimed, 'You noble woman.' I am sure she felt abundantly repaid for all she had undergone."

25. *Report of the Chicago Relief and Aid Society*, pp. v–vi.

26. Andreas, *History of Chicago*, vol. 2, p. 51.

27. A. T. Andreas, *History of Chicago*, vol. 2, p. 774. Elsewhere Andreas praised Mayor Mason as much for his appointment of Sheridan as Chicago's peacekeeper as he had for designating the Chicago Relief and Aid Society as the almoner of the city: "Being advised, furthermore, that criminals of all classes were pouring toward Chicago, thinking to be benefited by the confusion then reigning, he [Mason] earned the approval of all good citizens by calling upon the government of the United States for protection, and General P. H. Sheridan placed the city under martial law" (p. 51).

28. Hutton, *Phil Sheridan and His Army*, pp. 205–8. In addition to other active and retired army officers, Sheridan's party included James Gordon Bennett of the *New York Herald*, Charles L. Wilson of the *Chicago Evening Journal*, Anson Stager of Western Union, and New York financier Leonard Jerome, Winston Churchill's grandfather. Hutton describes this excursion by these representatives of order and discipline: "Covering almost two hundred miles in ten days, the hunters left a trail of empty champagne bottles and animal carcasses from Fort McPherson to Fort Hays, Kansas" (p. 208).

29. Philip H. Sheridan, *Report to the Honorable W. W. Belknap, Chicago, December 20, 1871* ([Chicago, 1871]), pp. 1–3. According to John J. Flinn, the regular police force at the time of the fire consisted of 310 men, half of whom were themselves burned-out and thus under severe personal and financial strain. They were genuinely in need of some assistance in patrolling the devastated city. *History of the Chicago Police*, pp. 123–25. The total number of men under Sheridan's command is hard to calculate precisely, but was probably under 2,500. For a brief overview of the organization of this force, see Andreas, *History of Chicago*, vol. 2, pp. 773–75. The famous detective Allan Pinkerton joined in this effort, sending his private army of Preventive Police to help guard the heart of the downtown. Pinkerton issued a broadside to "Thieves & Burglars" in which he warned, "Any person stealing or seeking to steal any of the property in my charge, or attempt[ing] to break open the safes, as the men cannot make arrests at the present time, they shall kill the persons by my orders, no mercy shall be shown them, but death shall be their fate." A copy of this notice is in the Prints and Photographs Department of the Chicago Historical Society. Pinkerton (1819–84) was born in Scotland but had been a resident of Chicago since 1842.

30. Philip H. Sheridan, *Report to the Honorable W. W. Belknap*, pp. 2, 20; *Personal Memoirs of Philip Henry Sheridan, New and Enlarged Edition With an Account of his Life from 1871 to his Death, in 1888 by Brig.-Gen. Michael V. Sheridan* (New York: D. Appleton, 1902), vol. 2, pp. 472–73.

31. Letters of John DeKoven (26 October 1871) and Phillip C. Morgan (11 October 1871), CHS Fire Narratives.

32. "Letter from Chicago," *The Christian Register* (21 October 1871); Bross, *History of Chicago*, p. 94. Andreas annotated his inclusion of Bross's comment: "Governor Bross is not the only one of our citizens who, in that fearful time, thanked God when the solid mass of blue coats and glittering muskets represented the barrier to the mob that these companies did—giving definite assurance of the might of the law in every gun and in every soldier." *History of Chicago*, vol. 2, p. 734.

33. In his communications, Sheridan stated that this public mind just after the fire "resembled that of a panic-stricken army," and that this was the source of all the stories of "incendiarism, robberies, murders, and lynching," which he called "the most absurd rumors." He described the newspaper reports of such goings-on as being "without the slightest foundation. There has not been a single case of arson, hanging or shooting; not even a case of riot or of a street fight." Sheridan, *Report to the Honorable W. W. Belknap*, pp. 1, 8, 16. Flinn also called the rumors and reports "exaggerated" and the result of the same combination of post-disaster distress and paranoia Sheridan cited, but he attributed the actual peace and calm of the city in part to the presence of Sheridan and the regular army. *History of the Chicago Police*, pp. 126, 129–30.

34. There was talk that Palmer, himself a Civil War officer who had served with Sheridan, was motivated by lingering resentments as well as his political ambitions.

35. Sheridan, *Report to the Honorable W. W. Belknap*, p. 7. Flinn generally praised the citizen patrols, dismissing the reports that they had shot several citizens, but he added, "Undisciplined, inexperienced, panicky and inclined to look with suspicion on every stranger who came along, they served to increase rather than to diminish the alarm of honest people in many quarters." *History of the Chicago Police*, p. 126.

36. Sheridan, *Report to the Honorable W. W. Belknap*, p. 20; *Report of the Select Committee on Governor J. M. Palmer's Messages of Nov. 15 and Dec. 9, 1871, Submitted to the House Jan. 6, 1872*, p. 12; Matthews, CHS. For more on the military occupation of Chicago, see Sawislak, "Smoldering City," pp. 63–80; and Lowell Dean Larson, "Constitutionalism in Crisis: The Case of the Great Chicago Fire," (M.A.T. diss., University of Chicago, 1962). Larson indicates that the legislature indefinitely postponed any final action.

37. Alan Trachtenberg, *The Incorporation of America*, p. 147. See Chapter 5, "The Politics of Culture," pp. 140–81. The pioneering work in this area is Raymond Williams, *Culture and Society, 1780–1950* (New York: Columbia University Press, 1958). On the significance of manners, see Kasson, *Rudeness and Civility*, and Halttunen, *Confidence Men and Painted Women*.

38. Quoted in McCarthy, *Noblesse Oblige*, p. 75. For Victorian suspicions— on both sides of the Atlantic—of democracy and materialism, see David D. Hall, "The Victorian Connection," in Howe, ed., *Victorian America*, pp. 89–90. Arnold (1815–84) was born in Otsego County, New York, of parents who had emigrated from New England. He studied law in Cooperstown and moved to Chicago in 1836, where he entered into partnership for about a decade with Mahlon Ogden, whose mansion survived the fire. Arnold became active in Free Soil and antislavery politics, serving in the Illinois General Assembly and the United States House of Representatives. He was a friend of Abraham Lincoln and, at the time of his own death, the former president's leading biographer.

39. Ogden quoted in Daniel Bluestone, *Constructing Chicago*, p. 8. Bluestone's interest throughout his book is in Chicagoans' attempts to find cultural forms—in gardens and parks, churches, skyscrapers, public buildings, and overall urban design—that reconciled the city's commercial character with what its citizens took to be their loftier ambitions.

40. While the literature of the fire repeatedly claimed that the future possibilities of Chicago were, if anything, strengthened rather than undermined by the fire, some writers in the days just before the calamity decried the spirit of speculation that was rampant everywhere, especially in Chicago, and which invited wholesale disaster. The *Chicago Evening Post* published the day before the fire an editorial whose title, "The Fever of Speculation," metaphorically classed this kind of economic activity with epidemic diseases that threatened the well-being of cities and the nation. The *Evening Post* warned that the country "has mortgaged the earnings of generations ahead, and given away the proceeds." *Chicago Evening Post* (7 October 1871), p. 2. For a more detailed discussion of the nineteenth-century critique of the culture of Chicago, see Smith, *Chicago and the American Literary Imagination*, pp. 1–12, 57–90, 171–76. See also Pauly, "The Great Chicago Fire as a National Event," p. 674; and Miller, *American Apocalypse*, p. 13.

41. *Harper's Weekly* 15 (11 November 1871). The descriptions of such damage had a double-edged quality, deeply regretting the irreplaceable losses but marveling that so young a city could have these treasures to lose. On these and similar losses, see Colbert and Chamberlin, *Chicago and the Great Conflagration*, pp. 344–45; Kogan and Cromie, *The Great Fire*, pp. 27–30. Chicago had no public library at the time of the fire, and one way in which the disaster indeed proved to be a blessing in disguise was that it spurred a drive in England to contribute books that were the basis of the collection of the city's first institution of this kind, housed temporarily in a converted water tank on the future site of the Rookery Building. In another turn of events, the Paris art dealer Goupil and Company—in coordination with a distinguished American committee of clergymen, artists, gallery owners, and businessmen—made a successful appeal to the artists of Paris and Dusseldorf to contribute paintings (carried across the Atlantic at no cost by the French Steamship Line) for sale in New York to benefit the stricken city. The collection included works by Breton, Gérôme, Lambinet, Meissonier, and Bougereau, among many others. Thus art literally came to the aid of Chicago. See *Chicago Relief from the Artists of Paris and Dusseldorf, 1872* (New York: Geo. A. Leavitt, 1872), which is the catalogue for the sale.

42. This was one kind of defense of Chicago's own special culture that has persisted well into the twentieth century and has been voiced by figures as varied as H. L. Mencken, Carl Sandburg, and, with qualifications, Saul Bellow.

43. J. B. Runnion, "Our Aesthetical Development," in *The Lakeside Memorial of the Burning of Chicago*, pp. 18–19. Runnion, along with James Sheahan, was an assistant editor to Horace White at the *Tribune*. In his survey of "Institutions of Art, Science, Literature," Sheahan's fire-history collaborator, George Upton, claimed that the finer things would have to wait until the more basic ones were back in place in Chicago: "Material growth always comes first; and the luxuries of literature and art only follow after the accumulation of wealth, and result from culture, which in its turn results from the leisure which wealth gives." Upton, "Institutions of Art, Science, Literature," *The Lakeside Memorial of the Burning of Chicago*, p. 80. See also Smith, *Chicago and the American Literary Imagination*, pp. 4, 58.

44. E. O. Haven, "Religious and Educational Institutions," in *The Lakeside Memorial of the Burning of Chicago*, pp. 80, 73–74. Haven hoped that Chicago would follow the example of the first New England settlements: "The Pilgrims built their meeting-house with their first dwellings. Chicago, if it has their spirit, while stores, hotels, breweries and saloons again arise, will give libraries, museums, schools and churches also a better resurrection." Haven (1820–81) was a Methodist bishop and prominent American educator who had been president of the University of Michigan before assuming the leadership of Northwestern from 1869 to 1872. He next served as secretary of the Board of Education of the Methodist Episcopal Church and then as chancellor of Syracuse University. Among his notable innovations at Michigan and Northwestern was the introduction of coeducation. See Rev. C. C. Stratton, ed., *Autobiography of Erastus O. Haven, D.D., LL.D* (New York: Phillips and Hunt, 1883).

45. Binckley found some hope, however, in the great untapped resources of Chicago: "The ambition of this city is still low, while its capacity, its means, and, above all, its prospects, are not much short of sublime. When transcontinental trade, by which the ancient world's extreme borders are to shake hands across America, is broached, grand as the idea is, Chicago may immediately lift her head above all competition. She may make pupils of the oldest cities of the world—Pekin, Bombay, Damascus; she may even teach London or New York; and she may lead Boston by the hand; but when it comes to anything by which man has been able to exalt himself in soul, this great city has not passed the stage of hands and knees. She is a follower." "The Chicago of the Thinker," in *Lakeside Monthly* 10 (October 1873), 265.

46. Horatio N. Powers, "The Chicago of the Connoisseur," in *Lakeside Monthly* 10 (October 1873), 281, 282, 284.

47. D. H. Wheeler, "The Political Economy of the Fire," *The Lakeside Memorial of the Burning of Chicago*, pp. 99–100. See chapter 3 n. 68, above.

48. Rima Schultz and Helen Horowitz indicate that there was some truth to Wheeler's contention about shifting generations. "While it is true that business resumed almost within twenty-four hours of the catastrophe, and many bravely reorganized," Schultz observes, "it fell to younger men to take the most active part in the rebirth" ("The Businessman's Role in Western Settlement," p. 255). Horowitz cites a letter written in 1885 by Ezra B. McCagg, one of the board members of the Relief and Aid Society, in response to young businessman and patron of the arts Charles Hutchinson's request for support for the Art Institute of Chicago: "It has seemed to me that the work of this kind to be done in this city . . . must devolve upon younger men than I am and to a large extent upon men who have not had their enthusiasm burned out of them. The fire of 1871 destroyed whatever I had set my heart on as however weak in itself yet perhaps the seed corns which in the end would bring a harvest, and left it all to be begun over again, and lame and weary and nearly hopeless I dropped out—and think I may not begin again." Helen L. Horowitz, *Culture and the City: Cultural Philanthropy in Chicago from the 1880s to 1917* (Lexington: University Press of Kentucky, 1976), p. 44. Attorney McCagg, who had been president of the Northwestern Branch of the Sanitary Commission and on the board of the

Chicago Academy of Design (the predecessor to the Art Institute), was only forty-six in the year of the fire, which destroyed his home and his extensive library, known for its collection of law books and of the writings and letters of early explorers and settlers in the Old Northwest (Andreas, *A History of Chicago*, vol. 2, p. 467). None of this proves that individuals who would have become painters and novelists and professors otherwise went into business, however. Horowitz in fact suggests that the fire helped inspire the civic renaissance that was part of the rebuilding. In any case, the last part of Wheeler's remarks appears to have been directed less at the fate of the current elite than at lost opportunities for elevating the lower classes.

49. "Disturbed by social forces they could not control and filled with idealistic notions of culture," Horowitz writes, "these businessmen saw in the museum, the library, the symphony orchestra, and the university a way to purify their city and to generate a civic renaissance" (p. x). See also Robert I. Goler, "Visions of a Better Chicago," in Susan E. Hirsch and Robert I. Goler, *A City Comes of Age: Chicago in the 1890s* (Chicago: Chicago Historical Society, 1990), pp. 106–8. While she concentrates on the last two decades of the century (Goler focuses on the 1890s), Horowitz traces the roots of this movement to the wartime work of organizations like the Sanitary Commission, which helped bring together successful men of affairs who shared an interest in the social uses of traditional high culture. Horowitz asserts that the fire was partly responsible for the "new cultural climate" in Chicago, though she views this climate mainly in terms of a "new burst of civic enthusiasm" generated by the "heroism and communal spirit" that were central to the fire legend, not in direct relation to fears of social disorder (p. 36). Kathleen McCarthy likewise sees the fire as a "turning point in Chicago's cultural development." While pointing out—as does Horowitz— that the dedication of leading businessmen to major cultural institutions after the fire was also often rooted in a democratic belief in the diffusion of culture, a genuine love of art and learning, civic pride, and community spirit, as well as unabashed boosterism, she also contends that the cultural benefactors of the post-fire era differed from their predecessors not only in the scale of their contributions but in their "desire to curb growing materialism and unrest." She further explains: "Laboring against a backdrop of endemic social and economic conflict, Chicago's self-made magnates sought to reunite class and caste in the collective pursuit of knowledge and self-culture." *Noblesse Oblige*, p. 75. Cultural philanthropy is the topic of all of Chapter 4 of this book, "Culture & Community," pp. 75–96.

On the building of a new permanent public library (which pre-fire Chicago did not have) as a result of the fire, in the broader context of elite concerns about social difference and control and their belief that institutions of culture would address these concerns, see also Bluestone, *Constructing Chicago*, pp. 164–71. Among this project's backers, as in so many other instances, were several board members of the Relief and Aid Society, including Nathaniel Fairbank, Marshall Field, and George Pullman. Bluestone argues correctly (pp. 207–8) that "genuine aspirations to genteel existence existed in a context of social class, with all the contradictions that entails," and that Chicago's elite "could not imagine a way of living above Mammon that did not require the buoyancy provided by wealth."

50. Goodspeed, *History of the Great Fires in Chicago and the West*, pp. 547–49.

CHAPTER FIVE

1. Letters of James W. Milner and Cassius Milton Wicker, CHS Fire Narratives; Frederick Francis Cook, *Bygone Days in Chicago: Recollections of the "Garden City" of the Sixties* (Chicago: A. C. McClurg, 1910), p. xi.

2. Hubbard, *Family Memories*, pp. 92–93. Whether Mrs. Hubbard classified the next generation of Chicago entrepreneurs, men like Field and Pullman and Dexter, among the "we" or the "them" is not certain.

3. Colbert and Chamberlin, *Chicago and the Great Conflagration*, pp. 254–55; see also Andreas, *History of Chicago*, vol. 2, p. 748. The fountain-rock, believed to be of Native American origins, was known as the Waubansie stone. It was acquired by Arnold at the Sanitary Fair and is now in the collections of the Chicago Historical Society. As Frederick Francis Cook elegantly pointed out, any claims old settlers might have made to having a settled culture ignored the fact that this "culture" was barely a generation old by the time of the fire. "We, of the earlier time," he recalled, "saw the things about us through a tenuous and almost colorless atmosphere—for we lived in a present without a past. Local history was then all in the making" (*Bygone Days in Chicago*, p. ix).

4. Charles Randolph, "Our Trade and Commerce. Development of Chicago in Wealth and Material Prosperity," in *The Lakeside Memorial of the Burning of Chicago*, pp. 12, 17–18. On the dynamics of collective and public memory, see Maurice Halbwachs, *On Collective Memory*, edited and translated by Lewis Coser (Chicago: University of Chicago Press, 1992); Paul Connerton, *How Societies Remember* (New York: Cambridge University Press, 1989); James Fentress and Chris Wickham, *Social Memory* (Oxford: Blackwell, 1992); and John R. Gillis, ed., *Commemorations: The Politics of National Memory* (Princeton: Princeton University Press, 1994). Halbwachs and Connerton are cited by Neil Harris in his own essay on the changing public memory of the Columbian Exposition, "Memory and the White City," in Harris, Wim de Wit, James Gilbert, and Robert W. Rydell, *Grand Illusions: Chicago's World's Fair of 1893* (Chicago: Chicago Historical Society, 1993), pp. 1–40.

5. Egbert Phelps, "The Fires of History," in *The Lakeside Memorial of the Burning of Chicago*, p. 86.

6. A typical comment: "Never before in the annals of history can such a parallel of destruction be found. The burning of Rome, London, Moscow, New York, Portland, and Paris were undoubtedly appalling, disastrous events; but pale into insignificance before the awful work of devastation which has resulted in the reduction to ashes of Chicago, the city of the world—the spot on which the eyes of all nations of the earth have been fixed with mixed envy and admiration ever since she started into existence." *Chicago Burned. An Authentic, Concise and Graphic Account of the Great Chicago Fire, October 8, 9 & 10, 1871, As seen by Eye Witnesses, together with Startling Heartrending Incidents* (Elkhart, Ind.: John F. Funk and Bro., 1871), p. 4.

7. W. W. Everts, "The Lesson of Disaster," *Chicago Pulpit* 2 (19 October 1872), 160–61. Everts was born in upstate New York in 1814. After a successful career in his native state, he accepted the call to a church in Louisville, which he left for Chicago in 1859 partly because of his pro-northern and antislavery sympathies. He led the First Baptist Church, which, according to Andreas, was in the years before the fire "the largest in membership and had the largest edifice of any Protestant denomination in the West." It was rebuilt after the disaster, then destroyed again in the fire of 1874. Andreas, *History of Chicago*, vol. 2, pp. 434–35.

8. Ross Miller writes: "Chicago was quickly transformed, even before any of the rebuilding began; it became the only American city whose myth of founding and development was absolutely contemporaneous with its modern condition." *American Apocalypse*, p. 12.

9. Colbert and Chamberlin, *Chicago and the Great Conflagration*, p. 278.

10. *New York Tribune* (13 October 1871), p. 2; F. B. Wilkie, "Among the Ruins," in *The Lakeside Memorial of the Burning of Chicago*, p. 51. Wilkie was a local journalist who in 1880 became the first president of the Press Club of Chicago. Cassius Milton Wicker wrote of the devastated landscape: "One is unable to form any idea of where he is—lost among the streets that contain not a house for miles." CHS Fire Narratives. The reflections on the ruins of Chicago repeatedly noted, above all, how total was the destruction of the center of the city, and how physical evidence of the past had been eliminated. Calculating the ruined area as being comparable to half the size of Manhattan, from the Battery to Central Park, or to the whole of the peninsula of Boston, Frederick Law Olmsted was struck by the thoroughness of the devastation. Olmsted, "Chicago in Distress," p. 303. Much more recently, the destruction caused in August of 1992 by Hurricane Andrew evoked a similar sense of disorientation. See "Alien Terrain Replaces What Was Once Home," *New York Times* (31 August 1992), p. 1.

11. Nathaniel Hawthorne, "Preface" to *The Marble Faun; or The Romance of Monte Beni* (Columbus: Ohio State University Press, 1968), p. 3; O. A. Burgess, "The Late Chicago Fire," p. 6.

12. Goodspeed's pen certainly was transported: "Arabia Petra looks upon us from the stone walls of the Post-Office, and the Catacombs of Egypt stare at us from the embrasure-like windows of the Court-House wings. Cleopatra's Needle and the Tower of Babel find duplicates in the water-tower and the smoke-stacks of ruined factories. Tadmor of the desert, with its sandy tumuli, appears on every hand in the crumbling piles of brick and mortar; the walls of ancient Jerusalem arise in the ruins of the great Central and Rock Island depots, and the pillared ruins of Cairo and Alexandria in the roofless front of Honore Block. The puzzler Sphinx is doubly reproduced in the one-time green lions of Ross and Gossage; while the Parthenon, the Acropolis, and the gladiatorial arena of ancient Greece and Rome find their counterpart in the fire-built ruins of last week's palaces." *The Great Fires in Chicago and the West*, pp. 56–57.

13. Sheahan and Upton, like Goodspeed, were unrestrained in their range of associations in their meditation on the ruins: "Here and there the vast bulk of

undestroyed buildings tower up, silent and uninhabited, like the watchtowers which Vathek saw at Istakhar. . . . Here there is no feeling of newness. It might be a page taken from middle age history. . . . It is so dark that one cannot see the ivy on the walls, but one knows that it is there, and if it were not so hackneyed, one would be apt to quote certain lines concerning Melrose Abbey." *The Great Conflagration*, pp. 256–57. Alfred Sewell likened the ruins to "a vast cemetery, in which a race of giants had been buried," adding that on returning home in the evening "we dreamed of walking amid the ruins of Pompeii and Herculaneum, of visiting the ruined Coliseum at Rome, and of starting on a tour to explore the ruins of the ancient cities of the Orient; and on waking next morning, we were for a time in a quandary whether we were in Pompeii, Nineveh, or Chicago." *The Great Calamity!*, pp. 71, 75–76. For several illustrations depicting individuals wandering among the ruins, see Colbert and Chamberlin, *Chicago and the Great Conflagration*, pp. 121, 241, 425, 432.

14. Sheahan and Upton, *The Great Conflagration*, pp. 262–63. Shortly after the fire, one reporter observed, "Photographers, alarmed by the process of speedy construction, are training their cameras upon every unprotected point of picturesque ruins." *New York Tribune* (13 October 1871), p. 2.

15. The library of the Chicago Historical Society contains a file on the Relic House, which includes a pamphlet evidently prepared by one of its owners, titled *The Relic House, 1871–1906. A Landmark of the Chicago Fire*. This curious building's final location was where Clark Street and Lincoln Avenue meet. For a photograph of the Relic House, flanked by foliage and surrounded by a picket fence, see Kirkland's *The Story of Chicago*, vol. 1, p. 334.

16. Sheahan and Upton, *The Great Conflagration*, p. 115; Luzerne, *The Lost City!*, p. 122. Anna Higginson wrote that "hundreds of children were born on the prairies the next few days," while a rambling letter written in pencil from a woman named Amelia to her sister excitedly described the death and ruin, and then continued: "the Doctors say that there was over five hundred births on the open Prairies on Monday and Monday night after the fire." This letter of November 5, like Higginson's of November 10, is in the CHS Fire Narratives.

17. When architect William Le Baron Jenney, who would become well known as one of the pioneers of the skyscraper revolution, was asked to design a fire monument, he first proposed a tower of salvaged relics, which was rejected by the city for not being dignified enough. His second proposal was a more conventional Gothic structure supporting a female figure holding a flaming torch, designed to celebrate what the *Tribune* called "the triumph of energy and enterprise, an example worthy of emulation to the end of time." Although a cornerstone was laid with great ceremony on October 30, 1872, the funds necessary to finish this project were never raised, and the partially completed monument was removed from its site in Garfield (originally Central) Park in the West Division. Miller, *American Apocalypse*, pp. 146–49; Pierce, *A History of Chicago*, vol. 2, p. 18.

18. Pierce, *A History of Chicago*, vol. 3, pp. 18–19, 475; Miller, *American Apocalypse*, pp. 23, 91–92. Helen Horowitz contends that the Inter-State Industrial Exposition was of great importance in the development of cultural institutions in Chicago because of its involvement of the business elite in such

enterprises and its increasing devotion of exhibition space in succeeding years to natural history and fine arts. She also states that the success of the building as a setting for concerts and opera inspired the most successful architectural marriage of culture and commerce in Chicago, the Auditorium Building. See *Culture and the City,* pp. 37–40. Fairbank served as chair of the Relief and Aid Society's Committee on Employment, while Avery was co-chair with Turlington W. Harvey of the Committee on Shelter.

19. On the fifteenth anniversary of the fire, a few months after the Haymarket bombing, a *Daily News* reported claimed to have found Mrs. O'Leary living on 50th Street near Halsted, where she refused to be interviewed. The euphemistic diction he employed tried to combine humor with an air of his and his readers' superiority over this living relic of a primitive Chicago essentially gone and forgotten: "The house has no front door, in lieu of glass clothing is stuffed into two or three windows, and long before a stranger reaches the place the pungent odor of distillery swill and the effluvium of cows proclaim that old habits are strong with Mrs. O'Leary and that she is still in the milk business." *Chicago Daily News* (8 October 1886), p. 2.

20. A copy of the poster is in the Prints and Photographs Department of the Chicago Historical Society.

21. *Nation* 13 (12 October 1871), p. 233. *The Ruined City* (p. 24) reached the same kinds of conclusions in its section on the effect of the fire on Wall Street: "One of the most instructive lessons of modern civilization is that no part of the world can suffer without entailing a greater or less degree of loss and ruin upon the remainder."

22. Some of this new calculus of modernity was implicit in the sudden reversals faced by the citizens of Chicago in the fire, which, as Frank Luzerne, with his irrepressible penchant for Gothic melodrama, put it, "in the silent watches of the night . . . brings death to their loved ones, poverty to their millionaires, dire want to all their people. The rich man of to-day is to-morrow a beggar; the happy wife and mother, widowed, childless, insane; husbands bereft, and lovers separated by the pathless ocean of death. Everything gone at one fell stroke, even before the fact of the destruction can be realized, and nothing left but the evidences of utter ruin!" Luzerne, *The Lost City!,* p. 20.

23. Luzerne, *The Lost City!,* pp. 18–19; *Chicago Times,* quoted in Andreas, *History of Chicago,* vol. 2, p. 718; *New York Sun,* quoted in *The Ruined City,* pp. 48–49.

CHAPTER SIX

1. Christine Meisner Rosen, *The Limits of Power: Great Fires and the Process of City Growth in America* (New York: Cambridge University Press, 1986), p. 140; "The Effect of Fire Upon Real Estate," in *Lakeside Monthly* 8 (October 1872), 261. On post-fire Chicago, see also Carl W. Condit, *The Chicago School of Architecture: A History of Commercial and Public Building in the Chicago Area, 1875–1925* (Chicago: University of Chicago Press, 1964), pp. 14–25; Homer Hoyt, *One Hundred Years of Land Values in Chicago: The Relationship of the Growth of Chicago to the Rise in Its Land Values, 1833–1933* (Chicago: University of Chicago Press, 1933), pp. 101–16; Mayer and Wade, *Chicago: Growth of a Me-*

tropolis, pp. 117–28; Pierce, *A History of Chicago,* vol. 3, pp. 17–19; and Richard Warren Shepro, "The Reconstruction of Chicago After the Great Fire of 1871" (Harvard College Senior Thesis, 1975). Daniel Bluestone offers a very informative discussion of the movement of churches away from the center of downtown as part of a new differentiation of business and residential real estate in Chicago. See *Constructing Chicago,* Chapter 3, "'A Parallel Moral Power': Churches, 1830–1895," pp. 62–103.

    2. On Medill's term in office, see David L. Protess, "Joseph Medill: Chicago's First Modern Mayor," in Paul M. Green and Melvin G. Holli, eds., *The Mayors: The Chicago Political Tradition* (Carbondale: Southern Illinois University Press, 1987), pp. 1–15.

    3. *Chicago Tribune* (16 January 1872), p. 1; Karen L. Sawislak, "Smoldering City," *Chicago History* 17 (Fall and Winter, 1988–89), 88; Rosen, *The Limits of Power,* pp. 100–103. The effectiveness of the regulations was undermined by the fact that much construction, including the wooden shelter houses built with Relief and Aid Society backing, had been completed already, and because the regulations were not enforced. In the days before the Common Council met to discuss fire limits, the *Tribune* maintained that the rapid rebuilding with wood was disgraceful (making Chicago seem like "a rude village on the frontiers of civilization") as well as dangerous, discouraging those who wanted to erect sound and attractive buildings. *Chicago Tribune* (7 January 1872), p. 4; (15 January 1872), p. 4. Sawislak's article, which has the same title as her dissertation, will subsequently be referred to as "Smoldering City" *CH.*

    The changes that were made in the building code to prevent fire were defeated by the public opposition, and it was not until a fire in July of 1874 that destroyed about sixty acres of prime downtown real estate south and west of Van Buren Street and Michigan Avenue led insurance companies to refuse coverage that the city moved to extend the fire limits to all of Chicago and take measures that included the purchase of new equipment, the improvement of the fire department, the implementation of fire inspections, and other safety measures. Pierce, *A History of Chicago,* vol. 3, pp. 308–9.

    4. Sawislak, "Smoldering City" *CH,* p. 93.

    5. The temperance enforcement effort reminded Flinn and others of the mayoral election in 1855, in which the victor was Know-Nothing candidate Levi D. Boone, for whom temperance reform had an explicitly anti-immigrant agenda. Boone's administration witnessed the so-called Lager Beer riots, which causes at least one death and several injuries and arrests before the city was put under virtual martial law. Sawislak, "Smoldering City" *CH,* pp. 93–98; Flinn, *History of the Chicago Police,* pp. 137–41, 156–57; Pierce, *A History of Chicago,* vol. 2, pp. 437–39; Perry R. Duis, *The Saloon: Public Drinking in Chicago and Boston, 1880–1920* (Urbana: University of Illinois Press, 1983), pp. 80–81. Medill, exhausted and frustrated by all the conflicts, resigned his office before completing his two-year term.

    6. Pierce, *A History of Chicago,* vol. 3, pp. 345, 240–42; Sawislak, "Smoldering City" *CH,* p. 101; *Chicago Tribune* (22 December 1873–6 January 1874). In his favorable account of the Relief and Aid Society in which he maintains that it "responded magnificently" to the fire, Otto M. Nelson admits that by 1873,

"The absence of new income perhaps inclined the society to be overcautious in dispensing its reserve," and open to the charge of imperiousness, overconfidence, and complacency. "The Chicago Relief and Aid Society," p. 66.

7. Louis H. Sullivan, *The Autobiography of an Idea* (New York: Dover Publications, 1956 [1924]), pp. 195-97.

8. Lucy E. Parsons, *Life of Albert R. Parsons with Brief History of the Labor Movement in America*, 2d. ed. (Chicago: Mrs. Lucy E. Parsons, 1903 [1889]), pp. 14-16; Paul Avrich, *The Haymarket Tragedy* (Princeton: Princeton University Press, 1984), pp. 13-14, 18-19. Avrich's outstanding book is the leading history of Haymarket, succeeding Henry David's *The History of the Haymarket Affair: A Study in the American Social-Revolutionary and Labor Movements* (New York: Farrar and Rinehart, 1936). On Lucy Parsons's extraordinarily long and difficult life, see Carolyn Ashbaugh, *Lucy Parsons: American Revolutionary* (Chicago: C. H. Kerr, 1976).

9. Pierce, *A History of Chicago*, vol. 3, p. 243; Avrich, *The Haymarket Tragedy*, pp. 17-18.

10. *Chicago Tribune* (25-26 July 1877); Avrich, *The Haymarket Tragedy*, pp. 28-33; Flinn, *History of the Chicago Police*, p. 185; Pierce, *A History of Chicago*, vol. 3, p. 250; Pinkerton, *Strikers, Communists, Tramps and Detectives* (New York: Arno Press and The New York Times, 1969), p. 396 (originally published in 1878 in New York by G. W. Carleton). Pinkerton was the author of several books that glorified his own career while chronicling his times.

11. The most comprehensive history of the railroad strikes is Robert V. Bruce, *1877: Year of Violence* (Indianapolis: Bobbs-Merrill, 1959). For more details on events in Chicago, see Pierce, *A History of Chicago*, vol. 3, pp. 244-53; Avrich, *The Haymarket Tragedy*, pp. 26-38; Floyd Dell, "Socialism and Anarchism in Chicago," in vol. 2 of J. Seymour Currey's *Chicago: Its History and Its Builders* (Chicago: S. J. Clarke, 1912), pp. 371-78; and Flinn, *History of the Chicago Police*, pp. 158-201. It is hard to find authoritative casualty figures or agreement on certain details of the 1877 strikes in Chicago, though the death toll in the city was probably as high as fifty, with dozens more injured. Flinn, who includes a double-page drawing of the melee between police and furniture workers, claims that the workers provoked the police. The raid prompted a successful suit by the workers that resulted in the condemnation of the police and the reaffirmation of the right of the union to peaceful assembly.

12. Thomas A. Scott, "The Recent Strikes," *North American Review* 125 (1877), 351-52; Bruce, *1877*, p. 225; Pinkerton, *Strikers, Communists, Tramps and Detectives*, p. 67. Pinkerton also included an illustration of the raid on the furniture workers (p. 398). The *Tribune* was more explicitly anti-Irish, calling one of the mobs "the worst scum of Bridgeport" (26 July 1877, p. 1). Flinn blamed the strike-related violence in Chicago in 1877 on "communists, socialists, vagrants, loafers, thugs, thieves and criminals in general." He maintained that early in the week, when the railroad strike first hit Chicago and before it was aggressively suppressed, "The communists were in their second heaven, the *canaille* was at the very summit of its glory. Chicago was apparently as completely in the hands of the revolutionary element as Paris ever had been." *History of the Chicago Police*, pp. 161, 163.

13. Scott, "The Recent Strikes," p. 357.

14. *Chicago Tribune* (26 July 1877), p. 3; Flinn, *History of the Chicago Police*, pp. 161, 179–83; Pierce, *A History of Chicago*, vol. 3, p. 252; Avrich, *The Haymarket Tragedy*, p. 35; Dell, "Socialism and Anarchism in Chicago," p. 377. On the relation between the strikes of 1877 and the building of urban armories, see Robert M. Fogelson, *America's Armories: Architecture, Society, and Public Order* (Cambridge, Mass.: Harvard University Press, 1989), especially pp. 52–53, 60–61. Collyer left Unity Church and Chicago in 1879 to become pastor of the Church of the Messiah in New York.

15. Pinkerton, *Strikers, Communists, Tramps and Detectives*, pp. 388–89.

16. Parsons, *Life of Albert R. Parsons*, pp. 17–21; Avrich, *The Haymarket Tragedy*, pp. 31–32.

17. Scott, "The Recent Strikes," p. 357. Scott's version of American history was conveniently flawed, since organized mobs had long been influential in American politics, including some "mobs," like the one that staged the Boston Tea Party, of which he might have approved. For an insightful discussion of American exceptionalist thinking in this period, including specifically its anti-urban dimensions, see Richard Slotkin, *The Fatal Environment: The Myth of the Frontier in the Age of Industrialization, 1800–1890* (New York: Atheneum, 1980), pp. 33–39.

18. Shelton Stromquist, *A Generation of Boomers: The Pattern of Railroad Labor Conflict in Nineteenth-Century America* (Urbana: University of Illinois Press, 1987), p. 24; David Montgomery, "Strikes in Nineteenth-Century America," *Social Science History* 4 (1980), 95. Montgomery argues that the backdrop of the Civil War and Reconstruction (which included the Chicago fire) infused the draft riots of 1863 and the railroad strikes of 1877 with their insurrectionary quality. He sees the draft riots and the railroad strikes, along with the eight-hour movement of the 1860s and 1870s as "parts of a continuous, largely unsuccessful, effort by American workers to intervene on their own behalf in the reshaping of national social and political life in a period when no ideological consensus legitimized the state" (97). While the angry mobs in Chicago in 1877 included working men and their families, it is misleading to see the rioting and vandalism as organized by unions, which, the criticism of business leaders notwithstanding, counseled discipline and restraint.

19. Parsons, *Life of Albert R. Parsons*, p. 21.

20. Montgomery, "Strikes in Nineteenth-Century America," p. 98.

21. A crucial episode in the alienation of many Chicago radicals (including Parsons, who through the 1870s had run unsuccessfully for alderman, county clerk, and congressman), was the protracted lawsuit required to seat socialist Frank Stauber after he was reelected alderman in 1880.

22. As Avrich explains, the linking of anarchism and revolutionary unionism became known as the "Chicago idea." *The Haymarket Tragedy*, p. 73.

23. As Bruce C. Nelson explains very well in *Beyond the Martyrs*, the rise of anarchism in the United States was a significant chapter in American immigrant and working-class history of the late nineteenth century, part of a national and international movement with important cultural as well as political dimen-

sions. See also his essay "Anarchism: The Movement Behind the Martyrs," *Chicago History* 15 (Summer 1986), 4–19; the discussion of anarchism in Avrich, *The Haymarket Tragedy*, pp. 55–177; and the many remarkable entries in *Haymarket Scrapbook*, ed. Dave Roediger and Franklin Rosemont (Chicago: Charles H. Kerr, 1986). In "The Knights of Labor in the Chicago Labor Movement and in Municipal Politics, 1877–1887" (Ph.D diss., Northern Illinois University, 1984), Richard Schneirov examines the relationship between the anarchists and the Knights.

24. *Chicago Tribune* (23 March 1879), p. 7; Avrich, *The Haymarket Tragedy*, pp. 43–46. The *Tribune*'s desire to characterize the rally as consisting of the worst of the foreign elements in the city was obvious: "Skim the purlieus of the Fifth Ward; drain the Bohemian Socialistic slums of the Sixth and Seventh wards; scour the Scandinavian dives of the Tenth and Fourteenth wards; cull the choicest thieves from Halsted, Desplaines, Pacific avenue, and Clark street; pick out from Fourth avenue, Jackson street, Clark street, State street, and other noted haunts, the worst specimens of female depravity; scatter in all the red-headed, cross-eyed, and frowsy servant-girls in the three divisions of the city, and bunch all these together, and you have a pretty good idea of the crowd that made up last night's gathering." This account went on, "That portion of the nationalities represented who are law-abiding citizens have too much decency and good breeding to be classed as carrying the same blood."

25. The fears that their homes might be attacked was nothing new among America's urban elite. Richard Bushman quotes an 1855 passage from George Templeton Strong's diary telling how "after demagogues harangued unemployed New York workmen," there were rumors that a socialist mob was sacking the Schiff mansion, where a ball attended by the city's "aristocracy" was taking place. *The Refinement of America*, p. 366.

26. Bartholdi's well-publicized statue had been assembled in Paris in 1884, disassembled and shipped to New York in 1885 for reassembly, and formally unveiled on Bedloe's Island in 1886.

27. *Alarm* (29 November 1884), p. 1; (2 May 1885), p. 1; *Chicago Tribune* (28–30 April 1885); Avrich, *The Haymarket Tragedy*, pp. 143–149.

28. Philip S. Foner, ed., *The Autobiographies of the Haymarket Martyrs* (New York: Humanities Press, 1969), p. 43. As Foner explains, these autobiographies were prepared and published in the weekly journal *Knights of Labor* after the guilty verdict. Plans to assemble them into a book went unfulfilled until Foner's edition.

29. Lucy E. Parsons, "A Word to Tramps," *Alarm* (4 October 1884), p. 1; *Abstract of Record. August Spies et al., plaintiffs, vs. the People of the State of Illinois, Defendants*, vol. 1 (Chicago: Barnard and Gunthorp, 1887), pp. 156–57. Parsons made similar statements in her public speeches. See Avrich, pp. 91, 135, 275. The *Abstract of Record*, which includes a second volume as well, is a printed transcript of the Haymarket trial that was prepared for the appeal of the verdict. Another transcript is "The Trial of the Chicago Anarchists: August Spies, Michael Schwab, Samuel Fielden, Albert R. Parsons, Adolph Fischer, George Engel, and Oscar Neebe for Conspiracy and Murder. Chicago, Illinois.

1886," in John D. Lawson, ed., *American State Trials,* vol. 12 (St. Louis: F. H. Thomas Law Book Company, 1919), pp. 1–319. A typescript record is in the Archives and Manuscripts Department of the Chicago Historical Society.

30. *Alarm* (15 November 1884), p. 1.

31. *Alarm* (15 November 1884), p. 1. When Sheridan had moved to Washington to succeed William Tecumseh Sherman as head of the army in November of 1883, a group of thirty-one grateful Chicago businessmen—including Anson Stager, Marshall Field, Philip D. Armour, Joseph Medill, Potter Palmer, and George Pullman—who had been through the "battles" of 1871 and 1877 with him, contributed over forty thousand dollars to a fund with which Sheridan purchased his home in the national capital. Until his death in 1888, Sheridan experienced a politically difficult command, but one of his accomplishments was to move troops from now unneeded former frontier encampments to posts near the nation's troubled cities. Hutton, *Phil Sheridan and His Army,* pp. 346–51.

32. *Alarm* (18 April 1885), p. 1. Dynamite, Parsons further explained at the trial, had the same leveling effect as did the introduction of gunpowder, which he described as "a democratic instrument" and "republican institution" that "immediately began to equalize and bring about an equilibrium of power." He continued his civics lesson, "So today dynamite comes as the emancipator of man from the domination and enslavement of his fellow-man. . . . Dynamite is the diffusion of power. It is democratic; it makes everybody equal." "The Pinkertons, the police, the militia," Parsons warned his personal demons, "are absolutely worthless in the presence of dynamite." His faith in this explosive, conveyed in these statements that had a ranting quality, bordered on the mystical: dynamite was "the disseminator of power. It is the downfall of oppression. It is the abolition of authority; it is the dawn of peace; it is the end of war, because war cannot exist unless there is somebody to make war upon, and dynamite makes that unsafe, undesirable, and absolutely impossible." [Spies et al.], *The Accused and the Accusers. The Famous Speeches of the Eight Chicago Anarchists in Court* (Chicago: Socialistic Publishing Society, n.d.), pp. 119–20. This booklet of transcripts of the convicted men's speeches before sentencing of October 7–9 was published in various versions to help publicize their cause and raise money for their continuing defense.

33. Dell, "Socialism and Anarchism in Chicago," pp. 391–92. See also Avrich, *The Haymarket Tragedy,* Chapter 12, "Cult of Dynamite," pp. 160–77.

34. There are many critical accounts of Bonfield's actions in discussions of Chicago in the period. The most outstanding defense appeared, not surprisingly, in Flinn's *History of the Chicago Police,* pp. 234–49, 338–47. Bonfield, who turned fifty in 1886, was born in New Brunswick and lived briefly in Buffalo, settling in Chicago with his family in 1844. He worked in a packinghouse and a glue factory and was a locomotive engineer for ten years before trying his hand unsuccessfully in his own businesses. He joined the police force in 1878 and rose very rapidly through the ranks.

35. Abbott (1835–1922) had left a successful New York legal practice in 1859 to become a Congregationalist minister and in 1881 had succeeded Henry Ward Beecher as editor of the *Christian Century,* which was renamed *The Out-*

look in 1893. In 1887 he followed Beecher as minister of the Plymouth Congregational Church in Brooklyn.

36. Having said all this, Abbott still found cause for faith in evangelical Christianity and the democratic process as means for making conditions better. "Repression is not the remedy," he contended, in direct rebuttal to much popular opinion, "We cannot suppress this growing discontent; we must remove its cause." And the way to do this was to give the laborer a greater stake in the social order through the meaningful exercise of the ballot and the establishment of cooperative corporations in which he had a stake, which would be "the first step toward the redemption of labor from the oppression of capital." Other reforms he suggested included the expansion of government services into new areas of health, housing, and education, and state ownership of major transportation and communication systems. Lyman Abbott, "Danger Ahead," *Century Magazine* 31 (1885-86), 51-59.

37. Newspapers were full of talk about the need to "preserve the peace and restore the supremacy of law," as the *St. Louis Globe-Democrat* put it in early April. The same day the *Louisville Courier-Journal* warned of "imminent peril which cannot be averted by tampering any longer with that lawless element which has assumed to act for labor." *St. Louis Globe-Democrat* and *Louisville Courier-Journal*, cited in *Public Opinion* 1 (1886), p. 7.

38. *Chicago Daily News* (30 April 1886) p. 1; *Chicago Tribune* (2 May 1886) p. 4. The article from the *Chicago Mail* and others like it are cited in Joseph M. Pasteris, "The Haymarket Riot of 1886: An Analysis of the Popular Press" (M.A. thesis, Northern Illinois University, 1966), p. 25.

39. *Chicago Tribune* (4 May 1886), p. 1.

40. Texts of both Spies's circular and of the call to the Haymarket meeting have been reproduced in several accounts of the event. For reproductions of both, see illustrations 11 and 12 (following p. 278) in Avrich, *The Haymarket Tragedy.*

41. *Chicago Tribune* (5 May 1886), p. 2. Harrison offered his opinion of the rally in his testimony at the Haymarket trial. See *Abstract of Record,* vol. 2, p. 175.

42. Grinnell (1842-98) was from Massena, New York. He arrived in Chicago in 1870 and was elected to his position in 1884. He won election to the Superior Court in 1887, resigning four years later to enter private practice.

43. Schaack was born in Luxembourg in 1843 and emigrated with his family to America in 1853, settling on a farm in Wisconsin. He started work at fifteen in a brewery in Cairo, Illinois, and then moved to Chicago in 1856, finding employment with a private detective force until joining the city department in 1869. He established a reputation for having arrested more notorious criminals than any other officer on the force (Andreas, *History of Chicago,* vol. 3, p. 112), and was promoted to captain in 1885. His book on Haymarket is *Anarchy and Anarchists. A History of the Red Terror and the Social Revolution in America and Europe* (Chicago: F. J. Schulte, 1889).

44. The charge that these men had worked together to set off the bomb was flimsy from the start. Four of the eight who stood trial—Parsons, Spies, Fielden, and Schwab—had actually attended the meeting. Only Spies and

Fielden were there when the bomb went off, while the two defendants who were in on the planning of the rally, George Engel and Adolph Fischer, were never in the Haymarket at all that evening, and two others, Oscar Neebe and Louis Lingg, were neither present nor had any role in organizing the meeting. Parsons, Spies, Fielden, and Schwab knew each other well and were familiar with Neebe. Spies had recently broken with Engel and Fischer, who moved in more radical circles that were more deeply committed to violent action. The most radical of all was Lingg, who at twenty-one was the youngest of the accused. He had arrived in America less than a year earlier, spoke little English, and was hardly known by the American Group.

45. Avrich, *The Haymarket Tragedy*, pp. 250–51; Herman Kogan, "William Perkins Black: Haymarket Lawyer," *Chicago History* 5 (Summer 1976), 85–94. Black (1842–1916) was from Kentucky but grew up in Danville, Illinois. He left Wabash College and training for the ministry to join the 11th Indiana Infantry Zouaves under Lew Wallace, and he later became captain of the 37th Illinois Infantry when he was still eighteen and served for over three years through several major battles, earning "a well-deserved reputation for faithfulness and bravery." After the war he decided to become a lawyer and settled in Chicago for good in 1867. Andreas, *History of Chicago*, vol. 2, p. 203.

46. Andreas, *History of Chicago*, vol. 2, p. 457. Gary (1821–1906) was born in Potsdam, New York, which was located in the same far north section of the state as Grinnell's home town of Massena. He had lived in St. Louis, Las Vegas (New Mexico), and San Francisco before coming to Chicago in 1856. He became judge of the Superior Court of Chicago in 1863, and remained on the bench until his death. Andreas also wrote: "In his court room good humor abounds, for he loves a keen encounter of wit, and is himself a most incorrigible punster." Among his papers in the Archives and Manuscripts of the Chicago Historical Society are a few poems of sentimental devotion and feeling written in his hand on his official stationery.

47. In all the trial lasted sixty-two days, fifty-four in session, of which twenty-one and a half were devoted to jury selection. Of 982 potential jurors called, 758 were excused, while the state used 52 of its 160 peremptory challenges. The prosecution called 111 witnesses, the defense 79. *Chicago Tribune* (21 August 1886), p. 3.

48. Avrich, *The Haymarket Tragedy*, pp. 372–73. Gompers had been particularly upset at the time of the riot that his young union's eight-hour campaign was halted by this act of violence, and he did not speak out during the trial. For his reaction to the bombing and his participation in the clemency campaign, see Gompers, *Seventy Years of Life and Labor*, ed. Matthew Woll (New York: E. P. Dutton, 1925), vol. 1, pp. 293–94; vol. 2, pp. 178–81.

49. *New York Tribune* (6 May 1886), p. 4; *Frank Leslie's Illustrated Newspaper* 65 (12 November 1887), 194; *Nation* 45 (10 November 1887), 366.

50. Russell, "The Haymarket and Afterwards: Some Personal Recollections," *Appleton's Magazine* 10 (October 1907), 410–11; *Chicago Tribune* (November 12, 1887), p. 1; Avrich, *The Haymarket Tragedy*, pp. 381–83. There is some slim evidence that a few anarchist sympathizers were willing to make a desperate attempt to free their comrades but that the condemned men rejected

this plan, believing that any new violence would only hurt the cause. Avrich (pp. 384–85) credits the memoirs and letters of anarchists William Holmes, Robert Reitzel, and Dyer Lum in this. These individuals could only gain by claiming, truthfully or not, that they could have mounted a bold escape but that, in Holmes's words, the city had ironically been saved by the "forbearance and mercy" of those on whom it had inflicted "persecution, treachery, imprisonment, torture, and murder."

51. *Chicago Tribune* (12 November 1887). There were numerous accounts of the executions, and these varied slightly in detail. For a description of the funeral, see Avrich, *The Haymarket Tragedy*, pp. 394–98.

52. Thure de Thulstrup (1848–1930) was a Swedish-born illustrator and painter who studied in Paris before emigrating to America in the mid-1870s. He specialized in military history, but his illustrations for the *New York Daily Graphic*, *Leslie's*, and especially *Harper's Weekly* (where he was on the staff for twenty years) included the inaugurations of four presidents and Grant's funeral. He also did several scenes of the Columbian Exposition and later became well known for his paintings of American colonial life. See Peter Hastings Falk, ed., *Who Was Who in American Art* (Madison, Conn.: Sound View Press, 1985), p. 162. The Haymarket drawing was based on sketches and photographs by H. Jeanneret.

53. Avrich, *The Haymarket Tragedy*, p. 223.

CHAPTER SEVEN

1. Joseph E. Gary, "The Chicago Anarchists of 1886," *Century Magazine* 45 (April 1893), 804. There is plenty of evidence that many other people at the time were well aware of the dramatic quality of Haymarket and the extent to which it engaged the public imagination. While the trial was still on, a theater manager in Chicago wrote to Judge Gary proposing to hang each of the condemned anarchists on his stage, one a night, and a roadshow offered several thousand dollars for one of the defendants' bodies in the hope of putting it on display around the country. Visiting Chicago with his new bride in October of 1887, President Cleveland reviewed a grand procession celebrating Louis Sullivan's greatest triumph in Chicago, the Auditorium Building, but he made a special request to see the spot where the Haymarket bomb was thrown. Mayor John Roche ushered him personally to the scene. The *Chicago Tribune* that appeared the morning of the executions described the mob surrounding the prison: "The women, who were in the majority, perhaps, were as a rule in high spirits and looked upon the impending tragedy as a sort of Barnum's moral show." Avrich, *The Haymarket Tragedy*, pp. 261, 377, 315; *Harper's Weekly* 31 (15 October 1887), pp. 743, 756; *Chicago Tribune* (11 November 1887), p. 7; Russell, "The Haymarket and Afterwards," pp. 400, 410, 411.

2. *The Accused and the Accusers*, p. 101; Schaack, *Anarchy and Anarchists*, p. 312.

3. Memoirs of the trial noted the effectiveness of such "silent witnesses," Frederick Trevor Hill speculating that they did far more to convict the accused than the testimony of the state's witnesses. During the final arguments, Hill noted, the state's exhibits "again spoke louder than any words." As the prosecu-

tion summed up the case, on a table "lay bombs of all descriptions, fulminating caps, shells, melting-ladles, and other tools of the dynamiter's trade, and in plain sight of the jury were the red banner and flags of the terrorists blazing with mottoes urging defiance of the law." In his book, Schaack devoted several of his illustrations to this evidence, including four pages of what he called "Banners of the Social Revolution," on which were inscribed such inflammatory declarations as "Every government is a conspiracy against the people," and "Workingmen, arm yourselves." Hill, "Decisive Battles of the Law," *Harper's Monthly Magazine* 114 (May 1907), 895, 896, 898; Schaack, *Anarchy and Anarchists*, pp. 69, 85, 91, 109.

4. *Chicago Tribune* (21 August 1886), p. 1; Gen. M. M. Trumbull, *The Trial of the Judgment. A Review of the Anarchist Case* (Chicago: Health and Home Publishing Company, 1888), p. 18; Trumbull, *Was It a Fair Trial? An Appeal to the Governor of Illinois by Gen. M. M. Trumbull, in Behalf of the Condemned Anarchists* (Chicago[?], 1887 [?]), p. 9. See also Leon Lewis's two pamphlets, *The Facts Concerning the Eight Condemned Leaders*, and *The Ides of November. An Appeal for the Seven Condemned Leaders and a Protest Against Their Judicial Assassination*, both published by Lewis in Greenport, New York, in 1887.

5. Sigmund Zeisler, an attorney for the Central Labor Union of Chicago and at twenty-six the youngest member of the anarchists' defense team, recalled that Black had "a strongly developed dramatic instinct," and that "he pictured to us in glowing colors the electrical effect which Parsons' sudden appearance would create in the courtroom and outside." After Grinnell upstaged him by interrupting to call for Parsons's arrest, Black responded, "This man is in my charge, and such a demand is not only theatrical claptrap, but an insult to me!" Avrich, *The Haymarket Tragedy*, pp. 276, 258–59; Hill, "Decisive Battles of the Law," p. 892; Sigmund Zeisler, *Reminiscences of the Anarchist Case* (Chicago: The Chicago Literary Club, 1927), p. 20. Once they established contact with Parsons, the anarchists' defense team debated among themselves whether he should surrender. According to Zeisler, Black "expressed his conviction that the presumption of guilt which had taken possession of the public mind would instantly change to a presumption of innocence, the benefit of which would extend to the other defendants; that as regards Parsons, it was, under the circumstances, unthinkable that the jury should find him guilty of murder."

6. *The Accused and the Accusers*, p. 42. These speeches varied widely in tone as well as length. Parsons in particular attempted to manage the courtroom drama within the restrictions forced upon him. He carefully groomed his mustache and dyed his hair to cover the fact that he was graying. He was given to flourishes and gestures, such as waving his red handkerchief to the crowds and pantomiming his own hanging after the verdict was announced. His supporters later proudly cited an article from the *Chicago Times* describing the effectiveness of his manner as he spoke in his own defense in July: "He pulled out of his pocket a bundle of notes, and began at the jury in tones which tokened that the speaker was primed for the finest speech of his life. Luckily for him the witness-chair was a swinging one. He held his notes in his left hand, and, together with the swaying of his body, gesticulated with his right arm. From low, measured

tones he went on from eloquence to oratory, and from oratory to logic, and from logic to argument." *Chicago Tribune* (21 August 1886), p. 1; *Chicago Times* (10 August 1886), cited in *The Haymarket Speeches as Delivered on the Evening of the Throwing of the Bomb, at Haymarket Square, Chicago, May 4, 1886, by August Spies and Albert R. Parsons* (Chicago: Chicago Labor Press Association, 1886), p. 2. The *Tribune* said similarly of Spies's performance in court that "his voice is agreeable and his slight accent is rather pleasant than otherwise, reminding one in some inexplicable way of the exquisit [*sic*] tones and charming accent of Modjeska, the titled Polish actress." *Chicago Tribune* (8 October 1886), p. 1.

7. George N. McLean, *The Rise and Fall of Anarchy in America* (Chicago: R. G. Badoux, 1890), p. 232. On the top are smaller insets showing the courthouse and prison. The reporting at the time of the executions was permeated with the language of the theater and of melodramatic fiction. The *Police Gazette* devised a special cover for its issue on the executions and what it called, in a typical description, "Chicago's tragedy of bombs and blood." Set diagonally across the masthead were the words, "The Last Act!" Below this was a drawing featuring a jailer adjusting the rope around Spies's neck as the other condemned men, already noosed and hooded, stand ghostlike in the background. The caption reads, "Ring down the Curtain." The *New Orleans Times-Democrat* responded to the verdict with one of the longest extensions of the theatrical metaphor. The fact that the executions were yet to take place indicates clearly how they were scripted in advance in the public imagination: "All the chapters in that dramatic and horrible Haymarket tragedy have been written save one; all the acts finished but the last. It was a drama attended by saturnalian lights and scenes. Act I represented the conspirators gathered in the ill-lighted gloom of their secret halls, under the folds of blood-red banners and among heaps of deadly bombs. Act II showed a wild mob turned loose on the streets, with murder in their flaming eyes, and the terrible weapons of assassins in their hands, or dead and wounded men lying amid the smoke of exploded bombs. Act III represents Justice standing as a Nemesis before a group of cowering criminals. Now there is a short *entre acte*. When the curtain rolls up again, with a nation as spectators, to show the final tableau in Act IV, it will disclose a row of gibbeted felons, with haltered throats and fettered hands and feet, swinging slowly to and fro in the air; then it will be rung down again, and the people will breathe freer, feeling that anarchism, nihilism, socialism, communism are forever dead in America." Four years after the hangings, socialist John Henry Mackay devoted three pages to a conceit describing Haymarket as an epic tragedy in three acts. The first begins with "[t]he trembling of the earth which presages the outbreak of the volcano" and both sides gathering for the conflict. It ends with the throwing of the bomb, as "the mad dance of the passions rushes past." The second act is "the quiet, hidden, but far more terrible struggle in the 'domain of the law,'" which ends with the executions. The third is prescriptive, an "unexpected epilogue" in which the masses rise up against their oppressors in an apocalyptic conflict without mercy, after which they uncover the graves of the martyrs and tell them, "You are avenged. Sleep in Peace." *National Police Gazette* 51 (26 November 1887); *New Orleans Times-Democrat* (21 August 1886),

cited in *Public Opinion* 1 (1886), 381; John Henry Mackay, *The Anarchists. A Picture of Civilization at the Close of the Nineteenth Century,* translated from the German by George Schumm (Boston: Benj. R. Tucker, 1891), pp. 223–25.

8. Louis P. Masur points out that the 1830s witnessed the movement from public to private executions. He attributes this, as well as the invention of the penitentiary and related penal reforms, to "a middle-class culture that dreaded vice, craved order, advocated self-control, and valued social privacy." He also sees this movement as related to fears about the instability and excitability of the urban population. "In principle," he writes, "private executions were supposed to protect the sensibilities of all citizens, eliminate a scene of public chaos and confusion, and permit the prisoner to die quietly penitent; in practice, they became a theatrical event for an assembly of elite men who attended the execution by invitation while the community at large was excluded." *Rites of Execution: Capital Punishment and the Transformation of American Culture, 1776–1885* (New York: Oxford University Press, 1989), pp. 8, 111. See also all of Chapter 5, "The Origins of Private Executions in America," pp. 93–116. Masur states that by the middle of the nineteenth century, the earlier organized opposition to the death penalty had stalled. Even at a time of other well-publicized executions, however, the Haymarket hangings had an extra public interest and spectacular quality all their own.

9. The *Alarm* and other anarchist publications were forced to suspend operations following the bombing. The paper, under the editorship of Dyer Lum, made an appeal for contributions in October of 1886, but it did not resume publication until the issue of November 5, 1887, six days before the execution.

10. Dexter described the association as "the bulwark of a conservative element" which Gary represented. "How needful is this bulwark at the present time I need not say," Dexter continued, "with the deep unrest that exists about us. When men armed with destructive theories seek their enforcement, which would speedily make for us an earthly hell, other professions will expostulate, but the law—and I say it with Judge Gary sitting in our midst—will hang!" Harry Barnard, *"Eagle Forgotten": The Life of John Peter Altgeld* (Indianapolis: Bobbs-Merrill, 1938), p. 193. Schaack claimed that between early May of 1886 and November 20, 1887, he received 253 reports from his operatives. Schaack, *Anarchy and Anarchists,* p. 206. Grinnell reportedly told the police, "Make the raids first and look up the law afterward!" Some of the funds were intended for the families of the dead and injured policemen, though the anarchists charged that they were also used to suborn perjured testimony. Avrich adds that these contributions continued until 1891. *Haymarket Tragedy,* pp. 221, 223.

11. Aveling, *An American Journey* (New York: John W. Lowell, 1887 [?]), p. 126. Aveling, who called the paper's coverage "indecent, undignified, and panic-stricken," was accompanied on his tour by his wife, Eleanor, the daughter of Karl Marx. In its edition of May 16, more than a week before even the indictment was in, the *Tribune* laid out the inevitable sequence in a four-part cartoon it called "The History of Anarchy in Chicago." The first panel, titled "PAST," was a scene of rabble-rousing. The second, "PRESENT," showed the anarchists in jail. The third, "FUTURE," was set on a gallows, while the fourth, "THE END," showed four fresh graves on whose headstones were the

initials of Schwab, Fielden, Parsons, and Spies. *Chicago Tribune* (16 May 1886), p. 9. The day after its issue on the executions, the paper congratulated itself for its reporting and distribution of the story, which it described as "one of the most complete and remarkable accomplishments in American journalism." Its press run of 103,802 papers, forty thousand of which went out in the "lightning mail" train at 2 A.M., was "the largest morning edition of any newspaper ever issued in Chicago," one "that should be secured and laid away by every person, not only for his own reference, but for the perusal of his grandchildren." *Chicago Tribune* (13 November 1887), p. 4.

The influence of local journalists evidently was even greater than Aveling charged, so that the shape of belief expressed in the papers before the bombing became the shape of action after. In his memoirs, Melville Stone, who ran the *Daily News*, claimed that following the bombing it was he who suggested to Grinnell the conspiracy argument that proved to be the foundation of the subsequent conviction of the anarchists. Stone recalled that he "at once took the ground" that the state's inability to name the bomb-thrower was "of no consequence." Since the anarchists "had advocated over and over again the use of violence against the police and had urged the manufacture and throwing of bombs, their culpability was clear." For Stone's version of his role, and the far different view of it in the anarchist literature, see Melville E. Stone, *Fifty Years a Journalist* (New York: Greenwood Press, 1968; originally published 1915), pp. 17–77; and *Life of Albert R. Parsons*, p. 230. Both versions are suspect.But there is little doubt of the centrality of the press's role in Haymarket and of the influence of Stone and the *Daily News* in particular. While he was in hiding, Parsons had sent through Stone a letter "to my fellow workers," expressing no regrets and pledging himself to the struggle, which was published in the *Daily News* on May 9. As for Stone, Paul Avrich notes that while "[f]ew men had done more to whip up feeling against the anarchists," he later "was . . . among the most active in the effort to save their lives." Avrich, *The Haymarket Tragedy*, pp. 243, 338.

12. See *Anarchy at an End* (Chicago: G. S. Baldwin, 1886); [F. O. Bennett], *Chicago Anarchists and the Haymarket Massacre* (Chicago: Blakeley Printing Company, 1887); and Paul C. Hull, *The Chicago Riot: A Record of the Terrible Scenes of May 4, 1886* (Chicago: Belford, Clarke, 1886).

13. Schaack's full title is *Anarchy and Anarchists. A History of the Red Terror and the Social Revolution in America and Europe. Communism, Socialism, and Nihilism in Doctrine and in Deed. The Chicago Haymarket Conspiracy, and the Detection and Trial of the Conspirators*. It is likely that Schaack's book was largely the work of journalists Thomas O. Thompson and John T. McEnnis, to whom Schaack credited in his preface "much of the literary form of this volume." Thompson worked for the *Chicago Inter-Ocean* and later the *Times* before serving Carter Harrison for six-and-a-half years as private secretary. He was also president of the Chicago Board of Education and a specialist on law, politics, and economics. Another lengthy pro-prosecution history was George N. McLean's *The Rise and Fall of Anarchy in America* (see n. 7 above).

14. Rev. Frederick A. Noble, D.D., *Christianity and the Red Flag* ([Chicago?], [1886]); *Chicago Tribune* (3 November 1887), p. 2. A Chicago paper car-

ried a summary of a sermon by the Reverend Frank M. Bristol delivered at the Grace Methodist Episcopal Church under the colorful headline, "PULPIT BOMBS." A clipping of this story is in a scrapbook on Haymarket presumably kept by some Chicago police sergeants that is now in the library of the Chicago Historical Society. Lewis F. Wheelock observes that very few ministers were outspoken on the injustices of the trial and that most clergy and religious publications were as nativist and antiradical, if more subdued in their choice of words, as the secular press. The clergy were generally sensitive to the plight of labor but still saw social improvement as resting on temperance, frugality, industry, and piety on the part of the worker, not on reform of the wage system. The urban church, he maintains, was at this time "undergoing a violent and rapid transition from a sectarian frontier orientation stressing individual needs and goals toward a more churchly, urbanized orientation" that emphasized group needs and goals. See "Urban Protestant Reactions to the Chicago Haymarket Affair, 1886-1893," (Ph.D diss., University of Iowa, 1956) p. 191. Henry F. May states that "few church papers balked at salutary bloodshed" as an answer to the bomb, whose "most striking immediate effect, . . . however, was to revive and increase hostility to labor in lay and clerical circles." *Protestant Churches and Industrial America* (New York: Harper and Brothers, 1949), pp. 101-2.

15. H. K. Shacleford, *The Red Flag; or the Anarchists of Chicago* (New York: Frank Tousey, 1886); A. R. Parsons, *Anarchism: Its Philosophy and Scientific Basis, as Defined by Some of Its Apostles* (Chicago: Mrs. A. R. Parsons, 1887), p. 3. Howells was particularly bitter about the importance of the press coverage of the case in sealing the verdict. Two weeks after the executions, he wrote to William Salter of the Chicago Ethical Culture Society, one of the leaders of the clemency movement, "What a squalid and vulgar oligarchy of half-bred scribblers we live under! Somehow their power must be broken." Howard A. Wilson, "William Dean Howells's Unpublished Letters About the Haymarket Affair," *Journal of the Illinois State Historical Society* 56 (1963), 15. On Howells and the Haymarket case, see also Edwin H. Cady, *The Realist at War: The Mature Years, 1885-1920, of William Dean Howells* (Syracuse: Syracuse University Press, 1958), pp. 69-80; and Kenneth S. Lynn, *William Dean Howells: An American Life* (New York: Harcourt Brace Jovanovich, 1970), pp. 88-92. On Whittier's decision, which his biographer Edward Wagenknecht describes as "about the only time he failed to speak out," see Wagenknecht, *John Greenleaf Whittier: A Portrait in Paradox* (New York: Oxford University Press, 1967), pp. 65-66.

16. *Abstract of Record*, vol. 1, p. 32; Lawson, "The Trial of the Haymarket Anarchists," p. 175.

17. *Chicago Tribune* (6 May 1886), p. 4; (6 June 1886), p. 6.

18. Hull, *The Chicago Riot*, pp. 22-27; Shacleford, *The Red Flag*, pp. 7-8; *New York Times* (4 May 1886), p. 1; Samuel P. McConnell, "The Chicago Bomb Case," *Harper's Monthly Magazine* 168 (May 1934), 730. McConnell was thirty-six at the time of the trial, and he had practiced law for fourteen years in Chicago. His father-in-law was one of Gary's colleagues on the bench, and McConnell himself was elected to the Circuit Court in 1889.

19. Halttunen, *Confidence Men and Painted Women*, pp. 14, 24.

20. Schaack, *Anarchy and Anarchists*, pp. 103, 110, 368, 83.

21. Lawson, "The Trial of the Chicago Anarchists," p. 312; Gary, "The Chicago Anarchists of 1886," p. 809.

22. *Louisville Courier-Journal* (10 April 1886); *New York Staats-Zeitung* (6 May 1886). Both are cited in *Public Opinion* 1 (1886), 7, 81. The statement of the Knights dissociating themselves from Haymarket appeared widely.

23. *Harper's Weekly* 30 (15 and 22 May, 1886), 305, 333. Morton Keller includes a selection of Nast's anti-communist illustrations dating from the 1870s in *The Art and Politics of Thomas Nast* (New York: Oxford University Press, 1968), pp. 167–74.

24. Noble, "Christianity and the Red Flag," pp. 2–3.

25. Schaack, *Anarchy and Anarchists*, pp. 26, 287.

26. Schaack, *Anarchy and Anarchists*, p. 125; Gary, "The Chicago Anarchists of 1886," p. 830.

27. In addition to entering into evidence Most's *Science of Revolutionary War*, the prosecution also presented to the court correspondence between the defendants and this most hated of German anarchists. Most had come to the United States in 1882 (where he remained until his death in 1906) after serving several jail terms and being expelled fro his homeland. *Science of Revolutionary War*, published a year before Haymarket, discussed in harrowingly dispassionate detail how the dedicated revolutionist could make and use explosives for the cause. "Most," Paul Avrich writes, "it would be no exaggeration to say, was the most vilified social militant of his time." The treatment of Most in the press, including drawings by Nast and others, expressed attitudes toward radicals generally. He was portrayed as a cunning and dangerous bomb-throwing terrorist, perversely determined to advance his social critique in an America where it did not apply; but he was also characterized as a coward who would run at the first sign of danger. In the weeks following Haymarket the cartoonists made much of an incident in which in the course of a raid New York police supposedly found him hiding under his lover's bed. Avrich, *The Haymarket Tragedy*, p. 61; *Harper's Weekly* 30 (22 and 29 May 1886), 335.

28. McLean, *The Rise and Fall of Anarchy in America*, p. 18.

29. *Chicago Tribune* (6 May 1886), pp. 2, 4; (30 May 1886), p. 4.

30. *New York Tribune* (6 May 1886), p. 4; *New York Times* (5 May 1886), p. 4; *Nation* 42 (13 May 1886), 392; *Pictorial West* 9 (August 1886).

31. The Nast drawing was published in the September 4, 1886, *Harper's Weekly* p. 564. Morton Keller views Nast's response to the Haymarket defendants as tied to his fears of current proposals in favor of soft money and the institution of an income tax, as well as of a "decreasingly untrustworthy political order," all of which particularly offended a sensibility such as Nast's, which was shaped by the Civil War: "The demand for new fiscal or tax policies, the strikes and riots were as one with the seeming decline of the Republican party into office-holding and ideological inconsequence; with the collapse of Radical Reconstruction and the other hopeful ventures of the Radical Republican era. Place-serving politics, Greenbackers and silverites, labor organizers and violent social revolutionaries alike posed threats to the unified social order that the

Civil War supposedly had created. They were a common danger to the triumphant, seamless union of 1865; and had to be resisted with the same determination that secession, that other great threat to unity, to law and order, had been
faced." *The Art and Politics of Thomas Nast,* pp. 244–46.

32. Lawson, "The Trial of the Chicago Anarchists," pp. 312–313. Schaack,
Anarchy and Anarchists, p. 27; McLean, *The Rise and Fall of Anarchy in America*
p. 238.

33. Lawson, "The Trial of the Chicago Anarchists," p. 174; Schaack, *Anarchy and Anarchists,* pp. 385–86.

34. Lucy Parsons depicted the scene of her husband on the gallows, where
he stood "like one transfigured," as a crucifixion and apotheosis: "No tragedian
that has paced a stage in America ever made a more marvelous presentation of a
self-chosen part, perfect in every detail. The upward turn of his eyes, his distant, far-away look and, above all the attitude of apparent complete resignation
that every fold of the awkward shroud only served to make more distinct, was
by far the most striking feature of the entire gallows picture." Lucy E. Parsons,
Life of Albert Parsons, p. 246.

35. Schaack, *Anarchy and Anarchists,* p. 479; Salter, *"What Shall be Done
with the Anarchists?"* (Chicago: Open Court Publishing Company, 1887), p. 12;
Trumbull, *Was It a Fair Trial?,* p. 3. Salter's comments came in a pamphlet that
included the text of a lecture of the same title he delivered in the Grand Opera
House on October 23, along with editorial criticisms from the *Chicago Daily
News* and Salter's reply.

36. *Chicago Daily News* (13 March 1886), cited by Dyer Lum in *A Concise
History of the Great Trial of the Chicago Anarchists in 1886. Condensed from the Official Record* (Chicago: Socialistic Publishing Company, n.d.), p. 190. Lum's
book was the fullest anarchist version of the case. On disagreements among the
lawyers and defendants, see Zeisler, *Reminiscences of the Anarchist Case;* Hill,
"Decisive Battles of the Law."

37. *The Accused and the Accusers,* p. 4.

38. *The Accused and the Accusers,* pp. 173, 177.

39. *The Accused and the Accusers,* pp. 91, 12, 11.

40. *The Accused and the Accusers,* p. 20; *The Autobiographies of the Haymarket
Martyrs,* p. 45. M. M. Trumbull, *Was It a Fair Trial?,* pp. 15, 18.

41. *Nation* 43 (26 August 1886), 167; *Graphic News* 1 (5 June 1886), 220.
The Cassidy drawing was titled "A Hint to Our Citizens." An illustration reproduced in the twenty-five-cent instant history of the case titled *Anarchy at an End*
(see n. 12 above) depicted the verdict as a bomb that blasted away the spirit of
anarchy, which was represented as a demon with a pointed tail twice the length
of his body, while *Frank Leslie's* May 15, 1886, issue featured an image of Uncle
Sam lighting the fuse of an enormous bomb to which were tied four unhappy
anarchists. On the bomb was the address tag, "OLD WORLD DIRECT," indicating that he was blowing these alien troublemakers back to Europe.

CHAPTER EIGHT

1. Of the two major immigrant groups in the city, the Germans slightly increased their representation among the foreign-born residents of Chicago in

the period between 1870 and 1890 (36.68 percent of the foreign-born population to 37.07 percent) while the percentage of Irish immigrants in the total
foreign-born population declined significantly (27.66 to 15.54 percent). One
should keep in mind the tremendous growth in the total population of the city
in this same period, including newcomers from a wider range of countries. The
absolute number of new arrivals from abroad was enormous, even though the
percentage of Chicagoans of foreign birth (as opposed to Americans of foreign
parentage) decreased in this same period and the percentage of Germans and
Irish in the total Chicago population fell from 17.73 to 15.19 percent and from
13.37 to 6.37 percent, respectively. (See Chapter 3 n. 43.) The most striking
relative increases in immigration from Europe over these same twenty years
were from Scandinavia (9.53 to 15.97 percent of foreign-born residents) and
Poland (.83 to 5.34 percent). By 1890, slightly more than 2 percent of Chicagoans were of Polish birth, while the Scandinavian-born population was
slightly higher than the Irish. For these and related figures, see Pierce, *A History
of Chicago*, vol. 3, pp. 20–22, 516. Some of this continuing rapid population increase was the result of the annexation of several surrounding towns in the late
1880s and early 1890s. Chicago, which encompassed a little over 35 square
miles at the time of the fire, extended over 185 square miles by the end of 1893.

2. Montgomery, *The Fall of the House of Labor*, p. 49.

3. John Higham, *Strangers in the Land: Patterns of American Nativism, 1860–
1925* (New York: Atheneum, 1968), p. 55. On the broader context of anti-
immigrant feeling in the 1880s, see Higham's Chapter 3, "Crisis in the Eighties,"
pp. 35–67.

4. Paul C. Hull, *The Chicago Riot*, pp. 8–9; Schaack, *Anarchy and Anarchists*, pp. 25–26.

5. Hull, *The Chicago Riot*, p. 8. Schaack, *Anarchy and Anarchists*, p. 26; *Chicago Tribune* (21 August 1886), p. 4. Just after the trial, the *Forum* published a
"Letter to the People of New York," in which Howard Crosby warned that the
city was now on "an inclined plane of disaster" caused by contentious outsiders. Even at the risk of being called Know-Nothings, Crosby said, it was time
to distinguish "between the respectable foreigner who comes among us and
becomes an American, and the foreigner who remains a foreigner, and yet
meddles with our domestic affairs, and endeavors to overthrow our institutions." He closed by pointing to the Haymarket verdict as a turning point. "The
condemnation and sentence of the anarchists at Chicago should be our signal
for a new position," Crosby wrote. "We shall still welcome most heartily virtue
and worth coming to us from across the sea, but we shall give no such welcome
to imported vice and violence, and when this latter sort appears in our streets
and attempts to assert itself, we shall choke it unto death." *The Forum* 2 (1886),
pp. 420–28. Crosby was a former professor of Greek at Rutgers who was a
prominent Presbyterian minister in New York, where he was also engaged in
education and temperance reform, as well as biblical scholarship.

6. Cited in Schaack, *Anarchy and Anarchists*, p. 526. Walker's comments followed his dramatic reading of an extract from Johann Most on the value of violence to the social revolution.

7. Schaack, *Anarchy and Anarchists*, pp. 207–8; Robert Wooster, *Nelson A.*

Miles and the Twilight of the Frontier Army (Lincoln: University of Nebraska Press, 1993), pp. 147–52. Four days before the execution of the anarchists, reports on the last stages of the Crow Indian War were on the same front pages that carried the news of the condemned men's final days, including the public debate over commutation. *Chicago Tribune* (7 November 1887), p. 1.

8. The women who attended anarchist meetings were "the most hideous-looking females that could possibly be found. If a reward of money had been offered for an uglier set, no one could have profited upon the collection." Some were "pock-marked, others freckle-faced and red-haired," while one seemed to be cross-dressed in her husband's boots. Another was six feet tall. "She was raw-boned, had a turn-up nose, and looked as though she might have carried the red flag in Paris during the reign of the Commune." Schaack, *Anarchy and Anarchists*, pp. 207–8.

9. The participants in an anarchist meeting in the dime novel *The Red Flag; or the Anarchists of Chicago* are likewise "unkempt and wild-looking" (p. 7). In John Hay's popular antilabor novel, *The Bread-Winners,* written following the strikes of 1877 and published two years before Haymarket, the deceitful labor organizer Andy Offitt has a greasy mustache that sets off his "oleaginous" expression and "reeking" black hair. *The Bread-Winners. A Social Study* (New York: Harper and Brothers, 1884), p. 74. Hay's book was published anonymously and first appeared serially in the *Century Magazine* in 1883. Richard Slotkin offers an insightful reading of this novel, which, in connection with the larger concerns of his book, he sees as an elaboration of "the symbolism that relates the Frontier catastrophe to the conflicts that threaten the metropolis." *The Fatal Environment*, p. 512.

Schaack in particular seemed incapable of saying enough about how dirty the anarchists were. His descriptions of radicals always stressed their long hair, filthy clothing, and instinctive aversion to personal hygiene. He read these as signs of nonconformity, sloth, and a psychopathic hostility to the decent and normal. Schaack closely linked dirt and insanity in his description of one figure at a secret meeting that was supposedly infiltrated by one of Schaack's spies: "He was a large man with a black beard and large eyes, and very shabbily dressed. He looked as though he had been driving a coal cart for a year without washing or combing. He also had the appearance of being on the verge of hydrophobia." Schaack scorned those citizens who, after the trial, worked for clemency and allowed their homes to be used for meetings to promote this purpose. In such respectable settings, "avowed Anarchists and Socialists spread their feet under mahogany tables and shuffled dirt-laden shoes over velvety rugs in houses that had hitherto sheltered owners who, on the streets and in the marts of trade, had denounced the anarchists in unmeasured terms." *Anarchy and Anarchists*, pp. 208, 623.

10. Mary Douglas, *Purity and Danger*, pp. 35–36.

11. *The Accused and the Accusers*, p. 167, 5; Lawson, "The Trial of the Chicago Anarchists," p. 199; Foner, ed., *The Autobiographies of the Haymarket Martyrs*, pp. 59–60; *August Spies' Auto-Biography; His Speech in Court, and General Notes* (Chicago: Nina Van Zandt, 1887), pp. 1–2. Spies's accounts of his life here and in *The Autobiographies of the Haymarket Martyrs* are substantially the

same. Spies came to America in 1872, a year before Fischer and Engel and seven years before Schwab. Neebe emigrated in 1865, three years before Fielden. Spies grew up in central Germany and was in training to become a government forester like his father when the latter's death ended his schooling. He lived briefly in New York before moving to Chicago in 1873, three years after Grinnell. See Avrich, *The Haymarket Tragedy*, pp. 121-22.

12. Like Parsons, Fischer was a printer. He was foreman of the composing room of the *Arbeiter-Zeitung*, where Schwab was associate editor. Spies opened a successful upholstery shop in 1876, the same year Engel and his wife started a toy store in their home, while Neebe had his own small yeast company. Lingg was trained as a carpenter but quit his factory job to work as a paid organizer for the International Carpenters' and Joiners' Union. Fielden hauled stone for a living, but was self-employed and owned his wagon and team. He had spent the day of the Haymarket rally making a delivery to Waldheim Cemetery.

13. Foner, ed., *The Autobiographies of the Haymarket Martyrs*, pp. 88, 65. That German workers fully understood they were stigmatized as "dirty" is clear. In 1899 the *Arbeiter-Zeitung* published a fictive "capitalist's diary" that revealed his candid views of a strike. The capitalist's first impression of the delegation of workers that came to see him is of the way they "trampled all over my good carpets from Brussels with their filthy boots." Hartmut Keil and John B. Jentz, eds., *German Workers in Chicago: A Documentary History of Working-Class Culture from 1850 to World War I* (Urbana: University of Illinois Press, 1988), p. 307.

14. Lawson, "The Trial of the Chicago Anarchists," pp. 25-27.

15. For more on Parsons's ancestry, see his brother's account in *Life of Albert R. Parsons*, pp. 1-2, as well as Foner, ed., *The Autobiographies of the Haymarket Martyrs*, pp. 27-28, and Avrich, *The Haymarket Tragedy*, pp. 3-4. Oscar Neebe was born in New York but raised in Germany.

16. *New York Times* (12 November 1887), p. 4. Parsons, Grinnell charged in his opening statement, had brought special "shame" to the nation "because . . . he was born on our soil," while in his closing address to the jury, Francis Walker called Parsons "the worst of all the defendants." To emphasize his point, Walker added, "He stood alone, the only American among the conspirators." "The Trial of the Chicago Anarchists," pp. 27, 158, 230. Frederick Trevor Hill argues that "the fact that [Parsons] was an American deepened the feeling against him." "Decisive Battles of the Law," p. 893.

17. Foner, ed., *The Autobiographies of the Haymarket Martyrs*, pp. 36, 59-60; *Alarm* (4 October 1884), p. 3; (4 April 1885), p. 3. References to Jefferson were everywhere in the writings of the Haymarket defendants, their associates, and their supporters. The title page of Parsons's posthumously published book on anarchism features a quotation from the third president, and Trumbull observed, "Had the Illinois rulings been good law in Jefferson's time, he might have been hanged at any period of his active political career. He was an anarchist; not an amateur speculative anarchist, but a physical force anarchist, and an avowed enemy of government." *The Trial of the Judgment*, p. 70. In another issue of the *Alarm*, an editorial titled "Anarchy" stated, "All men are born free and equal, with certain inalienable rights, among which are life, liberty and

pursuit of happiness," adding, "This doctrine fulfilled is pure Anarchism." *Alarm* (4 April 1885), p. 2. Their trial prompted the anarchists to increase their emphasis on the parallels between themselves and the founders of the Republic.

18. Black drew objections from Grinnell when he went a step further and likened the defendants to Jesus, whom he called "the great Socialist of Judea," the first to preach "the socialism taught by Spies and his other modern apostles." "The Trial of the Chicago Anarchists," p. 238. Swett quoted in Spies's *Auto-Biography*, p. 75. See also in the same vein Black's eulogy at Waldheim (*Life of Albert R. Parsons*, pp. 254–60) and his introduction to *The Autobiographies of the Haymarket Martyrs*, pp. 15–25. The often controversial Civil War general and Massachusetts politician Benjamin F. Butler, who agreed to serve on the three-man defense team that prepared the defendants' unsuccessful appeal to the United States Supreme Court, cited another kind of legal precedent. In a letter to Black a few months after the execution, Butler compared the Haymarket case to the "judicial murders" in Massachusetts almost two hundred years earlier of supposed witches, whom he called "the Anarchists of that day." The full letter is included in Parsons, *Life of Albert Parsons*, pp. 261–63. Aware of these defenses, the *Tribune* took pains to distinguish between John Brown and the condemned anarchists: "he proposed to lift up the poor black slaves and they to pull down white American freemen." *Chicago Tribune* (4 November 1887), p. 4.

19. *The Accused and the Accusers*, p. 89.

20. *The Accused and the Accusers*, pp. 43–44.

21. Among the large and growing number of studies of manhood, with particular reference to the late nineteenth century, see the essays collected in Mark C. Carnes and Clyde Griffen, eds., *Meanings for Manhood: Constructions of Masculinity in Victorian America* (Chicago: University of Chicago Press, 1990); and Elizabeth H. Pleck and Joseph H. Pleck, eds., *The American Man* (Englewood Cliffs: Prentice-Hall, 1980), Period III: "The Strenuous Life (1861–1919)," pp. 217–335; as well as E. Anthony Rotundo, *American Manhood: Transformations in Masculinity from the Revolution to the Modern Era* (New York: Basic Books, 1993). For more specific studies in regard to particular cultural practices and institutions, see Elliot J. Gorn, *The Manly Art: Bare-Knuckle Prize Fighting in America* (Ithaca, N.Y.: Cornell University Press, 1986), esp. pp. 132–44, 185–94; and Mark C. Carnes, *Secret Ritual and Manhood in Victorian America* (New Haven: Yale University Press, 1989). See also Bledstein, *The Culture of Professionalism*, pp. 106, 151–52, and the considerable literature that explores the cult of the strenuous life that arose in this period—reaching its peak near the turn of the century—partly in response to a heightened sense of routine, restriction, and devaluation of self-worth perceived by many males as a threat to their manhood. Edwin H. Cady, " 'The Strenuous Life' as a Theme in American Cultural History," in *New Voices in American Studies*, ed. Ray B. Browne et al. (Lafayette, Ind.: Purdue University Studies, 1966), pp. 59–66; John Higham, "The Reorientation of American Culture in the 1890's," *Writing American History: Essays on Modern Scholarship* (Bloomington: Indiana University Press, 1970), pp. 73–102; Lears, *No Place of Grace*, especially Chapter 3,

"The Destructive Element: Modern Commercial Society and the Martial Ideal," pp. 97-139. David Montgomery discusses the development of a code of "manly conduct" and the importance of a "manly bearing" among workers in *The Fall of the House of Labor,* pp. 22, 38, 204-5. Montgomery argues that "the union rules that codified craftsmen's norms" concerning standards and relations to one's employer and fellow workers "did not run back to time immemorial but, rather, had been forged in the fire of conflict during the depression of the 1870s. They represented new collective efforts to defend the autonomy and dignity of the craftsman against the growing power of the company." As large employers continued to assault the autonomy of craft, skilled workers in particular felt their manhood to be threatened.

22. *Alarm* (21 February 1885), p. 2; (5 September 1885), p. 3.

23. Avrich, *The Haymarket Tragedy,* pp. 190-93; Lawson, "The Trial of the Chicago Anarchists," p. 213. Lynn Hunt points out how the figure of Hercules as "a distinctly virile representation of sovereignty," the exterminator of all natural enemies of the revolution, was used to represent the radical conception of the people during the Terror. See *Politics, Culture, and Class in the French Revolution* (Berkeley: University of California Press, 1984), pp. 94-116.

24. McLean, *The Rise and Fall of Anarchy in America,* p. 9.

25. *Chicago Tribune* (5 May 1886), p. 1; (30 July 1886), p. 2; McLean, *The Rise and Fall of Anarchy in America,* p. 123. As self-appointed historian of anarchy and Haymarket, Schaack took it as his duty to depict the police, prosecution, and jury as men, and the accused and their supporters as cowards. Schaack claimed that the conspiracy was far wider than appeared, and that there was a plan to set off bombs in other spots in the city, but the anarchists "were all found lacking in courage at the critical moment." Schaack later boasted that with few exceptions (including Engel, Lingg, and Fielden), "the men who posed as the bloodthirsty bandits of Chicago" quickly lost their bluster and bravado after their arrest and broke down under questioning, becoming "arrant, cringing cowards when they found themselves within the clutches of the law." Schaack, *Anarchy and Anarchists,* pp. 148, 230-31.

26. Schaack, *Anarchy and Anarchists,* pp. 360-62. The strike in Hay's *Bread-Winners* ends when the sensible wives of workers assert themselves and tell their foolish husbands to call the silliness off.

27. Keil and Jentz, eds., *German Workers in Chicago,* p. 266.

28. *Alarm* (13 December 1884), p. 1. The article noted that Spies helped press charges, but that it was expected that nothing would happen. Avrich (*The Haymarket Tragedy,* p. 126) briefly notes that the officer in question was cleared.

29. *Alarm* (18 October 1884), p. 2; (18 April 1885), p. 1; (3 April 1886), p. 2. In his statement before sentencing, Spies said that the accused had "jeopardized our lives to save society from the fiend—the fiend who has grasped her by the throat; who sucks her lifeblood, who devours her children." *The Accused and the Accusers,* p. 7.

30. *Chicago Tribune* (23 June 1886), p. 1; (4 July 1886), p. 10. Part of the point of these scenes, however, was to show that, even if these men loved their families, they had betrayed them.

31. John Hay's handling in *The Bread-Winners* of the relationship between the cowardly and false labor organizer, Andy Offitt, and the upstanding but easily deluded worker, Sam Sleeny, was the fullest imaginative depiction of this idea. Offitt's radical politics are inseparable from his unnatural tendencies. Offitt secretly lusts after the girl Sleeny wants to marry, but Sleeny himself arouses unmistakably sexual and sadistic urges in the rabble-rouser. Sleeny's "shapely build, his curly blond hair and beard, his frank blue eye" are what "first attracted [Offitt's] envious notice." His "steady, contented industry" comes to "excite" in Offitt "a desire to pervert" this workman "whose daily life was a practical argument against the doctrines of socialism." *The Bread-Winners*, p. 86.

32. *Chicago Herald* (24 June 1886). The story continued, "The lady who is readiest admitted is the one who looks the prettiest." Aware that this practice had raised some eyebrows, Gary lamely explained in his article in the *Century* that he admitted his wife and other women to these privileged seats because they were the best place from which to hear the speeches to the jury.

33. "The Knight and the Lady: A Romance of the Strike," *Chicago Tribune* (1 May 1886), p. 16. Shelton Stromquist observes that locomotive engineers were, in fact, the most prestigious and independent of skilled railroad workers, and in many cases identified their own interests with their employers rather than with the broader cause of labor. *A Generation of Boomers*, p. 107.

34. *Chicago Tribune* (10 August 1886), p. 1.

35. John Kasson and Karen Halttunen discuss the difficulties nineteenth-century city-dwellers experienced in "reading" the many strangers they encountered. See Kasson, *Rudeness and Civility*, pp. 80–111; Halttunen, *Confidence Men and Painted Women*, Chapter 3, "Hypocrisy and Sincerity in the World of Strangers," pp. 33–55.

36. *Chicago Daily News* (20 January 1887), p. 1; *Chicago Tribune* (18 January 1887), p. 6, and (19 January 1887), p. 4.

37. *August Spies' Auto-Biography*, p. x. The Canute Matson Collection at the Chicago Historical Society includes a letter from Van Zandt's father importuning the sheriff to ease his daughter's distress by letting her see her husband. It is very difficult to decide what to make of this bizarre relationship from the point of view of either party. Writing twenty years after the executions, Charles Edward Russell, while sympathetic to the condemned men, was skeptical of the depth of Spies's feeling. As for Van Zandt, Russell concluded, "Doubtless she thought that her marriage to Spies would awaken public sympathy in his behalf; but in the storm of ridicule that arose his cause was really injured." Russell, "The Haymarket and Afterwards," p. 409. Nina Van Zandt survived Spies by fifty mainly unhappy years, which were complicated by her own sometimes erratic behavior. Though she remarried twice, she remained loyal to the memory of Spies and the other martyrs. See Avrich, *The Haymarket Tragedy*, p. 450.

38. Parsons, *Life of Albert R. Parsons*, pp. 241, 249–53. This contains a facsimile of Parsons's letter. Holmes made special note that she and Parsons's family were not foreigners by any definition, that in fact "the blood of revolutionary forefathers coursed in our veins, while the matron and officers . . . who

gave the order . . . had not been here long enough to speak our language correctly."

39. To the extent that the anarchists could be described in natural terms, their accusers declared, the proper metaphors were those of disease and disaster. Schaack offered a portrait of the anarchist Abraham Hermann, who was interrogated and imprisoned during the pre-trial round-up: "He was of dark complexion, wore a full black beard, had sharp, piercing eyes, and from thinking much on Anarchy, had come to present a sickly appearance." Schaack, *Anarchy and Anarchists*, p. 305. William Salter admitted that anarchy was a disease, but he said that it could not be dealt with by hanging every radical, since "like a ghastly cancer, it would appear again in time." Instead, it had to be cured. "If You do not," he warned, "you but drive it below the surface of society and in time it will rumble and shake and burst forth with volcanic force and reduce our State, our very civilization to ruins." Salter, *"What Shall Be Done with the Anarchists?"*, p. 19.

40. Noble, "Christianity and the Red Flag," p. 2.

41. *Alarm* (4 April 1885), p. 2. At the trial and after, the anarchists and their supporters continued to make such arguments. One prominent sympathizer, Colonel William Christie Benét, attorney and president of the South Carolina Club, cited Emerson in attacking the verdict: "The history of persecution is a history of endeavors to cheat nature, to make water run up hill, to twist a rope of sand." Quoted in *August Spies' Auto-Biography*, p. 90.

42. *The Accused and the Accusers*, p. 158; Foner, ed., *The Autobiographies of the Haymarket Martyrs*, p. 45.

43. *The Accused and the Accusers*, pp. 8, 11. In other instances, particularly in positing that the current social and economic hierarchy was the result of a dynamic competition that rewarded the most talented, many business leaders and social analysts advanced a Social Darwinist outlook that saw the natural order of things as anything but peaceful and settled.

44. *The Accused and the Accusers*, p. 10. British socialist H. M. Hyndman concurred: "Whichever way we look, in fact, we can see that the outbreak in Chicago was but a sputter of the hot volcanic lava below." H. M. Hyndman, *The Chicago Riots and the Class War in the United States* (London: Swan Sonnenschein, Lowrey, 1886), p. 7. This work was a pamphlet reprinted from the British periodical *Time*. M. M. Trumbull even offered a "scientific" formula to calculate the force of the social volcano: "The history of Europe shows that resistance to government restraint and political discipline has generally been greater than the act resisted. The square of the coercion expresses the quantity of resistance to it. We may plug up Vesuvius, but the pent up fires will split the earth open somewhere else." *The Trial of the Judgment*, pp. 59–60.

45. *Chicago Tribune* (14 November 1887), p. 2. Thomas was born in 1832 in what would become West Virginia and supported himself by farming while studying for the ministry. He came with his family to Iowa in 1855, and he was called to the pulpit of the Park Avenue Methodist Church in 1869, moving to the First Methodist Church in 1875, and then the Centenary Methodist Church two years later. His consistently liberal views caused great friction with

more conservative ministers, leading to a heresy trial in 1881 at the end of which he was expelled from the church. Backed by some twenty-seven subscribers who pledged $250 each, Thomas formed the People's Church, based on his liberal principles and open to visitors and the poor. Against the general trend in which churches moved out of the downtown and away from the commercial culture of Chicago, Thomas held his services first mainly in Hooley's Theater and then in the Chicago Opera House, as well as in McVicker's Theater. Andreas, *History of Chicago,* vol. 3, pp. 794–95, 827–29; Bluestone, *Constructing Chicago,* pp. 101–3.

46. Bonfield and Schaack, cited in the pamphlet *Anarchy at an End,* p. 90; *Chicago Daily News* (21 August 1886), p. 1; Lyman Abbott, *Reminiscences* (Boston: Houghton Mifflin, 1915), p. 401. Even some with deep misgivings about the conduct of the trial, such as Samuel P. McConnell, who was active in the clemency movement, admitted many years later in the pages of *Harper's* that "the hanging of these men did do away with the hysteria which had pervaded the body of the people," quickly adding, "And, aside from the injustice of such an occurrence, perhaps it did not matter who was hanged provided the public was satisfied." Others expressed the belief that the ends perhaps justified the highly questionable means. Writing in 1919, John D. Lawson prefaced his edition of the trial transcript by pointing out that the same interpretation of law would have hanged Wendell Phillips and William Lloyd Garrison, but then he conjectured that "it may be that our Government which today seems to be extremely lax in allowing Bolshevism and I.W.W. doctrines to be preached in all parts of the country might well study the result of the Chicago trial. For it is certain that for more than a quarter of a century this great metropolis was not again threatened with destruction from within its walls." McConnell, "The Chicago Bomb Case," p. 734; Lawson, *American State Trials,* p. vii.

47. *Chicago Tribune* (11 November 1887), p. 3. When a few weeks before his execution Parsons cited Patrick Henry in refusing to accept anything short of exoneration, William Salter observed in frustration, "The appeal of Parsons for liberty or death is pure bathos, and is in keeping with the theatrical nature of the man." Salter, *"What Shall Be Done with the Anarchists?",* p. 17.

48. John P. Altgeld, "Reasons for Pardoning Fielden, Neebe, and Schwab" [n.p., 1893], pp. 4, 49, 63.

49. Avrich, *The Haymarket Tragedy,* p. 339; *Chicago Tribune* cited in Pierce, *A History of Chicago,* vol. 3, p. 377–78. The first Democrat to be elected governor of Illinois since 1856, Altgeld had won the 1892 election (his rivals for the party nomination included John C. Black, brother of Haymarket attorney William P. Black) with an aggressive campaign that successfully brought together workers, ethnic groups, and moderates. On the lengthy history behind the pardon, see Barnard, *"Eagle Forgotten,"* pp. 183–267. Altgeld (who once had been heckled during a speech by Lucy Parsons) already had been branded an anarchist in the Republican press during the campaign for his prolabor sympathies, though he was never as radical as his reputation. It was widely rumored, however, that he would review the case if he won election. See Barnard, *"Eagle Forgotten,"* pp. 132, 156–62. Clarence Darrow had urged his friend Altgeld to correct the injustice done to the anarchists, but he felt that the gover-

nor was wrong in coming down so hard on Judge Gary. Writing in his autobiography many years later, Darrow stated that he was angrier at the United States Supreme Court than he was at Gary, since the justices refused to review the case even though they had the luxury of considering it collectively far from the scene and after a good deal of time had elapsed from the moment of initial terror over the bomb. "To severely blame Judge Gary meant blaming a judge for not being one in ten thousand," Darrow recalled, "and few men can be that and live." Darrow, *The Story of My Life* (New York: Charles Scribner's Sons, 1932), p. 102.

50. On the police scandals and the discrediting of Bonfield and Schaack, see Avrich, *The Haymarket Tragedy*, pp. 415–16; and Richard C. Lindberg, *To Serve and Collect: Chicago Politics and Police Corruption from the Lager Beer Riot to the Summerdale Scandal* (New York: Praeger, 1991), pp. 97–98. What disgrace they endured seems to have been only partial and temporary. See Chapter 11 in Avrich for their subsequent careers in Chicago.

51. Addams, *Twenty Years at Hull-House* (New York: New American Library, 1960), pp. 133–34. This was first published in 1910.

52. Collyer, quoted in the *Chicago Tribune* (14 November 1887), p. 3; *Harper's Weekly* 31 (26 November 1887), p. 851; Abbott, *Reminiscences*, p. 400.

53. J. Coleman Adams, "Is America Europeanizing?" *Forum* 4 (1887–88), 197; Pierce, *A History of Chicago* vol. 3, p. 464.

54. C. C. Bonney, *The Present Conflict of Capital and Labor. A Discourse* (Chicago: The Legal News Company, 1886), p. 25; *Chicago Tribune* (14 November 1887), p. 2. The publication of Bonney's sermon was underwritten by the Chicago Sabbath Association, "at the instance and expense of law-abiding citizens, who believe that its circulation among the masses will promote the best interests of both Labor and Capital, and the general welfare of the community" (p. 3).

CHAPTER NINE

1. *Ceremonies at the Unveiling of the Bronze Memorial Group of the Chicago Massacre of 1812* (Chicago: Chicago Historical Society, 1893), p. 7; *Chicago Tribune* (23 June 1893), pp. 1, 7. The Pullman mansion, which no longer stands, was located on the northeast corner of Prairie and Eighteenth, and the statue was originally placed at the east end of Eighteenth. The statue by sculptor Carl Rohl-Smith was subsequently inside the front lobby of the Historical Society's building on Clark Street at North Avenue, but has since been returned to an outdoor site on the west side of Prairie Avenue south of Eighteenth Street.

2. Stanley Buder, *Pullman: An Experiment in Industrial Order and Community Planning, 1880–1930* (New York: Oxford University Press, 1967), p. 5. Buder's book, long the leading full-length study of Pullman, concentrates on the history of the model town but also contains much information on the founder. For an illustrated brief account of the "raising" of Chicago in the 1850s, see Mayer and Wade, *Chicago: Growth of a Metropolis*, pp. 94–96. Liston Edgington Leyendecker discusses Pullman's career as a building raiser and mover in Chapter 2 of his *Palace Car Prince: A Biography of George Mortimer Pullman* (Niwot, Col.: University Press of Colorado, 1992), pp. 29–49. Much

of the biographical information on Pullman the man presented here is taken from Leyendecker and from Buder, as well as from discussions with Pullman scholar Janice L. Reiff. It was not until 1870 that Pullman's workers manufactured cars in his shops. Before that they modified cars built by other companies.

3. "A Visit to the States," *London Times* (24 October 1887), reprinted in Bessie Louise Pierce, ed., *As Others See Chicago: Impressions of Visitors, 1673–1933* (Chicago: University of Chicago Press, 1933), p. 242.

4. *Ceremonies at the Unveiling of the Bronze Memorial Group*, p. 17. In some instances, the busy Pullman's contributions to civic causes were mainly financial and symbolic rather than personal. For example, Andreas (*History of Chicago*, vol. 2, p. 145) explained that Pullman Company vice-president C. G. Hammond actually handled most of his boss's duties as treasurer of the Relief and Aid Society following the fire. When Sheridan withdrew his troops, however, Pullman himself wrote a handwritten note to Mayor Mason requesting around-the-clock police guards for the Society's offices since "[t]he large amount of money on deposit with the continued crowds of applicants at the door for relief passes &c renders this necessary to preserve order." In response to an invitation to the White House, Pullman told his friend President Grant that he "experienced personally little inconvenience or pecuniary loss" from the fire. Letters of George M. Pullman to Roswell Mason and Ulysses Grant (23 October and 22 November 1871), George M. Pullman Collection, Archives and Manuscripts Department, Chicago Historical Society. On Pullman and the Haymarket anarchists, see Avrich, *The Haymarket Tragedy*, pp. 223, 366. Regarding Pullman's support for the fair, see Leyendecker, *Palace Car Prince*, pp. 123, 197.

The Commercial Club was organized December 27, 1877, five months after the national railroad strike. The central purpose of its membership, which was limited to the sixty leading businessmen in the city, was to advance "by social intercourse and by a friendly interchange of views the prosperity and growth of the city of Chicago." See Pierce, *A History of Chicago*, vol. 3, p. 190.

5. "An Industrial City—Pullman, Ill.," *Scientific American* 50 (3 May 1884), 279. The article was adapted from a recent story in *Western Manufacturer.*

6. These statistics and description of the town are based on [Duane Doty?], *The Story of Pullman* (Chicago: Blakeley and Rogers, 1893); Mrs. Duane Doty, *The Town of Pullman. Illustrated. Its Growth with Brief Accounts of Its Industries* (Pullman, Ill.: T. P. Struhsaker, 1893); the 1884 article in *Scientific American;* and Buder, *Pullman*, especially Chapter 7, "Social Characteristics of Workers and Residents," pp. 77–91. Pullman was not the only company to build sleeping cars, but it was unquestionably the leading one. On the distinctions between kinds of laborers in the work force, see n. 28 below. While Pullman was an innovator in the organization of the workplace, his heavy reliance on skilled labor and the apparent absence of a comprehensive close analysis and precise breakdown (along with time-motion studies) of the manufacturing process in the works differentiates him from more "scientific" managers of the decades ahead.

7. Liston Leyendecker maintains that the widely circulated legend—which the company did not deny—that Pullman got his earliest major positive public-

ity when he offered the first car built in his shops to the Lincoln funeral train is probably untrue. *Palace Car Prince*, p. 77. According to his granddaughter, Pullman's private car was sixty-seven feet long and included an observation room with chairs and a large double sofa; a private suite with an extension sofa bed and an adjoining dressing room with wardrobe and lockers; a dining room and lounge with sofa, an eight-foot table with chairs, a desk, and an organ; a dressing room and bath with a tub; storage space for luggage; servants' quarters; and a pantry and kitchen. Florence Lowden Miller, "The Pullmans of Prairie Avenue: A Domestic Portrait from Letters and Diaries," *Chicago History* 1 (Spring 1971), p. 146. Pullman's expectation that his loaning this car to noted people would produce favorable publicity was well-founded. For example, when *Harper's Weekly* reported on President and Mrs. Cleveland's visit to Chicago and other cities in 1887, during which they traveled in Pullman's coach, it included a separate article on the car itself (which, the journal pointed out, had also carried Presidents Grant and Arthur). It placed an illustration of President and Mrs. Cleveland in their luxurious accommodations on the cover of the magazine and, inside, a diagram of the coach as a whole. The article also marveled at the glittering chandeliers, the handsome oak furniture, and the old-gold carpet. *Harper's Weekly* 31 (8 October 1887), 721, 731.

8. See, for example, the description of the approach to Pullman by train by the *London Times* reporter who visited in 1887: "Riding down the line of the Illinois Central, over the flat land and among the succession of villages which have grown up between Chicago and Pullman," he wrote, "the visitor alights at one of the best station buildings seen on the line, and finds the new settlement is in front of him, spreading far out on either hand." The reporter then described the "fine hotel, which is a model of artistic design and worthy of the largest city; and across the park, with its ornamental grounds and lake, . . . the extensive shops, with their clock spire and huge water tower rising high above." The whole town, he assured his countrymen, "like the Pullman coach, is a model of neatness and elegance," with flower beds and lawns around the shops, and solid walls around the whole grounds which "give them quite an English air." "A Visit to the States," p. 245. For an extended discussion of the view of Chicago from the train in this period, see Smith, *Chicago and the American Literary Imagination*, pp. 107–20.

9. *Chicago Times* (28 May 1882), Pullman Company Scrapbooks in the collections of the Newberry Library (hereafter PSNL), Miscellaneous Scrapbooks, Series A, vol. 7. For an account of a similar ceremonial visit a year later, see "The Wonders of Pullman, in *New York World* (15 April 1883), PSNL Town Scrapbooks, vol. 1. See also Buder, *Pullman*, pp. 54–56, and, for more public relations events staged by the company, pp. 12, 20, 22, 29, 55, 93. Leyendecker also discusses Pullman's publicity efforts.

10. [Doty?], *The Story of Pullman*, pp. 11, 4–5, 33. Doty also edited the company-run town paper, escorted reporters and distinguished visitors on tours of Pullman, and spoke widely outside the town in its behalf. For more on Doty, see Buder, especially pp. 108–9.

11. Pullman quoted in Mrs. H. E. Starrett, "Pullman—A Social and Industrial Study," *Weekly Magazine* (16 September 1882), PSNL Miscellaneous

Scrapbooks, Series A, vol. 7. Pullman testified right after the strike that the company's aim was a return of 6 percent on the rent, but that it actually returned closer to 4.5 percent, and, by the summer of 1894, only 3.82 percent. The company's annual dividend was 8 percent. *Report on the Chicago Strike of June-July, 1894, by the United States Strike Commission* (Washington, D.C.: Government Printing Office, 1895), p. 530.

12. "An Industrial City—Pullman, Ill.," p. 279.

13. "A Western Utopia," *Christian Register* (1 February 1883), PSNL Town Scrapbooks, vol. 1; Paul de Rousiers, *American Life* (1892), quoted in Pierce, *As Others See Chicago,* p. 264. Most other newspaper and magazine articles before the strike made the same points about the Pullman idea.

14. *Hour Weekly Journal* (5 August 1882), PSNL Miscellaneous Scrapbooks, Series A, vol. 7; *Chicago Times* (10 January 1891), PSNL Series A, vol. 14. The *Omaha Daily Free Press* of September 9, 1882, in an article subtitled "Pullman, or Fairyland," assured its readers that if Pullman was a fairyland, it was also "a city or hive in which there is not one drone—all are workers; drones cannot gain a footing in this elyseum [*sic*] of the west" (PSNL Miscellaneous Scrapbooks, Series A, vol. 7). In statements to stockholders and to the general public, spokesmen for the company pointedly rejected the idea that Pullman was in any way engaged in philanthropy.

15. [Doty?] *The Story of Pullman,* p. 34.

16. "A Western Utopia," *Christian Register* (1 February 1883), PSNL Town Scrapbooks, vol. 1; *Frank Leslie's Illustrated Weekly* (27 April 1889), PSNL Miscellaneous Scrapbooks, Series B, vol. 9.

17. *Railroad Gazette* (6 July 1882), PSNL Miscellaneous Scrapbooks, Series A, vol. 7.

18. *Hour Weekly Journal* (5 August 1882).

19. Charles Dudley Warner contended that if the "only valuable result" of Pullman was "an 'object lesson' in decent and orderly living," then "the experiment will not have been in vain." Warner, "Studies of the Great West. IV. Chicago," *Harper's New Monthly Magazine* 77 (June 1888), 126.

20. "An Industrial City," p. 280; *Pall Mall Gazette* (7 February 1884), PSNL Miscellaneous Scrapbooks, Series A, vol. 8; *Arcade Mercantile Journal* (11 October 1890), p. 4. The Chicago Public Library, Special Collections Division. The *Arcade Mercantile Journal* was a weekly house organ begun in the late 1880s. It changed its name to the *Pullman Arcade Mercantile Journal* in April of 1892. It was devoted to promotional town and company news, local social doings, genteel literature, features and anecdotes, useful and obscure fillers, and plenty of advertisements, mainly for local merchants. Duane Doty was the editor, though he was not listed on the masthead. Buder, *Pullman,* pp. 84–85.

21. Although these ceremonies were less grand and formal than the dedication of the theater, once more a special train conveyed a "large and brilliant assemblage" of Chicago's elite from downtown for the evening. More than the theater, the five-room skylit library on the second floor of the Arcade, furnished with Wilton carpets and eleven cherrywood double bookcases holding more than five thousand books and periodicals, expressed the Pullman ideas of com-

bining the ideal with the practical and managing the problem of labor through shrewd benevolence. The company would later point out the relatively high number of technical works and the low proportion of novels in the collection, and it would defend the three-dollar annual user's fee as a way to avoid charity and teach operatives to value the cultural opportunities of the town. For a description of the theater dedication, see *Chicago Tribune* (10 January 1883), p. 6; and James Gilbert, *Perfect Cities*, pp. 131–33.

Swing (1830–94) was one of a group of clergymen with whom Pullman, who was raised a Universalist (two of his brothers became Universalist ministers), was friendly. Swing officiated at the wedding of Pullman's daughter and eldest child Harriet in 1892. Described on one occasion as "the Emerson of our American pulpit," he moved to Chicago in 1866 to lead what became the Fourth Presbyterian Church, which burned down in 1871 (he published a recollection of the fire in *Scribner's* in June of 1892). His career was in many ways very similar to that of H. W. Thomas of the People's Church (see n. 45, Chapter 8, above). His sermons received wide attention and were soon printed regularly in the newspapers, but his resistance to orthodox dogma led to a highly publicized heresy trial in the mid-1870s. He resigned to form his own more theologically liberal congregation, taking many of his congregants with him into his new Central Church, which he committed to what he saw as moral Christian work suited to the needs of a large modern city. A strong voice in support of stern treatment for the Haymarket accused, Swing counted among his friends and sponsors some of the most prominent business and professional men in the city, including Wirt Dexter, Leonard Swett, Nathaniel Fairbank, William Bross, Joseph Medill, and A. T. Andreas, and they helped him build in downtown Chicago the Central Music Hall, which could hold some three thousand people and was used for many other kinds of public events as well as his worship services. He died in October of 1894, a few months after the Pullman strike, during which he stood by George Pullman. Pierce, *A History of Chicago*, vol. 3, pp. 429–32; Andreas, *History of Chicago*, vol. 3, 802–4.

22. *Chicago Tribune* (12 April 1883), p. 7. Volume 1 of the Pullman Town Scrapbooks contains other full reports on the dedication that appeared in the *Saturday Evening Herald* and the *Inter-Ocean*.

23. Wright (1840–1909), the son of a minister, had served under Phil Sheridan in the Civil War before establishing a successful law practice in Massachusetts, which, as the most industrialized state in the nation, had instituted the country's first bureau of labor statistics. He became chief of that agency in 1873, and held the post until 1888, the last three years simultaneously with his federal appointment, a job he kept for almost twenty years. In his distinguished career he also directed the eleventh census (1890), served as president of the American Statistical Association for more than a decade, and was the first head of Clark College. Wright was a pioneering social scientist as well as a public servant who devoted his expertise to a range of living and working conditions, including divorce, crime, and pauperism. For more on his career, see James Leiby, *Carroll Wright and Labor Reform: The Origin of Labor Statistics* (Cambridge, Mass.: Harvard University Press, 1960).

24. Wright et al., *Pullman* (Boston: Wright and Potter, 1885), pp. 4, 10, 17, 22–23. This was one of several different versions in which the report was published. Much of it was also reprinted in Mrs. Doty's book.

25. Wright, "Pullman," pp. 8, 19, 14, 25–26.

26. Some town residents did not work for the Pullman Company, and a number of operatives did not live in the town. While most of the employee residents were workers in the shops, several managers and their families lived in the more expensive housing. For a more precise breakdown, see Buder, *Pullman,* Chapter 7, "Social Characteristics of Workers and Residents," pp. 77–91. There was a bar in the Hotel Florence, but for all practical purposes it was unavailable to most operatives. On the combination of reform idealism and conservative fear in the public-health movement, see Bledstein, *The Culture of Professionalism,* p. 182.

Pullman's innovations were not limited to his model town. In 1873 the company constructed a downtown office building that featured a restaurant, library, and sitting rooms for employees and their families in the hope that this would be "productive of harmony and good feelings, while it will interest them more in the work for which they are employed . . . [and] make them more useful." Bluestone, *Constructing Chicago,* pp. 141–43. The grander design by Solon Beman that was built in the early 1880s at Adams and Michigan developed these ideas even further, and, like the model town, it set aside space for residences in the form of apartments. On this building, see Bluestone, pp. 117–18, 149; Gilbert, *Perfect Cities,* p. 141; and Leyendecker, *Palace Car Prince,* pp. 176–77.

27. Joseph Kirkland, *The Story of Chicago,* vol. 1, p. 400.

28. Buder, *Pullman,* p. 94. "Operatives," a term used quite generally in discussions of Pullman, has a more precise meaning that is important in the history of labor and the organization of manufacturing in the late nineteenth-century. The operative was a person of limited skill and training who repeatedly performed the same defined task in a complex and highly rationalized system of production dictated entirely by employers, often following the recommendations of management experts. The rise of the operative, a worker as interchangeable as the parts that he (or, as was often the case, she) handled, represented a victory by management over labor in the struggle for control of the workplace. "Unlike either the craft worker," David Montgomery writes, "whose training and traditions permitted considerable autonomy in the direction of his own and his helpers' work, or the laborer, who applied his portable muscle power wherever and whenever directed, the operative was a specialist, bound to repetition of the same task in the same place. Because the operative's work was easily defined and measured, it was compensated more often by the piece than by the day or the hour." Montgomery explains that the operative should be understood neither as an ideal type nor as an intermediate figure between the skilled and unskilled worker, "but as a historical development of ever increasing importance in the reshaping of the working class as the century progressed," beginning with the textile and clothing industries right after the Civil War. He points out that in the early 1890s, by the company's own description,

operatives made up about one-fifth of the Pullman work force, craftsmen about three-fifths (down from an earlier high of about three-fourths), and laborers about one-fifth. He notes that the piecework system that was instituted by the company in response to the depression of 1893 diminished the distinction between craftsmen and operatives. Montgomery, *The Fall of the House of Labor,* Chapter 3, "The Operative," pp. 112–70, especially pp. 115–16, 126–31.

29. [Doty?], *The Story of Pullman,* p. 9. In fact the company probably expected people to behave better on the train than at home since Pullman's cars were likely to be more luxurious and more scrupulously maintained. A typical newspaper article from the mid-1870s told its readers that the cars had reached "the acme of splendor," and went on in lengthy and loving detail to describe the black walnut paneling, gilt and silver-plated ironwork (including the spittoons), tapestry curtains, plush velvet upholstery, magnificent carpets, generous lighting, and other convenience and safety devices. *Pueblo* (Colorado) *Chieftain* (30 August 1876), PSNL Miscellaneous Scrapbooks, Series A, vol. 4.

30. *Report on the Chicago Strike,* p. 602.

31. Starrett, "Pullman—A Social and Industrial Study."

32. [Doty?], *The Story of Pullman,* pp. 31–34.

33. Doty, *The Town of Pullman,* p. 4.

34. Wright, *Pullman,* pp. 15, 17–20, 23–24; Starrett, "Pullman—A Social and Industrial Study."

35. James Gilbert examines the relationship between Pullman's religious background and his attitude toward the malleability of the worker. He also notes the broader influence of the industrious evangelical culture of the farms and small towns of antebellum New York and New England on the generation of Chicago leaders among whom Pullman was so prominent. See *Perfect Cities,* pp. 147–49, 37–42.

36. Wright, *Pullman,* pp. 24, 18; *St. Louis Spectator* (30 September 1882), PSNL Miscellaneous Scrapbooks, Series A, vol. 7; Charles Dudley Warner, "Studies of the Great West," p. 126.

37. *Report on the Chicago Strike,* p. 529; *Chicago Daily Inter-Ocean* (16 October 1885), PSNL Miscellaneous Scrapbooks, Series B, vol. 1; *Philadelphia Public Ledger and Daily Transcript* (3 April 1884), PSNL Miscellaneous Scrapbooks, Series B, vol. 1. The Pullman Company took frequent and detailed censuses of the local population. The 1885 annual report counted 3,752 men, 1,945 women, and 2,906 children in 1,381 families, with an average household size of 6.9. *Chicago Daily Inter-Ocean* (16 October 1885), PSNL Miscellaneous Scrapbooks, Series B, vol. 1. The annual reports proudly cited increases in both the number of employee savings accounts in the Pullman Bank and in the balances in these accounts.

38. Wright, *Pullman,* pp. 5–6.

39. Ely, "Pullman: A Social Study," p. 463.

40. [Doty?], *The Town of Pullman,* pp. 29, 26.

41. *Report on the Chicago Strike,* p. 602.

42. *Chicago Tribune* (12 April 1883), p. 7.

43. In this respect Pullman perhaps felt more genuinely "paternal" to some

of his stockholders than to his employees. The company's literature emphasized its solidity by pointing to the high number of charitable institutions, trusts, and widows that owned shares.

44. Jane Addams, "A Modern Lear," in *The Social Thought of Jane Addams,* ed. Christopher Lasch (Indianapolis: Bobbs-Merrill, 1965), p. 112. According to both Leyendecker and Gilbert, Pullman's own home life was luxurious but less than happy. He was an easily irritated man who doted on Florence and was fond of her sister Harriet, but he was never close to his twin sons, whose purposelessness and irresponsibility angered and distressed him. His business duties and his wife Hattie's hypochondriac pursuit of various cures and regimens—perhaps brought on by neglect—meant that they spent a great deal of time apart, though they apparently were never estranged and remained affectionate.

45. Warner, "Studies of the Great West," p. 127. Pullman did promote quickly those individual workers he judged to be outstanding employees, and he helped a few set up their own businesses. Similarly, the company repeatedly pointed with pride to those cases in which workers saved their wages (preferably in the Pullman Bank) and bought their own homes in nearby communities. But the prospect of George Pullman willingly selling any property in the town was always remote.

46. *Report on the Chicago Strike,* p. 529; Ely, "Pullman: A Social Study," p. 463; "Pullman's Great Work," *Chicago Times* (10 January 1891), PSNL Miscellaneous Scrapbooks, Series A, vol. 14.

47. For another view of paternalism in Pullman, see Richard Sennett, *Authority* (New York: Alfred A. Knopf, 1980), pp. 62-77. Liston Leyendecker argues that Pullman became more and more aloof from his employees through the years, and that his closest personal link to the work force was broken in 1886 when his brother Albert, who as second vice president dealt with operatives, left the company. *Palace Car Prince,* pp. 214-15.

48. Buder, *Pullman,* pp. 36-37; Almont Lindsey, *The Pullman Strike: The Story of a Unique Experiment and of a Great Labor Upheaval* (Chicago: University of Chicago Press, 1942), pp. 32-33. Charles Reade (1814-88), though little read nowadays, was a well-known dramatist and novelist in the United States as well as in Britain. From the mid-1850s he devoted several works to different causes, including the humane treatment of inmates in prisons and lunatic asylums. As a reform-minded writer, he has been frequently linked in his authorial intentions, if not in artistic skill, with Dickens. Reade mixed melodramatic plots with factual material he clipped from various sources and kept in scrapbooks for reference when writing his exposés of social wrong. Reade published *Put Yourself in His Place* serially in the *Cornhill Magazine* during 1869-70 and produced a version for the stage, titled *Free Labour,* before its publication as a book. The familiarity of Reade's novel to late nineteenth-century readers is indicated by the fact that Ely also mentioned it in his 1885 article on Pullman in *Harper's,* apparently without knowledge of its influence on Pullman, and Thomas Nast made explicit reference to it in a drawing sympathetic to business that appeared in *Harper's Weekly* in March of 1871. For more on Reade, who shortly before his death became involved in a plagiarism scandal, see Wayne

Burns, *Charles Reade: A Study in Victorian Authorship* (New York: Bookman Associates, 1961), and Thomas Mallon, *Stolen Words: Forays into the Origins and Ravages of Plagiarism* (New York: Ticknor and Fields, 1989), Chapter 2, "A Good Reade: Malfeasance and *Mlle. de Malepeire*," pp. 41–88.

49. Charles Reade, *Put Yourself in His Place* (Boston: Dana Estes, n.d.), p. 3.

50. Reade, *Put Yourself in His Place*, p. 58.

51. James Gilbert discusses Pullman's inability to understand the world he helped create in *Perfect Cities*, p. 145.

52. *Chicago Herald* (7 May 1883, 13 January 1886), PSNL Town Scrapbooks, vol. 1; (31 May 1890), PSNL Miscellaneous Scrapbooks, Series A, vol. 13; *Philadelphia Evening Bulletin* (9 February 1886), PSNL Miscellaneous Scrapbooks, Series B, vol. 1.

53. *Alarm* (13 December 1884), p. 1; *Chicago Tribune* (1 October 1885), PSNL Town Scrapbooks, vol. 1. On the strike talk, see also the *Chicago Daily News*, the *Chicago Herald*, and the *Chicago Mail* of October 1, as well as the *Alarm* of October 3. The company spokesman said that while there had been a good crowd, it was smaller than reported, that no more than a tenth of it actually worked at Pullman, and that none of the company's "best men" were there, for they were satisfied with the wage reductions.

54. According to Buder, Ely was asked to write the article after a complicated series of events that included Henry Demarest Lloyd's refusal to let the magazine run a greatly edited article that he had written a few years earlier, Cornell University president Andrew White's agreeing to write in Lloyd's place and then backing out of the assignment, and White's recommendation of Ely. Buder, *Pullman*, pp. 99–101.

55. Ely, "Pullman: A Social Study," pp. 452–53, 455.

56. Ely, "Pullman: A Social Study," pp. 461–63. A newspaper story from 1891 described Pullman as looking more like "a modern university" than a factory town, and them moved into the by-then standard discussion of Pullman as the answer to the capital-labor riddle: "Art, education, flowers and music, comfortable, and even elegant homes were provided in the belief that workmen living under such influences would produce a higher grade of workmanship." "Pullman's Great Work," *Chicago Times* (10 January 1891), PSNL Miscellaneous Scrapbooks, Series A, vol. 14.

57. Ely, "Pullman: A Social Study," pp. 455, 458, 463.

58. Ely, "Pullman: A Social Study," pp. 463–65.

59. Ely, "Pullman: A Social Study," pp. 460–61, 465–66.

60. *New York Sun* (25 January 1885), PSNL Town Scrapbooks, vol. 1; *Nation* (29 January 1885), PSNL Town Scrapbooks, vol. 1. Several newspaper articles of the same time also criticized the "luxurious dependence" of the Pullman workers and smaller problems, such as Pullman's insistence on charging enough rent for the Greenstone Church to make it "pay," undermining religion in the town. The *Buffalo Express* published a letter to the editor defending Pullman against Ely's attacks, citing the report of Wright and his colleagues and praising the town as "a city where debauchery and crime can not find permanent lodgment within its borders." The editor responded that Ely's article made it clear that the danger of the Pullman plan was "inherent in the very

'idea' itself." No resident could feel a stake in the community or permanent interest in it. "There can be no local attachment to Pullman, no pride in haling from that well-ordered town, on the part of the operatives who live there." *Philadelphia Times* (1 February 1885), *Chicago Herald* (4 February 1885), PSNL Town Scrapbooks, vol. 1; *Buffalo Express* (15 February 1885), PSNL Miscellaneous Scrapbooks, Series B, vol. 1.

James Brady Smithson sees Pullman "first and foremost, as an experiment in community," explaining, "That is, the impact of the model town in its own day as well as its enduring significance today is a consequence of the fact that the model town was an effort to recapture community within industrial society and by means of industrial organization." He views the failure of Pullman largely in terms of the conditions of its existence: "lack of closure and susceptibility to influences outside of the control of the company," including influences resulting from its location in Chicago; "conflict of loyalties on the part of the company, especially between shareholders and workers"; the "high degree of formality, rationality, and resulting inflexibility"; and the "capricious and unilateral definition of responsibility for workers." Smithson maintains that the town was built at a moment of balance in the history of American industrial policy between an orientation toward the local community and social accountability that characterized earlier experiments, and one toward the expanding national and international marketplace. See "The Incorporation of Community: An Analysis of the Model Town of Pullman, Illinois, as a Social Experiment" (Ph.D diss., Cornell University, 1988), pp. 3, 220, 243.

61. Warner admitted that the town's "interference with individual responsibility" was perhaps "un-American." Still, when he contrasted "the dirty tenements, with contiguous seductions to vice and idleness, in some parts of Chicago, with the homes of Pullman," Warner was glad that this experiment had been undertaken. "It may be worth some sacrifice," he reasoned, "to teach people that it is better for them, morally and pecuniarily, to live cleanly and under educational influences that increase their self-respect." Warner, "Studies of the Great West," p. 127. Warner offered the same rationalization for company ownership that Pullman himself forwarded, that it would take time for the worker to develop good habits, and that with the "full evolution" of the Pullman idea, when "laboring people will voluntarily do . . . what they have here been induced to accept," they would be allowed to purchase property in the town. *St. Louis Spectator* (30 September 1882), PSNL Miscellaneous Scrapbooks, Series A, vol. 7.

CHAPTER TEN

1. The European examples most often cited were the Krupp works in Germany, Guise in France, and Saltaire in England. The railroad strikes of 1877 and the development of the national economy through the 1880s prompted other employers besides George Pullman to take progressive measures to deal with the labor problem. For instance, while some railroad managers maintained that only the market could determine wages, others moved to establish insurance programs, reading rooms, YMCAs, and related benefits to promote

the welfare of their employees, reduce the appeal of unions, and prevent strikes. See Stromquist, *A Generation of Boomers,* pp. 234–51.

2. See John S. Garner, *The Model Company Town: Urban Design through Private Enterprise in Nineteenth-Century New England* (Amherst, Mass.: University of Massachusetts Press, 1984); John S. Reps, *The Making of Urban America: A History of City Planning in the United States* (Princeton: Princeton University Press, 1965), Chapter 15, "The Towns the Companies Built," pp. 414–38. Citing the example of the yearly years of Lowell, Massachusetts, and its unique experiment with young women in its work force, Garner observes, "Long before the advent of Pullman, and prior to a time when laws obligated companies to observe safety and health standards, paternalism was viewed as a means to protect labor" (p. 54). Discussing the founding of nearby Gary, Indiana, in 1908 by United States Steel, Sam Bass Warner, Jr., writes, "The industrial satellite city, a mill town set within a metropolitan region where workers could live and labor in their own community instead of commuting to work, was a characteristic type of the era." *The Urban Wilderness* (New York: Harper and Row, 1972), p. 105. On the possible influence of Pullman on Ebenezer Howard and, through him, the Garden City movement of the late nineteenth and early twentieth centuries, see Stanley Buder, *Visionaries and Planners: The Garden City Movement and the Modern Community* (New York: Oxford University Press, 1990), pp. 27–28.

3. The distinctive features of the discussion of social, and especially urban, disorder in America reflected this country's particular history, geography, demography, and values. The most important concerns in this discussion were the bewilderingly sudden and apparently uncontrollable growth of cities like Chicago, uneasiness about the limits of what was once thought to be an inexhaustible supply of natural resources, the enormous influx of immigrants and the changing ethnic composition of this population, the appearance of large corporations and labor unions and the accompanying increase in strikes, and the perceived threat that all of these posed to democratic tradition and to America's special historical destiny. Such concerns were the most pressing subject of American literature and social thought from 1877 to the turn of the century.

4. Frederic Cople Jaher, *Doubters and Dissenters: Cataclysmic Thought in America, 1885–1918* (Glencoe, Ill.: The Free Press of Glencoe, 1964) provides a good analytical survey of this literature.

5. Gronlund, *The Cooperative Commonwealth* (Cambridge, Mass.: The Belknap Press of Harvard University Press, 1965); Strong, *Our Country: Its Possible Future and Its Present Crisis* (New York: Baker and Taylor, 1885). The Belknap edition of Gronlund's book is a reprint of the original 1884 text published by Lee and Shepard in Boston and Charles T. Dillingham in New York, but it also includes the introduction to the revised 1890 edition. The Danish-born Gronlund, after a brief time in Milwaukee, came to Chicago and was admitted to the Illinois bar in the late 1860s before moving to New York a decade later. While his book found a following among "respectable" reform-minded readers, it was also advertised for sale in some anarchist publications at the time, as were the works of Richard T. Ely.

6. John L. Thomas, *Alternative America: Henry George, Edward Bellamy, Henry Demarest Lloyd and the Adversary Tradition* (Cambridge, Mass.: The Belknap Press of Harvard University Press, 1983). See also Thomas's earlier essay, "Utopia for an Urban Age: Henry George, Henry Demarest Lloyd, Edward Bellamy," in *Perspectives in American History* 6, ed. Donald Fleming and Bernard Bailyn (1972), pp. 135–63.

7. *Progress and Poverty* is a ponderous theoretical analysis of the current socioeconomic order that only well into the second half of the book presents the virtues of the Single Tax on land with which its author became so closely identified. *Wealth Against Commonwealth*'s attack on large corporations is exhaustively substantiated with specific detail and citations from legal cases, legislative proceedings, commission reports, and other official documents. *Looking Backward* is a futuristic vision of Boston, America, and the world in the year 2000 reorganized into a productive and harmonious society. George was deeply attached to his Single Tax as an all-encompassing solution, and he was suspicious of the causes of socialism and labor to which Lloyd in particular was increasingly sympathetic.

8. Strong, though certainly more conservative than the others, was hardly an unquestioning supporter of the current economic order. He attacked the use of technological innovation to pursue exploitative monopoly and the emergence of a permanent and degrading class system which disregarded the humane needs of workers and created catastrophic strife between corporations and powerful trades-unions. And, like so many others, Strong equated his cause with the most crucial contest to save the nation: "What the campaign in Pennsylvania was to the Civil War, what the battle of Gettysburg was to that campaign, what the fight for Cemetery Hill was to that battle, such is the present opportunity to the Christian civilization of this country." Strong, *Our Country*, p. vii.

9. Pullman's luxury railroad cars, especially the sumptuous coaches of the kind in which he traveled and which he built on special order for the very rich, seemed to substantiate *Looking Backward*'s opening conceit that compared American society in the 1880s "to a prodigious coach" bearing the few well-to-do members of society "which the masses of humanity were harnessed to and dragged toilsomely along a very hilly and sandy road." Edward Bellamy, *Looking Backward, 2000–1887* (New York: Random House, 1982), p. 5.

10. For his part, Gronlund certainly rejected the Pullman "solution" of industrial reform through private ownership, but his call for a humane and efficiently administered bureaucracy to manage modern industrial life sounded like the Pullman idea in many of its particulars, from his proposal that human manure be piped from the city to farms in the country to his belief that what he called "family-exclusiveness" and "family-prejudice" had to be broken down through the community's assertion of its superior claim over children. Gronlund, *The Cooperative Commonwealth*, p. 200.

11. To some degree this is also true of Strong, who argued in *Our Country* that the only way to prevent social disintegration was to save the city's soul, and that this would necessarily involve some practical as well as spiritual work in behalf of the poor. In *The New Era; or the Coming Kingdom* (1893), Strong again

made the case for the primacy of what he saw as the values of Anglo-Saxon Christendom, arguing that improvements in hygiene and housing reform—of the kind George Pullman enacted—were a necessary foregrounding for spiritual progress. Five years later he devoted an entire book to the urban challenge. Certain now that the city would "control the nation," he was all the more determined that "Christianity must control the city; and it will." Turning to the language of public health, Strong predicted that "Twentieth century Christianity" would be the "remedy" for the epidemic of intemperance, infidelity, materialism, and mechanization that was plaguing society. "When living cells which disregard the laws of the organism enter it, and there multiply, there results typhoid fever, small-pox, diphtheria, or some other zymotic disease," he wrote. "If these intruders become numerous enough to overcome the law-abiding cells of the body, the result is anarchy, which is death." Josiah Strong, *The New Era; or the Coming Kingdom* (New York: Baker and Taylor, 1893), p. 193; *The Twentieth Century City* (New York: Baker and Taylor, 1898), pp. 180-81, 124-25.

12. Henry George, *Progress and Poverty* (New York: Robert Schalkenbach Foundation, 1955), pp. 9, 6, 443, 7. Thomas points out that Book X, titled "The Law of Human Progress" (with a section on "How Modern Civilization May Decline"), both belonged to a long-standing American fascination with catastrophe and looked ahead to the *"fin de siècle* obsession with cataclysm which in the next two decades swept across the whole of Western society." *Alternative America,* p. 27.

13. James D. Hart, *The Popular Book: A History of America's Literary Taste* (New York: Oxford University Press, 1950), pp. 175-76.

14. Henry George, *Social Problems* (New York: Robert Schalkenbach Foundation, 1939), p. 5. See also *Our Country,* pp. 108-9.

15. Expressing a xenophobia that linked him to Strong and which distinguished him from Bellamy and Lloyd, George also discussed cities in the same figurative language of dirt and disease that would become a regular part of the attacks on the Haymarket accused. Places like Chicago were dumping grounds of what he called the "human garbage" (made all the worse by the fact that this "garbage" could vote) in the urban tenements who were "hurrying modern society toward inevitable catastrophe." George, *Social Problems,* pp. 5-6, 116, 237.

16. *Progress and Poverty,* p. 456. As Thomas points out, George's place (along with Bellamy and Lloyd) in American thought is based less on his achievement as a persuasive social and economic theorist than as a representative of an adversary culture. But he was truly remarkable in the way his work anticipated key developments that followed, including increased social violence and accompanying cataclysmic thought, the rise of the Social Gospel and Progressivism, and the literature of urban anomie.

17. For more on the sources of the novel, see *Alternative America,* pp. 170-72.

18. Hart, *The Popular Book,* pp. 170-71. Many other utopias share with *Looking Backward* a vivid depiction of the city in disorder and distress along with an ideal vision of how it might be.

19. Bellamy, *Looking Backward,* pp. 10, 170, 173.

20. Bellamy, *Looking Backward,* p. 25. In Bellamy's sequel to *Looking Backward,* titled *Equality* (1897), he devoted a special section to the topic of "What Became of the Great Cities," whose projection of an ideal community is similar to George's. Now a small urban elite no longer exploits humbler producers and consumers, and cities have ceased to be the "great whirlpools" they once were when they "drew to themselves all that was richest and best, and also everything that was vilest, in the whole land." With the dispersal of markets of exchange, advances in technology, and the development of more widely placed cultural institutions, we learn, the urban population itself greatly diminished (as George also predicted it would with the application of the Single Tax on land), allowing for massive urban renewal featuring a "low, broad, roomy style" of architecture. In addition, "Parks, gardens, and roomy spaces were multiplied on every hand and the system of transit so modified as to get rid of the noise and dust, and finally, in a word, the city of [the late nineteenth century] was changed into the modern city." *Equality* (New York: AMS Press, 1970), pp. 290–95.

21. Bellamy, *Looking Backward,* p. 38.

22. From his position on the editorial staff of the *Chicago Tribune* as well as in the writings he published elsewhere, Lloyd attacked the abuses of capital and praised labor unions until illness and continuing friction with editor Joseph Medill caused him to resign in 1885. Horrified by the Haymarket bomb but equally appalled by the obvious injustice of the trial, Lloyd selflessly tried to save the anarchists from execution. He was in the last delegation that appealed to Governor Oglesby for clemency just before the hanging, and on the evening of the executions he retreated to his home in Winnetka to mourn, singing with his family a "Hymn to the Gallows" that he had written himself. His actions lost him friends and led his father-in-law, William Bross, to make sure that Lloyd would never have any control over the Bross fortune. Avrich, *The Haymarket Tragedy,* pp. 373–75; Thomas, *Alternative America,* pp. 79–80, 145–48, 207–10.

23. Henry Demarest Lloyd, *Wealth Against Commonwealth* (New York: Harper and Brothers, 1894), p. 2.

24. Lloyd, *Wealth Against Commonwealth,* p. 510. As Thomas points out, Lloyd, Bellamy, and George all viewed current events in light of the fall of Rome. See Thomas, *Alternative America,* pp. 1–6. The historical example of the fall of Rome, whether cited directly or through the mediation of Gibbon or Macaulay or others, was one of the most widely shared ideas of the period, appearing in literary forms from dime novels to *The Education of Henry Adams.* In his address to the reader at the outset of *The Cooperative Commonwealth,* for example, Gronlund warned that, without radical change in the current social order, barbarism would ensue, and he advised his audience not to be misled by signs of wealth when "possibly the under-current is, nevertheless, carrying us swiftly backwards." He continued: "Suppose you had told a Roman citizen in the age of Augustus that his proud country *then* had entered on its decline,—as every schoolboy now knows it had,—he would have thought you insane. Now, the many striking parallels between that period and the times in which we are living must have forced themselves on your attention, if you are of a reflective turn of mind, as we assume you are. You will have observed the same destruc-

tive forces to which History attributes the fall of pagan Rome busily at work under your very eyes" (pp. 5–6).

25. As noted earlier (Chapter 9, n. 54), *Harper's Monthly* accepted a revised version of this article in 1882, but then expanded it so extensively that, when he saw the galleys in 1884, Lloyd angrily refused to let *Harper's* publish it, and, through a complicated sequence of events, Richard T. Ely prepared his "social study" of the town. The article by Ely, who became a friend and ally of Lloyd, was much more critical than Lloyd's. Buder, *Pullman*, pp. 100, 238 n. 1.

26. Henry D. Lloyd, "Pullman," typescript, Henry Demarest Lloyd Papers (Microfilm Edition), State Historical Society of Wisconsin, Reel 20, "Articles and Addresses, 1859–1888," pp. 3, 4, 11. These quotations are from the original article that Lloyd prepared. The revised version that Lloyd rejected is also included in this collection.

27. Lloyd, *Wealth Against Commonwealth*, p. 499.

28. The discussions centering on Twain's sources and intentions in this uneven novel have long absorbed readers. Daniel Carter Beard's illustrations, strongly influenced by Beard's desire to merge Twain's ideas with those of Henry George, and which evidently won Twain's enthusiastic approval, complicate things further. When the book appeared, its critical reception was mixed, but it was warmly greeted by followers of both George and Bellamy. For more on sources of the novel and the discussion that surrounds it, see Henry Nash Smith's introduction to the University of California Press edition, edited by Bernard L. Stein (Berkeley, 1979), pp. 1–30; the excellent collection of supplemental materials in the critical edition edited by Allison R. Ensor (New York: W. W. Norton, 1982); and Beverly R. David, "The Unexpurgated *A Connecticut Yankee:* Mark Twain and His Illustrator, Daniel Carter Beard," *Prospects* 1 (1975), 99–117. The University of California edition includes the Beard illustrations. See also Henry Nash Smith, *Mark Twain's Fable of Progress: Political and Economic Ideas in "A Connecticut Yankee,"* (New Brunswick: Rutgers University Press, 1964).

29. See the excerpts from Howard G. Baetzhold, *Mark Twain and John Bull: The British Connection* (Bloomington: Indiana University Press, 1970), in Ensor, pp. 342–60. On Twain's views on the labor question, see Louis J. Budd, *Mark Twain, Social Philosopher* (Bloomington: Indiana University Press, 1962), excerpted in Ensor, p. 404.

30. Smith, *Mark Twain's Fable of Progress*, pp. 4, 38. Smith begins his analysis by placing Twain's novel in the context of two contemporary novels of business in an urban industrial age, Charles Dudley Warner's *A Little Journey in the World* and William Dean Howells's *A Hazard of New Fortunes*, describing the subject of all three as "the transformation of men and institutions by rapid industrial development," which "is the central fact of modern life." Smith also contends that Twain's book is "the first literary effort of any consequence to treat the entrepreneur sympathetically" (pp. 36–37).

31. Twain, *A Connecticut Yankee*, pp. 184–85, 226.

32. Twain, *A Connecticut Yankee*, pp. 128–29, 443–45.

33. Twain, *A Connecticut Yankee*, pp. 203, 466. In his more optimistic moments earlier in the novel, Hank speculates on the proper form of government,

and here he sounds in some ways as if believes in the Pullman example. "Unlimited power *is* the ideal thing—" Hank argues, "when it is in safe hands. The despotism of heaven is the one absolutely perfect government." Hank does admit, however, that the despot would have to be "the perfectest individual of the human race, and his lease of life perpetual" (pp. 127–28). Hank realizes the impossibility of perfection and the potential for an earthly despotism to become the worst form of government as well as the best, so he opts for a democratic republic—based on the assumption that he will be its leader.

34. Twain, *A Connecticut Yankee*, pp. 229, 318, 128, 458–61, 476, 480.

35. As Henry Nash Smith and others have pointed out, at the suggestion of his friend poet Edmund Clarence Stedman, Twain deleted from the typescript several hundred words which describe the complex methods by which Hank computes the exact weight of the dead flesh from the Battle of the Sand-Belt. Smith also indicates, however, that contemporary readers, including Howells, were considerably less shocked by such passages than modern critics. See Smith's introduction to the University of California Press edition, pp. 20–21.

36. There were a number of single-tax communities inspired by Henry George, probably the most noted being Fairhope on Mobile Bay. In October of 1894 *Harper's Weekly* featured—on the same page as an obituary of David Swing—a story on a Nationalist cooperative colony called Pacific City that had attracted 500 Americans to a remote location in Mexico on Topolobampo Bay in the Gulf of California. Here on the shores of this *"terra incognita,"* the magazine reported, "a handful of enthusiasts are trying to carry out the most advanced ideas of co-operative life as outlined in Edward Bellamy's book, *Looking Backward.*" While factionalism, jealousy, and isolation threatened the future of this undertaking, the conditions of the time were enough to make it merit the same kind of special attention Ely claimed that Pullman deserved. "The experiment, as it can only be called such," the article concluded, "is being watched with interest by a people grown thoughtful during a period of business depression, many of whom are eagerly looking for some system that promises freedom from the nightmares of modern industrial and social conditions." *Harper's Weekly* 38 (13 October 1894), 977; Donald Drew Egbert and Stow Persons, eds., *Socialism and American Life* (Princeton: Princeton University Press, 1952), vol. 2, p. 319. The Topolobampo area had been the scene of earlier experiments of the same kind that attracted attention in the troubled cities that inspired them. In January 1887, while it was covering the wedding plans of August Spies and Nina Van Zandt, the *Tribune* reprinted a story from the *San Francisco Chronicle* it titled "A Communistic Utopia." This told of a party of thirteen setting off to build a town "where crime will be unknown, poverty a rank impossibility, labor light, and all will dwell in a state of unalloyed happiness and comfort." Here women would have equal rights, hard currency would have no place, bachelors would be fined, and lawyers and drunks would not be tolerated. "Capital will no longer be in conflict with labor, political corruption will be wiped out, and all evils of existing governments will be eradicated." The town would follow the plan of civil engineer and railroad entrepreneur A. K. Owen, who might have been influenced by Pullman. It was to be "neat as a

pin," with paved and landscaped streets and parks throughout. Factories, businesses, markets, and housing would be located in different sections, connected by free cable cars and pneumatic tubes. Public buildings would include baths, theaters, and places of amusement. *Chicago Tribune* (26 January 1887), p. 5.

37. As Michael Ebner points out, the one time in its more than a century of history when Fort Sheridan was used for its original purpose was when its soldiers were sent to occupy Chicago during the Pullman strike. *Creating Chicago's North Shore: A Suburban History* (Chicago: University of Chicago Press, 1988), pp. 140-44. Fort Sheridan in some ways was evidently a less regulated and peaceful community than Pullman. Ebner reports that there was a great deal of controversy in 1893 when Highwood legalized the sale of liquor, wine, and beer in this otherwise teetotal area, leading to complaints by local residents about the soldiers' rowdiness on payday.

38. Addams and Lloyd became close friends, working together on many projects, and George addressed an enthusiastic audience in the Hull-House gymnasium, which, Addams remembered, "fairly rocked on its foundations under the enthusiastic and prolonged applause which greeted this great leader and constantly interrupted his stirring address, filled, as all of his speeches were, with high moral enthusiasm and humanitarian fervor." Addams, *Twenty Years at Hull-House*, pp. 77-78; "The Objective Value of a Social Settlement," in Addams et al., *Philanthropy and Social Progress* (New York: Thomas Y. Crowell, 1893), pp. 27-28.

39. Addams, "The Subjective Necessity of Social Settlements," in *Philanthropy and Social Progress*, pp. 4, 22; "The Objective Value of a Social Settlement," p. 52; *Twenty Years at Hull-House*, pp. 158-59.

40. Addams noted in this regard that it was vital to help new arrivals "to preserve and keep for them whatever of value their past life contained," but also "to bring them in contact with a better kind of Americans," which included not only the settlement volunteers but also educated members of their own ethnic group. "The Objective Value of a Social Settlement," p. 35. Addams also was concerned with the social importance of sanitation. For a time in the early 1890s Addams herself became garbage inspector of the nineteenth ward and helped organize incineration and recycling projects. *Twenty Years at Hull-House*, pp. 203-4.

41. Karl Baedeker, ed., *The United States, With an Excursion into Mexico: A Handbook for Travelers, 1893* (New York: DaCapo Press, 1893; reprint of the original edition published in Leipzig and New York), p. 286; Moses P. Handy, ed., *The Official Directory of the World's Columbian Exposition* (Chicago: W. B. Conkey, 1893), pp. 781, 785, 795; Buder, *Pullman*, pp. 147-48. For a photograph of the model of Pullman, see Rossiter Johnson, ed., *A History of the World's Columbian Exposition*, vol. 3 (New York: D. Appleton, 1898), p. 241; *Chicago Tribune* (1 November 1893), PSNL Miscellaneous Scrapbooks, Series B, vol. 4. The 1893 Pullman annual report also includes a handsome color foldout featuring the cars on exhibit at the fair. There are several clippings on Pullman's support for the fair in PSNL Miscellaneous Scrapbooks, Series A,

vols. 12 and 13. James Gilbert maintains that Pullman was "[o]ne of the three or four great tourist attractions of Chicago during the Exposition year," and that 10,000 of its visitors were from foreign countries. *Perfect Cities*, p. 135.

42. In his perceptive discussion of the relationship between world's fairs and the cities that mounted them, Neil Harris calls the major fairs of the late nineteenth century "testaments to the power of an urban dream, the first such dream to emerge in our country, for we still celebrated, rhetorically, the virtues of the countryside." The Chicago fair was "the Exposition as Heavenly City, a purified reflection of the actual character of the late nineteenth-century metropolis." "Great American Fairs and American Cities: The Role of Chicago's Columbian Exposition," in *Cultural Excursions: Marketing Appetites and Cultural Tastes in Modern America* (Chicago: University of Chicago Press, 1990), pp. 112, 115.

43. A composite portrait of the Secret Service Corps, with Bonfield prominently in the center, is featured in Joseph Kirkland and Caroline Kirkland, *The Story of Chicago*, Vol. 2 (Chicago: Dibble, 1899), p. 224.

44. Henry Van Brunt, "The Columbian Exposition and American Civilization," *Atlantic Monthly* 71 (May 1893), pp. 584, 583, 579.

45. For a discussion of the fair in these terms in the writings of several authors, including Theodore Dreiser, see Smith, *Chicago and the American Literary Imagination*, pp. 141–46. Some pointed to the cultural confusion of the commercial exhibits and attractions of the Midway, purposely located outside the White City proper, as a better reflection of the city as it actually was.

46. Montgomery Schuyler, "Last Words About the World's Fair," *Architectural Record* 3 (1893–94), pp. 299–300. In an often-quoted passage, Louis Sullivan bitterly maintained in his autobiography that, far from being an emblem of a finer world, the fair revealed Burnham's betrayal of modern architecture and democratic idealism, "a naked exhibitionism of charlatanry in the higher feudal and domineering culture, conjoined with expert salesmanship of the materials of decay." Sullivan, *The Autobiography of an Idea*, pp. 321–22. Sullivan's tirade against what he called "[t]he selling campaign of the bogus antique" (p. 324) went on for several pages. In a related manner, Henry Adams's equally well-known remarks on the fair in *The Education of Henry Adams* regarded it as a reflection of contemporary conditions, focusing on the exposition as a reflection of the chaos and contradictions of modernity.

47. Bellamy, *Looking Backward*, pp. 72–73.

48. W. D. Howells, *Letters of an Altrurian Traveller*, ed. Clara M. Kirk and Rudolf Kirk (Gainesville, Fla.: Scholars' Facsimiles and Reprints, 1961), p. 23; Debs quoted in Trachtenberg, *The Incorporation of America*, p. 218.

49. Addams, *Twenty Years at Hull-House*, p. 136; Thomas, *Alternative America*, pp. 283–84. Addams recalled in particular a congress on cooperative community experiments that met at Hull-House in the world's fair summer at which Lloyd, "who collected records of coöperative experiments with the enthusiasm with which other men collect coins or pictures," was the central figure. An "old time co-operator" attending the congress denounced some of Lloyd's ideas as being too similar to "'cut-throat business' and declared himself in favor of 'principles which may have failed over and over again, but are nevertheless as

sound as the law of gravitation.'" Lloyd and Adams "agreed that the fiery old man presented as fine a spectacle of devotion to a lost cause as either of us had ever seen, although we both possessed memories well stored with such romantic attachments." *Twenty Years at Hull-House,* p. 109.

50. Henry Demarest Lloyd, "No Mean City," in *Mazzini and Other Essays* (New York: G. P. Putnam's Sons, 1910), pp. 201–3.

51. Lloyd, "No Mean City," pp. 203, 204, 214.

52. Lloyd, "No Mean City," pp. 220–22, 224, 229–31. For a discussion of "No Mean City" in the context of Lloyd's career and his times, see Thomas, *Alternative America,* pp. 285–87.

53. Buder, *Pullman,* pp. 110–14. For more on the annexation movement in Chicago at this time, see Pierce, *A History of Chicago,* vol. 3, pp. 331–33. On the country as a whole, see Jon C. Teaford, *City and Suburb: The Political Fragmentation of Metropolitan America, 1850–1970* (Baltimore: The Johns Hopkins University Press, 1979), Chapter 3, "The Consolidation of the Metropolis, 1850–1910," pp. 32–63.

54. *Chicago Evening Journal* (17 February 1888), PSNL Town Scrapbooks, vol. 1. *Chicago Herald* (31 May 1890), PSNL Miscellaneous Scrapbooks, Series A, vol. 14.

55. Lloyd, *Wealth Against Commonwealth,* pp. 7, 181; Strong, *The Twentieth Century City,* pp. 124–25.

56. "The primary perception, which George shared with Bellamy and Lloyd, together with a large number of social critics after the Civil War," Thomas explains, "was that of an essentially rural republic, pastoral, small-town, run according to village values." They each desired a social order "that was still eighteenth-century in its stress on balance, measure, proportion, scale, and symmetry—a view of America as a complex of crossroads and neighborhoods, rooted in the land, truly productive and wholly satisfying." Thomas, *Alternative America,* pp. 119–20.

CHAPTER ELEVEN

1. Jane Addams, *Twenty Years at Hull-House,* p. 158; "A Modern Lear," p. 107.

2. M. A. Lane, "The Distress in Chicago," *Harper's Weekly* 38 (13 January 1894), p. 38.

3. In an article headlined "Where Peace Reigns," one local paper confidently observed, "Just now, when the whole country is trembling with the fever of a diseased labor condition, one finds a sort of satisfaction in studying the status of a town that is based and founded on labor, and yet one in which there is no serious clash between the interests of those who work for wages and the men who live from the profits of labor employed." *Chicago Sunday Herald* (29 April 1894), PSNL Miscellaneous Scrapbooks, Series A, vol. 17.

4. The *Times* reported that the company made matters worse by denying that there were any problems. Management supposedly now would not permit any charity work in the town, even though it was badly needed, because to do so would be to admit that the Pullman experiment was failing. Neither charity nor destitution were "contemplated in the theory upon which the town of Pullman was founded and is controlled." The town had become Pullman's "idol, his fet-

ich," a place where "[e]verything must be right because it is Pullman." *Chicago Times* (10–14 December 1893), PSNL Miscellaneous Scrapbooks, Series A, vol. 17. The *Sunday Herald*'s report on Pullman's peacefulness dismissed such stories as evidence of "the sensational in newspaper making." Ely's article in *Harper's* had cited as an example of the company's putting its concern for its own image ahead of the well-being of residents its refusal to allow a resident to found an organization for the poor and needy out of fear that this might make it appear that there was pauperism in the town. According to Buder, in 1892 the average length of residence in Pullman was four-and-a-quarter years. In September of that year, of 6,324 operatives, 13 percent owned their own homes and 22 percent rented outside the town. Buder, *Pullman*, pp. 81–3.

5. Buder, *Pullman*, p. 149. For a summary of strike action among Pullman workers, see Leyendecker, *Palace Car Prince*, pp. 180–81. In fairness to the company, it should be noted that it did not raise rents in good times, nor did it aggressively try to evict tenants who fell behind. There seems to have been little public discussion of whether the landlords of operatives outside of Pullman should reduce rents.

6. *Chicago Tribune* (15 May 1894), PSNL Strike Scrapbooks, vol. 1.

7. *Chicago Mail* (25 May 1894), PSNL Strike Scrapbooks, vol. 1; *Chicago Tribune* (12 June 1894), p. 6. The Civic Federation described itself as a "non-partisan, non-sectarian association, inviting the co-operation of all the forces that are now laboring to advance the municipal, philanthropic, industrial and moral interests of Chicago." Its leadership included banker Lyman Gage, who had worked to bring the city together after Haymarket and to make the world's fair a reality; Mrs. Potter Palmer, wife of real estate magnate Potter Palmer and head of the Board of Lady Managers at the fair; and Edward S. Dreyer, who was on the original Haymarket grand jury and later was one of those most fervent in appealing for the pardon, which he personally delivered to the state prison in Joliet. In May the Industrial Committee of the Federation appointed what it called "a board of conciliation" to help deal with "labor difficulties." Included on the board were Jane Addams and Henry Lloyd. Letter of Ralph M. Easley to Henry D. Lloyd (12 May 1894), Henry Demarest Lloyd Papers (Microfilm Edition), State Historical Society of Wisconsin, Reel 5, "Correspondence, General."

8. The General Managers Association had been inactive since the mid-1880s but was reorganized under new leadership early in 1893, almost simultaneously with the formation of the American Railway Union. Both developments were based in the recognition by the respective memberships that their individual interests would be best served by a common national strategy. Stromquist, *A Generation of Boomers*, p. 251.

9. *Chicago Times* (28 June 1894), PSNL Strike Scrapbooks, vol. 1.

10. Hopkins was perhaps the most notable case of an operative whose talent and initiative George Pullman tried to develop and reward. He started as a laborer in the lumberyards, but Pullman quickly promoted the highly capable employee and helped him get started in his own stores in the Arcade. Hopkins's highest post in the company was paymaster. A Democrat, Hopkins favored annexation to Chicago and helped carry Pullman for Cleveland in 1888. See

Almont Lindsey, *The Pullman Strike: The Story of a Unique Experiment and a Great Labor Upheaval* (Chicago: University of Chicago Press, 1942), pp. 80–81. This book is the most detailed history of the strike. For a brief summary, with excellent visual material on the town and the walkout, see Susan E. Hirsch, "The Metropolis of the West," in Hirsch and Goler, *A City Comes of Age,* pp. 76–82. On Altgeld's role in the strike, including his sympathy toward the Pullman residents suffering from the strike (whom he visited personally and for whom he helped raise contributions in the summer of 1894), his antagonism toward George Pullman and the Pullman Company, and the sharp criticisms he endured for his stance, see Barnard, *"Eagle Forgotten,"* pp. 271–317.

11. Grover Cleveland, *The Government in the Chicago Strike of 1894* (Princeton: Princeton University Press, 1913), p. 2. The article appeared in *McClure's* in July 1904.

12. See Lindsey, *The Pullman Strike,* pp. 206–7, for disputes between Miles and Major General John M. Schofield, commander of the army, on the placement of troops. In all, Cleveland sent out two-thirds of the army, or about 16,000 troops, along with some sailors and marines to deal with the strike across the nation. See Edward M. Coffman, *The Old Army: A Portrait of the American Army in Peacetime, 1784–1898* (New York: Oxford University Press, 1986), p. 251.

13. *Chicago Inter-Ocean* (7 July 1894), quoted in Lindsey, *The Pullman Strike,* p. 208.

14. John M. Egan called the charge that men were recruited by the railroads to burn cars "the vilest rot." *Report on the Chicago Strike,* pp. 158, 282; *Chicago Times* (30 June 1894), PSNL Strike Scrapbooks, vol. 2; Eugene V. Debs, "The Federal Government and the Chicago Strike," in *Writings and Speeches of Eugene V. Debs* (New York: Hermitage Press, 1948), p. 150. Debs originally prepared this last article as a response to Cleveland's essay in *McClure's,* but it was rejected, and he published it instead in the socialist journal *Appeal to Reason* in August of 1904. Almont Lindsey writes, "They [the mobs] were prepared to take advantage of any situation that would yield excitement and plunder. Unemployment and insecurity—products of the panic of 1893—had fostered a spirit of recklessness and despair, which in turn must have contributed to the recklessness of the crowds that assembled as much from curiosity as from any desire to do violence." *The Pullman Strike,* p. 205. The composition of the various mobs and their motives is hard to figure precisely, especially given the eagerness of the railroads and the government to pin the blame on Debs and the unions, and Debs's inability to restrain each and every worker no matter how eloquently he argued that disorder could only harm the union in the public eye. Lindsey sees no firm proof of agents provocateurs, but notes that there is some evidence that a few of the cars were fired by deputy marshals and that, though the railroads were careless in protecting their property, nothing very valuable was damaged. It is also possible that even if they did not deliberately plan the violence, the 5,000 belligerent and unprofessional deputies who were hired and armed by the railroads were as much a provocation as a deterrent to disorder.

15. Lindsey, *The Pullman Strike,* pp. 208–10. The main reason for the lack of wider union solidarity was that the strike seemed at this point to be a lost

cause, but the personal, philosophical, and tactical disagreements among different unions and their leaders complicated the issue. On the intricate union politics of the time—and the tensions between Debs and Gompers in particular—see Nick Salvatore, *Eugene V. Debs: Citizen and Socialist* (Urbana: University of Illinois Press, 1982), pp. 135-37.

16. Debs, "How I Became a Socialist," in *Debs: His Life, Writings and Speeches* (Girard, Kans.: The Appeal to Reason, 1908), p. 82.

17. Wright served as chairman ex officio, while the other two members were John D. Kernan of New York and Nicholas E. Worthington of Illinois (the law prescribed one member from the local state).

18. *Report on the Chicago Strike*, pp. xxiii, xlii; *Chicago Tribune* (13 November 1894), PSNL Strike Scrapbooks, vol. 9. The Commission set the cost of destroyed property and of the marshals at just under $700,000, the loss of earnings by the railroads at $4,672,916. It calculated that about 3,100 Pullman employees lost at least $350,000 in wages, and that some 100,000 workers on the twenty-four railroads centered in Chicago lost an estimated $1,389,143. *Report on the Chicago Strike*, p. xiii. The report is a remarkable document, not only for the bluntness of its findings, which had the effect of countering the anti-union feeling in official circles, but as a coherently focused collection of testimony by principals and other parties deeply involved in the strike and the events surrounding it.

19. Harry Perry Robinson, "The Humiliating Report of the Strike Commission," *Forum* 18 (1894), 526, 523.

20. *Chicago Evening Post* (11 May 1894), PSNL Strike Scrapbooks, vol. 1; *Chicago Tribune* (11 July 1894), PSNL Strike Scrapbooks, vol. 4.

21. "Social Unrest and Disorder," *The Chautauquan* 19 (April 1894), 224.

22. *Washington Chronicle* (1 July 1894), PSNL Strike Scrapbooks, vol. 2.

23. *Railway Age* (29 June 1894), PSNL Strike Scrapbooks, vol. 2. Even if they would explain the sources of the Chicago strike quite differently, the strike commissioners agreed with the appropriateness of the metaphor. Condemning strikes, boycotts, and lockouts as barbarisms, their report explained, "They are war—internecine war—and call for progress to a higher plane of education and intelligence in adjusting the relations of capital and labor." *Report on the Chicago Strike*, p. xlvi.

24. *Harper's Weekly* 38 (28 July 1894), 698. One commentator said that the current crisis was more severe than that in 1861, "for the more earnestly I have tried to grasp the situation, the more have I become convinced that we are fast drifting into a more appalling crisis even than the civil war." He claimed that society itself was not as threatened by the Civil War as it was in the current instance. H. von Holst, "Are We Awakened?" *Journal of Political Economy* 2 (September 1894), 485. Herman Eduard von Holst, who had held distinguished professorships in history in Germany, was one of the first major appointments at the University of Chicago, where he arrived in 1892. He was the author of books on the constitutional history and law of the United States.

25. *Chicago Tribune* (30 June 1894), PSNL Strike Scrapbooks, vol. 2.

26. *Report on the Chicago Strike*, p. 192.

27. Reverend William H. Carwardine, *The Pullman Strike* (Chicago:

Charles H. Kerr, 1894), pp. 118-19; *Chicago Tribune* (21 May 1894), PSNL Strike Scrapbooks, vol. 1. See also Stephen G. Cobb, "William H. Carwardine and the Pullman Strike" (Ph.D diss., Northwestern University, 1970). Some journalists themselves wondered about the broader damage caused by the indiscriminate use of certain terms. The *Chicago Dispatch* worried that Chicago was being slandered by all the talk of anarchy and anarchists, and observed, "Lawlessness has occurred but lawlessness is not anarchy, nor is ever lawbreaker an anarchist." The *Review of Reviews* published an article specifically on the promiscuous use of the term, claiming, "The point has been reached where certain newspapers would hardly be disposed to admit a difference between Trades Unionism and Anarchism." *Chicago Dispatch* (10 July 1894), PSNL Strike Scrapbooks, Vol. 4; "'Anarchist' as an Epithet," *Review of Reviews* 10 (August 1894), 255.

28. W. F. Burns, *The Pullman Boycott. A Complete History of the Great R.R. Strike* (St. Paul: The McGill Printing Co., 1894), p. 312; Carwardine, quoted in *Chicago Tribune* (21 May 1894), PSNL Strike Scrapbooks, Vol. 1; Carwardine, *The Pullman Strike*, pp. 23, 49. Carwardine's charge that Pullman was un-American was part of a speech he repeated several times. The *Chicago Times* of June 16 reports an address he delivered to the Single Tax Club in which he says essentially the same thing the *Tribune* quoted him as saying in late May. PSNL Strike Scrapbooks, vol. 1.

29. Walter Blackburn Harte, "A Review of the Chicago Strike of '94," *Arena* 10 (September 1894), 501; *Chicago Times* (30 June 1894), PSNL Strike Scrapbooks, vol. 2.

30. Debs, "Proclamation to the American Railway Union," in *Writings and Speeches of Eugene V. Debs*, p. 2; Burns, *The Pullman Boycott*, p. 16. T. Burke Grant seized on Pullman's decision to leave Chicago during the strike to compare him both to arrogant slaveholders and to decadent and doomed foreign royalty: "He called for the police to preserve his pictures and his plate. He rang for the obeisant darkey, who, even in this trying and rebellious period, approached his master with a low salaam, to order out his sumptuous palace car— the same that carried the Grand Duke Alexis of Russia on his hunting tour in the West, and, gorgeously attired, the Prince of Pullman, like Louis XVI, fled from the populace whose passions and whose power he defied." Grant, "Pullman and Its Lessons," *American Journal of Politics* 5 (August 1894), p. 197. John Merritt Driver further emphasized the slavery parallel when he expressed the hope that the book would be a second *Uncle Tom's Cabin*. "May its plain, honest facts," Driver wrote, "banish the flagrant misinformation with which the secular and even the religious press has been teeming for weeks, and may it be the mission of this book to stir the heart of this whole nation until the 'white slaves' of industrial tyranny be emancipated and receive the treatment becoming the sons and daughters of the Most High." Driver, Introduction to Carwardine, *The Pullman Strike*, p. 7. In 1890 the *Chicago Herald* quoted a Pullman worker who bitterly complained, "About the only difference between slavery at Pullman and what it was down South before the war, is that there the owners took care of their slaves when they were sick and here they don't." *Chicago Herald* (31 May 1890), PSNL Miscellaneous Scrapbooks, Series A, vol. 13.

31. Chicago *Times* (19 May 1894, 30 June 1894), PSNL Strike Scrapbooks, vols. 1, 2.

32. *Chicago Herald* (31 May 1890), PSNL Miscellaneous Scrapbooks, Series A, vol. 13; Gibbons, *Tenure and Toil; or, Land, Labor, and Capital,* 2d ed. (Chicago: Law Journal Print, 1894), p. 190.

In 1866, at the age of eighteen, Gibbons came to America from Ireland. He was educated at Notre Dame and established a successful legal career in Iowa before moving to Chicago in 1880. From 1893 to his death in 1917, he was a judge on the Illinois Circuit Court. *Tenure and Toil* is less significant for the accuracy of its observations or the value of its proposals than as one more substantial piece of evidence for the widespread feeling that something was basically and dangerously wrong with American society.

Less well known than the books of George, Gronlund, Bellamy, and Lloyd, Gibbons's work was close to them in spirit, and his attack on the model town was similar to Ely's. He maintained that the city was both cause and effect of much contemporary social disorder because of its concentration of capital and people. Convinced of the importance of private property to a settled order, he wished to make certain that every individual could have his own plot of land on which to build his life, and that it was necessary to limit the amount of property any one person or corporation could amass. To achieve this goal, Gibbons called not for Henry George's Single Tax on land, but for a progressive tax on wealth, an attack on trusts, and the distribution of the vast tracts of real estate owned by the government, railroads, large farms, private individuals, and corporations. Not satisfied with simply making this land available to the surplus urban population, Gibbons would virtually require any man over twenty-one unable or unwilling to work to be relocated, at public expense if necessary, to a parcel suitable to the size of his family. Here, with strict rules as to how he was to work and pay for the land, he would begin life again as a yeoman farmer.

33. Samuel Gompers, "The Lesson of the Recent Strikes," *North American Review* 159 (August 1894), 204; *Report on the Chicago Strike,* p. 195.

34. *Chicago Herald* (15 May 1894), PSNL Strike Scrapbooks, vol. 1; *Report on the Chicago Strike,* pp. 161–62; Debs, "The Federal Government and the Chicago Strike," pp. 151–52.

35. *Report on the Chicago Strike,* pp. xxxviii, xxii.

36. Buder, *Pullman,* p. 156; *Report on the Chicago Strike,* p. 602.

37. C. H. Eaton, "Pullman and Paternalism," *American Journal of Politics* 5 (December 1894), pp. 572, 577. Eaton accompanied Pullman when he sought refuge at Castle Rest, his home in the Thousand Islands, in July of 1894. On Eaton and Pullman, see Buder, *Pullman,* p. 239, n. 6; and Leyendecker, *Palace Car Prince,* p. 227. The discussion of paternalism at this time went beyond the Pullman strike. The same issue of the *American Journal of Politics* had another article on "Dangers of Paternalism," which, its author claimed, were most apparent in socialism, in protective legislation, and in big government, all of which the author perceived as threats to liberty and individualism.

38. T. C. Crawford, "The Pullman Company and the Striking Workmen," *Harper's Weekly* 38 (21 July 1894), 686–87.

39. Carwardine conceded that Pullman was a talented and honest business-

man, but he attacked the attitude which demanded "that we regard him as a benefactor to his race, as a true philanthropist, as one who respects his fellowmen, who regards his employees with the love of a father for his children." The same personal qualities that had made him successful, "untempered with nobler elements," had led to the "present predicament." As matters stood now, "Determination and resolution have turned into arrogance and obstinacy." Carwardine, *The Pullman Strike*, pp. 23, 24, 28.

40. *Report on the Chicago Strike*, p. xxvii.

41. T. M. Cooley, "The Lessons of the Recent Civil Disorders," *Forum* 18 (1894), 1–19; "Some Lessons of the Great Strike," *Harper's Weekly* 38 (21 July 1894), 674; "The Lesson of the Recent Strikes," *North American Review* 159 (August 1894), 180–206; Grant, "Pullman and Its Lessons," 190–204; J. W. Mason, "Pullman and Its Real Lessons," *American Journal of Politics* 5 (October 1894), 392–98. The *North American Review* article was in four parts that were individually authored by Nelson Miles, Wade Hampton, Harry P. Robinson, and Samuel Gompers.

42. *Report on the Chicago Strike*, p. xxvii.

43. Albert B. Hart, "Are Our Moral Standards Shifting?"; Charles W. Eliot, "Some Reasons Why the American Republic May Endure." *Forum* 18 (1894–95), pp. 513–22, 129–45.

44. T. Burke Grant, "Pullman and Its Lessons," p. 192.

45. As editor of the *Review of Reviews*, Stead had in February of 1890 selected Twain's *A Connecticut Yankee* as the journal's Novel of the Month. Stead maintained that the book was "the latest among the volumes whereby Americans are revolutionising the old country," and he linked it in this regard to the "social-democratic movement" best exemplified by the "land nationalisation theories" of Henry George that "have gained a firm hold of the public mind," and by Edward Bellamy's *Looking Backward,* "which has supplied our people with a clearly written-out apocalypse of the new heaven and the new earth that are to come after the acceptance of the Evangel of Socialism." Twain's novel, Stead declared, "is a third contribution in the same direction." Stead, cited in Ensor, ed., Norton Critical Edition of *A Connecticut Yankee*, pp. 331, 332–33.

46. William T. Stead, *If Christ Came to Chicago! A Plea for the Union of All Who Love in the Service of All Who Suffer* (Chicago: Laird and Lee, 1894), pp. 73, 75. See pp. 85–90 for his specific discussion of Pullman. Stead spoke of the justifiable antagonism the Pullman workers felt toward an employer who ruled them, as Ely had charged, like a German sovereign. So proud of how he kept his town well-organized, tidy, and free of vice, Pullman did not realize how little the purity enforced in Pullman did to eliminate the "baneful influences" he (and Stead) abhorred. The town's highly publicized moral probity was an illusion, since its restrictions did not discourage or diminish vice so much as move it to other places close by, such as neighboring Kensington, nicknamed "Bumtown," and the forty saloons and gaming houses on its main street. "There," wrote Stead, "the moral and spiritual disorder of Pullman was emptied, even as the physical sewage flowed out on the Pullman farm a few miles further south" (p. 89). Stead's book took its title from a conference he convened in the Central Music Hall in November of 1893 that focused, in his words, on "the question

whether, if Christ were to come to Chicago to-day, He would find anything in Chicago that He would wish to have altered." While he criticized the city and many of its commercial leaders during his stay and after, Stead still expressed special hope for Chicago's future. One of the final chapters of *If Christ Came to Chicago!* presented a utopian vision of the Chicago of the twentieth century. Stead laid out his thoughts on Chicago most succinctly in an unpublished article in which he wrote: "Whether or not Chicago will ever become the ideal city of the world is for the future to say; certainly she, more than any other city, has the opportunity at her feet. She is not laden down by any *damnosa hereditas* of the blunders and crimes of the past; her citizens are full of a boundless élan, and full of faith in the destiny of their city. They have a position of unique prominence in the heart of the New World. They have the incentive of the aspiration of the World's Fair; they have at their head a young and capable chief magistrate, who has set himself against the worst evils which afflict city life in America. It seems to me that nowhere on the whole of the earth's surface, for one of my ideas and aspirations, could I have been more profitably employed than I was in Chicago in the winter of 1893-94." See Frederick Whyte, *The Life of W. T. Stead,* vol. 2 (New York: Houghton Mifflin, n.d.), pp. 43, 53.

47. Stead then turned to imagery that even more specifically recalled the horrors of 1871: "The edifice of our competitive commercialism built four-square to all the winds that blow, massive, imposing, impregnable, has taken fire. But the door is locked, and neither is there any key forthcoming to unlock the wards of the great gate through which the inmates might go free. The world watches and sickens with horror; but the fire burns, the flames mount higher and higher, and there seems to be no escape." He went on to blame Pullman for withholding the key. W. T. Stead, *Chicago To-Day; or, the Labour War in America* (New York: Arno Press and the New York Times, 1969), p. 5. This is a reprint of the edition originally published in London in 1894 by William Clowes and Sons for the *Review of Reviews.*

48. W. T. Stead, *Chicago To-Day,* p. 261; "Incidents of Labour War in America," *Contemporary Review* 66 (July 1894), 75-76.

49. Published a decade before *The Jungle,* Bech-Mayer's novel is similarly dedicated "To the Wage-Earners of America." It was issued by the new pro-labor publisher Charles H. Kerr, who also published Carwardine's work, and included an end note calling for agents to help distribute "books like this one that expose acts of oppression and injustice, and books that point to some way for bringing about better social conditions." Once settled in Pullman, the Wrights quickly discover that things are not as appealing as they first seemed. A Scottish laborer who boards with them tells the Wrights that the fair was an exhibition of the skill and intelligence of the worker, but it was managed by those "who trample him under foot" and who committed "wholesale robbery" that escaped prosecution because "the thieves were too big." All the talk of the fair elevating and educating the worker was just more hypocrisy. Those who praised the exposition "set up an incessant cry about all those wondrous chances for labor to see and profit by seeing, while it was a fact that the laborer sat in his home, bitter, despairing, without a cent for car-fare or for admit-

tance." Nico Bech-Mayer, *A Story from Pullmantown,* illustrated with sketches by Capel Rowley (Chicago: Charles H. Kerr, 1894), p. 29.

50. "Those meetings of the workingmen from Pullmantown came to many as a voice from above. Many a suicide was prevented, many a heart-broken man and woman found strength to keep up the struggle by witnessing the self-sacrificing zeal of those workingmen in their efforts to unite. They forgot that they were artists in painting, and unskilled laborers, geniuses in mechanical work, and drudges in the clay of the brickyard; they only knew that they were all wage-earners, and what money one of them had was the other one's too, until they either starved together or bettered their conditions." Bech-Mayer continued in the next paragraph, "Therefore those evening meetings became meetings of true religion to those who took part in them." Bech-Mayer, *A Story from Pullmantown,* pp. 89, 77–78.

51. Wade Hampton, "The Lesson of the Recent Strikes," 194. Hampton had been congressman and senator before resigning to become a Confederate officer. He was elected governor at the end of Reconstruction and then senator, but was at the time he wrote the article commissioner of Pacific Railways, having lost his Senate seat to a populist coalition in 1890.

52. W. G. Sumner, "Industrial War," *Forum* 2 (1886), 1–8. Others had no problem in using a more worldly version of the language of redemption, morality, and patriotism to take a hard stand against the strikers and in favor of the reassertion of the rights of property. In a direct response to T. Burke Grant, J. W. Mason conceded that "from a moral standpoint" George Pullman may have been as remiss as his men, but Mason concluded that the workers were finally more deeply at fault because "morals cannot be enforced or inculcated by acts which do violence to moral laws and the laws of the country." "Pullman and Its Real Lessons," p. 392. Edgar A. Bancroft made the same argument when he maintained that if a reform movement gained public attention and aid in proportion to its ability to paralyze industry and cause industrial war, "we may as well abandon all claim to intelligence, self-control and morality." Bancroft, *The Chicago Strike of 1894,* p. 69.

53. "More than any previous railroad strike," Shelton Stromquist writes, "the Pullman boycott brought about the broad application of federal authority in its suppression. None of the tools of federal intervention were new with this crisis: troops, injunctions, and contempt of court citations had been tried before. But never before was the scale of federal intervention as great, and never before had it been as masterfully coordinated with a well-organized association of general managers." *A Generation of Boomers,* p. 256.

54. *In re Debs,* in *United States Reports. Cases Adjudged in the Supreme Court at October Term, 1894,* J. Bancroft Davis, Reporter (New York: Banks & Brothers, 1895), pp. 586, 582, 592.

55. W. L. Sheldon, "The Place of the Labor Leader," *American Journal of Politics* 5 (July 1894), 152.

56. Charles King, "The Future of the Army," *Harper's Weekly* 38 (30 June 1894), 615. After all, King continued, the most serious enemy was the army of the "dirty" within the country: "[A]re our revolutionists, recruited confessedly

from the masses ashore, to suddenly take to that element with which they of all people seem least acquainted, and considerately do their battling on the water?" The answer was obviously no, which meant that the army was the only hope in a time of aggressive agitators and spineless civil authorities: "[J]ust so long as human greed and human passions stand as they have stood since creation, just so long as demagogues and dynamiters and weak-kneed or weak-minded executives are prevalent in our land, just so long will there be danger from without and peril from within—invasion, insurrection, or rebellion—that can only be held at bay by eternal vigilance, by ceaseless preparation. And when the clash shall come, as come full well it may, just as in '61, on every field, in the seat and toil and shock of battle, shoulder to shoulder "regular," guardsman, and volunteer shall face the mob or fight the foe, and never until the millennium comes let any man believe 'the work of the army is done.'" The discussion of the proper size of the army was a continuing topic of concern among officers, government officials, and other commentators at this time.

57. Stromquist, *A Generation of Boomers*, p. 274.

58. *Report on the Chicago Strike*, p. 163.

59. John Swinton, *A Momentous Question: The Respective Attitudes of Labor and Capital* (Philadelphia: Keller, 1895), pp. 17, 209.

60. Gompers, "The Lesson of the Recent Strikes," 205.

61. *Report on the Chicago Strike*, pp. xlix, xlvii; Carroll D. Wright, "The Chicago Strike," *Publications of the American Economic Association* 9 (1894), 505, 518–19.

62. W. G. Sumner, "The Absurd Effort to Make the World Over," *Forum* 17 (1894), 93, 102, 95. Sumner the social scientist claimed to find "a rational and orderly process of development beneath the fragmented experiences of American life," offering himself as "the professional expert who defined the limits of the possible in a given social instance [unlike] the amateur reformer who wished to make the world over by moralizing every issue." Bledstein, *The Culture of Professionalism*, pp. 326–27. Bledstein also applies this observation to such people as Frederick Jackson Turner and E. A. Ross.

63. Thorstein Veblen, "The Army of the Commonweal," *Journal of Political Economy* 2 (June 1894), 457–61.

64. Stromquist, *A Generation of Boomers*, p. 231, 257–63. Olney also endorsed the Strike Commission's call for arbitration of major disputes and drafted the Erdman Act, which passed in 1898, outlawing the black-list, yellow-dog contracts, and employer interference in a worker's choice of union. By this point even railroad executives generally accepted the principle of at least voluntary arbitration.

65. Addams, *Twenty Years at Hull-House*, pp. 158–61.

66. Addams, *Twenty Years at Hull-House*, pp. 160–1; "A Modern Lear," pp. 108–9.

67. Addams, "A Modern Lear," p. 113.

68. Addams, "A Modern Lear," p. 117.

69. Addams, "A Modern Lear," p. 122.

70. Allen F. Davis, *American Heroine: The Life and Legend of Jane Addams* (New York: Oxford University Press, 1973), pp. 113–14; Lasch, *The Social*

Thought of Jane Addams, p. 106. Robert B. Westbrook discusses the effect of the strike on John Dewey in relation to the ideas of both Henry Demarest Lloyd's "No Mean City" and Jane Addams's "A Modern Lear." Dewey arrived at the height of the strike to take his new position at the University of Chicago. He felt great sympathy with the plight of the workers and was disturbed "by the hostility to the strikers expressed by intellectuals and academics." Westbrook adds that the strike "was not only a radicalizing experience for Dewey, it also illustrated a key point in his democratic theory, for it opened to view the moral shortcomings of a paternalistic brand of 'welfare capitalism' which failed to cultivate workers' capacity for autonomous participation in social life." *John Dewey and American Democracy* (Ithaca: Cornell University Press, 1991), pp. 83–91.

71. *Report on the Chicago Strike,* p. xliii.

72. Wooster, *Nelson Miles and the Twilight of the Frontier Army,* pp. 198–201. Wooster comments that Miles's conduct during the strike "displayed none of the talents that had marked his leadership against the Confederates and the Indians."

73. Miles, "The Lesson of the Recent Strikes," pp. 186, 187. Miles ended his essay: "In brief, let us not blow down the beautiful arch of our sovereignty—the hope of humanity, the citadel of liberty, independence, the temple of happiness for all mankind. Rather let us follow the avenues of peace, intelligence, and true manhood for the improvement of our condition as a nation and a people; upholding, supporting, and maintaining the supremacy of law and civil government, and cherishing and protecting in all its grandeur and benevolence the blessed inheritance vouchsafed to us by the Fathers" (p. 188). Miles did not explain how he would classify a "small town" like Homestead, Pennsylvania, and other similar nonurban settings of major industrial strife. For other discussions of the strike as a violation of cherished principles, see Edgar A. Bancroft, *The Chicago Strike of 1894* (Chicago: Gunthorp-Warren Printing Company, 1895), and Joseph Nimmo, Jr., *The Insurrection of June and July 1894 Growing Out of the Pullman Strike at Chicago, Ill.* (Washington: Age Printing Company, 1894). Bancroft read part of his work to the Illinois State Bar Association, and he relied on legal documents relating to the strike; Nimmo originally presented his findings as a talk to the National Statistical Association, of which he was vice president, Section of Railway Transportation. He estimated that the damages to the American economy by the strike were greater than those of the Civil War.

74. "Some Lessons of the Great Strike," *Harper's Weekly* 38 (21 July 1894), 674; *Nation* 59 (5 July 1894), 1.

75. General Miles, who was insatiably ambitious for publicity and promotion, had invited Remington to accompany him in his investigation of the conditions of the northern Cheyenne in the fall of 1890. Remington's alcoholism had proved an inconvenience, but he published the laudatory article hoped for in *Harper's Weekly* in December of 1890. Wooster, *Nelson A. Miles and the Twilight of the Frontier Army,* p. 177.

76. Frederic Remington, "Chicago Under the Mob," "Chicago Under the Law," "Withdrawal of the U.S. Troops," *Harper's Weekly* 38 (21, 28 July, 11 Au-

gust 1894), 680–81, 703, 748. On Remington's virulent xenophobia and desire for apocalyptic violence, both of which attitudes were unfortunately all too typical of the time, see David McCullough, "Remington the Man," in Michael Edward Shapiro and Peter H. Hassrick, eds., *Frederic Remington: The Masterworks* (New York: Harry N. Abrams, 1988), p. 28. Ben Merchant Vorpahl points out that Remington's first published work of fiction, "The Affair of the – th of July," which appeared in *Harper's Weekly* on February 2, 1895, expressed what he wished had happened at Pullman. Narrated by a young military officer, the story depicts a bloody showdown between the army and foreign-born revolutionaries in a Chicago from which the respectable population has fled. Vorpahl sees in the story the influence of Twain's *A Connecticut Yankee* and, more persuasively, of Donnelly's *Caesar's Column*. "In short," he writes, "confronted with an event that failed to meet the requirements of his imagination, Remington constructed a fictitious event to replace it." *Frederic Remington and the West. With the Eye of the Mind* (Austin: University of Texas Press, 1978), pp. 167–73.

77. Captain Charles King, *A Tame Surrender: A Story of the Pullman Strike* (Philadelphia: J. B. Lippincott, 1894), p. 211. There is some risk in making too much of historical melodrama like *A Tame Surrender*, but some of its unexpected elements were significant. Captain King, who applauded the breaking of the strike, was suspicious of large corporations. The soldier-gentleman hero of the novel criticizes the Pullman company for not reducing management salaries and rents when it cut workers' wages. "It has simply said to its wageworkers," he explains, "'You alone are the ones to suffer. You and your families and your cares and troubles are nothing to us.'" He expresses "respect and sympathy" for "the struggles, the self-denial, the charity, the patience, the helpfulness" of the workers (as opposed to their leaders). When someone suggests that the workers should be organized and controlled like the army, this military man rejects the idea since it would lead to a dangerous and unconstitutional standing force controlled by such corporations as the railroads, which, if anything, treated their employees worse than did the military, and, unlike the army, cut their pay when times were hard. *A Tame Surrender*, pp. 154–55, 157. Besides urging restraint in the use of military force and organization in civilian society as a means of assuring order, King acknowledged the admirable qualities of the working class as such, and not simply as potential members of the middle class. The book argues for the merging of the best that is in American society. In a plot line that recalled the Haymarket-era story "The Knight and the Lady," the heroine of the book has a working-class background, and her marriage to the hero—after his family realizes her nobility of character (she is described without condescension as a "sturdy little aristocrat")—seems to offer some hope for the future stability of the city.

78. *Chicago Tribune* (12 June 1894), p. 5. One should keep in mind how much Swing was committed to urban life, and that people like him could be great advocates as well as critics of Chicago. In situating his Central Church in a downtown theater building, Swing, with the support of many members of the city's elite, had refused to accept the dichotomy between business and home, commerce and faith, implicit in the move of other congregations away from the central city. As Daniel Bluestone points out, because the cost of attending his

services was less than pew rentals in other leading churches, he preached his liberal notions to a more diverse congregation than did many other ministers, calling for a greater mutual understanding across class lines. Bluestone, *Constructing Chicago*, pp. 98-101.

79. *Report on the Chicago Strike*, p. 641.

80. Miles, "The Lesson of the Recent Strikes," pp. 187-88.

81. Hampton, "The Lesson of the Recent Strikes," p. 194; Goldwin Smith, "'If Christ Came to Chicago,'" *Contemporary Review* 66 (September 1894), 387; Stead, *If Christ Came to Chicago!*, p. 410. Stead was, however, making this remark in praise of the kind of community he felt Jane Addams was establishing in the Hull-House neighborhood.

82. Boyer, *Urban Masses and Moral Order in America*, p. 98; Gibbons, *Tenure and Toil*, p. iii; Francis G. Peabody, "Colonization as a Remedy for City Poverty," *Forum* 17 (1894), 52-53. Peabody (1847-1936) had earlier been appointed by Harvard to the position of Parkman Professor of Theology. A moderate who emphasized the responsibilities of the wealthy in bridging the separation between capital and labor, he published *Jesus Christ and the Social Question* in 1900.

83. "What's the Matter With Chicago?" in *Writings and Speeches of Eugene V. Debs*, pp. 50-54. Debs explained that he wrote this article, which was originally published in the *Chicago Socialist*, after reading the answers by spokesmen from different classes who were responding to this question as raised by William E. Curtis, correspondent of the *Chicago Record-Herald*. Believing that the supposed labor leaders and workers whose opinions were solicited "take the prize in what would appear to be a competitive contest for progressive asininity," he decided to formulate a response himself. The Rockefeller letter, dated June 19, 1897, is quoted in Ray Ginger, *The Bending Cross: A Biography of Eugene Victor Debs* (New Brunswick: Rutgers University Press, 1949), p. 201. Ginger comments: "If Debs had intended this letter as dramatic irony, it might have been called a stroke of genius, but he was completely sincere." See also Salvatore, *Eugene V. Debs*, p. 164.

84. Bryan, quoted in *Documents of American History*, ed. Henry Steele Commager, 8th ed. (New York: Appleton-Century-Crofts, 1968), vol. 1, p. 627.

85. Henry George, *Progress and Poverty*, p. 390; *Social Problems*, p. 29.

86. Turner and his wife arrived a few days before his July 12 session and stayed in a dormitory of the University of Chicago, located just north of the Midway, but he did not get a chance to do much sightseeing (he even passed up a chance to see Buffalo Bill's Wild West Show) since he still had to finish his essay. On George's anticipation of the ideas of Turner, see also John L. Thomas, *Alternative America*, pp. 128-29; and Richard Hofstadter, *The Progressive Historians: Turner, Beard, Parrington* (New York: Alfred A. Knopf, 1968), p. 58. On Turner in Chicago, see Ray Allen Billington, *Frederick Jackson Turner: Historian, Scholar, Teacher* (New York: Oxford University Press, 1973), pp. 124-31.

87. Frederick Jackson Turner, "The Significance of the Frontier in American History," in *The Frontier in American History* (New York: Henry Holt,

1920), pp. 1–38. As Billington notes, Turner probably read only a portion of his essay, which did not receive much notice at the time he gave it. He read it again in December at the State Historical Society of Wisconsin, which was the first to publish it.

88. "The Chicago Drainage Canal," *Harper's Weekly* 38 (1 September 1894), 827.

89. *Arcade Mercantile Journal* (4 October 1890), p. 1. Chicago Public Library, Special Collections Division. Hofstadter, *The Progressive Historians* (pp. 48–50), perceptively links Turner's talk to the publication—in Chicago in 1894—of Hamlin Garland's literary and cultural manifesto *Crumbling Idols,* which championed the imaginative qualities of the middle western and western farm and village as subject and inspiration while criticizing eastern and European standards as no longer relevant to the development of American art and social thought. Garland himself settled in Chicago, which he saw as the appropriate cultural capital of America, and devoted some of his fiction to depicting how the common citizen-farmer was being driven off the land. The writers of rural background who were most closely associated with Chicago's distinguished literary achievements at the turn of the century, whatever their criticisms of the city, often offer a far more devastating critique of life in the countryside. See Smith, *Chicago and the American Literary Imagination,* pp. 5–6, 11.

90. *Chicago Tribune* (9 October 1893), pp. 1, 12. A copy of the Chicago Day poster is in the Prints and Photographs Department of the Chicago Historical Society. The attendance figure is from the *Tribune* of October 29. The second largest single-day attendance total, on the Fourth of July, was 283,273. The final total was 27,529,400, which fell just short of the record set by the Paris fair of 1889. *Chicago Tribune* (31 October 1893), p. 1. The count on Chicago Day (and the totals for other days) included visitors entering more than once.

91. *Chicago Tribune* (29 October 1893), pp. 1, 3; (30 October), p. 1, 3. Kevin Tierney, *Darrow: A Biography* (New York: Thomas Y. Crowell, 1979), pp. 88–116; Clarence Darrow, *The Story of My Life,* pp. 62–73.

92. *Chicago Tribune* (6 July 1894), p. 7; "The Burning of the World's Fair Buildings," *Harper's Weekly* 38 (21 July 1894), 687. Of additional interest here is that public health officials attributed an outbreak of smallpox—the kind of outbreak avoided after the fire because of health measures taken by the Relief and Aid Society—to the crowds visiting the fair. Thus one of the effects of the disaster was to escape at least one sort of crisis that the triumphs of the fair supposedly helped cause. See Robert W. Rydell, "A Cultural Frankenstein? The Chicago World's Columbian Exposition of 1893," in Harris et al., *Grand Illusions,* pp. 166–69. Rydell's work in this essay, and in his earlier *All the World's a Fair: Visions of Empire at American International Expositions, 1876–1916* (Chicago: University of Chicago Press, 1984), focuses on the exposition as a planned demonstration of the superiority of the elite white Protestant culture already dominant in most aspects of life in the nation.

93. H. H. Van Meter, *The Vanishing Fair,* ill. William and Charles Ottman (Chicago: The Literary Art Company, 1894), pp. 21, 23.

EPILOGUE

1. The literature of both progressivism and modernism in America is extensive, and the former in particular has become deeply conflicted. For discussions of the difficulties of defining both terms, see Daniel T. Rodgers, "In Search of Progressivism," *Reviews in American History* 10 (1982), 113–32; and Daniel Joseph Singal, "Towards a Definition of American Modernism," *American Quarterly* 39 (1987), esp. pp. 7–8.

2. Henry Adams, *The Education of Henry Adams* (Boston: Houghton Mifflin, 1918), p. 498; George, *Social Problems*, p. 3.

3. William James, "What Makes a Life Significant," *The Writings of William James. A Comprehensive Edition*, ed. John J. McDermott (Chicago: University of Chicago Press, 1977), pp. 647–48. This essay, which was based on a lecture, appeared in *Talks to Teachers on Psychology: and to Students on Some of Life's Ideals* in 1899.

4. William James, "On Some Mental Effects of the Earthquake," in *Memories and Studies* (New York: Longmans, Green, 1917), pp. 213, 211. This essay was first published in *Youth's Companion* in June of 1906.

5. Career reformer Frederic C. Howe, for example, explained in his influential work *The City: The Hope of Democracy* (Seattle: University of Washington Press, 1967; originally published by Charles Scribner's Sons in 1905) that he had moved from the opinion held by leading businessmen, that democracy had to be controlled for the good of urban order, to the belief that the best "hope" was to extend it. Howe was influenced by Henry George in formulating his arguments that certain changes had to be made in the economic basis of city life for social democracy to succeed. In recent years Dewey and others (including figures like Howe) have been criticized for their alleged complicity with political and business leaders and other explicitly management-oriented reformers who, in the name of efficiency, organization, and expertise, advanced the cause of state and corporate power to the detriment of social democracy. For a discussion (including a defense) of Dewey in these terms, see Westbrook, *John Dewey and American Democracy*, pp. 185–89.

6. Rev. David Swing, *A Story of the Chicago Fire* [Chicago: H. H. Gross, 1892,], pp. 29, 36. Like much booster literature, the promotional material for the fire cyclorama stressed quantity as much as quality, informing viewers that this titanic and remarkably detailed sequence of scenes (which, in the absence of actual photographs, became in some books the visual record of the fire) cost $250,000 and was prepared by a group of eleven artists from Europe and America who in the service of art, history, and the city went through nearly two tons of paints and oils. For more on the cyclorama, including photographs of selected panels, see Kogan and Cromie, *The Great Fire*, pp. 64–5, 86–87, 88–89, 92–93. Cycloramas were a popular form of urban entertainment in the period, presenting enormous historical or biblical scenes mounted in a circular building that afforded the viewer a breath-taking range of vision. The fire cyclorama competed with another depicting the Battle of Gettysburg.

7. "Chicago Historical Society Program for Celebration of the 50th Anni-

versary of the Great Chicago Fire" (typescript); Chicago Association of Commerce, "Preliminary Announcement, Semi-Centennial Observance of the Chicago Fire"; "Report, Semi-Centennial Observance of the Chicago Fire," 20 October 1921 (typescript); *Chicago Commerce* (13 and 27 August, 1921). The festival play, as interpreted in a synopsis in the program, shows that the view of the fire as a test of morality, character, responsibility, and control, expressed so strongly a half-century earlier, was alive and well. These reports, announcements, programs, and related documents are in the library of the Chicago Historical Society.

8. See Paul Boyer's analysis of these pageants of the Progressive era, particularly the widely influential "Pageant and Masque" that Perce MacKaye staged in St. Louis in 1914. *Urban Masses and Moral Order in America*, pp. 257–60, 278, 281.

9. Eugene V. Debs, "The Martyred Apostles of Labor," in *Debs: His Life, Writings and Speeches*, p. 264. See the pamphlet, *In Memoriam of the Martyrs of the Working People Murdered at Chicago on November 11, 1887*, issued by the Committee on Agitation of the International Workingmen's Association, which is in the library of the Chicago Historical Society. The Society's collections also contain broadsides announcing rallies in several English cities featuring prominent European radicals. See also Keil and Jentz, *German Workers in Chicago*, pp. 223, 263–65, 271–76, 363–66. The richest group of republished materials relating to the heritage of Haymarket throughout America and the world is in Section III of Roediger and Rosemont, *The Haymarket Scrapbook*, pp. 173–251.

10. William J. Adelman's historical tour guide of Haymarket, *Haymarket Revisited* (Chicago: Illinois Labor History Society, 1976), includes a section on Waldheim. Adelman claims that at least some part of the remains of other legendary radicals, including Joe Hill and Big Bill Haywood, have also been placed near the monument, several without any markers.

11. A pamphlet, full of advertisements and including a brief history of Haymarket and an honor roll of participants, titled *Twenty-second Anniversary and Memorial Entertainment, Under the Auspices of the Veterans of the Haymarket Riot*, was published in connection with a 1908 reunion. The pamphlet, the resolutions presented to Judge Gary, and photographs of ceremonies beside the police statue, are in the holdings of the Chicago Historical Society.

12. *Chicago Tribune* (7 October 1969), p. 1; (5 October 1970), p. 1. On the history of the police monument, see Paul Avrich, *The Haymarket Tragedy*, pp. 430–31; Adelman, *Haymarket Revisited*, pp. 38–40; and Jeff Huebner, "Haymarket Revisited," *Reader* (10 December 1993), pp. 1, 14–25.

13. Leaflets in the author's collection.

14. Centennial poster in the Prints and Photographs Department of the Chicago Historical Society. The inscription on the monument substitutes "are throttling" for "strangle."

15. Ginger, *The Bending Cross*, p. 195.

16. *Chicago Tribune* (24 October 1897), p. 1. There had been two threats to Pullman's life by troubled individuals in 1895 that the authorities handled easily. The *Tribune* reported that the family's concerns about grave robbers stemmed from a recent incident in New York in which merchant A. T. Stewart's

body had been stolen and held for ransom, and a failed attempt to steal the body of Lincoln. Leyendecker states that Mrs. Pullman contested the will and had it altered in order to support her twin sons more comfortably, but the erratic and profligate behavior that so alienated their father continued. One died of pneumonia at twenty-six, the other in a coaching accident at thirty. *Palace Car Prince*, pp. 259–60.

INDEX

Abbott, Lyman, 118–19, 125, 170, 172, 326 n. 35

Adams, Henry, 271, 362 n. 46

Adams, J. Coleman, 172

Addams, Jane: on Haymarket trial aftermath, 171–72; and Hull-House, 221–23; on Pullman, 200–201; on Pullman Strike, 232, 235, 255–58; on World's Columbian Exposition, 226; other references, 270, 361 nn. 38, 40, 362 n. 49

Alarm: arguments for anarchism, 154, 156, 167, 339 n. 17; on sexual violation of workers, 160–62; on violence, 115–17, 116; other references, 112, 114, 133, 204, 332 n. 9

Alexander II, Czar, 138

Alger, Horatio, 94

Altgeld, John Peter: election as governor, 344 n. 49; and Haymarket trial, 170–71, 178, 276; and Pullman Strike, 236, 237, 239, 260; other references, 224, 267

American Economic Association, 253

American Group of Chicago anarchists, 112, 114

American Journal of Politics, 245, 368 n. 37

American Railway Union: dissolved, 277; and events of Pullman Strike,

233–37; other references, 240, 242, 244, 252, 364 n. 8

Amnesty Association, 123

Anarchists: Abbott on, 119; on anarchy as natural, 167–68; and cultural memory of Haymarket, 276; executions, *see* Haymarket bombing executions; Gary on, 135; in Haymarket bombing, 120–22; Nast on, 136, 140, 335 n. 31; Pullman as answer to, 187; Pullman Strike leaders accused of being, 239, 367 n. 27; rhetoric of violence, 115–18, 167; rise of, 111–15; trial for Haymarket bombing, *see* Haymarket bombing trial; other references, 178, 207, 211

Anarchy and Anarchists (Schaack), 121, 131, 134–35, 138, 141, 333 n. 13

Anarchy at an End (book), 336 n. 41

Andreas, Alfred T.: on Chicago Fire, 20, 31, 60–61; on Gary, 122; on Mason, 76, 313 n. 27; on Sheridan, 77; other references, 299 n. 18

Arbeiter-Zeitung, 112–14, 117, 120, 133, 160, 339 n. 13

Arcade Building, 181, 189, 223, 229, 348 n. 21

Arcade Mercantile Journal, 188, 266, 348 n. 20

Architecture: and Chicago Fire, 46; City Beautiful movement, 225; in Pull-

381

1-16-33